Contents

Section One — Beliefs in Society

Theories of Ideology 2
Theories of Science 4
Theories of Religion 6
Religious Organisations 8
Religion and Social Position 12
Religiosity in the Contemporary World 14

Section Two — Global Development

Theories of Development 16
Theories of Globalisation 18
Strategies for Development 20
NGOs and International Bodies 22
Urbanisation and Industrialisation 24
The Environment 26
War and Conflict 27
Aspects of Development: Demography 28
Aspects of Development: Education 30
Aspects of Development: Health 31
Aspects of Development: Gender 32
Aspects of Development: Employment 33

Section Three — The Mass Media

Ownership and Control of Mass Media 34
Theories about Mass Media 36
Selecting and Presenting the News 38
Censorship and Violence 40
Media Representations 42
Mass Media and its Audience 46
New Media 50
Globalisation and Popular Culture 51

Section Four — Power and Politics

The Nature and Distribution of Power 52
The Modern State 54
Political Parties and Participation 56
Voting Behaviour 58
The Influence of the Media 59
Old and New Social Movements 60
Political Action and Protest 62
Protest and Identity 64
Globalisation 66
Ideology and Political Action 68

Section Five — Crime and Deviance

Defining Crime and Deviance 70
Theories of Crime and Deviance 72
Measuring Crime 80
Patterns of Crime 82
Victims, Prevention and Punishment 84
Recent Issues in Crime and Deviance 86
Suicide 88

Section Six — Stratification and Differentiation

Stratification 90
Class Inequality and Stratification 92
Changes in the Class Structure 96
Inequality, Stratification and Gender 98
Inequality, Stratification and Ethnicity 100
Inequality, Stratification and Age 102
Inequality, Stratification and Disability 103
Social Mobility 104

Section Seven — Education

The Role of the Education System 106
Class and Differential Educational Achievement 110
Gender and Differential Educational Achievement ... 112
Ethnicity and Differential Educational Achievement . 114
Education and the Economy 116
The Education System and State Policy 118

Section Eight — Sociological Theory & Methods

Research and Sociological Theory 122
Consensus Structuralism 124
Conflict Structuralism 125
Social Action Theory 126
Modernity and Postmodernity 127
Feminism 128
Feminism and Realism 129
Sociology and Social Policy 130
Stages in the Research Process 132
Research Design 134
Ethics in Research 136
Quantitative and Qualitative Methods 138
Issues about Validity 142
Quantitative and Qualitative Analysis 144
Mixed Methods 145
Sociological Research: Crime and Deviance 146
Sociological Research: Stratification and Difference . 152

Do Well in Your Exam

Do Well in Your AQA Exam 158
Do Well in Your OCR Exam 162

Glossary 166
Index 170

We deliberately haven't put answers in this book — because there are lots of valid ways to answer essay questions. Instead, we've put in a section about how to do well in your exam — which includes some sample exam answers.

Theories of Ideology

These pages are about the many different ways people have used the concept of **ideology**. ***This section is for AQA only.
If you're doing OCR, you can go straight to section 3 on page 34.***

The term **"Ideology"** has several meanings

Antoine Destutt de Tracy first used the word **ideology** in 1796 to describe what he called a new '**science of ideas**' which
he saw emerging after the French Revolution. Since then the term has been used in several different ways.

> **Ideology has been defined in a large variety of ways**
>
> 1) As a set of **political beliefs**, e.g. socialism, liberalism.
> 2) As the **ideas** and **beliefs** of a **particular social class**.
> 3) As the **dominant ideas** and **beliefs** of the **ruling class**.
> 4) As the **official beliefs** of a **political system**, e.g. in totalitarian (dictatorial) regimes like Hitler's Germany.
> 5) As a set of beliefs that represent a **total view of reality**, e.g. religious fundamentalism.

It's not easy to **pin down** just one workable definition for 'ideology' — but it's important you understand how the word has
been used by some **prominent thinkers**.

Your **Social** and **Political** perspective **Influences** how you define **Ideology**

When someone uses the word 'ideology' their **perspective** will give you a clue as to what they mean. E.g.

Marxists	See ideology as the set of ruling ideas that **keep workers in their place**.
Feminists	See ideology as both the set of ideas that **keep women oppressed** (patriarchal ideology), and a potentially **liberating set of beliefs** (feminism).
Liberals (pluralists)	Tend to see ideology as **totalitarian** and **oppressive** — e.g. Stalin's Russia and Hitler's Germany both had official ideologies which were repressive. Pluralists **reject** the idea that there can be a **monopoly of truth**.

Karl Marx said *Ideology* was a *False Picture* imposed by the *Ruling Class*

Karl Marx (1818-1883) believed the most important force in society was **class conflict** between the workers and the
ruling class. In *The German Ideology* (1970, New York: International Publishers, written 1845) Marx and Engels said:
"The **ideas** of the **ruling class** are in every epoch the **ruling ideas**."

1) In capitalist societies, workers are employed to **produce goods** which are sold by their employers for a **profit**.

2) Only a **bit** of this profit ends up in the **workers' wages** — most of it's **kept** by the employer.

3) Marx said if workers were allowed to notice the **unfairness** of this they'd **revolt**.

4) Ruling ideas (or **ideology**) are needed by the ruling class to make a grossly unfair system **appear fair** and **legitimate** and therefore keep it going.

5) Marx claimed that ideology creates a '**false consciousness**' for the workers. It gets them to **believe** that the system and their **position** within it are both **fair** and **just** by **mystifying** and **falsifying** their picture of reality.

6) The function of ideology for Marx then was to keep the workers in their place and **stop them rebelling**.

7) According to Marx only the ruling class has an ideology because only they have the need to **create illusions**.

Cissie was sure she'd never
knowingly mystified the proletariat.

Theories of Ideology

The *Marxist* view of *Ideology* was developed by *Gramsci*

Antonio Gramsci (1891-1937) was a Marxist who called the domination of ruling class ideology in society '**hegemony**'.

1) Hegemonic ideas don't just rule — they **dominate**. Other values and ideas still exist in society, but **don't** get taken **seriously**. Ruling class ideas become '**the common sense of the age**'.

2) Nobody questions 'common sense' and so **nobody questions** the **ruling class's right to rule**. Gramsci argued that the ruling class's ideology becomes **entrenched** in all areas of social life — e.g. religion, art, law, language, education. This makes it difficult to challenge.

"....the ruling class not only justifies and maintains its dominance, but manages to maintain the active consent of those over whom it rules." (**Gramsci**, 1971, *Selections from the Prison Notebooks*, London: Lawrence and Wishart).

3) The **struggle** against hegemony for Gramsci had to be an **intellectual** one with socialist thinkers developing an alternative '**proletarian hegemony**' (proletarian = working class).

Gramsci wrote most of his theories in prison, in the 1930s. His prison notebooks were published much later. That's why the date of publication is well after he died.

Althusser argued there were *Ideological State Apparatuses*

1) The neo-Marxist **Althusser** argued that elements of society like the education system, mass media and religion were **Ideological State Apparatuses** (ISAs).

2) The ISAs are a tool of capitalism used to **justify**, **maintain** and **reproduce** class inequalities.

3) For example, according to Althusser, education **transmits** and **reproduces** an ideology about what it means to be working class, what it means to be middle class, and what everyone's **place in society** ought to be.

Karl Mannheim identified *Two* types of *Ideology*

Mannheim (1929) argued that ideology can be defined in two ways.

1) A set of beliefs used to **justify** and **perpetuate** an existing social order (a ruling class ideology).

2) A **utopian** set of beliefs about how the world **could be organised** in the **future**. Utopian ideologies tend to be formed by **oppressed groups** who want **radical change**.

According to Mannheim both types of ideology **distort reality** — the former is a distortion to create the illusion of **fairness** in society, the latter is just a '**wish image**' of what the future might be like.

- **Marxism** could be seen as a **utopian ideology** with its vision of an ideal future society after the ruling class has been overthrown. The ideal vision is used to **criticise existing society**.

- **Functionalism** could be seen as a **ruling class ideology** as it seeks to **justify existing society** with its emphasis on **agreement**, **consensus** and **stability**.

Benji's idea of rebranding their petrochemical products organisation as "Benji's Bag o' Fun™" was little more than a wish image.

Practice Questions

Q1 List four different ways in which the word ideology has been used.
Q2 According to Marx, what is the purpose of ruling class ideology?
Q3 Explain what is meant by false consciousness.
Q4 Why aren't hegemonic ideas challenged in capitalist society, according to Gramsci?
Q5 What two types of ideology does Mannheim identify?

Exam Question

Q1 Assess the view that functionalism is a ruling class ideology. (33 marks)

Explain the different theories — and get top Marx...

The trick is to remember that ideology doesn't have just one definition that you can reel off, but is used in lots of different ways by different sociologists depending on their... er,... ideological perspective.

Theories of Science

*These pages examine theories of science in relation to other types of **belief system**, and discuss the debates surrounding their similarities and differences.*

The **Traditional View** is that **Science** is **Objective** and **Evidence-Based**

Many scientists claim there is a clear **distinction** between **science** and other ways of viewing the world. A recent example is **Richard Dawkins**, who in *The God Delusion* (2006) made the following observations about science and religion:

"Fundamentalists know they are right because they have read the truth in a holy book... The truth of the holy book is an axiom, not the end product of a process of reasoning. The book is true, and if the evidence seems to contradict it, it is the evidence that must be thrown out, not the book. By contrast, what I, as a scientist, believe... I believe not because of reading a holy book but because I have studied the evidence... When a science book is wrong, somebody eventually discovers the mistake and it is corrected in subsequent books. That conspicuously doesn't happen with holy books."

Exhibit A: not painted blue due to the outcome of an evidence-based enquiry.

> **The traditional view of science**
>
> 1) **Science is objective** — the scientist is **neutral**.
> 2) Scientific enquiry is **evidence-based** — conclusions are based on evidence, not **preconceived ideas**.
> 3) Scientific enquiry is **'open'** — ideas which are **tested** and proved wrong are rejected and **more accurate** ideas replace them.

This **Traditional View** of science has been **Challenged**

Michael Lynch (1983) argued that science is **far less objective** than scientists claim.

1) Lynch studied scientists experimenting on lab rats and concluded that the scientists were more **influenced** by their **existing theories** than may have been expected.

2) When **'anomalies'** occurred — i.e. results they were not expecting — they were often put down to **errors** in the photographs they were studying, rather than as **evidence** towards a new theory or hypothesis.

Science can be viewed as a **Belief System** like **Religion**

Polanyi (1958) suggested that a **belief system** was made up of **three factors**. Science can be viewed as fitting this model.

> 1) **A circularity of beliefs** — each idea within the belief system is explained in **relation to others**. If one is challenged or fails it is **defended** by reference to another, to **avoid changing** the belief system.
>
> 2) **Supporting explanations are given for difficult situations** — if any **evidence** is shown to **contradict** the belief there will be a reason to explain it (as with the anomalies in the experiments Lynch observed).
>
> 3) **No alternative belief systems can be tolerated** — a **sweeping rejection** of religion could be seen as an example of this.

Sociology can be treated as a **Science**

Positivists like Comte believe that sociology is scientific. It consists of **gathering information** about the social world, **classifying data**, and **drawing conclusions** about '**the social laws**' which govern human society.

The positivist **Durkheim** claimed that by using the technique of **multivariate analysis**, 'social facts' could be uncovered.

1) Multivariate analysis is the attempt to **isolate** the impact of **independent variables** (the factors affecting something) on the dependent variable (the thing being affected).

2) For instance, the level of working class achievement in school might be the **dependent** variable, and material deprivation and teacher labelling the **independent** variables.

3) Durkheim believed that by complex, in-depth **statistical analysis** the independent variables could be measured and a **social law established**.

The early positivists used an **inductive** approach. This means they first **collected data on their topic**, which they **studied** and **analysed**. From this they composed a **theory** or **hypothesis**. They then **tested** their hypothesis and drew **conclusions**. If their results were **repeatable** (i.e. if people repeated their experiment and got the same results), the hypothesis was considered a **social fact**.

Theories of Science

Popper said scientists should use the Deductive Approach and Falsification

The **deductive approach** is similar to the inductive approach, only in reverse — it starts with the theory, which then leads to the investigation. **Karl Popper (1959, 1963)** argued that theories or hypotheses could spring from anywhere, such as **flashes of inspiration** ('eureka moments') or even from **dreams**.

Popper said the positivists were **wrong** in their belief that theories could be **proved** to be **true**. He had a different idea of scientific method —

1) Popper rejected the idea that there are **permanent social laws** governing human behaviour. He claimed that any 'law' could at some point be **falsified** (proved wrong), no matter how many times it has been 'proved' correct in the past.

2) The famous example he gave was the hypothesis '**all swans are white**,' which can be 'proved' thousands of times until you encounter a **black swan**.

3) Popper said the aim of science and social science should be to constantly **strive to falsify** theories. This '**falsification**' of theories arguably distinguishes science from religion and other supernatural belief systems.

"Don't believe the hype."

Gomm argued that scientists' work should be viewed in its Social Context

Roger Gomm (1982) argued that the theories scientists produce are in part a product of their **social context**, and that scientists tend to try and **prove** rather than falsify their theories.

Gomm gave the example of **Darwin** and his **theory of evolution** to explain this.

1) Gomm suggests Darwin's theories of **natural selection** and the **competitive struggle** for the survival of the fittest were **not supported by all of the evidence**.

2) Darwin therefore missed the opportunity to '**falsify**' aspects of his theories. Gomm suggests the reason for this was **ideological** rather than scientific.

3) Gomm argued that the 'survival of the fittest theory' slotted neatly into the **Victorian capitalist ideology** of free market economics, individualism, and the minimalist approach to welfare of the time. Gomm therefore emphasised the importance of placing 'science' in its **social context**. Scientific knowledge can be seen, at least in part, as **socially constructed**.

Kuhn challenged the idea that science is Objective

Thomas Kuhn (1962) introduced the idea that scientists, at certain times in history, work in a **paradigm**.

1) A paradigm, according to Kuhn, refers to the **framework** of **accepted ideas** in which scientists operate. It might include ideas on **truth**, **validity** and **methodology**.

2) Kuhn argued that scientists will tend to work within the paradigm and so seek evidence which **supports** it. This will continue until **anomalies** are so strong as to trigger a **paradigm shift** or **scientific revolution**.

3) When this happens, a new '**normal science paradigm**' is established and the process begins again.

Working within the paradigm can be seen as similar to Polanyi's first factor of a belief system — circularity of beliefs (see p. 4).

Practice Questions

Q1 According to Dawkins, what distinguishes science from religion?

Q2 What are the three factors which make up a belief system, according to Polanyi?

Q3 What is the difference between an inductive and a deductive scientific approach?

Q4 What is meant by falsification?

Exam Questions

Q1 What does Kuhn mean by a paradigm, and how is it important in the theory of science? (18 marks)

Q2 To what extent can religion and science be seen as different varieties of belief system? (33 marks)

Study this page — it'll help you do your experiments Popper-ly...

...or perhaps not. You see, science is a funny thing — you think it's a clean break from the superstition and mummery of the past, and yet it all turns out to be the product of inspiration and whimsy. I wonder what Richard Dawkins dreams of...

Theories of Religion

Sociologists disagree about religion. Some think it's great and stops society descending into chaos — others think it's just there to oppress people. God doesn't seem to have much to do with it.

Marx said Religion helps to Oppress Workers and Inhibits Social Change

1) Karl Marx said that in **capitalist** society there was a **conflict of interests** between the **ruling class** and the **working class** because the ruling class **exploit** the working class to get the most profit out of them (see p. 2).

2) But — there's **something stopping** the working class from **uniting** and **overthrowing** the ruling class. Marx argued that the working class are in a state of **false consciousness**. This means they're **not aware** of **how unfair** society is.

3) This is where **religion** comes in. Marx is **very critical** of religion. He said it's one of the things that **keeps** the working class in a state of **false consciousness**. He said, "**Religion is the opium of the people**" (1971, *Critique of Hegel's 'Philosophy of the Right'* Cambridge: Cambridge University Press, written 1843) This means that it **dulls the pain** of oppression like **opium** — a **drug** which kills pain. It doesn't take the oppression away, though.

> **Marx said that religion justifies social inequality**
>
> 1) People have **the afterlife** to **look forward** to if they're **good**, so they **don't break the rules** and don't challenge the capitalist system.
>
> 2) Religion **consoles** people with the **promise of life after death** and so they **put up** with their **suffering** here **on Earth** more easily.
>
> 3) Religion often tells people that their **position is decided by God**. This encourages false consciousness by blaming God instead of **blaming capitalism**.
>
> 4) If **God is all-powerful** he could **do something** about the suffering **if he wanted to**. He **doesn't do anything** — so people think this must be **how society is meant to be**.

Marx believed religion was both a way of oppressing people and a way of cushioning the effects of oppression.

Marxism says that religion **passes on beliefs** that **oppress the working class**. It argues that religion is a **conservative** force which prevents revolution — it keeps things the same. The **rich stay rich** and the **poor** keep on working. It's a neat **social control**.

But... there are problems with applying this Marxist view to today's society. Fewer people go to a place of worship than in the past — if people **don't go to worship**, it's **hard** for them to be duped by formal religious ideology. Also, religion can bring about **change**, but traditional Marxists tend to ignore this.

Functionalists see religion as Maintaining Harmony and Social Cohesion

Functionalists also see religion as something that **inhibits change** and helps **keep society as it is**. But they think this is a positive role, which creates **social order** based on **value consensus**.

1) **Durkheim** studied **Aboriginal** society and suggested that the **sacred worship of totems** was equivalent to **worshipping society itself**. Durkheim said that sacred religious worship encourages shared values.

2) **Malinowski (1954)** looked at how religion deals with situations of **emotional stress** that **threaten social order**. Unpredictable or stressful events like births and deaths create **disruption**. Religion **manages these tensions** and promotes stability.

Religions have ceremonies for dealing with birth and death.

3) **Parsons** wrote in the 1930s and 1940s that religion provides **guidelines** for human action in terms of "**core values**". Religion helps to **integrate** people into a value consensus and allows them to **make sense of their lives**.

4) Functionalist **Bellah (1967)** suggested the idea of **Civil Religion**, which is when secular (non-religious) symbols and rituals create **social cohesion** in a similar way to religion. **Flags**, famous **political figures** and even **royal deaths** bring about some kind of **collective feeling** that generates **order** and **stability**.

Functionalism ignores **dysfunctional** aspects of religion. There are **religious conflicts** all over the world. Religion can be a source of **oppression**. Religion can also bring about **change**, and functionalism ignores that as well.

But in some cases Religion can Encourage Social Change

1) Marx's good pal **Engels** reckoned that in **some circumstances** religion could actually be a **revolutionary** force. Sometimes **religion** is the **only means of change** because all other routes have been blocked.

2) **Early Christian sects** opposed Roman rule and brought about change. **Jesus** himself encouraged social change.

3) In the 1960s and 1970s, **Catholic priests** in **Latin America** criticised the bourgeoisie and preached **liberation theology** — using religion to free people from oppression. This led to **resistance** and **social change** — in 1979, revolutionaries threw out the oppressive government in **Nicaragua**. Neo-Marxist **Otto Maduro (1982**, *Religion and Social Conflicts* New York: Orbis Books**)** studied liberation theology. He said religion is "often one of the main available channels to bring about a social revolution".

4) Reverend **Martin Luther King** and the **Southern Baptist Church** resisted oppression and segregation, bringing about **political** and **social rights** for black people in **1960s America**.

5) In Iran, **Islamic fundamentalism** encouraged **social change**. In 1979, there was a **revolution** against the Shah, led by followers of the Shia Ayatollah **Khomeini**. Khomeini set up a **religious government** that followed Sharia law.

Theories of Religion

Weber said that Religion can Create a Capitalist Work Ethic

Weber's book *The Protestant Work Ethic and Spirit of Capitalism* looked at how the **religious** ideas of **Calvinism** brought about social change. Weber spotted **two important things** in Calvinism:

1) **Predestination:** This is the idea that your **life** and whether you're going to heaven are **predetermined** by **God**. Calvinists believed only a **few** were **chosen** for heaven. This created **anxiety** — no one knew if they were chosen.

2) **Ascetic Ideal: Working hard** in your job was a **solution** to this anxiety. Success might be a sign that you were chosen for heaven. Early Calvinists lived a **strict** and **disciplined** life of hard work and simple pleasures.

Weber claimed that the ascetic ideal helped create an ethic of **disciplined hard work**. This is the **spirit of capitalism**. Not only was there a build-up of **capital**, there was the right **work ethic** for capitalism. Religion **indirectly** brought about change.

However, **Eisenstadt (1967)** contradicts Weber's theory by claiming that capitalism occurred in **Catholic** countries like Italy **before** the **Protestant Reformation happened** and before the ideas of **Calvin ever came out**.

Feminists point out the Sexism in Religion

However, menstruation is seen as taboo in many religions.

1) Women's capacity to **have babies** gives women an **important role** within religion, in terms of bringing **new life** into the world. Women's role as **primary caregiver** is seen as **important** by traditional religion — it's the job of a mother to raise her children to **believe in God** and worship God. Feminists say this **traps** women in **traditional** roles.

2) Because women are **sexually attractive** to men they're perceived to be **distractions** from worship. Many religions believe in giving worship to God through a denial of sexuality (e.g. priests in the Roman Catholic Church have to be **celibate**). Religions have historically seen women as "**temptresses**" of men — think of Eve and the apple.

3) Women are **excluded from power** in many religious organisations.

4) Feminists argue that religious texts **transmit messages** to readers through stories that reflect and uphold a **patriarchal** society. This patriarchal ideology says that women are part of the profane and imperfect, and maintains the **conformity** and **submission** of women.

    profane = opposite of sacred or holy

5) **Simone de Beauvoir (1953)** saw religion as **exploitative** and **oppressive** towards women. She thought that religion promotes the idea that if women **suffer** in their present lives, then they'll receive **equality in heaven**, which allows women to **put up with** being treated as **inferior** to men in the hope of gaining in the afterlife. Spot the **similarity** to **Marx's** ideas on religion — just swap "women" for "working class" and you're there.

There are Problems with Feminist Anti-Religious Views

1) Women are not necessarily **passive victims** of religious oppression. Women may **actively resist** oppression — e.g. in **Afghanistan** under the Taliban it was forbidden for girls to go to school, so women educated girls in secret.

2) Religion **isn't necessarily patriarchal**. For example, **veiling** can have **positive functions** for Muslim women. The veil can **affirm Muslim identity** and **protect** women from sexual harassment in public.

3) Patriarchy within a society may be transmitted by other social and cultural activities, not by religion.

Practice Questions

Q1   In what ways does Marx say religion justifies social inequality?

Q2   What is the role of religion, according to functionalists?

Q3   What two aspects of Calvinism favoured a strong work ethic, according to Weber?

Q4   Give three examples of feminist views of sexism in religion.

Exam Question

Q1   Evaluate the view that there is sexism in religion.   (33 marks)

The function of religion is to give you someone to pray to before exams...

There's an awful lot to learn here, I'll be honest. To make it easy on yourself, take each kind of theory individually. Once you've read it through, what Marxists and functionalists think about religion ought to be no big surprise. The next step is to learn the key names and studies. Cover up each subsection and work on it until you can remember the names and ideas.

Religious Organisations

Religious groups organise themselves into different forms. They differ in leadership, relationship to the state and politics, how they worship and who they appeal to. Sociologists have put forward different classifications of religious organisations.

There are **Four Key Concepts** in the Study of Religion

Religious Belief	Thinking that the world is controlled by supernatural forces — normally a god or group of gods.
Religious Commitment	Carrying out religious actions, such as praying or singing religious songs.
Religious Membership	Being part of a formal religious institution — a church, sect, cult, etc.
Religiosity	The level of an individual's connection with all aspects of religion — belief, commitment and membership.

1) A person's religiosity is the **balance** between their **religious experience** and their **religious beliefs**.

2) Some people attend church for social reasons, even though they don't believe in a god — their religiosity emphasises **membership** and **commitment**.

3) Others believe in a god but never go to church — their religiosity emphasises **belief**.

A **Church** is a well-established **Religious Organisation**

Sociologists often use a **typology** (a set of "**ideal types**") to categorise and analyse religious organisations. It is important to remember that these are **ideal** types — perfect **pure** models. **Real** religious organisations may include features of **more than one type**.

Social historian **Ernst Troeltsch (1912)** distinguished between different types of religious organisation, and used the word **church** to mean a **large religious organisation**. He said churches usually have four main features:

1) A church claims **monopoly over the truth** — it says its claims are **absolutely true** and others are **false**.

2) Churches have a **complex rigid hierarchy** and a **bureaucratic structure** with lots of **rules and regulations**.

3) Churches often have a **close relationship** to the **state**. Some nations have an official national religion — Weber used the term "**ecclesia**" for this.

4) They are closely integrated into **mainstream society**. Churches act as a **conservative** force, resisting change. This is why the **upper classes** are more likely to join — even though churches are **universal** and **inclusive in principle**.

Examples of churches include the **Roman Catholic Church**, the **Church of England** and the **Episcopal Church**.

Troeltsch studied churches in **16th century** Europe. **Steve Bruce (1995)** says that Troeltsch's points don't always apply to today's churches because there's **religious pluralism** these days. Nowadays, the Church of England doesn't claim a monopoly over the truth and it isn't always conservative.

Religious pluralism = lots of different types of religious groups.

Sects are Small, Radical Religious Movements

Troeltsch defined sects as being almost the **opposite of churches**. Few religious groups fall into the category of sect.

People who are **dissatisfied** with mainstream religion can be attracted to a sect. Sects are often formed by people **splitting off from a church** because they **disagree** with the church's **practices** or **theology**.

1) Sects claim a **monopoly over the truth** and are intolerant towards other religious organisations.

2) Sects have **no complex hierarchy**. They often have a **charismatic leader** who **persuades** members to **follow his or her teaching**.

3) Sects are **small**. Their members follow with **total commitment**, and they can be **manipulated** by the sect's leader.

4) Sects are separate from the state — they're in **opposition** to mainstream society. Sects can sometimes offer an alternative way of life for **deprived** and **marginal** groups.

Examples of sects include the **early Methodists** and **Calvinists** (although over time these have become more mainstream). This category also includes **extremist** groups like the **People's Temple** in America who were led to mass suicide by Jim Jones, or the **Branch Davidians** led by David Koresh.

These extremist groups are generally called cults in everyday language. Watch out though — in sociology, cult means something else...

Religious Organisations

Denominations are Subsets of Churches

Troeltsch **originally classified** religious organisations into **churches** and **sects**.
The term "**denomination**" was added later.

1) Denominations don't usually claim **a monopoly over the truth**. They see themselves as a **possible route to the truth**. They are **tolerant** towards other religious organisations.
2) Like a church, they have a **hierarchy** and **bureaucratic structure**, but it isn't as complex.
3) They have a reasonably **large membership**, but not as large as an established church.
4) Members of denominations are usually **not as loyal** as members of churches.
5) Denominations **aren't closely connected to the state**. They get involved in society and **comment** on **current events**.

Denominations don't usually claim a monopoly over the truth — in general they prefer chess.

Examples of denominations are **modern Methodists** and **Baptists**.

Cults are Mystic Movements — Often Wrongly Defined

Bruce (1995) defined cults as movements without a fixed set of beliefs. They emphasise the **inner power** of the **individual** and **mysticism**. Cults are usually loosely knit and don't have a hierarchy.

Fundamentalism Provides Meaning and Certainty in Periods of Uncertainty

Fundamentalism involves the **fundamental, literal interpretation** of religious texts. Fundamentalist groups **strictly** and **fervently** follow their beliefs. Fundamentalists seek **change** to create a more **conservative** society and advocate a return to '**traditional values**'. These groups often have **charismatic leaders**.

In both of the following examples, **fundamentalism** provides **certainty** and **meaning** in periods of **uncertainty**.

1) Islamic Fundamentalism in Iran

Iran was a **traditional** society that **quickly modernised** under the **Shah**. **Women** wore **Western clothes**, alcohol was freely available and there was **secular education**. There was also **inequality** in society — the upper class were **very rich**, and working class areas were **neglected**.
Traditional Muslims were **unhappy** about the direction that Iranian society had taken, and saw the Shah as **corrupt**. They started to oppose the Shah, led by a **fundamentalist** religious leader called **Ayatollah Khomeini**. There was a revolution in 1979 and the Ayatollah came to power. He established a society based on **Islamic Sharia law** — alcohol was banned, there were harsh punishments for crime, and women were required to cover their bodies in public.

2) Christian Fundamentalism

The **New Christian Right** in **America** argues that American society is in **decline** and in a state of **moral crisis**. They think this is caused by **liberal reforms** — e.g. easy **divorce**, legalised **abortion**, **gay rights** and **secular education**. The New Christian Right **oppose** the teaching of **evolution** in schools, because it disagrees with their fundamentalist interpretation of the Bible. They started some **universities** that offer not only degrees, but also a strict **Christian education**. They promote their views through **mass communication**, e.g. TV and Christian publishing.

Practice Questions

Q1 What do sociologists mean by 'religious commitment'?
Q2 Give the key characteristics of a cult.
Q3 Give two examples of fundamentalist religious movements.

Exam Questions

Q1 Identify and explain two features of a church. (6 marks)

Q2 Identify and explain two features of a denomination. (6 marks)

Lots of religions don't condone sects before marriage...

*Don't assume you already know what a church is, what a sect is, etc. Sociological definitions can be a bit different from the everyday definitions. So **learn them**. Obviously, not all religious groups will fit neatly into one of these categories — but most will.*

Religious Organisations

The term "new religious movement" (or NRM for short) includes a huge range of movements from diverse sources.
They've increased significantly in number since the 1960s. They don't always fit the old church-sect-denomination-cult divisions.

New Religious Movements can be Affirming, Rejecting or Accommodating

Sociologist **Roy Wallis (1984)** identified three types of new religious movement:

World-rejecting movements cut themselves off from society — similar to sects

1) World-rejecting movements are very **critical** of wider society and are often in conflict with the state.

2) **The Unification Church**, better known as the '**Moonies**', is one example of a world-rejecting movement.

3) World-rejecting movements require **total commitment**. They demand **significant lifestyle changes**. Members often turn away from family and friends — world-rejecting movements have developed a reputation for "**brainwashing**" members. It's often hard to leave a world-rejecting movement.

World-affirming movements are tolerant of other beliefs — similar to cults

1) They're similar to **self-help** and therapy groups — they try to "**unlock spiritual power**". **Transcendental Meditation** is an example of a world-affirming movement.

2) World-affirming movements seek **wide membership**.

3) World-affirming movements **don't require** especially high levels of **commitment**.

World-accommodating movements are traditionally religious — similar to denominations

1) World-accommodating movements often come from **traditional** religions.

2) They try to rediscover **spiritual purity** lost in traditional religions. **Pentecostalism** is a movement within Christianity that aims to bring the Holy Spirit back into worship.

3) World-accommodating movements allow people to carry on with their **existing lifestyle**.

The Growth of New Religious Movements isn't Easy to Explain

The **interpretivist** idea is that **new religious movements (NRMs)** provide **certainty** in times of **uncertainty**.
When there's uncertainty, new religious movements have **greater appeal** and **grow** in numbers.
Here are some of the **uncertainties** that people face:

1) **Marginality** — inequality, immigration and racism may **marginalise** some groups. So, some new religious movements may help marginalised people **make sense** of their situation, and may promise a better life after death as **compensation**. **Weber** called this the "**theodicy of disprivilege**".

2) **Relative deprivation** — the concept of marginality doesn't explain why **white, middle class groups** join new religious movements. Although they aren't absolutely poor or deprived, some middle class people may see themselves as **deprived in comparison to their peers**.

3) **Social change** — transformation of society can result in **anomie** and **uncertainty**. The breakdown of **community**, the process of **secularisation** (see p.14), **cultural diversity** and bad news such as **terrorist attacks** may generate uncertainty.

4) **Modernity and post-modernity** — the **alienation** of capitalism, the increasing amount of **red tape**, bureaucracy, and disillusionment with work may create **uncertainty**. The choice people have in constructing their identity may create **uncertainty** and a **crisis of identity**.

> anomie = a state of confusion where there is a lack of agreed norms and values.

Melton (1993) didn't agree that NRMs emerged in periods of uncertainty. He looked at the founding dates of non-conventional religious organisations in the US. **Rapid growth** took place in the **1950s** — in a period of **stability** and **certainty**. Why do these sociologists never agree...

Wallis (1984) explains the appeal of the three different kinds of new religious movement

1) **World-rejecting movements** grew in numbers in the 1960s. There was a lot of **freedom** for people, but also **uncertainty**. It was a period of **radicalism** with lots of alternative world views — often called the "sixties counterculture". Some people got **disillusioned** with this counterculture and wanted more **concrete** beliefs.

2) **World-affirming movements** develop as a means of coping with a **crisis of identity** in more successful groups (e.g. the middle class). They try to unlock **human potential** and help people solve their problems. **Bruce (1995)** claims that they're a response to the **rationalisation** of the modern world where it's hard to find satisfaction from work.

3) **World-accommodating movements** appeal to those who are dissatisfied with existing religion.

Religious Organisations

Millenarian Movements *Look Forward to the* Apocalypse

1) **Millenarian** movements are a type of NRM that claim that members will achieve **salvation** through a **cataclysmic** event — a major disaster. Millenarianism is connected to **apocalypticism**, which is the belief that **divine forces** will **overthrow** the existing social order.

2) The **Ghost Dance** of the indigenous **Plains Tribes** in **North America** is a traditional example of a **millenarian** movement. The tribes believed storms and earthquakes would return the buffalo to the prairies and end ethnic divisions.

3) Millenarian movements are associated with **deprived groups** or areas where there has been **radical social change**.

The return of Changing Rooms.
Enough to make anyone believe the end is nigh.

New Age Movements *are Cultural*

1) **New Age movements** are close to cults and world-affirming movements. New Age ideas often aren't linked to an organisation, but spread through a **culture**, e.g. **dowsing**, **feng shui**, **crystal healing, neopaganism** and **reiki**.

2) **Heelas (1996)** claims that New Age beliefs are dedicated to "**self-spirituality**" and the development of the self.

3) **Bruce (1995)** highlights **three themes** to New Age movements: **New Science** rejects many claims of traditional science, **New Ecology** is concerned for the environment, and **New Psychology** sees the self as sacred.

New Age Movements *Appeal to People Already* Examining *their* Identity

1) New Age beliefs appeal to people who have **turned away from traditional religion**. New Age beliefs say that people can find salvation, peace or perfection **inside themselves**. Modern society is more **individualistic** than before — **individual beliefs** are **trusted more**, and **authority** is **trusted less**.

2) New Age movements help some people cope with the **uncertainties** of modernity. In the modern world, people have a lot of **different roles**. New Age beliefs can help people find a sense of **identity**.

3) New Age beliefs often appeal to middle class people working in "**expressive professions**" — actors, writers, social workers, counsellors, therapists etc. New Age beliefs appeal to **women** more than men, and **middle class** more than working class.

4) New Age movements may also reflect a **cultural change** in mainstream society. People are surrounded by non-conventional ideas like horoscopes, feng shui and homeopathy. **Mass communication** gives us an awareness of different movements.

5) New Age is quite a **postmodern** thing. In a **postmodern** society of **choice** and **diversity** people can **pick and mix** from all kinds of New Age philosophies to help them construct their own identity.

> There are more and more belief systems in society. "**Spiritual shoppers**" are people who **sample** different systems of belief to find the **best fit**. This is an **individualistic** and **consumerist** attitude.

Practice Questions

Q1 Give two examples of New Religious Movements.

Q2 Give two of the 'uncertainties' that help make New Religious Movements popular.

Q3 What are the three types of New Religious Movement that Wallis identified?

Q4 What three themes did Bruce identify in New Age movements?

Exam Questions

Q1 Identify and explain two characteristics of New Religious Movements. (6 marks)

Q2 Assess the view that New Religious Movements are created in periods of uncertainty. (33 marks)

Yup, moving your furniture around counts as religion...

It's not just going to a traditional place of worship that counts as religion. Deranged groups who think the world's going to end tomorrow, and all sorts of wishy-washy lifestyle stuff is also seen by sociologists as evidence of religious belief.

Religion and Social Position

Religiosity is related to age, gender, ethnicity and social class.

Religiosity varies by Age

Age affects how religious people are.

1) People **under 15** and **over 65** are more likely to be involved in religious activity. However, participation by those under 15 usually takes the form of **Sunday school** and **religious playgroups**.

2) The **over 65** group is the **most religious** in terms of **belief**. They aren't necessarily the most likely to practise their religion by going to church, because of difficulty with mobility.

3) However, some recent studies claim that the **elderly** are **increasingly losing faith** in God.

4) **Middle aged** groups are more likely to get involved in **world-affirming movements**.

5) **Sects** and **cults** are more likely to be populated with **young adults**.

- **Sects** often appeal to young adults by messages of **friendship** and **companionship** — this can be attractive to those who are experiencing forms of **anomie** (lack of social/moral standards) and **detachment** from the world, and those who have few responsibilities (e.g. marriage).

- **Cults** appeal to the **inner thoughts** and **feelings** of young adults who are often alienated from the primary cultures of society. **Cults** are attractive to individuals who are often already engaging in **counterculture** activity.

6) Young adults may be less religious than older people because of the way that society is changing. An increase in **rationalisation** means they feel less **need** for religion to explain things.

Religiosity varies by Gender

1) **Women** are **more likely to attend church**, and more likely to say they belong to a religion (**British Social Attitudes Survey, 1991**). This has often been explained by women's traditional role as **primary caregiver**. Going to **church** and **raising children** to be **religious** is traditionally seen as an **extension** of that role.

2) **Differential socialisation** is also a factor. The argument goes that girls are socialised to be **passive** and to **conform** — which fits in with the behaviour of more **traditional** and **conservative** religious groups.

3) Another argument is that **women** simply **live longer**. More women are on their **own** as they get older, and they may **turn to religion** for a sense of community. **Older** people are **more religious anyway**.

4) More **men** than **women** have **turned away** from organised religion in the 20th century.

Feminists' view of religion

1) **Beauvoir (1949)** claimed that the **images of gender** in Western religion deceive women into thinking they're **equal** when they're not. Women are sometimes portrayed as "**nearer to God**" than men by religious imagery and so are **duped** into believing their **sufferings** on earth will be rewarded with **equality** in heaven (see p. 7).

2) **Jean Holm** (Holm and Bowker, eds., 1994, *Women in Religion* London: Continuum) outlined how many contemporary religions both **exploit** and **subordinate** women and give men **dominant organisational roles**. She suggested this secondary status has its origins in **biology** and **sexuality** — "Menstruation and childbirth are almost universally regarded as polluting."

Women often have Significant roles in New Religious Movements (NRMs)

1) Women generally **participate** in **sects** more than men.

2) Also, many sects and NRMs were **established** by **women**, e.g. one of the founders of the Seventh Day Adventists was Ellen White, and the Christian Science movement was founded by Mary Baker Eddy.

3) **Glock and Stark (1965)** have argued that the gender difference in membership of NRMs is because **deprivation** (social, physical and mental) is **disproportionately** experienced by **women**.

4) **Bruce (1995)** suggests that men are more interested in NRMs that advocate **esoteric knowledge**, *esoteric = elitist and specialist* — women are more interested in subjects that can be classified as **New Science**, **New Ecology** and **New Spirituality**.

5) Some sociologists claim that **New Age** movements appeal more to women, because they emphasise "**feminine**" characteristics such as healing, caring and cooperation.

Remember, some NRMs have **narrow beliefs** about **women's role** in society, and therefore may **not appeal** to women. For example, some new evangelical right wing Christian movements believe that women should not work outside the home.

Religion and Social Position

Religiosity Varies by Ethnicity

The 1994 PSI Fourth Survey of Ethnic Minorities (**Tariq Modood et al**, published **1997**) found that, in England and Wales, nearly all **ethnic minority groups** are **more religious** and participate more in religion than white groups.

1) Religion maintains a sense of **community** and **cultural identity** within ethnic minority groups.

2) **Johal (1998)** claims that in a multi-faith society such as the UK, **religious identity** has become of key importance to members of ethnic minorities.

3) **Davie (1994)** argued that identification with a **religious organisation** was important to Indians, Pakistanis and Bangladeshis in the UK because it gave a sense of cultural identity and a feeling of **belonging**.

- **Modood** found that Pakistani and Bangladeshi Muslims in the UK identified themselves primarily as **Muslim**.
- Many young Muslims have a deeper **knowledge of Islam** than their **parents** do.
- Many Muslim girls feel more **liberated** by wearing headscarfs and dressing modestly because they are not subjected to the same **stereotypes** and values as non-Muslim girls.

i.e. rather than British, Pakistani, or Bangladeshi

4) **Afro-Caribbeans**, who are mainly Christian, attempted to incorporate themselves into the established churches of the UK but found **racism** within many congregations. One way to tackle this was to develop their own churches and ways of worshipping — e.g. Pentecostal churches.

5) **South Asians**, however, had to establish their faiths in a country with **radically different** systems of belief. Religion acted as a **support mechanism** for new immigrants, allowing them to share their culture. South Asians **quickly established** religious organisations — mosques, Sikh gurdwaras, etc. **Bruce (2002)** calls this **cultural transition**.

6) **Modood (1994)** and **Saeed (1999)** found some evidence for a decline in religious practice among Asians in the UK.

Religiosity Varies by Class

1) The **middle class** is disproportionately **Anglican** and **Quaker** compared with a more **Roman Catholic** or **Methodist** working class (this can be partly explained by their popularity in Victorian industrial areas). This pattern can be seen across many countries such as the U.S. and this would seem to back up Marx and Weber's opinions on Protestantism and capitalism.

2) Religious participation is greater in the **middle classes**, partly because religious affiliation is seen as a **desirable** social characteristic. Church is an opportunity for **social networking**.

3) Some argue that participation in **denominations** and **sects** is based on **class position**, claiming that there are middle class denominations and working class denominations.

4) **Bruce (1995)** found that cults are primarily middle class — in his opinion because they fulfil spiritual needs for people who have little financial pressure.

Lisa follows the cult of the Flying Spaghetti Monster. Well, it's hard not to believe in the thing when it's sitting on your head.

Practice Questions

Q1 Suggest why young adults participate more in sects and cults.

Q2 What role does religion play in upholding patriarchy, according to feminists?

Q3 Suggest why middle class people participate more in cults.

Exam Questions

Q1	Identify and explain two gender differences in religiosity.	(6 marks)
Q2	Assess the view that religious identity is of key importance to ethnic minorities.	(33 marks)

"Ah no, this is the women's church. Men's church is next door"...

Well, obviously it's not quite like that. The examiners will expect you to know how religion relates to age, gender, ethnicity and class, and also how religious participation relates to those things. You should mention a few studies too — no, don't kid yourself that you can remember them all — what did Glock and Stark argue? What about Johal? Davie? Saeed? Ha!

Religiosity in the Contemporary World

As the world changes, so too do religions and patterns of religiosity.

Globalisation *affects religion in* Different Ways

Peter Beyer (1994) claimed that **globalisation** has had three very different impacts on religion.

1) **Marginalisation** — religion has been **pushed out** of politics and public life and into the **private sphere**.

2) **Particularism** — religion has been used by groups who feel **threatened** by globalisation. They use it to express a sense of identity through a mix of **fundamentalism** and **nationalism**.

3) **Universalism** — globalisation can result in the emergence of an understanding of **common values** between religions. Beyer gives the example of **religious environmentalism**, in which many faiths come together in **common concern** for protecting a 'God-created' world.

Secularisation *is When* Religion Loses Its Influence *Over Society*

Bryan Wilson (1966, *Religion in Secular Society,* London: CA Watts) defined secularisation as a "**process whereby religious thinking, practice and institutions lose social significance**". Secularisation is said to be a result of the social changes brought about by **modern, urban, industrial society**.

Elizabeth worshipped bureaucracy...

The "founding fathers" of sociology **predicted secularisation**.

1) **Auguste Comte** claimed that **science** was the **final stage** in the **development of human thought**. He said modern society would be dominated by **science** and not religion.

2) **Max Weber** believed that **modern society** would be the age of **technology, rationality** and **bureaucracy**. He said rationality and efficiency **sweeps away magic, myth** and **tradition**.

Church Attendance *and* Membership *is in Decline*

Counting bums on pews gives **supporting evidence for secularisation**:

1) **UK church membership** and **attendance** has gone down — the number of people who **go to church** has fallen by almost 1 million in the last 20 years.

2) Attendance at ceremonies such as **baptisms** and **marriages** has also dropped. Just **27%** of babies were baptised in 1993, compared to **65%** in 1900.

Measuring secularisation by counting **bums on pews** has **limitations**:

1) People may **attend church** but **not believe in God**. They might attend a service, baptism or wedding out of friendship for the people involved, for respectability or because of family duty. Or even to get their kids into a certain school.

2) **Davie (1994)** argued people may **not attend church** because of their **lifestyle** even though they believe in God. Church attendance **doesn't** tell you about **belief**. The 2001 census found 72% of people identified themselves as Christians.

3) To make comparisons with the past you have to use **old statistics**, which may not be reliable.

Pluralism *Gives People* Choice

Religious pluralism means **diversity** in types of religious organisations and beliefs in society. As a result of this diversity the **established, national church loses its influence** in integrating people into **shared values**. **Multicultural** societies are more likely to have religious **pluralism**.

> Some sociologists see pluralism as evidence against secularisation
>
> 1) The increase in New Age movements since the 1980s can be seen as proof that the sacred is becoming important again — this is called resacrilisation, by the way.
>
> 2) It can be argued that pluralism is evidence of religion being transformed. It shows a trend towards individuation — people being free to search for their own religious meanings (to become "spiritual shoppers").

> Other sociologists see pluralism as supporting evidence for secularisation
>
> 1) Pluralism gives people choice. People might feel freer to choose to reject religion altogether.
>
> 2) Although some people in modern society have joined new religious movements, they are still a small proportion of the population. Some sociologists claim the growth in NRMs has been overestimated.

Postmodernists like **Lyotard (1984)** argue that people have lost faith in the old **metanarratives** of organised religion and politics. A metanarrative is a 'big' explanation that **makes sense** of the world, such as communism or Christianity. Postmodernists argue that organised religion has become **less influential** in postmodern society. **Zygmunt Bauman (1992)** suggested that a **religious vacuum** has been left behind — a "**crisis of meaning**". He argued that this vacuum is being filled by **new and diverse types of religiosity** such as New Age movements.

Religiosity in the Contemporary World

Desacrilisation is Where Supernatural Belief is Less of a Force in Society

1) **Weber** predicted **desacrilisation** (see glossary) in his idea of **disenchantment**. He thought that magic and myth were less important in modern society. Similarly, **Bruce (1995)** sees **science** and rational explanations as **undermining religion**.

2) Instead of turning to the supernatural or religion to **explain our problems**, we might turn to **science**. We demand pills when we are ill and we use science to explain natural disasters.

3) However, the **death** of a loved one, **injustice**, **natural disasters** and **terrorist atrocities** still sometimes lead people to prayer and faith in the supernatural. Modern science **can't explain everything** to everyone's satisfaction.

4) **Postmodernists** claim that we've moved **beyond scientific** rationality and we now **mistrust science**.

The Church May have Lost Some Functions and Become Disengaged

1) **Differentiation** is where **society becomes more specialised** so each **institution** in society has **fewer functions** than in the past. For example, the **church** used to have an important **educational** function. But since the 19th century more separate institutions have developed for this role and state involvement has increased. **Bruce (1995)** argues that religion becomes less important in society as some of its previous functions are taken over.

2) **Disengagement** is when the church becomes **separated from the state**. As a result, it has **less influence**.

3) **Parsons (1974)** claims that although the church may have lost its functions and become disengaged from the state and politics, religion can still be **significant in everyday life** and encourage **shared values** in society.

4) Religion is still closely linked to **politics** in the **Middle East** and **Northern Ireland**.

Some religious institutions have become 'secularised'

1) **Secularisation** of **religious institutions** is when the church becomes **less religious** in its beliefs to **fit in** with the rest of **society**. For example, many churches will now allow divorced people to marry.

2) American sociologist **Herberg (1956)** thinks church attendance shows **commitment to community** and not religion — people go to church to **meet up with friends** and to feel like **part of something**.

3) Remember that **not all religious institutions** have become more **secular**. The **New Christian Right** don't compromise their beliefs to fit in with society — they're against divorce, homosexuality and premarital sex. The more extreme end of the religious right are also against women working outside the home.

Secularisation is Very Difficult to Measure

There's more about sociological research methods in Section 8.

1) There are lots of different **measures of secularisation**. Some are more valid and reliable than others. **Surveys** show **high levels of religiosity**, but **quantitative measurements** of **church attendance** are **low**. **Different religious groups** measure membership in **different ways**, anyhow.

2) The term **secularisation** is a general term that's sometimes applied just to Christianity. It's important to know **what's being measured** — the decline of **religion in general** or the decline in **Christianity** in particular.

3) It's difficult to measure the significance of religion and make comparisons because sociologists use **different definitions of religion**. Some sociologists use **substantive definitions** which say **what religion is** — e.g. "religion is belief in the sacred". Some sociologists use **functional definitions** saying **what religion is for** — e.g. "religion is for creating value consensus".

4) To measure whether society has become **more secular** you have to compare it to **the past**. Some sociologists argue that we see the past as a **golden age** of religion where **everyone** believed and **no one** was sceptical. This is **far too simplified**.

5) Research into secularisation can also be rather **ethnocentric** — e.g. focusing on **Christianity** and what the **predominantly white British mainstream** does. Islam, Hinduism and Sikhism are also changing and developing in different ways.

Practice Questions

Q1 How does religious pluralism provide supporting evidence for secularisation?

Q2 What is meant by desacrilisation?

Q3 Define the term disengagement, with reference to religion.

Exam Question

Q1 Identify and explain two problems with measuring secularisation. (6 marks)

Bruce (1995) sees surnames as completely unnecessary...

There are lots of different sides to secularisation, and lots of ways to measure it. There's some clear evidence both for and against the secularisation thesis — which you need to learn. Oh, and by the way, the Bryan Wilson with the theory on secularisation isn't the Brian Wilson who was in the Beach Boys. Not that you thought he was. I'm just saying, like.

Theories of Development

*This whole section is for **AQA**. Ignore it if you're studying OCR. There are different ways of defining and measuring development and underdevelopment, and tons of theories to explain why some countries are more developed than others.*

The Exact Words used to Describe Development are Important

1) The term '**development**' is used to mean economic growth, industrialisation, and high living standards, e.g. high life expectancy and universal education. Countries which have achieved this are called **MEDCs** (More Economically Developed Countries). Countries which haven't are called **LEDCs** (Less Economically Developed Countries).

2) Richer countries are also referred to as **developed**, poorer countries as **developing**. **Underdeveloped** countries have developed less than other countries with the same resources.

3) All these terms are **ethnocentric**. They define development in terms of 'Western' ideals.

4) Another set of labels that's often used is '**First World**' and '**Third World**'. These expressions are **out of date**. The First World was wealthy countries like the USA and Japan. 'Third World' was used to describe the poorest countries.

5) The terms **North** and **South** are also used to describe differences between countries. These terms are more neutral. They don't imply that it's better to be Northern or Southern. They're not very accurate though. Australia is a 'Northern' country in the Southern hemisphere and China is a 'Southern' country in the Northern hemisphere.

If someone says a theory is ethnocentric they usually mean it looks at everything from a Western viewpoint and assumes Western values are superior to the values of other cultures.

Development is Measured in Different Ways

1) Capitalists argue that **economic indicators** such as **Gross National Product (GNP)** are the only effective ways of defining a country's potential for developing (along capitalist lines).

2) However, GNP doesn't tell you how wealth is **distributed**. In a country with a high average GNP per capita (per person) there may be a **minority** living in **deprivation**.

3) Economic indicators also ignore **externalities** caused by economic progress — e.g. pollution.

4) Some claim development is better measured by **social factors**. They measure development using **lists** of **basic human needs** — e.g. the Human Development Index (HDI), Human Poverty Index (HPI) and Physical Quality of Life Index (PQLI). Unlike economic indicators, these can show that there is deprivation even in 'developed' countries.

GNP = economic value of goods and services produced by a country over a year.

Development Theories have their foundations in Marx, Durkheim and Weber

1) **Marx** said that capitalism and industrialisation were about obtaining the **maximum** amount of **profit**. Capitalists in developed countries **exploit** underdeveloped countries to get **raw materials**, and to get a wide **market** for the goods produced by capitalism. Marx thought that capitalism would give way to **communism**.

2) **Durkheim** argued that societies would **progress** through **industrialisation** and that the most developed nations were those which had industrialised first. Durkheim saw the West as the most advanced society, and thought underdeveloped countries could improve their progression by taking on the **characteristics** of Western countries.

3) **Weber** argued that society was becoming more **rational** and **bureaucratic** — people needed to make more choices and come up with new, scientific ideas to solve social problems like deprivation. Less developed societies would need to copy Western **attitudes** in order to allow progress and economic development.

Modernisation Theory says countries Progress towards Liberal Capitalism

Modernisation theory says that **all countries** move **towards liberal capitalism**. **Undeveloped** countries are seen as **inferior** to **developed** countries that have achieved a higher rate of **production**, **consumption** and **wealth**.

Rostow (1971) suggested that all countries go through a five-stage process of development:

1) Basic, **agricultural** society.

2) **Transition**, or preparing for 'take off' — farmers produce a surplus and make money from selling cash crops. Small towns develop, and there's some industry on a very small scale.

3) **Industrialisation** or 'take off' — rapid growth of manufacturing. People move from rural to urban areas.

4) **Drive to Maturity** — lots of investment, and the right social conditions for growth. Large cities develop.

5) **Mass consumption**, or 'developed economy' — wealth spreads, people buy more and the service sector grows.

The explanation for poverty and underdevelopment is insufficient agricultural surplus to fund investment, insufficient investment in technology, and not enough hard-working business people to create opportunities.

Kerr (1962) focused on **cultural factors** — he believed that countries need Western-style politics and social values in order to develop, and they should replace traditional culture with Western values.

Theories of Development

Neo-liberalism believes in using Free Trade to help countries Develop

1) Neo-liberalism says that government intervention **distorts** the natural economic processes of the **free market**. Neo-liberals like **Friedman (1962)** believe **free market trade** can be used to help countries develop.

2) Organisations like the International Monetary Fund and World Bank favour neo-liberalism. They point to **Newly Industrialised Countries** (NICs) such as the '**tiger economies**' to prove that removing tariffs (charges for importing and exporting) and encouraging free trade can lead to development. 'Tiger economies' are South East Asian countries including Singapore and Hong Kong that have experienced a period of growth over the last 20 years.

Modernisation Theory and Neo-liberalism are both criticised

Both theories are criticised for being **ethnocentric** (arguing for the superiority of Western culture and industrialisation), and critics say this leads them to distort the true history of Western involvement in developing countries.

Neo-liberals and modernisation theorists also argue that Western methods of development are easily imitated and likely to succeed — which isn't necessarily true. In fact, the tiger economies got into serious economic trouble in 1997 after attempting to **extend too far** and **too fast**.

Dependency Theory says Developed countries Exploit Underdeveloped ones

1) **Dependency theory** was a reaction **against modernisation theory**. The key dependency theorist is **Frank (1967)**.

2) The theory says that developed countries **exploited** underdeveloped nations during colonial times (especially in the 1800s) when they controlled them as part of an **empire** (see p.20), and prevented them from industrialising.

3) When the underdeveloped nations got political independence, they were often still **economically dependent** upon their former imperial rulers. The poor nation's main trading partner is often its former colonial ruler. The theory says richer developed nations organise trading relationships in their favour. They set the price for goods.

4) **Dependency theory is Marxist** — it argues that **workers** in the poorest nations are **exploited** by the **ruling class**. They're paid very low wages, so the profits from the goods they make and grow go to the ruling class. Developed nations pay a low market price for the goods, and the goods are sold in the developed nation for a profit.

5) The theory goes on to say that profits pass from **workers** in **satellite areas** (less developed agricultural areas), to the **ruling class** in the **metropolis** (major cities, the former outposts of colonial power), and out to **developed nations**.

The theory doesn't fully define what development is or give realistic suggestions for how the situation can be resolved. It also doesn't explain why **socialism also exploited** and created dependency — e.g. the Eastern European satellite states depended on Russia. Dependency theory is criticised for being **deterministic** — it assumes that **everyone in LEDCs** will be **exploited**, and it doesn't accept that some LEDCs might **choose** capitalism, instead of being pushed into it.

World Systems theory says there's One Global Economy

1) **Wallerstein (1974)** suggested World Systems theory, which treats the entire world as one economy, rather than looking at development country by country. World Systems theory divides the world into **core** (developed countries), **semi-periphery** (e.g. South Africa, Mexico) and **periphery** (e.g. Ethiopia).

2) According to the theory, **core** countries make **full use** of the global economy, and can affect any other country — in other words, they have a global '**reach**'. Core countries are the ones which get the most out of capitalism. The core takes up all the surplus profits generated by the whole world — periphery and semi-periphery countries.

3) World Systems theory says the **semi-periphery** countries are **exploited** by the core countries, but they also **exploit** the **periphery** countries. In the theory, because they exploit as well as being exploited, they aren't fully "on the same side" as the periphery countries — no unity amongst the exploited means no united action to change the system.

This theory is also criticised for being too **deterministic**. It doesn't allow for **individual countries' characteristics**, and it still holds up the **core countries** as the model for perfect development.

Practice Questions

Q1 What are the five stages of development according to Rostow?

Q2 What is the central idea of dependency theory?

Exam Question

Q1 Compare and contrast dependency theory and world systems theory as explanations of underdevelopment. (18 marks)

Singapore and Hong Kong have stripy economies that go 'RAAAR'...

And they go stalking through the jungle, swishing their tails... or they would, if they weren't just boring old economies. Important reminder — don't use the terms 'first world', 'second world' and 'third world' — the second world doesn't exist since the USSR collapsed. Pages 20-21 will help with all this — they give some of the historical background to colonialism, and its effects on trade.

Theories of Globalisation

This fine pair of pages is about international trade and globalisation. Globalisation has economic, political and cultural aspects. No, don't switch off, this really isn't that boring. Honestly. Look, there's a photo of a burger and everything.

Globalisation has resulted in a Global Economy as well as National Economies

Giddens notes that **technological change** has transformed the way people live — global **communication** and **travel** are now easy. Goods can be **transported** across the world, and **information** can be transferred across the world **instantaneously**.

1) **Globalists** (sociologists who believe that society is becoming globalised) argue that **international trade** and investment have caused national economies to blend together into a **global economy**.

2) **Transnational Corporations** (**TNCs**) operate across national boundaries. They tend to have their headquarters in MEDCs and set up production in countries where there's **cheaper labour**, in order to maximise their profits.

3) **Fröbel et al (1980)** first referred to the **New International Division of Labour** — manufacturing tends to be done in developing countries, and knowledge-intensive work is done in MEDCs. **International division of labour** also means that **different stages of production** can be done in **different countries** — the car industry is a good example.

4) **TNCs** have a **positive** effect — they bring **jobs** and **investment** to developing countries, which can help with their national strategy for development. There's also a benefit for **international consumers** — cheap consumer goods.

5) However, some argue that this is a new form of **exploitation**. **Neo-Marxist** critics of globalisation say that the people of the developing world are turned into '**wage slaves**' for the capitalist system.

6) TNCs aim to create **global markets** for the goods they manufacture. They affect cultures throughout the world.

7) **TNCs** also have an effect on the **business culture** of host nations. TNCs can be categorised as three types — **ethnocentric** (headquarters in country of origin runs everything and sets corporate culture), **polycentric** (managed locally, according to guidelines set by headquarters) or **geocentric** (management is integrated across all countries).

> **Weberian sociologist Ritzer (1993) writes about global standardisation and 'rationalisation'.**
>
> 1) He refers to a '**McDonaldisation**' of production across the world. He says products are made with the same values as a **fast food** outlet: the product is made in **assembly line** conditions, it must be **inexpensive** to make and must be **standardised** at all times, across all the countries where it's made and sold. A Big Mac® is the same everywhere.
>
> 2) Ritzer picks out five themes within this McDonaldisation — **efficiency**, **calculability**, **predictability**, increased **control**, and the replacement of **human** workers by **machines**.

There's also Globalisation in Politics

1) Politics is increasingly carried out on an **international** level, rather than a national level.
2) The United Nations is responsible for enforcing international law, and peacekeeping etc.
3) There's increased **international political cooperation** — e.g. the **European Union**.
4) **International** non-governmental organisations (**NGOs**) coordinate **aid** and **campaigning**.

Sweet, juicy global standardisation.

Increased Communication spreads Cultural Goods across the world

1) The increase in **international media** communication in the last few decades has meant that cultures that were once local have become international and global. British and American pop music is everywhere. American and Indian films are seen internationally.

cultural goods = films, clothes, food, music, books etc.

2) Postmodernists argue that this allows people to consume a **plurality** of cultures. They think that globalisation leads to **hybridity** (a **pick and mix** of cultures) rather than one culture being imposed over another.

3) Critics point to the concentration of the **production** of cultural goods in the hands of a few large **TNCs** which have a lot of power in developing countries. They fear that TNCs will replace traditional culture with Western culture to try and **create new markets** for **Western cultural goods**. Critics refer to cultural globalisation as **cultural imperialism**.

4) Those who believe in the **positive** effects of cultural globalisation argue that it's a **two-way process**. Western culture is transmitted to new societies, and other identities and cultures get passed on to societies in MEDCs. An example of this would be the increase in screenings of **Bollywood films** in Western mainstream cinemas.

Theories of Globalisation

Global Organisations are seen by some as More Powerful than Governments

1) TNCs operate in **many countries** — they have a global reach. Many are as powerful as nation states in economic terms, and some critics point to their perceived lack of respect for local cultures as a key feature of globalisation.

2) National governments often find it hard to **control** TNCs and are **reluctant** to act against the interest of the TNC. The host nation **risks losing large numbers of jobs** if the TNC decides to pack up and **move to another country**.

3) **International political agencies**, such as the **United Nations** and the **European Union (EU)**, have taken some power and decision-making away from national governments.

4) Critics claim that this means nation states lose the ability to **determine their own future**, as they must constantly **negotiate** with other governments and agencies to try and get the best policy for the nation.

Leslie Sklair (2000) sees globalisation as a form of **transnational capitalism** (capitalism which crosses national boundaries). He thinks it isn't worth analysing nation states — power is held by TNCs, bureaucrats and global media.

There's Evidence to say that the role of the Nation is still as Important as ever

1) **Realists** point out that **national interest** still determines **most policies** within a nation and in international negotiations. For example, the US has so far refused to agree to the terms of the Kyoto Protocol (an international environmental strategy) **partly** because it's not in the interests of the US because of the potential effects on employment.

2) **Hall (1995)** argues that in a global world, **national identity** becomes very **important** to people as a way of ensuring there are still differences between the countries of the world. As a result, the nation state can be strengthened.

3) Increasing fears over the loss of power from national government to the EU has meant that many people in the UK are even more determined to protect the **sovereignty** of the nation.

4) There's a trend towards **devolution** — i.e. giving power to local bodies, as has happened with the Scottish Parliament and Welsh Assembly. Nations **within** the UK have reasserted their identity and control over key issues and policies.

You can protect her from the EU — but you can't protect her from this year's floral trends...

Practice Questions

Q1 Explain why some theorists say we now have a Global Economy.
Q2 What is the New International Division of Labour?
Q3 What is McDonaldisation?
Q4 Why do critics of cultural globalisation refer to it as cultural imperialism?

Exam Questions

Q1	What are the arguments for and against the view that we live in a 'McWorld'?	(9 marks)
Q2	Critically evaluate the argument that economic globalisation benefits less developed societies.	(18 marks)
Q3	"Despite globalisation, identity, culture and power are held by local communities and nation states rather than international organisations and agencies." Explore the arguments for and against this statement.	(33 marks)

So the world is turning into McDonald's? I reckon Ritzer was just hungry...

Hallucinations and bizarre fantasies are common during extreme hunger. But seriously, globalisation is a big thing in Sociology. Giddens is obsessed by it. It's a many-armed beast, is globalisation, with cultural, technological, political and economic aspects. Pretty much everything we buy has some kind of global connection. Think of how much stuff has 'Made in China' stamped on it.

Strategies for Development

There are different sociological perspectives on development strategies. And unfortunately, you have to know them all.

The **History** of **Colonialism** has shaped **International Trade Relations**

1) A colony is a territory that's **controlled** by a **foreign power**. Back in the 16th and 17th centuries, **European** countries began to **colonise Asian**, **African** and **American** territories. The height of colonialism was in the **19th century**.

2) European nations colonised foreign territories for three main reasons:

- Colonies were **economically important**. **Raw materials** and **food** were sourced in the colonies, and taken back to Western Europe to fuel **industrial-capitalist development**.

- Having **colonies** and building up an **empire** added to a nation's **power** and **influence** — the colonising country could put military bases and trading ports in the colony.

- Europeans also saw colonialism as a way of "**civilising**" native people. They saw traditional Asian, African and American cultures as **inferior**, and tried to **replace** them with Western values, including Christianity.

3) Colonialism strongly shaped **economic development** in the colonies. The colonisers set up plantations to grow **cash crops** such as coffee and cotton. They used slaves and low-paid labour and sold the crops for high prices in Europe.

4) Former colonies are often **under-industrialised**, because they were used only for primary sector industries such as agriculture and mining. Former colonies didn't get the chance to develop **manufacturing** industry.

5) Former colonies which rely on **agricultural exports** are hit hard by **global recession** — when the **market price** of cash crops drops, their **national income drops**.

Many **LEDCs** face a **Debt Crisis** — they spend more on **Debt** than **Investment**

Throughout the 20th century, **LEDCs** have had to **borrow money** from **richer nations** and **international organisations** both for survival and for development. The **World Bank** and **International Monetary Fund** (IMF) have lent large sums of money to LEDCs to fund development projects.

The World Bank and IMF are groups which loan money to fund development projects in member countries. It's not just LEDCs who borrow money — the UK has taken out loans from both organisations.

1) If you ask for a **loan** from your **local bank**, it'll come with a set of conditions — you have to pay **interest**, you have to pay a certain amount **back** each month. If you don't pay enough off each month, the **interest** starts to **pile on**, and you can find yourself in **financial trouble**. If you stop paying altogether you could even **lose your home**.

2) It's exactly the same with **nations**. Many poor countries spend **more** repaying **debts** and the interest that's built up on their debts than they spend on their own **infrastructures**. As **Hayter** points out, that's **not good** for **development**.

Dependency theory puts the crisis down to colonialism, corruption and greed

1) Dependency theorists argue that many countries are poor because **colonialism** restricted their economic development. Countries that gained independence were forced to **borrow money** to fund development.

2) Dependency theorists also argue that **aid** doesn't go to the right place — much of the money that's donated disappears, either because **governments embezzle** it (i.e. steal it for themselves) or invest in products that **don't help** a country to develop (e.g. **weapons**). This leaves an **investment gap** that has to be filled with **loans**.

3) In the 1980s and early 1990s, the **richest nations** and the **international lending organisations** significantly raised levels of **interest** paid on loans. Countries had to **borrow more** to meet **interest payments**. Dependency theorists think this rather suited the West as they saw an **increase** in the **debt owed** to them — they were suddenly looking at receiving a lot **more money** in debt repayments from the poorer nations.

There's an ongoing **campaign** to **reduce debt**, or **scrap** debts entirely. Many countries have had their **total debt** reduced, but this hasn't **yet** made a significant impact on the absolute poverty experienced by people within the poorest nations.

International Trade and **TNCs** can help **Development**

A recent view is that **trade** is more productive in development strategies than **aid**. This view is influenced by the New Right.

Not all trade-based strategies are due to New Right theorists, though — e.g. the **fair trade movement** aims to **insulate** agricultural workers in developing countries from the **ups and downs** of the world market. Fair trade businesses pay farmers a fixed '**fair**' price for their crops, whatever the global market price is. Neo-liberals claim that fair trade is just **aid under another name**, and say that **subsidies** don't encourage producers to be efficient and enterprising. They'd rather leave it to the free market.

1) TNCs can have both **positive** and **negative** impacts on development in LEDCs and NICs. They **provide investment** to developing countries, which can help with their own national strategy for development. They also provide **jobs**, which increases the host nation's **wealth**. Workers in the host nation have increased **spending power**.

2) TNCs can cause **rapid economic growth** which can be **too fast** for a host nation's **infrastructure** to cope with.

3) Those who define development in **quality of life** terms are concerned about **working conditions** in TNC factories.

Strategies for Development

Aid can be given in Three Different Ways

The United Nations recommends rich countries should give <u>0.7%</u> of their <u>GDP</u> in aid. In fact, very <u>few</u> developed countries meet the UN target. The UK gives around 0.4% of GDP.

1) **Bilateral Aid** is where a **government** gives **direct financial support** to another **government** that needs help (e.g. Malawi).

2) **Multilateral Aid** is from **international bodies** such as UNESCO, the World Health Organisation, the International Monetary Fund (IMF) and the World Bank. Multilateral aid can be either **grants** or **loans**. The IMF and World Bank give **loans**, and charge **interest** on the loans.

3) **Non-Governmental Organisations** (NGOs) give logistical support and direct financial donations. They get their money from the **public**. Examples of NGOs are Oxfam and Christian Aid.

Different Theories have Different Views of Aid

Modernisation theory says aid helps LEDCs 'Westernise'

1) **Modernisation theory** believes that developed countries should give **aid** to countries that are prepared to accept Western styles of development, i.e. **industrial capitalism**.

2) Modernisation sees aid as having a **'trickle-down effect'**. The argument is that aid goes to the elites of LEDCs, and the elites create wealth and prosperity. Associated factors such as **employment** and **increased standards of living** should **filter down** to **local economies** and **local people**.

3) Modernisation theorists were largely justified in the mid-20th century, as many poor countries (newly independent from colonialism) received aid and experienced **growth** and **success**. However, growth stalled later, and in some countries the poverty gap increased rather than decreased.

Neo-Marxist dependency theorists see aid as a tool to serve capitalism

1) Aid is often **tied** (given with conditions attached). A common condition is that local markets should be opened up to **free trade**, allowing foreign companies (including TNCs) to import and export goods without trade or customs levies. Neo-Marxists view this very **negatively**, believing that LEDCs are often exploited economically by TNCs.

2) **Bilateral aid** often requires the **recipient** nation to **buy goods** from the **donor** nation, or employ **technical experts** from the donor nation. These requirements help the **donor** nation.

3) Critics of Western aid such as **Teresa Hayter (1971, 1981, 1989)** see it as a tool for the richest countries to **politically influence** LEDCs. **Western** countries tended to give aid to countries with **right wing** governments rather than to countries with **socialist** or **communist** governments. This happened a lot during the Cold War.

4) To get a loan from the World Bank or IMF, LEDCs have often had to agree to make **political** and **economic changes** called **'Structural Adjustment Programmes'**. These are often **industrial-capitalist** in nature (e.g. privatisation of state-run services). Evidence shows that some of these programmes **haven't succeeded** in developing poor nations.

New Right theory says that aid creates dependency

1) **New Right theorists** generally don't believe in giving anyone 'something for nothing'. They argue that aid teaches LEDCs to be **dependent** on MEDCs, rather than standing on their own two feet. They say that LEDCs start to see aid as a right, rather than as a safety net, or last resort.

2) **Neo-liberals** believe that aid mucks about with the proper operation of the **free market** — they think that the free market is the best way of encouraging development, through **enterprise** and **investment**.

Practice Questions

Q1 What are the causes of debt according to dependency theorists?

Q2 What are the three types of aid that are given to less developed countries?

Q3 Explain how the 'trickle-down effect' works, according to modernisation theory.

Exam Question

Q1 "Aid is merely a tool for spreading capitalism across less developed countries." Assess sociological views on this statement.

(33 marks)

Lend us 20 million euros, would you...

You've probably heard Bono banging on about debt in developing countries, unless you've been in a cave on the moon with cushions strapped to your ears. You might even have heard him there — being a rock star, his voice does carry a fair way. You probably haven't heard of all the theories and sociologists' names on these pages, though, so you'll need to learn them for later.

NGOs and International Bodies

These pages look at the impact that international organisations have on the developing world — and it's a bit of a mixed bag.

NGOs and **Charities** used to provide mainly **Emergency Aid**

NGOs (non-governmental organisations) are private organisations carrying out campaigning, aid and development work. They are economically and politically **independent** from **government**.

1) **NGOs** and **charities** such as Oxfam, Save the Children® and the Red Cross/Red Crescent mainly respond to **emergencies** — e.g. the 1984 **famine** in Ethiopia, the crisis in the **Darfur** region of Sudan and the 2004 **tsunami** in South East Asia.

2) **Disaster and emergency relief** is obviously a **short-term** thing. It's different from **long-term development strategies**. That being said, economic and social development **can't take place** where large numbers of people are starving or homeless. It's essential to **fix** the **immediate damage** before going on to **plan strategies** for the long term.

3) NGOs also participate in **development**. They develop **local communities** through education and village clinics and work with **governments** and **businesses** to coordinate national development.

Four stages of NGO and charity involvement

1) Relief and aid	**Food** programmes, **urgent** medical care
2) **Community development**	Community **health centres**, community **education**
3) **Systems development**	Working with **government** and **private business**
4) **People's movements**	Encouraging **locally managed development**

NGO Activity has **Increased** over the last 50 years

The number of NGOs has grown massively in the past 50 years, as has the range of their different aims and structures. **Robbins (2005)** suggests a number of reasons for this:

1) **Better communications** — for example, the **internet** has made it easier for NGOs to organise, publicise and plan.

2) **Raised public awareness** — the extensive **mass media coverage** of global development issues and crises has raised public awareness of global humanitarian issues.

3) **Funding** — some national governments have increased funding to NGOs as an alternative to taking action themselves on development issues. This is because of a **neo-liberal** belief in **private** over state action. The increase in funding has also been driven by the belief that NGOs are more likely to **deliver results**.

4) **Expertise/Responsiveness** — NGOs have **developed networks and expertise**. They have a reputation for getting assistance where it is needed quickly, and for being **less likely** to be **corrupt** than some government bodies.

International Agencies try to help countries **Develop**

1) The **IMF** (International Monetary Fund) is an organisation made up of 185 countries which provides **loans** to states going through **financial difficulties**. It also provides **advice** to the governments of LEDCs on handling their economies.

2) The **World Bank** provides **grants and loans** to help developing countries build **infrastructure** (the things that society needs to function and grow — roads, electricity, a telephone network, etc.) and alleviate **debt problems**. It also advises LEDCs on how to make their **economies grow**.

The main criticism of these agencies is that they attempt to impose an **ideologically biased** model of development on poorer countries. They favour **neo-liberal free market economics** (see p.16-p.17) — but this **may not** be the best approach for all the countries they try to help.

To get **Loans** countries have to accept certain **Conditions**

Structural Adjustment Programmes (SAPs) are designed to promote **private-sector economic growth**. The World Bank and IMF link aid and debt-repayment assistance to the country's willingness to make free-market economic reforms, including:

1) The **deregulation** of private sector business and industry to remove limits on foreign investment and competition.

2) The **privatisation** of state-owned industries.

3) **Currency devaluation** to encourage foreign investment.

4) Tight **restrictions on government spending** on education and health.

5) **Reducing taxes** on businesses.

6) Gearing the economy for the **export market** rather than the domestic market.

SAPs were introduced in the early 1980s. From 1999, they have been partially replaced by **Poverty Reduction Strategy Papers (PRSP)**. These are documents, agreed with the **IMF** and **World Bank**, which outline the country's **social and economic strategy**. PRSPs put more emphasis on the country's sense of **ownership** and **involvement** in the policies adopted.

NGOs and International Bodies

SAPs have been criticised as an *Ideologically Driven* development programme

Hong (2000) has argued that the impact of SAPs has been negative on LEDCs. She argues it's led to:

1) **Increased poverty** — the result of **low pay** and **regressive taxation** (tax that hits the poor harder than the rich).

2) **Poor social conditions** — caused by **low funding of state health** and **social care provision**. Also caused by low pay and poor working conditions due to **lack of regulation**.

3) **Corruption** — liberalisation has **reduced** the amount of **regulation**, and provided an **open door for corrupt practices**.

4) **Environmental damage** — production for the **export market** rather than the domestic market has resulted in damaging practices such as **monoculture** (growing one crop exclusively), **deforestation** to make way for plantations of 'cash crops', and increased **carbon emissions**.

5) **Social unrest** — Hong cites the example of **Sierra Leone** where the combination of grinding poverty and the lack of services and welfare led to serious upheaval in the 1990s.

Not all the activities of *International Organisations* are so *Controversial*

1) In 2005 the **G8** — an organisation made up of eight of the richest countries in the world — **wrote off the debts** of 18 of the poorest developing countries.

2) **Dalmiya and Schultink (2003)** argue that the work of the **World Health Organisation** (WHO) — the section of the UN that deals with public health matters — has significantly **reduced disease** and **improved nutrition** in the developing world.

Transnational Corporations are huge businesses operating across borders

Some **transnational corporations** (**TNCs**) are richer than many nation states. The **impact** of such corporations on LEDCs can therefore be **immense**. There's more about TNCs on p.18 and p.33.

TNCs have been **criticised** for their activity in LEDCs. Harmful practices include:

Isabella wasn't colouring outside of the lines — she was just 'operating across borders...'

- **Driving down prices** paid to producers in LEDCs followed by **profiteering** when these lower costs are not passed on to consumers in the developed world.

- **Exploiting their workforce** in LEDCs, by using unregulated markets to pay very low wages for very long hours.

- Having a **negative impact** on the enviroment.

There are *Potential Benefits* to TNC activity

Contreras (1987) suggests that TNC activity in the developed world can lead to **significant benefits**. For example:

1) Increased government revenue through tax increases, which can in turn be spent on **health and education**.

2) The **advanced technology** that TNCs bring with them can provide a **catalyst** to further economic growth in the economy.

3) TNCs increase **employment opportunities** and therefore income.

4) TNCs need **skilled workers**, which provides impetus for improvements in education and training.

Practice Questions

Q1 Give four reasons for the growth in the number of NGOs in the last 50 years.

Q2 List the potentially negative effects of Structural Adjustment Programmes according to Hong (2000).

Q3 What are the potential benefits to the developing world of the activities of TNCs?

Exam Question

Q1 Evaluate the arguments for and against the model of aid and development pursued by the IMF and World Bank. (18 marks)

You're gonna have to learn this stuff — you can bank on it...

The SAPs are a big ol' bone of contention with a lot of people — while the IMF and World Bank would claim they're just trying to help, some see them as part of a big conspiracy to spread Western values throughout the globe. For me they're another crazy acronym to learn and love. It's worth getting to grips with both sides of the argument — no matter what your opinion.

Urbanisation and Industrialisation

Some sociologists say that cities are a focal point for modernisation, investment and economic development. Others say that development in cities doesn't help the poor, and damages the environment too much. The rest just live in them and leave it at that. Those last ones are my favourite type of sociologist. There don't seem to be enough of them.

Urbanisation goes along with Industrialisation

Urbanisation means the increase in **urban populations**, compared to **rural populations**. During periods of industrialisation, people have **migrated** from rural areas to urban areas in search of **work**.

Industrialisation means the change from **agriculture** and small-scale cottage industry to large-scale manufacturing in factories. Factories are **centralised workplaces** — they require people to move to where the work is.

In Western Europe, there was a **rapid increase** in urban populations in the **19th century** as a result of **job opportunities** offered by the **Industrial Revolution**. In Mexico, industrialisation and urbanisation happened in the **20th century**.

Modernisation theory argues that Urbanisation is key to Development

1) In modernisation theory, the growth of cities symbolises the triumph of Western models of development and Western ideals. The city is seen as a place that rejects traditional goals and aspirations and replaces them with notions of **meritocracy**, **activism** and **individualism**.

2) **Hoselitz (1964)** argues that the **cities** encourage people to **work**, and contribute to the economy, because the system within **urban** areas is focused on **achieved status** (success based on achievement rather than social position) and **meritocracy** (allocation of people to positions in society based on **ability** rather than **family**).

3) Critics of this theory argue that it is **ethnocentric**, because it's based on Western cities, Western capitalism and Western ideals.

4) Additionally, it's seen as rather **unclear** in places — it doesn't say **how** power, wealth and development move from urban areas into rural areas, it just **assumes** that they do.

Some see Development as the move from Rural Lifestyles to Urban ones

1) Some sociologists, especially modernisation theorists, see development as the shift from the characteristics of **rural** life to **urban** life.

2) Taking this view means that it's **easy** to measure development — it's just a calculation of how **urbanised** society has become. This can be measured by counting the number of **cities** and urban townships, and the numbers of **people living, working** and **socialising** within them, and comparing it to the number of people who live, work and socialise in the countryside.

Dual Economy theory says that Rural and Urban economies are Separate

1) **Dual economy** theorists argue that urbanisation leads to two very **different** types of society within one country — **rural** society and **urban** society. They function as **two separate economies** with little connection between them.

2) The **rural** economy is **localised** and focused on **subsistence**. The **urban** economy is **national** and **international** and focused on **economic growth** and development.

3) The theory is based on the idea that **colonialism** pushed progression in **urban** areas at the expense of **rural** areas, which became marginalised. See p.20 for more on colonialism.

4) It's a useful theory to explain the point that the needs and problems of **urban** areas are very **different** to **rural** areas.

5) However, **critics** point to the fact that dual economy theory still assumes that rural economies are 'backward'.

Dependency Theory — Poverty in LEDC cities is caused by Colonialism

1) Dependency theorists believe the cities described by modernisation theorists don't exist. They say cities in LEDCs aren't success stories of meritocracy and achieved status, where hard work always brings big rewards. They're actually polarised between the '**haves**' and the '**have nots**'. They blame **colonialism** for this.

2) Dependency theory says that urbanisation doesn't bring solutions to the developing world, just more problems, e.g. **inequality**, **urban poverty**, **bad public health**. The developing world doesn't have the infrastructure to deal with them — there's poor health care, limited access to education, and little social security (if any at all).

3) According to the theory, only the parts of the city where **capitalist elites** live and work are anything like the modernisation theory model of a city. Those parts were **designed** under colonialism to house the **colonial elite**.

4) The theory says LEDC cities depend on trade with rich nations, and serve rich nations rather than their own people.

5) Dependency theory **ignores** countries where urbanisation actually **has** brought **economic benefits** for the people.

Urbanisation and Industrialisation

The Two Main Approaches to Industrialisation are ISI and EOI

ISI is short for **Import Substituting Industrialisation**. The developing nation works to substitute **home-grown alternatives** for goods it used to import. **Trade tariffs** and **taxes** are used to **protect** the locally manufactured goods from **foreign competition**. A state applying ISI has to be **interventionist** — protecting markets, patrolling borders and overseeing the industrialisation process.

EOI stands for **Export Orientated Industrialisation**. The developing country focuses on producing **consumer goods** for **export**. There is **high demand** for the goods from MEDCs, which have **moved away** from labour-intensive manufacturing. LEDCs have **cheaper labour costs** and can sell their products at attractive prices.

ISI has Advantages and Disadvantages

On the plus side, **ISI** helps LEDCs become **less dependent** on the developed world.
They can **target** and **plan** their own economies and **invest the profits** they make in further development.

But on the down side...

1)   With **no foreign competition** local industries have no incentive to be competitive.
Businesses can become **inefficient** and **corrupt** or even fail.

2)   **Protectionist policies** (i.e. refusing to buy goods from abroad) can **aggravate potential customers**, who may in turn **refuse to buy** the developing country's goods.

3)   With **no real incentive to expand** their business, some firms **cut wages** as an easy way of boosting profits. This can drag down wage levels in the country as a whole.

EOI has Positive and Negative Effects too

Saving for one of these?
That's fierce tiger economy...

EOI has worked very well for some Newly Industrialised Countries (NICs) like **South Korea**, **Hong Kong**, **Taiwan** and **Singapore** — sometimes referred to as the '**tiger economies**'. People living there now enjoy a much **improved standard of living** and **health**.

But the focus on export markets can mean the manufactured goods are **too expensive** for the domestic population to buy. **Fierce competition** in international markets can lead to **wage cuts**.

Industrialisation can bring Too Many People to the Cities

Rapid industrialisation can lead to **massive social problems** as workers move from the countryside to work at new city factories. **Webster (1984)** described this as **over-urbanisation**. Over-urbanisation is caused by **push** and **pull factors**.

Push factors	Pull factors
Poverty	Chance of employment in new factories
Loss of land	Better access to education in towns
Natural disasters	Perception that there are better opportunities
War and civil war	Escape constraints of family, religion, culture
RESULT: people leave the countryside	**RESULT: people move to the city**

Newcomers often can't afford ordinary city housing and build temporary homes in **shanty towns**. The shanty towns don't get any of the usual city **services** like a proper **water** supply, **health care** or **policing**. Standards of living are **extremely low**.

Practice Questions

Q1   What is industrialisation?

Q2   What is the dual economy theory?

Q3   Give examples of two 'push' and two 'pull' factors which can contribute to over-urbanisation.

Exam Questions

Q1	Outline and explain two features of urbanisation in the developing world.	(9 marks)
Q2	Evaluate the effectiveness of alternative strategies for industrial development in the developing world.	(33 marks)

And the city streets are paved with gold and diamonds — honest...

When you look at interpretations of urbanisation, remember that modernisation theory and dependency theory are pretty much opposite. So, given that modernisation theory says that cities are wonderful and promote development, dependency theory must say they're awful. If modernisation theory says something is black, dependency theory says it's white. And so on.

The Environment

There's a major downside to LEDCs attempting to become more economically developed — the negative impact it has on the environment. Sociologists have suggested different ways of managing the damaging effects of industrialisation, but they mostly agree that it's hard to balance building a successful economy and being environmentally friendly.

LEDCs Contribute to and Suffer from Environmental Problems

Deforestation

Rainforests are logged for **hardwoods** or to make way for **agriculture**. They are disappearing fast — a **fifth** of the **Amazon** has already been **deforested**. Rainforests **release oxygen** and **absorb carbon**, which helps hold back climate change. Deforestation also causes **species loss**.

Water pollution

The World Health Organisation (WHO) estimates that an average person needs **20 litres of clean water** a day for drinking, cooking and washing. In 2001, 1 billion had **no access** to piped water. **Kingsbury (2004)** suggests that water is scarce in some areas due to **industrial pollution**.

Desertification

Poor farmers may have no choice but to **over-cultivate** and **over-graze** their land. Eventually the land is **exhausted** and turns to desert. The process is called **desertification**. It can lead to **famine** and **species loss**.

Climate change

CO_2 **emissions** have increased as the developing world becomes industrialised. **Fossil fuels** (oil, coal and gas) are used to power the **industrialising economies**. As countries become wealthier and more industrialised there is more use of **motor vehicles** and more CO_2 is emitted.

Decline in biodiversity

If present trends continue, one, or even **two thirds** of the world's plants, animals and other life forms could be **extinct** by the end of the century. This could lead to total **ecosystem collapse**, making food production impossible and leading to widespread starvation.

Industrialisation is a major cause of Environmental Damage

1) Industrialisation creates air, water and land **pollution**, and uses up **natural resources**.

2) Rapid urbanisation results in **overcrowding**. Urban **infrastructures** often **can't cope** with the influx of people. Rural-urban migrants settle in makeshift **squatter** settlements without proper **water supply** or **sanitation**.

3) Urban areas are polluted by **industry** and by **motor traffic**. This affects **public health**.

4) The new **international division of labour** means that polluting heavy industry is concentrated in LEDCs.

5) LEDCs don't have **equal access** to "clean" technology — e.g. equipment to reduce air pollution from power plants.

There are different Theoretical views on how to Manage the Environment

The neo-liberal view

Countries need to calculate the **costs** and **benefits** of any development strategy. If a country works out that the **environmental cost** of a development strategy is **too high**, then they won't pursue that strategy. But this may make them **less competitive** in the **global market**.

The structuralist view

Structuralist theories argue that the developing world would do more about environmental issues if it was **debt-free**. As long as the developing world is struggling to **catch up economically** the **economy** will always **take priority** over the environment.

Structuralist theories are the ones that say the structure of society is responsible for social problems. Marxism is a structuralist theory.

Some sociologists argue that Sustainable Development is the solution

Sustainable development is development that aims not to harm the environment.

The Neo-Marxist **Redclift (1987)** points out that the idea of sustainable development is **only needed** because development is defined in **economic** terms and characterised by trading **natural resources** for **money**. Redclift also says that some environmentalists **claim** to support sustainable development but don't give enough priority to relieving **poverty**.

War and Conflict

If you're worried that pollution and global warming might destroy the planet in the next hundred years or so, don't panic— there's a good chance we won't have to wait that long. A good, old-fashioned war could destroy the planet in no time at all. Wars tend to take place in LEDCs — and make it even harder for those countries to develop.

War and Violence *are widespread in the* Developing World

1) Since the end of the Second World War around **25 million people** have died in warfare. The vast majority of these deaths have taken place in **LEDCs**.

2) In 1993, there were **52 wars** taking place, involving 42 countries. In another 37 countries, **violence** (often **political**) was widespread. That makes a total of 79 countries involved in wars or other widespread violence. Of these **79** countries, **65** were **LEDCs**.

3) **Dan Smith (1994)** suggested that **MEDCs** are much **less likely** to be engaged in war and violence. The countries in the lower two thirds of the development tables were **most likely** to be **involved in violence** or conflict.

4) Smith concluded that **development aimed at generating wealth** is essential to reduce the threat of war and violence in developing countries.

5) Smith also highlighted **links** between **national debt** and the **likelihood of being involved in war** or conflict. Of those LEDCs with national debt it was the 85 per cent with the worst levels of debt that were also most affected by war, violence and conflict.

Conflict creates long-term problems

- Infrastructure (e.g. transport and communication networks) is often damaged, setting development back by many years.
- People flee their homes and can no longer work or grow food.
- In camps for displaced people, diseases often spread quickly.

KPA / Zuma / Rex Features

A camp for internally displaced people (IDPs) in the DR Congo.

Poverty, Social Division and Weak Government *can lead to war*

1) **Frances Stewart (2002)** says that while many conflicts may have an ethnic, cultural or religious dimension, the underlying causes of most are **economic**.

2) Economic causes of war could include **political**, **economic** or **social inequalities**, **poor government services**, high **unemployment**, **land disputes** and disputes over scarce **resources** like water due to environmental degradation.

3) According to Stewart, a possible solution to these problems is **inclusive development** with the aim of **reducing divisions** between rich and poor and **tackling unemployment**.

The conclusions of Smith and Stewart contrast sharply with neo-liberal theories of development. Neo-liberals would favour free markets, low taxes, encouraging enterprise and wealth generation over actively intervening to tackle the causes of conflict.

Practice Questions

Q1 Name three types of environmental damage caused by industrialisation.

Q2 What is sustainable development?

Q3 Have more people died in conflicts in developing or developed nations?

Q4 List three economic factors that can cause wars and conflicts to break out.

Exam Questions

Q1 Assess the view that economic development must come before environmental issues. (18 marks)

Q2 Critically evaluate the argument that economic development can be an effective strategy for reducing conflict in developing countries. (33 marks)

Make tea not war...

Ross Kemp and John Simpson seem to get on alright in war zones, but I think I can safely say the rest of us would rather sit at home with a cup of tea and a biscuit. When sociologists look at war and conflict they're interested in a) what causes the violence, and b) the effects conflict has on future development. There's an easy short answer to b) — not good.

Aspects of Development: Demography

Demography is the study of population change. It's been a big thing in World Sociology since, well, forever.

Population is growing Fast in the Developing World

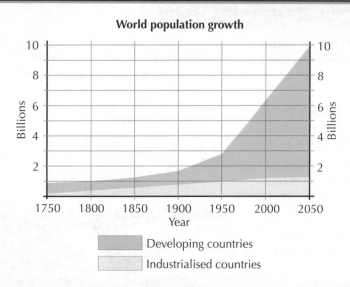

World population growth

This chart* shows **world population growth** since 1750, and predicts what could happen between now and 2050.

Population is growing much **more quickly** in the **developing world** than in the industrialised nations.

* Based on a 1997 graph by Philippe Rekacewicz, UNEP/GRID-Arendal from http://maps.grida.no/go/graphic/world_population_development

Malthusians and Modernists say High Population Growth must Stop

Malthus (1798) thought that population growth could cause **problems** — a population could grow faster than its capacity to feed itself. He pointed out that limited resources would cause death, which would balance the birth/death equation.

Neo-Malthusian **Ehrlich (1968)** believed that the '**population explosion**' was putting too much stress on the resources of the world, leading the developing world, in particular, to experience problems such as famine and malnutrition. He believed over-population was damaging development and the environment.

1) The work of Malthus and Ehrlich has been used by **modernisation theorists** who argue that over-population in the developing world is one of the biggest obstacles to development. Any economic surplus has to be spent on feeding the population and building an infrastructure to cope with increased population, instead of on industry.

2) Modernisation theorists argue that the solution is to persuade governments to **promote birth control**, and for **Western governments** and **international organisations** to **fund birth control** programmes.

3) Modernisation theorists also suggest that money should be spent on **educating women**, because educated women tend to have fewer babies.

4) Ehrlich has even suggested that men in the developing world who have had 3 children or more should be **sterilised**.

5) **USAID** (The United States Agency for International Development) currently spends around US$425 million a year on **family planning programs** worldwide.

6) Countries like **China** and **Singapore** have used **legal restrictions** and **economic incentives** to encourage their citizens to have fewer children.

Most attempts to Lower Birth Rates have Failed

1) Some religions, including **Islam** and **Roman Catholicism**, discourage or do not approve of using contraception. Many people who practise these faiths prefer not to use contraception.

2) **Harrison (1990)** notes that the fastest rates of population growth in the developing world are found in **Muslim** countries where traditional ideas about **women** and the **family** predominate.

3) **Feminists** have suggested **significant progress** will not be made on population control until developing countries become **less patriarchal** and the position of **women** in society improves so they are able to **take control over their own bodies**.

4) Much of the evidence does suggest that making contraception and contraception advice available is not enough. It needs to go hand in hand with **changing the position of women in society**.

Aspects of Development: Demography

Ehrlich's Theory of over-population has been Criticised

Carnell (2000) showed that Ehrlich's predictions about population growth were wrong. The population is growing more **slowly** than Ehrlich thought.

Harrison (1990) points out that the **birth rate** isn't the cause of population growth. Population growth is actually caused by a **decline** in the **death rate**, especially the infant mortality rate. People are having the same number of babies, but **fewer** are **dying**. Harrison does agree with Ehrlich that population growth threatens the environment, though.

People are having the same number of babies — only now they take up less space...

Marxists say Population Growth is Not the Problem

1) **Marxists** would say modernisation theorists blame the wrong people for population growth. Modernists say over-population is the fault of the **governments** of the developing world, **religious organisations** and the **people** themselves. Marxists blame the **global capitalist system**.

2) Modernists believe over-population is a problem because they assume Malthus was right when he said growing populations can outstrip food supplies. The Marxists believe the real cause of starvation and famine is not over-population but **unfair distribution of world resources**. There is enough food for everyone, but capitalist market forces mean food goes where the money is and not where it is needed most.

Other theorists also Support Redistributing Resources

1) There's not a lot of evidence that **food resources** aren't coping. **Food production** has **increased**, and the world has the capacity to produce **more** food than it produces now, although it might be difficult to do this sustainably. **Boserup (1965)** said that **population increase** determines **agricultural change**, so that agricultural production always keeps up with the population.

2) **Dependency theorists** argue that the West continues to take the very best resources a developing nation has, leaving the inhabitants with little land of any quality. **Land reform** and **redistribution** to the poor would be a better solution than population control.

3) **Adamson (1986)** says focusing on population growth can distract us from the **real causes** of poverty and starvation. He believes the real causes are an unfair distribution of resources. We should look at the developed world's contribution to these problems, e.g. **over-consumption**, **environmental damage**, and **economic exploitation** of the developing world.

4) **Adamson** also suggests that poverty **causes** high population. Poverty forces parents to see children as **economic assets** who will bring money into the household and support them in **old age**. Where there are high levels of infant mortality parents have more children to increase the chances of at least one surviving into adulthood.

Adamson points out that, in 1986, an American used up on average 300 times more energy than a Bangladeshi.

Some believe Population Growth can Encourage Development

1) Some theorists see population growth not as a problem but as a **cause of development**. As population growth creates pressure on resources it encourages people to **innovate** and find ways to be more **productive**.

2) A good example would be **Britain** in the 19th century where many historians see population growth as a major **cause of industrialisation**.

Practice Questions

Q1   Why do modernists believe over-population is an obstacle to development?

Q2   Why have policies aimed at reducing population in the developing world had limited impact?

Q3   What positive effect does an increasing population have according to some theorists?

Exam Question

| Q1   Evaluate the view that rapid population growth is a significant obstacle to development. | (33 marks) |

Malthus thought we had problems in 1798...

... imagine if he could see us now. The world's population was only about 1 billion then — it's over 6 times that now. Sociologists disagree about what's to blame for over-population — too many babies, too few deaths, capitalism...the list goes on. Anyway, soon we'll have bigger issues than arguing about the causes 'cause the world will be full and there won't be any room to lie down.

Aspects of Development: Education

You might not be in the mood to believe this, but good education has been proven to improve standards of living, raise participation in civic activities and make for a happier, harder-working populace. In the last 50 years, developing countries have spent more of their budgets on improving the education of their people — with mixed results.

Good Education *improves the* Living Standards *of people in LEDCs*

Education is necessary for **development**. In Rostow's model of development (see p.16), an educated workforce is necessary for industrial take-off. Many other sociologists, in particular **functionalists** and **modernists**, also think education is very important for development.

1) **Economic development** requires expert, technical knowledge on a local level. Not all expertise can be brought in from other countries. International organisations and MEDCs are generally keen to see LEDCs **train** their own people in the **specialist skills** required for the long-term development of a country.

2) Education also gives people the **values** and **attitudes** required in the process of development. Literate, numerate people can fully understand what action is required for development and **participate** in deciding what action to take in their communities and their country.

3) Education can act as a **unifying force**. It can give people a common set of **values** and ideas about their country, which helps to overcome class, ethnic and religious **differences** in a country.

4) Many people in the developing world are keen to participate in education because they want to obtain **achieved status** — a qualification, improved employment opportunities, etc. Education acts as an **empowering** tool for groups in society that have traditionally been **excluded** from **social mobility**, e.g. women and the poor.

Universal Education *is still* Unavailable *for many in the* Developing World

1) **External aid** and increased **investment** in the developing world has led many countries to introduce **universal education** — but provision is often **patchy**.

2) Some countries have universal education for **primary school** age (up to about 11 years old), some have universal education up to 14 or 16 years old, and some still haven't introduced universal education.

3) Even in countries that have **universal education** as a policy, not every child **actually goes to school**. This is because of other **family commitments** and needs — e.g. children may be required to **work** on the **family farm**.

4) In many countries, parents still have to **pay school fees** to get their child into school. Also, **school supplies** aren't provided by the state like they are in the UK. Families have to **buy** books and other resources.

The Growth *in* Education *doesn't mean* Quality Education

Much of the **increase** in education has had to be supplied by education **systems** that were designed to meet the **basic needs** of a **few**. Basic education systems have been put under **strain**.

Lessons aren't always of **high quality**. Some education doesn't provide enough **useful knowledge**.

The Growth *in* Education *has raised problems with* Employment

1) While young people are in schools and colleges being educated, they're not out **working** and contributing to the **local** and **national economy**.

2) Because more people are studying and fewer people are working, governments get less revenue from income tax. Governments have less money coming in but have to **pay out more** to **provide education**.

3) Bright, educated people from rural areas tend to **migrate** to the **cities** to look for jobs. This contributes to **over-urbanisation** and urban **overcrowding**.

4) The more educated citizens **sometimes struggle** to find **employment** in their own country, or they can simply earn a lot more by moving away to countries that have **better job prospects** — this is called the "**brain drain**", by the way. The end result is that the country **fails to develop** because the educated have **left**, to use their education elsewhere.

Marxist Dependency Theorists *see* Education *as* Cultural Imperialism

Dependency theorists really frown on the idea that education **trains** people for **development**. They **strongly disapprove** of education that gives people the **values** and **attitudes** that are needed for "imperial-capitalist" (i.e. Western) development — they call this **cultural imperialism**.

Dependency theory sees **education** as a potential **tool** for keeping people **culturally** and **economically dependent** on the developed world — it trains them to get the kind of **jobs** that **benefit TNCs** and the **developed world**.

Aspects of Development: Health

At the start of the 21st century, health in the developing world is still poor compared to the developed world. Good health care provision is essential for the development and protection of people in the developing world.

Physical Quality of Life Index (PQLI) Measures Health and Education

1) **David Morris** developed the PQLI in **1979**. It measures **infant mortality**, **literacy** and **life expectancy**. It's useful for sociologists concerned with development as a social issue rather than an economic issue.

2) The PQLI also allows you to compare trends across countries. However, there are problems in collecting reliable data.

Education, Poverty and the role of MEDCs all impact on Health in LEDCs

1) Poverty forces people to suffer poor **public health** and a **bad diet**.

2) It also prevents them from gaining a good quality of **health care**. Universal free health care is **rare** in the developing world — people usually have to **pay** to see a doctor. There are also **not enough doctors** and **nurses** to go around.

3) The lack of good **health education** in the developing world means many people (particularly those in traditional, rural areas) do not know how to **prevent disease** and are not aware of **basic treatments**.

4) Some drugs companies sell drugs in the developing world that are **banned** in the **West** for **safety** reasons. Or they may set the **price** of life-saving drugs so **high** that many in LEDCs can't afford them.

5) **Western products** may be used **inappropriately**. For example, **baby formula milk** is heavily advertised in LEDCs. Some mothers don't have access to **clean water** to make the milk with, so many babies die from **infections** and poor mothers may **water down** the formula too much (to make it last longer), resulting in **malnutrition**.

6) Also, TNCs that have set up in the developing countries often pay little attention to the environment, or health and safety. For example, the Bhopal poison gas leak of 1984 happened because safety procedures were inadequate.

> **Example: HIV/AIDS in South Africa**
> - **Insufficient health education** in poor areas meant people **didn't know** how HIV was transmitted.
> - Clinics could be a **day's walk** away.
> - **Transnational drugs companies** refused to allow local drugs companies to make **cheap versions** of anti-HIV drugs. This was overturned by the courts in 2001.
> - In the 1990s, the **South African government** was **reluctant** to **distribute** anti-HIV drugs.

They doubted that HIV caused AIDS.

There are different Theoretical Views about Health Inequalities

Modernisation theorists and **functionalists** believe **Western** medicine is **superior**, and that Western medicine and **health education** can **solve** the problems of **high infant mortality** and **low life expectancy**. **Rostow (1971)** said **high-tech medicine** used in the developed world should be **transferred** to developing nations so that **quality health care** can be provided.

Marxist **Navarro (1976)** believed that high-tech Western health care is not the immediate priority for the developing world. Poor nations need to focus on **basic health procedures** to **save lives** and **improve quality of life**. Doctors from these nations need to be encouraged to stay and work in their own countries, not to migrate to MEDCs for better pay.

Dependency theory blames **colonialism** and **exploitation**. Colonialism introduced European diseases to Africa, America and Asia. Colonialism also replaced food crops with cash crops, resulting in malnutrition. Dependency theory also blames the developed world for **poverty** and **debt**.

Practice Questions

Q1 What are the advantages and disadvantages of universal education?

Q2 What is PQLI?

Q3 What do modernisation theorists argue is crucial for development in health?

Exam Questions

Q1 How can education be used as a tool for development in the developing world? (18 marks)

Q2 Critically evaluate the argument that the health concerns of the developing world have largely been caused by the policies of the developed world. (33 marks)

This subject is certainly draining my brain...

With every page my head feels emptier and emptier, and soon there'll be nothing left. Anyway, it's those dreaded words 'cultural imperialism' again. It's really hard to think about development without slipping into some kind of 'them and us' thinking — either assuming that the West knows best, or assuming that the West is all bad, and that poor countries should be left to get on with it.

Aspects of Development: Gender

Recently, sociologists (particularly feminists) have pointed out that women and men experience development and under-development in different ways. And you know what that means — more radical feminists. Should be interesting.

There's **Gender Inequality** in the **Developing World**

Evidence from studies into gender in LEDCs shows that in many cases women get a worse deal than men.

- Women have **lower life expectancy** than men in **some countries** (usually women live longer than men).
- Women are **paid less** than men.
- Women get **less education** than men.
- Women's **health** is **poorer** than men's health, and women have **less access** to health care than men do.
- There's even a **greater chance of abortion** if a foetus is **female**.
- Women have very poor **reproductive rights**. They don't get to choose whether to have children or how many because local **religious attitudes** are against contraception and abortion.

The Gender Empowerment Measure (GEM) is a indicator of the progress made by women in a society

1) The GEM focuses on **social indicators** of gender equality — female and male participation in **decision making**, **economic participation** and **economic power**.

2) In other words, it monitors whether women have the right to **vote**, how many women there are in **parliament**, how many women have **top management jobs** and the **GDP per capita** of the **female population**.

3) This measure has continually shown that women haven't reached **social equality** with men.

The Gender-related Development Index (GDI) measures several development-related factors

1) The GDI measures **life expectancy**, **literacy**, years in **school**, number of **women in work** and **women's income**.

2) It has a more **positive** story to tell about women and development. Sure, men still generally have better income, literacy and so on, but women have **improved** in most of the categories measured.

3) **Women's literacy** and **numeracy** has improved, and the chance of **death** during or after **childbirth** has **fallen**.

Women may feel the **Negative Side Effects** of development **More** than **Men**

1) According to Marxist feminists, women experience a **dual burden** of **paid work** and **domestic responsibilities**.

2) When a country **industrialises**, men go from **one** form of work (agriculture) to **another** form of work (manufacturing industry), but women go from **one** form of work (housework and childcare) to **two** forms of work (housework and childcare plus a paid job outside the home).

This is quite simplified, and it's a broad generalisation anyway.

3) Women in LEDCs often work **longer hours** than **men**, in poor conditions.

Technology can change **Women's Employment Patterns**

1) **Swasti Mitter (1995)** writes about the impact of **ICT** on **female employment** in LEDCs. She says that computer technology can be a real **boon** to women — it allows them to work from home and work **flexible hours**.

2) Many ICT jobs which have been outsourced to NICs from MEDCs go to women — e.g. **call centre jobs**, **data entry**, **medical transcription services**.

3) Mitter points out that many women in LEDCs like India, Malaysia and Brazil now work in ICT, but they're concentrated towards the **bottom end** of the work ladder.

Radical Feminists argue that **Development Benefits Patriarchy**

1) Some radical feminists see development as a tool to make women more **dependent** upon men.

2) Radical feminists say TNCs actively seek to employ women as they are cheaper, more efficient and more docile.

3) If women do experience **improvement** in their position in society, e.g. **greater life expectancy** through better **health care** or **increased income**, it's because the **patriarchy** of the developed **world** allow it for **productivity** reasons.

Radical feminism can be **criticised** for failing to see the **exploitation** experienced by **men**.

Socialist Feminists believe **Socialism** can bring **Equality** to poorer countries

1) Socialist feminists argue that socialism can bring about a society that **isn't gendered** — i.e. that treats men and women **equally**. They push for **socialist revolution** that totally **changes** the way people see 'men's jobs' and 'women's jobs', as well as moving ownership of the means of production from capitalists to workers.

2) Socialist feminist **Mies (1986)** argues that traditional Marxism and capitalism both **undervalue** the work women do.

Aspects of Development: Employment

Employment is another thorny development issue. Big international companies often move their factories, call centres or whatever it is they need, to developing countries because wages are cheaper there. That means jobs for local workers, but many people would say the workers aren't treated fairly. Looks like nothing is ever straightforward in sociology.

Developing Countries Encourage TNCs to Relocate

TNCs are large businesses that operate in several countries around the world. TNCs are a feature of globalisation.

1) **Labour costs** are much much lower in LEDCs than in the developed world. As a result, many **TNCs** (transnational corporations) prefer to set up factories abroad, or pay companies in LEDCs to make goods on their behalf.

2) Many LEDCs have actively encouraged TNCs to do this by setting up **Export Processing Zones** (EPZs), also known as **Free Trade Zones** (FTZs).

3) In the EPZs, companies may be offered **tax breaks**, **training grants**, **low regulation** and **low wage costs**. **Trade unions** are often banned.

4) There are now **more than 800** of these zones in the developing world. Most are in Asia, South America and Central America, with over 100 in Mexico and over 100 in China.

Busan in South Korea — a free trade zone and the world's fifth busiest port.

Conditions Favour the TNCs, not the Workers

Typical EPZ industries include **garment-making** and assembling **electronic goods**. Workers are not usually directly employed by the TNCs. They work for **local manufacturers** who have to **compete** to win contracts from the TNCs. The manufacturers' main concern is to **keep costs down**. This can lead to very **poor working conditions**.

1) Often **hours are long** and **pay is low**. In the garment industry, workers in Bangladesh received the lowest wages in 2008 — US$0.22 per hour. Mexican workers were better paid, earning $2.54 per hour. In Europe, workers in Hungary doing similar work earned around $4.45 per hour.

2) **Health and safety** issues, and basic comforts like breaks or washrooms, may be **ignored**.

3) Many firms use **flexible** or **casual labour** which means that workers have almost **no job security**. They are employed on **short-term contracts** — often on a weekly or even daily basis.

4) Highly paid jobs like marketing and design are usually done at the TNC's sites in MEDCs. Workers in the LEDC factories tend to have **basic unskilled jobs**. There's very little training or chance of progression.

5) In EPZs, **women** usually make up the majority of employees. In garment making it can be up to 90%. Because women usually earn less than men in LEDCs, it can be argued that the TNCs are **profiting** from women's **lower status**. Some companies in EPZs also use **child labour**.

6) When **trade unions** are **banned** or restricted, it's hard for workers to campaign for better pay or conditions. Governments are scared of losing the TNCs so come down hard on **strikes** and **demonstrations**.

7) Even though wages are low there are plenty of people willing to work. In this situation employers have **no incentive** to offer a better wage.

There are Arguments For and Against the special Zones

1) Marxists like **Fröbel** (**1980**) are highly critical of EPZs. They see them as a new version of **exploitative colonialism**.

2) **Globalists** say that EPZs benefit world consumers as a whole by **keeping prices down**.

3) **Wages** in EPZs look low compared to what people are paid for the same work in industrialised nations. However, they're often **relatively good** when compared to average wages in the developing world.

Practice Questions

Q1 What do the GEM and the GDI suggest about gender inequality? Why do they differ?

Q2 Why do TNCs locate manufacturing in LEDCs?

Exam Question

Q1 Assess the argument that women are disadvantaged in the developing world. (18 marks)

Relocation, relocation, relocation...

Employment, health, education, gender issues, the environment, demography... There can't be many issues that global development doesn't touch on. The most important thing to get straight about this section is the difference between Marxist, modernist and dependency theories. Once that's clear you can pretty much predict what they'll say on a particular issue.

Ownership and Control of Mass Media

The mass media is one of the most powerful influences in modern society because it's part of all our lives. The study of the mass media has had to change just to keep up with new developments. **This section is for both AQA and OCR. Whee.**

The Mass Media Communicates with a large Audience

1) **Traditionally**, the **mass media** is defined as "the methods and organisations used to communicate to a large audience". That definition covers things like radio, television, cinema and newspapers quite nicely.

2) However, since the 1980s there have been **huge changes** in the media. There are a lot more **specialist** media outlets communicating with smaller, **niche groups** rather than to the whole "mass" of the public — e.g. subscription TV channels for fans of particular football teams, special interest magazines, podcasts about special interest topics.

3) Also, new media such as blogs, email and texting allow audiences to **interact** with the media. Communication isn't **one-way** any more. Some media are more of a **multi-way network**, e.g. mobile phones and the internet.

4) We still use the term "**mass media**", though. There's some debate about what counts as mass media — for example some theorists would count all mobile phone technology, but others would only include it when it's used to communicate to a large audience. So, sending a text to a friend wouldn't count, but **subscribing** to a service that sends you football scores by text **would** count, and so would reading an online news site on your phone.

5) Some theorists include a lot more things when they talk about "media". **Marshall McLuhan (1964)** included **any** kind of technology that helped people communicate — even cars and clocks.

> Well, OK, I suppose a car lets you drive from A to B to have a meeting, and a clock lets you be on time.

Learn these Key Media Concepts — Determinism and Censorship

> **Determinism means that developments in technology and the media actually change society.**
> **McLuhan (1964)** suggested that developments and changes in **communication** were the **main force for change** in society.
> He believed that the **nature** of the media had a much **bigger effect** on society than the **content** of the media.
> He thought that communication technologies actually affected the way audiences **see** the world, and the way they **think.**

> **Censorship means controlling the content of the media.**
> Media messages which are considered **harmful** or **offensive** to society can be **removed** before the audience receive them. Censorship can be done for moral, political or security reasons. There's loads more about censorship on pages 40-41.

Sociologists Analyse and Research the Mass Media (and its effects)

> **Content Analysis — measuring how often a word, phrase or theme is used in a piece of media**
>
> 1) In the social sciences, content analysis means **formal**, **quantitative** measuring. For example, you could **count** how many times a news report used the words "economic crisis". It's most suited to **written texts**, or to **transcripts.**
>
> 2) Content analysis can also be used to investigate the **relationship** between two phrases or themes.
>
> 3) The main **downside** of content analysis is that it **takes a long time**. It also doesn't take **context** into account.

> **Semiotics — studying the signs and codes of media**
>
> 1) A sign is **anything** that can be used to **mean something else** — e.g. a word or an image. Semiotic analysis looks at the **meanings** of the signs in a piece of media.
>
> 2) **Advertisements** are particularly open to semiotic analysis. Ads use **signs** to associate their product with **positive ideas**, e.g. attractiveness, happiness and success. They don't **directly** say, "buy this product and you will be happy".
>
> 3) Semiotic analysis is open to **subjectivity** and **bias**. The **values** of the researcher may influence how they **interpret** a sign, or the **relative importance** they place on different signs in a piece of media.

> 1) A sign can have a very <u>simple meaning</u>, e.g. the written word "cows" means, well, the idea of cows (the technical term for this kind of meaning is <u>denotation</u>).
>
> 2) A sign can also <u>suggest meaning</u>, e.g. a photo of a couple holding hands on the beach at sunset means the idea of romance (this kind of meaning is <u>connotation</u>).

> **Experiments — studying how an actual audience respond to media**
>
> 1) One example would be to monitor people's **behaviour** after viewing a violent film.
>
> 2) Short experiments like this don't tell you about **long-term media effects**. People also tend to **behave differently** when they know they're in an **experiment.**
>
> 3) **Audience research** means things like showing media to a **sample audience**, then **interviewing** them or giving them a questionnaire. You have to **formulate good interview questions** to get useful and **meaningful** results and **avoid bias.**

Ownership and Control of Mass Media

The Media is *Owned* by a *Few Powerful Companies* and *Individuals*

The **same companies** often own **different forms of media** — e.g. film studios, TV stations, radio stations, newspapers, social networking websites. This is called **cross-media ownership**. It's often not publicised.

1) Media companies **diversify** — they buy other companies that make **different kinds of media**, and they also buy companies in **other business sectors**.

- Rupert Murdoch's **News Corporation** owns TV stations, newspapers, book and magazine publishers and websites including myspace® and Photobucket.

- In Italy, **Silvio Berlusconi** owns three national TV channels, an advertising agency and a magazine publisher. He part owns a banking company and a cinema firm. He also owns football club **AC Milan**.

2) Some media companies **own media** in **several different countries**. News Corporation owns newspapers in Australia, Britain and the USA. They own TV networks in Australia, Europe, Asia, North and South America.

3) Over the last 30 years, media ownership has become concentrated into fewer and fewer hands. Research by **Bagdikian (2004)** found that the American media was now mostly owned by just **five huge corporations** — TimeWarner, Disney, News Corporation, Bertelsmann and Viacom®.

The individuals who own and control those companies have **huge power and influence** in society. They can **control** the information we receive **if they want to**. A **great example** is Italy, where media company owner **Silvio Berlusconi** just happens to be the **prime minister** as well. **He owns a lot of media outlets** and some people claim he is able to use them to **control the reporting** of his political party and the opposition.

Marxists say *Media Ownership Controls Media Content*

1) **Traditional Marxism — media owners control what we see in the media**

The idea is that the owners of the media **exploit their power position** to **manipulate** the content of the media. Capitalist media owners **tell news editors** what **stories** to cover and what **views** to put across. There's a lot of **anecdotal** evidence about newspaper proprietors **personally telling** the **editors** of their newspapers **what view to take on important stories**. The media ends up putting across views that **serve the interests of capitalism**.

2) **Neo-Marxism — the media reflects the ideas of the ruling class (including media owners)**

Neo-Marxist theory is **more complicated** — it says that control over the media is **indirect**. Neo-Marxism says the **world view of the elite class** is **broadcast** and **reinforced** by the media. The **values** and **ideas** of the **ruling class** are presented as the **natural, common-sense** views to have. This is called **"cultural hegemony"** — i.e. one set of ideas **dominating** over other ideas.

Pluralism says the *Media Reflects* the *Values* and *Beliefs* of Society

The pluralist view is that **society gets the media it wants** — media outlets have to **respond to market demand** or they'll go out of business. In other words, it **doesn't really matter** who **owns** the media — it's the **market** that matters. Pluralists do realise that the media will express **some opinions more than others**, though. Pluralists reckon this isn't because of bias from journalists, editors or owners — it's only a reflection of the **most common** views in society.

Practice Questions

Q1   What is meant by the term "media determinism"?

Q2   Give one drawback of semiotic analysis.

Q3   What is cross-media ownership?

Q4   Describe the traditional Marxists' view of media ownership and control.

Exam Question

Q1   Outline and assess the view that media owners have little control over media output.   (50 marks)

I own my own TV — I've got the receipt for it and everything...

All through this section there are examples of sociological media research using the methods described on the last page, and there's tons more about sociological methods in Section 8. The debate on media ownership is interesting. I've got to say — if I owned a newspaper I'd be awfully tempted to use it to spread my own views. Just casually like, nothing blatant.

Theories about Mass Media

*These two pages focus on ideology and theory and mention things like "neo-Marxism" and "pluralism". They concentrate on the ways in which **ideology influences the media** and its content.*
These pages are for both AQA and OCR.

Traditional Marxists say media serves the Economic Power of Ruling Classes

1) According to **traditional Marxism**, the media presents what's **important** and **relevant** to the **ruling class**. For example, stocks and share prices are featured on national news bulletins but only a small percentage of the population have a lot of shares. Marxists say that the poor are ignored by the media because they don't have money to buy the things that capitalism sells.

2) Marxist theory says that it's the "**logic of capitalism**" that the institutions in society will always be used as instruments of power by the capitalist class. It's all about serving the interests of capitalism.

3) For example, advertising is in magazines and on TV to **create the demand for goods** produced in the **capitalist economy**. Advertising also gives the idea that there's a wide range of choice for the consumer when, in reality, a few companies own the vast majority of products.

4) **Herbert Marcuse (1964)** was a Marxist who reckoned that the media promotes **consumerism** and gives people "**false needs**" — the belief that they "need" things that they don't really need.

There's more about Marcuse on page 61.

> Marxist sociologist **Miliband** (**1969**, *The State in Capitalist Society,* London: Weidenfeld and Nicolson) thought that the media encourages the proletariat to be **subordinate** and happy to serve the bourgeoisie. Remember what Marx said about **religion** being the **opium of the people** — keeping the working class **subdued** and in support of a system which works against their interests. Well, Miliband reckons that the mass media is "**the new opium of the people**".

Some Neo-Marxists say the Ruling Class Indirectly Control media content

In Marxist thought, one of the key powers of the ruling class is the power to **control ideas**, **values** and **attitudes**. The mass media is a useful tool for doing this. The values of the ruling class have dominance in society — this dominance is called **hegemony**.

This theory says that the **ideas** and **values** of the ruling class are **spread** by the mass media, and presented as if they're the most ← natural, obvious, common-sense things to assume and believe.

> "The ruling ideas are the ideas of the ruling class."
> Marx and Engels (1985, *The Communist Manifesto* Harmondsworth: Penguin, first published 1848).

1) Media content is controlled by an **approval process** — articles written by journalists are given the OK by editors. **Editors** are mostly from **white, middle class backgrounds** so they **select content** which **reflects** their own values. The idea is that they do this **unconsciously** — they **don't even realise that they're doing it**. Which is a bit odd and a bit scary. (Journalists also tend to come from middle class backgrounds — that's who newspapers and broadcasters tend to employ.)

2) Some events are given **less media coverage**, and some are **left out completely**. Marxists believe that people who work in the media are **trained** to present a **certain view of the world**. This view becomes natural and "obvious" to them and the audience. Neither the media workers nor the audience are conscious that the media are pushing a certain view.

3) This neo-Marxist view doesn't say that **alternative** views are **suppressed** — it says they're **allowed**. This gives the impression that all views get a fair shout — which makes it seem OK and perfectly fair for the dominant view to stay on top. Alternative views are often made to look silly or immature.

4) Marxist sociologists say the control of ideas **doesn't just happen in news** or factual programmes. For example, family entertainment programmes are presented as light-hearted fun but they present a specific **idea of British family life**.

Gerald liked to get good press.

Critics of Marxism don't think all journalists think the same way, and they point out that not all media stories are covered from the same viewpoint.

They also say that the media **doesn't** always **reflect** the opinions of the **dominant class**. For example, some people thought the BBC reports about government evidence for weapons of mass destruction in Iraq undermined those in power rather than supported them.

Pluralists point out that media audiences aren't completely stupid, and don't all believe everything they see on TV and read in the papers.

Theories about Mass Media

Pluralism — media content **Reflects Diversity** in society

The pluralist view is that society is made up of lots of **different** and **interacting** parts and the state oversees them to keep them in check. Pluralists think that the **content of the media reflects the values of society**. The **free market economy** is the key to a pluralist media — any media which reflects the values in society will be **popular** and stay in business, any that doesn't will go ti... er, bosoms up. This is how pluralist theory says the media **regulates itself**.

Nick Jones (1986) studied reporting of strikes

Jones studied the reporting on **industrial disputes** by the **UK media**. He concluded there was balanced and equal reporting. Individual reports may have been biased but the overall picture was **neutral**. He said apparent bias was down to the opposing sides managing to get good media coverage — the media were happy to publicise any relevant view.

Pluralism is criticised for **assuming** the diversity and neutrality of the mass media and **not showing evidence** for it.

Critics of pluralism point out that studies are often **carried out by people who work in the media**. Jones is a BBC Radio news journalist. This means that the research **might not be impartial**.

Katz and Lazarsfeld (1955) studied media before a US election

They wanted to find out how much the **media** influenced people's **political opinions** and votes. They concluded that the influence of the media is rather **unpredictable** and is often severely **limited**. They believed it was difficult to influence people through the media. People don't all get exposed to media messages, and don't always pay attention. People's attitudes can completely distort their understanding of a message. People also paid more attention to what their spouse, parents, co-workers and friends said than what the media said.

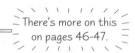

There's more on this on pages 46-47.

Postmodernism — media content gives society a **Consumerist Identity**

1) Postmodernism says that **consumption** is **more important** than **class** identity. It sees Marxist views about economic power as irrelevant nowadays.

2) The postmodern view says that people's **identity** comes from **what they buy** and what kind of **culture and media** they **choose to consume**. Postmodernists think the media has a very important part to play in **showing people what they can buy** and what kind of **lifestyles** they can choose from.

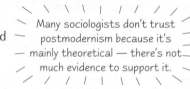

Many sociologists don't trust postmodernism because it's mainly theoretical — there's not much evidence to support it.

3) Postmodernists also say that there's **no dominant set of ideas**. Postmodernism sees society as presenting many choices and many alternative opinions. There isn't a "unified culture" but many voices adding their opinions and one view is not seen as better or worse than another. Therefore there is **no dominant ideology**.

French postmodernist theorist **Jean-François Lyotard (1979)** said that the key thing about the postmodern condition was the rejection of what he called "**grand narratives**" (or **metanarratives**). Grand narratives are large-scale theories and philosophies — ideas like "progress is inevitable" or "a Marxist revolution will end capitalism".

4) French postmodernist **Baudrillard** believed that media images actually **take the place of reality** — see p.49.

Practice Questions

Q1 What do traditional Marxists think advertising is for?
Q2 What is hegemony?
Q3 Why do Neo-Marxists think that alternative, anti-establishment views are allowed on TV and in the papers?
Q4 What do pluralists think regulates the media?

Exam Question

Q1 Identify and explain two criticisms of the Marxist view of the relationship between media and audience. (9 marks)

CGP — subconsciously disseminating Cumbrian values since 1995...

Hmm. Subtle. Anyway, the big difference between Marxist and pluralist views is whether the media controls the audience or whether the audience controls the media. You've got traditional Marxists, who think the media's all about making profits for capitalism, and you've got neo-Marxists who say it passes on ruling class values without even meaning to.

Selecting and Presenting the News

Sociologists have studied the news as an example of how the media works because it reaches so many people. It's the main source of information on the World for most of the population. The news is a social product full of ideas and values — it's not an objective reality out there waiting to be discovered by journalists. **For both AQA and OCR.**

News *is influenced by* Practical Constraints *— time, space and money*

The news is **presented** to us as the most **factual**, **objective** form of media — the reporting of what's happened in the world that day. In reality, newspapers, radio and television run to very tight **deadlines** and **constraints** which **influence** what finally appears as the news.

1) **Time constraints** mean the most **easily available stories** make it onto the TV/radio news or into the newspaper. Editors and journalists have **contacts** they use **again and again** for convenience, meaning a **limited number of viewpoints** are used. Also, all news organisations have a "news diary" of regular events. This means they can plan coverage of regular events in advance.

2) **Technical constraints** influence the news. Some places are **easier** to get **cameras**, **microphones** and **journalists** into and these are the places **top stories** will tend to come from. A story will rise and fall in significance **partly** on **how easy it is to report**.

This can lead to, for example, disasters in far-flung places being ignored or under-reported.

3) News organisations all run to a **budget**. Stories and reports from **places where they already have reporters** or **established contacts** are **cheaper to produce**. Many newspapers **can't afford** to have **many reporters** of their own so they **buy stories from news agencies**. These agencies then have a **huge influence** over what becomes news.

4) **Competition** affects the **selection** of the news. Newspaper editors are more likely to publish stories that they believe will make their newspaper the most **popular** that day. It's very important for newspaper editors that their paper **sells more** than their rivals. News stories that can be **sensationalised**, or **celebrity gossip** are often popular.

It's common these days for celebrities, politicians and groups in society to issue **press releases**. Press releases give the story **straight to the newsroom**, which makes it much more likely to be used because it **saves time and money**.

Also remember that stories have to shrink or expand to **fit the space available**. The same story could be on page 2 one day and page 17 the next, depending on **what else has happened** or what else is available to report.

Key studies are **Cohen and Young (1981)** and **Grossberg et al (1998)**. Both refer to the above as common practices in the media.

News *is influenced by the* Values *and* Practices *of* Journalists

Journalists who report the news learn to follow **certain rules** and ideas, which tend to be based on what they believe the general public want to hear about. Sociologists have referred to these as "**news values**". There are different types of news values which influence the news the media chooses to report.

Bureaucratic news values:
News should be **current**.
News should be **simple**.
News should be **brief**.
Big news is better than **small news**.

Cultural news values:
News should be **unexpected**.
News should focus on **important people**.
News should be **relevant to the audience**.
Bad news is preferred to **good news**.

The relative importance of the different news values to an individual journalist will depend partly on the type of publication or programme they work for.

Two key practices used by journalists which you must know are **agenda-setting** and **gate-keeping**.

Agenda-setting

Journalists and **editors** "control the news agenda". News **only becomes news** when **journalists** and **editors select it** as news. When a story is selected, journalists choose what **angle** to take when reporting it. This has a **direct effect** on how the audience will **perceive** the story. Agenda-setting may not be **conscious**. It comes from **learnt practices** of journalism — usually based on what **catches the audience's attention**.

Gate-keeping

This comes from work by **Gans (1979)** which describes how the editor decides **which stories are featured** and **how much space** is given to each story. Gans says it's like a gate — the editor opens it for some stories and closes it for others. **Dutton** (**1986** *The Media*, London: Longman) concluded from his research: "editors fulfil a filtering role since there is usually an excess of material available to fill limited newspaper or broadcasting space".

Selecting and Presenting the News

Case Study of Selection and Presentation of News

The Glasgow University Media Group studied television news

The Glasgow University Media Group (GUMG) studied **television news** over a long time span (1970s and 1980s) to look for evidence of bias. They focused in particular on coverage of workplace **strikes**. They used **detailed content analysis** of **television news bulletins**.

GUMG have a neo-Marxist perspective.

Finding	Examples
The **selection of news** was biased in favour of dominant class values. →	**Picket line violence** was **reported more** than police violence.
The **voice-overs** were biased in favour of dominant class values. →	**Leading terms** such as **"trouble-makers"** and **"pointless strike"** were used.
Management were given **more access** to the media than strike leaders. →	Television interviews with management were **more frequent** and longer than those with strike leaders.
The **filming** and **editing** was biased in favour of the police. →	Cameras were often placed **behind police lines** showing the police viewpoint.

The work of the GUMG is used to demonstrate **bias in the news** and in the **values and assumptions** of the people who **produce** and **construct** the news. Their work is **highly respected** because they've studied **a lot of news** in **great detail**. Remember though, this study was done in the 1970s, so think before you start blithely applying it to the news today.

The **image** of the news as **objective** reporting of fact makes this bias more **important** and more **powerful**. When people **think the news is unbiased**, they're **more likely to believe it**. ← *This is linked to postmodernist ideas about reality, see p.49.*

New Media have had an Impact on the Selection and Presentation of News

1) People don't sit down and spend a whole coffee break reading an **online** newspaper — they tend to click on what look like the most **intriguing, juicy headlines**. Editors therefore tend to **select interesting**, **scandalous** or **wacky** stories and present them with a headline that makes them appear **even more** interesting, scandalous or wacky.

2) Audiences can **"have their say"** on news stories via text and email. This **interactivity** seems popular with news editors. They may **select** stories that will **stir up** a big response, and **invite audience response** when **presenting** them.

3) TV news can feature **viewers' own photos** or **video footage** of news events — taken on mobiles and emailed in.

4) An online or TV news provider with a **global audience** has to try to select news items that are globally **relevant**.

News is Influenced by Society — it's Socially Constructed

There's more about new media on p50.

1) All media sociologists agree the **news is socially constructed** but they disagree over whose values are behind the social construction of news — those of the dominant class or those of the majority of society.

2) From a **pluralist** perspective, **practical constraints** are more significant in influencing the content of the news than ideological bias. The values of journalists are the **common values in society**.

3) From the **Marxist** perspective, the **ideological influences** are most important, and practical constraints can't be separated from ideology. Journalistic values are part of the **dominant ruling class ideology**.

Practice Questions

Q1 Describe what is meant by "news values".

Q2 Explain how the process of gate-keeping takes place in news production.

Q3 Give two examples of ways that new media technology has influenced the presentation of the news.

Q4 What is meant by the term 'socially constructed' in relation to the news?

Exam Question

Q1 'Journalists create rather than discover the news.' To what extent does the sociological theory and evidence you have studied support this viewpoint?

(33 marks)

It's funny how the day's events always exactly fill the newspaper...

You think you know what news is, and then you read these pages. Suddenly, you know a lot more about news, but it isn't so clear-cut any more. News is as much of a social construct as anything else. People choose what to put in the papers and on the telly, and people aren't unbiased and neutral — they're affected by all sorts of social factors, and all sorts of ideas.

Censorship and Violence

All governments control the media to a greater or lesser extent. The media reaches a large section of the population on a regular basis and it's influential in changing behaviour and attitudes — so it's not surprising there's some control and regulation over media content to protect the public from being misled or manipulated. **For both AQA and OCR.**

The Media can be Self-Regulating

Different branches of the media have different ways of **making sure content and practices** are kept to a **good standard**.

1) In Britain the press is "free". This means all **newspapers** and **magazines** are **commercial**, not funded by the state. There's **no obligation** for the press to be **impartial** or **unbiased** — in fact many daily newspapers **openly support** a particular **political viewpoint**.

2) The press set up their own organisation, the **Press Complaints Commission (PCC)**, to monitor standards and to deal with complaints. The PCC can order newspapers to print apologies if a complaint's been upheld. A **frequent beef** people have with the PCC is that when apologies are printed they're often in tiny print at the bottom of an inside page — even when the initial story was on the front page with a **MASSIVE HEADLINE**.

3) **Broadcast media** (TV and radio) are **more regulated by the government**. They also often publicise **standards of their own** which **their journalists** have to stick to.

The Media must Obey the Law

Both **public** (BBC) and **commercial** broadcasting are subject to **legal guidelines** and **restrictions**.

1) There are **laws** restricting **what can be shown on TV and when**. There is a "**watershed**" of **9pm**. Before 9pm you can't show **nudity**, **sex**, **violence** or **bad language**. After 9pm a **warning** must be given before programmes that have nudity, sex, violence or bad language.

2) UK television is required by law to be **impartial** — unlike the press. For example, in 2004, a public inquiry strongly criticised the **BBC** for its **reporting** of issues relating to **Iraqi weapons of mass destruction** (WMDs). The reporter involved, as well as the Chairman and Director General of the BBC, resigned as a result.

3) In **1989** TV and radio broadcasters were **banned** from using **words spoken by members** of **11 political and paramilitary groups** in **Northern Ireland**, including **Sinn Fein**. The ban was in place for **five years** — during that time the words of Sinn Fein politicians were spoken by **actors**.

4) The **law of libel** makes it **illegal** to make **defamatory** or **damaging** comments about **anyone**. Anyone and any organisation can be **sued** for **writing** (libel) or **saying** (slander) defamatory or damaging comments. This includes newspapers, magazines, internet sites, TV, emails — even repeating comments initially made by someone else. Media providers often use **lawyers** to check **controversial material** before it is printed or broadcast.

Charters and Legal Contracts restrain the media

1) The **BBC** was established by a **charter** which all its TV and radio content has to stick to. The BBC has to be "**independent**, **impartial** and **honest**" at all times.

2) The BBC has to **follow the rules** of its charter to get **funding** from the government. It has 12 **governors** to make sure it sticks to the charter.

3) **Commercial TV and radio broadcasters** don't have to follow this charter. Before they can broadcast they have to get **legal contracts** which tie them to certain standards. These contracts run for several years and are **issued by the government**.

4) In January 2004 **Ofcom** was established as the **new government regulator** to oversee the conduct of **all communications industries**. It deals with complaints and it can **fine** or **close down** broadcasters who break the rules.

After cracking her knee on the desk, South West Tonight's Sheila Green struggled to time-delay a torrent of foul language until after the sport and weather.

Ever heard a presenter **panic** if a guest swears on TV or radio — this is because broadcasters are **heavily fined** for breaking regulations "regarding **standards of taste and decency**". One way to avoid this problem is to broadcast on a **time delay** so you can bleep out the swearing.

The Power of Advertising is a Restraint on Commercial Media

Commercial media need **funds from advertising** to **survive** — they'll always be careful not to have **bad publicity** or content which advertisers don't like. If content doesn't fit with the advertiser's image the media outlet is likely to **adapt the content** rather than **risk** losing an advertiser.

Censorship and Violence

There are **Several Arguments** about **Violence** in the **Media**

Some sociologists argue that violence in the media has an effect on people

1) Early studies by Bandura, Ross and Ross (see p.46) show that children would **copy violent behaviours** they'd seen on film. This is often called "**copycat violence**".

2) Some sociologists say that violence on TV and film **desensitises** viewers to real violence. Seeing violence in the media makes people **less shocked** by violence in **real life**.

Other sociologists disagree with these ideas

1) **Catharsis theory** says that watching violence on screen **gets violent thoughts out of the viewer's system**. Watching a good gore-fest makes you **less likely** to grab a chainsaw and rampage through your own neighbourhood. So said **Feshbach and Singer (1971)** in their study of boys aged 8-18. Boys who watched aggressive and violent TV were less aggressive themselves.

2) **Buckingham (1993)** said that audience members actively interpret film and TV violence, and **make their own minds up** about the rights and wrongs of what they see on screen. Even young kids do this.

3) Some sociologists think that watching violence is a "**rite of passage**" for young people, especially boys. It's a phase they go through to prove they **aren't kids** any more.

4) **Morrison (1999)** makes a really important distinction between **serious, disturbing violence** and **light-hearted comedy violence**. For example, a photo of a prisoner of war getting shot in the back of the head is serious while *Jackass* and the cartoon *South Park* contain light-hearted violence. It's a darn obvious difference when you see it like that, but a lot of research has ignored it.

Cohen (1973) first used the term "**moral panic**" to describe how media reporting identifies something as a **serious threat to society**. **Martin Barker (1984)** analysed a 1980s moral panic about low-budget violent horror films known as "**video nasties**". These videos were **blamed** for violent crime, and the tabloid press predicted an **epidemic of violence** if they weren't banned.

Ferguson (2008) claims that the **generation gap** fuels moral panics about **video games** — most anti-game campaigners are **older** than most gamers, and often have **never played** the games they are complaining about. He says that research linking video games and violent behaviour is **flawed** and even **biased**.

For more on moral panics see page 45.

Censorship of Violence in the media is a Tricky Area

1) There are clear regulations for public broadcasting which all programmes and films have to follow. Films can't be shown on TV or in cinemas in the UK, or released on video or DVD until they've been **passed by the British Board of Film Classification (BBFC)** and given a **grading** which tells you **how old you have** to be to watch the film — U (Universal), PG (Parental Guidance), 12, 15 or 18.

2) Classification of most **video games** is **voluntary**. Video game producers often choose to submit violent games to the BBFC for classification, as a way of showing that the game is not intended for children. Games containing human sexual activity or extreme violence have to be submitted for classification.

3) Censorship doesn't actually stop material being produced. The **internet** has been used to distribute **violent** and **pornographic** material which would be banned from other media outlets.

Practice Questions

Q1 Explain the difference between public and commercial media.
Q2 Name two legal controls which both public and commercial media have to adhere to.
Q3 What differences are there in how print and broadcast media are regulated?
Q4 Describe the regulatory arrangements for the BBC.
Q5 Explain what Feshbach and Singer (1971) said about the effect of watching violent TV on boys.

Exam Question

Q1 "The media is regulated to protect the public from biased and inappropriate media in Britain today."
Evaluate this statement with reference to at least two forms of media.

(33 marks)

TV makes me violent — I have to slap the telly to make it work...

Imagine — TV might be even worse if there weren't any controls or regulation... The question of whether violence on TV makes kids more violent and aggressive is an old one. There are those who say it does, and those who say it doesn't necessarily. Kids can be a lot more clever at telling the difference between real and pretend than you'd think.

Media Representations

The role of the media in representing social groups is very influential. These pages look at the images of particular social groups, how they're formulated and what effect they might have. **For OCR and AQA.**

Stereotypes *are* Inaccurate Generalisations

Stereotypes are **generalisations** about **social groups**. They are **inaccurate** and often **derogatory** — e.g. "Women can't read maps", "Gay men are camp", "Chinese women are submissive".

Stereotypes *are* Socially Constructed — *often with* Binary Opposition

Binary Opposition means looking at the world in terms of pairs of opposites

1) We like to see the world in terms of **opposites** — e.g. male/female, gay/straight, good/bad.

2) According to **Levi-Strauss (1963)** we apply this system of **binary opposition** to the world in such a subconscious way that it **appears** to be entirely natural. However he suggested that it isn't natural at all — instead the sets of binary opposites have **socially constructed meanings**.

3) Levi-Strauss pointed out that these pairs of binary opposites aren't equal. One half of the pair is culturally marked as being **more positive** than the other. For example, in the binary opposition of male/female, male is culturally determined as positive. It's the dominant half of the pair. Levi-Strauss thought that we subconsciously relate **all binary oppositions** back to the two opposites **good/bad**.

4) The **media** often **perpetuates** these binary oppositions — e.g. by portraying stereotypes of women as caring and men as macho breadwinners.

Defining something as "the other" means saying it's different and foreign — and it implies it's a bit inferior

1) **Edward Said (1978)** suggested that academics in the West define the East as "the other" when they study Eastern culture. He said when they do this, they imply that Eastern culture is somehow inferior to Western culture.

2) A social group can define another group as "other" in order to **promote social cohesion** within their **own** group. It's **them and us**. The media often do this, e.g. in newspaper stories about immigration.

3) The idea of "the other" goes with the idea of **binary opposition**. The **dominant** half of the binary pair is seen as the **normal**, standard, regular version. The half of the binary pair perceived less positively is the **"other"**.

Media Messages *go through* Four Stages *from* Production *to* End Effect

In "sociology speak" this is called the **process of message trajectory**.

Stage 1 — Media Message is formulated by editors

Media messages are **formulated** (put together) by those in **powerful positions** in media institutions. These individuals aren't usually members of the social groups which the media stereotypes. For example, very few media editors are female, disabled, black, working class, openly gay, under 25 or over 65.

Stage 2 — Media Message content reflects groups in power

The content of the media **reflects the values** of the people who **formulate** it. Groups who aren't in power have **limited representation** in the media.

"Look," said Saskia. "Do you see what I see?"
"Golly," said Rupert. "Working class people on the telly. Whatever will they think of next?"

Stage 3 — Media Message is received by the audience

The messages are then **received** by the audience and **interpreted** in different ways — depending on **context** and **experience**.

Stage 4 — Media Message affects the role and treatment of social groups

Opinions and behaviour of **individuals** and **institutions** in society are **influenced** by **messages in the media**. The **impact of the media** depends on how you view the **interaction between media and audience**. It's all very theoretical.

There's plenty of detail about this on pages 46-49.

You need to **know these four stages** and to be able to give **examples** for the **social groups on the following three pages** (gender stereotypes, class stereotypes, disability stereotypes, ethnic stereotypes, age stereotypes and sexuality stereotypes). You can choose other groups but you'd need to **do your own research** to find your own examples.

Media Representations

Media Messages about Gender are Stereotyped

1) Most **editors** are **men**. **Croteau and Hoynes (2000)** found that in the mid 1990s in the US only 6% of top newspaper management were women and only 20% of top TV management.

2) Women **don't appear on the media as often as men**. Research by **Cumberbatch (1990)** found 90% of all advertising voice-overs were male and 66% of all people in adverts were male.

3) Women in the media are often presented as **ideals** for other women to aspire to. **Naomi Wolf (1990)** and **Susan Orbach (1991)** both reckon that the rise in eating disorders in women is a direct result of this.

4) The media tends to portray women in a limited range of roles. **Tuchman (1978)** argued there were only two female roles portrayed in the media: **domestic** and **sexual**. **Ferguson (1983)** researched **women's magazines**, and found they gave **advice and training** on being (stereotypically) **feminine** — i.e. **sexual**, **domestic** and **romantic**.

5) Some advertising portrays men as **incompetent** at the stereotypically female **domestic tasks** of housework and cooking.

6) Women are often represented as **victims** by the media — of sexual violence, domestic violence etc.

7) Action films portray **men as violent**, and show male violence in a **positive** way.

8) **Gauntlett (2002)** identified a **change** in media portrayal of masculinity — he found that some **men's magazines** mirrored the format of **women's magazines**, with advice on health, looking good, and attracting the opposite sex.

9) Postmodernists like **Hermes (1995)** think people can **reject media messages** about gender.

Some sociologists say there are Class Stereotypes in the media

1) Media **editors** and **executives** are almost all **middle class**.

2) **Middle class** people **appear on TV** more often than working class people, both on **dramas** and on **news** programmes.

3) **Drama roles** for working class characters are mostly limited to **soap operas**. **Upper class** characters are often seen in **historical costume dramas** — which tend to give a **romantic** picture of life and class.

4) **News** often represents **working class** people as a **source of trouble** — "anti-social behaviour", riots, strikes, crime, etc. From a neo-Marxist standpoint, the **Glasgow University Media Group (1982)** suggest that the media are perpetuating the view that the working class are trouble to ensure the dominance of capitalist ideology (see p.39 for more on this).

Glennon and Butsch (1982) looked at 40 years of families on TV in the USA

They found that only **4% of sitcoms** featured a family where the head of household was a **manual worker**.
In real life, **36%** of American families were like this. Nearly **half** the **TV families** had a **professional** as head of household.
In real life, only 25% were like this. Most of the TV families were wealthy and glamorous.
Glennon and Butsch thought that most **working class dads** were portrayed as **stupid** and **comical**, for the audience to laugh at.

This is their opinion, not necessarily what the TV audience thought.

Research from **Medhurst (1999)** showed that when middle class students were shown the programme 'The Royle Family' they thought it was an **accurate** portrayal of **working class life**.

Stuart Hall (1982, 1992, 1996) thinks that the media has always portrayed the **middle classes** in a **positive** light and the **working class** in a **negative** light. He says that the media has reinforced people's class identities — which keeps the divide between the classes going strong.

Practice Questions

Q1 Write a summary of the four stages of a media message in no more than four sentences.

Q2 Give two examples of social groups which have been identified as being subject to stereotyped media portrayal.

Q3 List two pieces of research which illustrate the argument that the media is a patriarchal institution.

Q4 What are Stuart Hall's views about the portraying of class by the media?

Exam Question

Q1 With reference to sociological studies, assess the view that the mass media is biased in its portrayal of women. (18 marks)

Learn the studies — you'll need them...

Remember, it's not just women who are stereotyped by the media. Men are also portrayed in a limited way, which tends to be as a strong, capable breadwinner. Most dramas which contain violence generally portray men as the aggressors, and they're more likely to be shown as criminals too. So, if a question asks about gender stereotypes, remember to talk about men as well as women.

Media Representations

*The media sends out stereotypes about disabled people, ethnic minorities, young people, old people and gay people. That's a lot of people. The sections on **disability** and **sexuality** are for **AQA only** — the rest is for **OCR and AQA**.*

Disabled people are Under-represented in the media

1) Disabled people are **poorly represented** in **powerful positions** in the media. Those who do hold powerful positions tend to have specialised in disabled issues — e.g. Peter White, the radio journalist.

2) There's really **very little representation of disabled people** in the media at all. Government statistics show that about 20% of the adult population has some form of disability, yet the Broadcasting Standards Commission (1999) reported that people with disabilities only appeared in **7% of television programmes** and had only **0.75% of all speaking roles**.

3) **Roles** for disabled people are very **limited**. Research by **Cumberbatch and Negrine (1992)** looking at British television over six weeks found the roles for disabled people were based on **pity** or **comedy**. They found that **disabled actors** never appeared **just as actors** playing a person who **just happened to have a disability**, only in **roles particularly about disability**. However, there are **some positive portrayals** of disabled people in films and on TV — e.g. of deafness in *Four Weddings and a Funeral*.

4) **Audience response** depends on people's **actual experience** of disability. Cumberbatch and Negrine researched audience responses as part of their study. They concluded that people with limited or **no real-life experience** of disability **accepted** the media images with **little concern**. People **with experience** of disability were **critical** of the media and **rejected** stereotyped images.

Media representations of Ethnicity are often Stereotyped

1) New technology means there are more satellite and digital TV channels. Lots of small specialised channels have developed. Many of these **cater for specific ethnic minorities** and they're managed and controlled by people from those ethnic minorities (e.g. Zee TV, Bangla TV, Punjabi TV). However, there aren't many people from ethnic minorities in positions of **power** in **mainstream media**.

2) **The Broadcasting Standards Commission (1999)** found that terrestrial and satellite television portrayed ethnic minorities in **42% of programmes**, and ethnic minorities made up 7% of all people with speaking parts. However, the range of roles was **restricted**. The highest percentage representation was in **children's programmes**.

3) A government report **'Viewing the World' (2000)** suggests that media coverage of less economically developed countries (LEDCs) often tends to portray them as **starving** or in **conflict**. The stereotype here is that people in those countries are unable to solve their problems and need the West to "**rescue**" them.

4) Tabloid newspapers sometimes stereotype some ethnic minority groups as being a **problem** or a **threat**. **Van Dijk (1991)** made a detailed content analysis of **headlines** in five British national newspapers. He argued that there was often an **association** in the headlines between **ethnic minorities** and **violent** and **negative language**.

5) Media portrayal of ethnic minorities can also be part of a media representation of **multiculturalism** (e.g. TV and newspaper coverage of the Notting Hill carnival). Some representations of multiculturalism are **utopian** (i.e. suggesting that everything's perfect) and some admit there are problems, e.g. *Bend It Like Beckham*.

6) **Cottle (2000)** points out that media portrayals of ethnic minorities reinforce views of non-whites as the "**other**" (see page 42). He also criticises media portrayals of multiculturalism, saying that they gloss over problems such as power imbalances between different ethnic groups, and the historical effects of colonialism and racism.

7) **Audience response** to ethnic minority stereotypes varies depending on the **real-life experience** of the audience. People don't swallow media stereotypes if they know better themselves. People can also **use the media** in the process of constructing their identity.

Hartmann and Husband (1974) analysed children's response to media

They compared the responses of children in two parts of Britain and found that in the **area with low ethnic mix**, children **believed negative media content** and thought of "race relations" in terms of conflict. In the **area with a high ethnic mix**, children **rejected media stereotypes** in favour of their own experience.

Media Representations

Images of Young and Old are Stereotyped in the media

1) The **people with power** in media organisations tend to be **older**. It takes **time** to get **experience**, so this makes sense.

2) There's often a sexist **double standard** in the way older people are represented in the media. The **older** a **woman** gets, the **less likely** she is to get a leading film role or a TV presenting job. It's a different story for men. In films, older male actors like Sean Connery and Harrison Ford are "allowed" to be romantically paired with cute young women. There are lots more **older men presenting TV programmes** than there are older women.

3) **Biggs (1993)** focused on entertainment programmes and found lots of representation of older people. However, they were often in stereotyped roles of "forceful", "vague" and "difficult" — especially in sitcoms. In America, **Signorelli (1989)** studied television characters and found that both young and old were under-represented on prime-time television. TV was biased towards **middle-aged** people.

4) **Featherstone and Hepworth (1995)** found that magazines aimed at older people tended to push an image of "youthful" old people — enjoying holidays and sports, wearing fashionable, "young-looking" clothes, etc.

5) There are also **stereotypes** relating to **young people**. **Children** are represented as **innocent**. Slightly older "**youth**" are often seen as a **social problem** — prone to drug abuse, binge drinking, petty crime and unplanned pregnancy.

Stan Cohen (1973) described how **media reporting** of expected "trouble" could **create a moral panic**.

Moral panic — public demands that something is done about it

Small group behaves in a deviant way → Media report the story → Media report similar stories again → Original group labelled as threat to social order → More people join in with deviant behaviour

Cohen used the example of the **Mods and Rockers** in the 1960s. The media reported that there would be **fights** between two youth subcultures — the Mods and the Rockers. Lots of people turned up to fight or watch, partly because of the **media publicity**. The public then **panicked** over reports of how many people turned up to fight.

You can easily find **contemporary** examples of a moral panic — e.g. the concern over trouble at **So Solid Crew** gigs. The possibility of **gun violence** led to some shows being cancelled because **media reporting** of the concern led to **panic**.

The Mods and Rockers struggled to make contact amongst the horde of onlookers.

Representations of Sexuality in the media are Stereotyped

1) Gay men are often stereotyped as "**camp**". TV shows often use "camp" gay characters as **comic relief**.

2) Homosexual relationships and heterosexual relationships are shown differently in the media. For example, much more explicit heterosexual sex is shown on television than homosexual sex. **Coronation Street** and **EastEnders** have both had storylines involving a **gay kiss** which got widespread media attention. You don't get any outcry in the papers when a **man and a woman** kiss on a soap opera.

3) There was a **political** aspect to early **media reporting** of **HIV/AIDS**. It was initially openly characterised as a "gay disease". A tabloid newspaper headline in the 1980s referred to AIDS as a "gay plague". However, according to **Cricher (2003)**, later representation of AIDS and gay men changed from the anti-gay message to a safe sex message.

Practice Questions

Q1 Briefly explain the findings of Cumberbatch and Negrine (1992).

Q2 Give an example of newspaper bias in relation to ethnic minorities in Britain.

Q3 How does real-life experience affect how people respond to stereotypes in the media?

Exam Questions

Q1 Outline and assess the view that the media are biased in their representation of ethnic minorities. (50 marks)

Q2 With reference to sociological studies, evaluate the claim that the media are ideologically biased. (18 marks)

Learn these studies... in fact learn ALL the studies... in the world... EVER...

If you do a question on media audiences and ethnicity, disability, age or sexuality, you have to be prepared to mention some sociological studies to back up your points. It's the only way to get the marks. The stuff on these pages makes you think a bit. British society, and the media especially, has a way to go before it treats everyone equally.

Mass Media and its Audience

The media constructs and sends out messages to the public — but the impact of the messages depends on how the audience responds. People can accept media messages, or dismiss them as complete rubbish. **For OCR and AQA.**

The *Hypodermic Syringe* Model — Media *Directly Influences Audience*

Way back in the **1920s**, when **radio** and **newspapers** were just starting to get **important** in society, sociologists developed theories about how the media affected people.

1) The **hypodermic syringe model** says the media **injects** its message into the mind of the audience in the same way as drugs are **directly injected** into the body. The idea is that the media is **so powerful**, its message **directly influences** the individual and they're **powerless** to **resist** the message or **reject** it.

2) This theory says that **all individuals** in the audience are **affected** in the **same way**.

> In **1938**, Orson Welles recorded a radio production of H G Wells' story *The War of the Worlds* in which Martians invade Earth. The broadcast included **fictional news bulletins** reporting the Martian invasion. Some radio listeners **believed** the fake bulletins were true, and **panicked**. This was used as **evidence** of the **dangerous** and **direct power of the media**, and it created concern in society. For the people who believed in the hypodermic syringe model it was proof enough.

3) Some sociologists decided that the hypodermic syringe model was **too simplistic** to explain how adults view media content. It did stay popular as a theory of how the **media** can **influence children**, though.

4) **Bandura, Ross and Ross (1963)** played children a **film of a man hitting a doll**. They then left the children to play with the **same doll** which they'd seen on the film. The children who'd seen the violence on film hit the doll, while those who hadn't seen the film played with the doll in a non-violent way.

Critics of the hypodermic syringe model think it treats people as **passive** and very easily led. They also point out that **not all audience members react in the same way** to the same piece of media. Studies showed this as far back as the 1920s.

> Don't assume that this theory is dead in the water. Think about the **concern** that **fictional TV** and **film violence** can cause violent acts in society. In 1993, two boys were convicted of **killing two-year-old James Bulger** when they were ten years old. When the judge was summing up he said that "exposure to **violent video films may in part be an explanation**" for the boys' actions. Media reporting of the murder case created a **moral panic** about violence in films and the effect of the media on children. **Barker (2001)** criticised this panic, and pointed out that there was no actual evidence to show that the two child murderers had actually seen the video in question.

The Media Message is *Interpreted* and *Passed On* by *Key Individuals*

The **two-step flow model** was developed in the 1950s. It says that the media does influence people, but **not everyone is influenced directly**.

1) The **first step** is the **media message** reaching an audience member. All simple so far.

2) The important **second step** is how their **understanding** of the message is **shaped** by **social interaction** with other audience members. For example, if workers in an office chat about a soap opera during their coffee break then these discussions affect individuals' opinions of the storyline and characters.

3) **Katz and Lazarsfeld (1955)** said that there were **key individuals** in each community whose reaction **directly influenced others**. These **"opinion leaders"** openly expressed their reaction and opinions, and others **followed** their lead. Katz and Lazarsfeld studied **media influence on American voters**. They concluded that most people followed the opinion leader's views on who they should vote for, but the opinion leaders themselves often got their **ideas straight from the mass media** messages.

4) It doesn't have to be just two steps — a message can go through several stages of interpretation. **Hobson (1990)** studied an office environment and found that a few **key individuals** influenced what the others watched on television and their **reactions** to the programmes. These opinions were **passed on** to another bunch of colleagues. A **social norm** of what to watch **spread** through the **whole office**. **New recruits** had to **conform** to fit in.

Did you see X Factor?

It's easy to imagine this happening in a school or a workplace: "Did you see Big Brother?" "Isn't she such a COW?" "He loves himself, doesn't he?". If you don't watch the programme, you're left out of the conversation. If you don't agree with the ~~big-mouth~~ opinion leader, you're made to feel a bit of an outsider.

Mass Media and its Audience

Social and Cultural Context affect how an Audience Responds to the Media

1) The **Cultural Effects theory** introduced the idea that **social context** is important when looking at the effects of the media. In short, it claims that **different people** interpret the media in **different ways**.

2) The idea is that an audience **interprets the media** in the **context** of the **culture** they already belong to. This means that the effect of the media is quite complex — it's not the same for everyone.

3) "**Culture**" refers to the **small, subcultural groups** an individual belongs to and also to the **wider, general culture of society**. For example, in England an individual's response to Arsenal winning the Premiership will **depend** on whether the **individual** supports Arsenal. But audience response to media reports of **England winning the World Cup** would be broadly **similar** for most of the population because there's a **cultural norm** of supporting your country's sports teams.

> Here's a **second look** at the audience response to the *War of the Worlds* broadcast — this time from a **cultural effects viewpoint (Cantril, 1940)**.
>
> 1) The response was **caused** by the **cultural context** in which it was heard. If it was on the radio **today** it wouldn't create the same response.
>
> 2) At the time of the broadcast there was **insecurity** in American society because of a **financial crisis** and the move towards **war in Europe**. Radio programmes were **frequently interrupted for news reports**, and there was a general expectation of bad news.
>
> 3) People **wouldn't have been surprised** to hear a **real report** of bad news interrupting a drama programme on the radio. This made it **more likely** that some members of the audience would **believe** the story.

We interrupt this A2 Sociology Revision Guide...

The neo-Marxist **Stuart Hall (1980)** argued that the media has **dominant ideological** messages '**encoded**' into it, but that people of different backgrounds can, to an extent, '**decode**' these messages in different ways — with varying degrees of **agreement** or **opposition** to the ideology expressed.

The Effects of media messages Build Up Over Time

1) Media effects can build up over time to **create** or **reinforce** cultural **norms**.

2) For example, **images of women** in the media create **stereotypical images** and place **expectations** on girls and women. There's been a long-running campaign by some feminists to remove pictures of **topless women** ("Page Three Girls") from national newspapers, because they argue that these images reinforce the dominant view that it's OK to objectify women as sex objects.

3) Some theorists think it's not just the **content** of the media that has a long-term effect on society — the **technology** of the media has a long-term effect on society. **Marshall McLuhan** (**1964**, *Understanding Media* New York: McGraw-Hill) claimed that media technology actually had a **greater effect** on society than media content.

4) It's **difficult** to **objectively measure** long-term media effects, so the discussion of long-term effects is mostly theoretical.

> The big catchphrase to remember from McLuhan is "**The medium is the message**".

Practice Questions

Q1 Briefly explain the hypodermic syringe model.

Q2 In which study did psychologists show children a film of a person hitting a doll?

Q3 Define the two steps in the two-step flow model.

Q4 Explain what's meant by the term "opinion leader".

Q5 Briefly explain cultural effects theory.

Q6 Explain what is meant by the statement: "the medium is the message".

Exam Question

Q1 Evaluate the claim that audiences are passive in their response to media messages, with reference to at least two sociological theories.

(18 marks)

The hypodermic syringe model — it gets right under your skin...

You read one theory and think, "ah, that explains it", then you read the next theory and think, "ah, that explains it" — and they're two totally contradictory theories, so they can't both be right. I suppose they can both be right some of the time, or they can give you a part of the picture. The most important thing is that you can write about them in the exam.

Mass Media and its Audience

Here's more about how people interpret what they see and hear from the mass media. Some sociologists think people can be quite active in deciding what media messages they want to see and hear. **These pages are for AQA and OCR.**

Audiences *Actively Use* and *Interpret* the Media to *Suit Their Own Needs*

Some theories argue that the audience responds **actively** to media content and messages.
There's a switch from "what the **media** does **to** people" to "what **people** do **with** the media".

Uses and Gratifications Theory

1) This theory was developed by theorists such as **Blumler and Katz (1974)** and says that people **use** the media to **meet their needs**. The audience **actively chooses** what media to experience, using such cutting-edge tools as free will and the remote control. Everyone chooses for themselves, so each person's media diet is **unique**.

2) A good example is the study of **soap opera audiences** by **McQuail (1972)**. He looked at how audiences used **Coronation Street** to fulfil a need for **social companionship**. Many audiences felt part of the characters' lives and felt interest and concern for what would happen next in a storyline.

3) **Lull (1990)** listed the social uses of television in the UK — and found men, women, young and old all used the media to meet different needs.

4) Uses and gratification theory is **functionalist** — it says the media exists to serve the **needs** of the public.

Selective Filter Model

In media language "to engage with" a piece of media means to find it interesting and pay attention to it — to be "into" it.

1) This theory says the audience **choose** which media to **experience** and also **control** which parts of the media message to pay attention to and **engage with**. The audience pick out the parts of a message which **fit in with their view of the world** and **ignore the rest**.

2) **Fiske (1988)** says individuals become very **experienced readers of the media**. He says that individuals can understand one "**media text**" in several **different ways** on several **different levels** — and in relation to other "**media texts**" on the same subject.

3) **Klapper (1960)** argued that to get its message across the media has to go through **three selective filters: selective exposure** — people only consume the media they want and are able to get, **selective perception** — people ignore messages they don't want to hear, and **selective retention** — people tend to remember only what they agree with. Klapper argued that this meant it's easier for the media to **reinforce** what people think than to **change** their minds about something.

"Media text" means a piece of media — a TV programme, a newspaper article, a magazine article, an advert. Academics really like to call things "texts" for some reason. Oh well, if it makes them happy...

4) This model emphasises the **power of the individual** to control his / her experience of the media and says that people use media in a **sophisticated** way. It's kinda postmodern in that way. However, it's been criticised for **overestimating** the control of the individual over very **powerful media messages**.

Structured Interpretation Model

1) This theory says there's a **dominant interpretation** of media messages which audiences go along with. Like the other two theories, individuals actively **pick** which media they **engage with**, but this theory says the process takes place in a **social context**. The social context creates a "**preferred reading**" of the media message (by "reading" they mean "interpretation"). For example, a film is written, presented and promoted with a **preferred reading** in mind — the makers of a film like *Slumdog Millionaire* want you to find the love story **moving** and **convincing**, not stilted and laughable.

2) **Different social groups** have **different dominant interpretations** of the same text. So, this theory isn't the same as earlier theories which saw the audience as a mass who all respond in the same way.

3) **Morley (1980)** studied how the television audience responded to one **news programme** — *Nationwide*. He showed the same programme to several **different social groups** and found that their responses to the programme **varied** hugely, **but within each group** most **individuals responded in the same way**. Trade unionists saw it as biased towards management, and management trainees saw it as pro-union.

Mass Media and its Audience

Postmodern Theory *says the audience gets* Lots of Meanings

1) **Postmodernists** say that there are **many, many meanings** to any social or cultural aspect of life. They say there **isn't any aspect of life** where there's one single, objective **truth** or **reality** that absolutely everyone experiences.

2) The **postmodern audience pick** and **choose** between a range of images, messages, ideas and meanings.

Postmodern Theory *also says the* Media Takes *the* Place *of* Reality

1) The development of the mass media and technology have meant everyday life is **chock-full of images** and messages competing and **conflicting** with each other. The media presents so many different images and stories **woven into everyday life** that the boundary between **reality and the media** is **blurred** — the **media becomes reality**.

> The explosion of **reality TV** and the **obsessive interest** people have with **soap stars** are good examples of this. With **reality TV, real** people get put in an **unreal situation** which is presented as **real**, and the audience follows it like a **soap**. With a soap, **pretend** characters get treated by the press and by audiences **as if they're real**.
>
> There's an example with **news media** — when something's on the news, it seems like that "**proves**" it's real and true. Images on the news can be taken out of context, though. And news is **influenced** by all kinds of factors (see pages 38-39). The news isn't **objective truth**. But the news is presented as reality, and **becomes reality**.

2) This idea is related to a philosophical idea of a thing called a **simulacrum**. A simulacrum is something that **looks real**, but **isn't**. It's like a copy but **without any kind of connection** to the **original**. Postmodernist theorists say that these simulacra actually replace reality.

Postmodernism can kind of make your head swim.

3) French postmodernist **Jean Baudrillard (1981, 1994)** suggested that **everything** had been replaced by simulacra. He called this replacement of reality **hyperreality** — he said that hyperreal images seemed **more real than real** and that meant they took over from reality. He suggested that **obviously made-up images** were used to give people the impression that they could **tell reality from a simulacrum** when in fact they **couldn't**.

> "Disneyland is presented as imaginary in order to make us believe that the rest is real, when in fact Los Angeles and the America surrounding it are no longer real, but belong to the hyperreal" — Jean Baudrillard (1994 *Simulacra and Simulation* Ann Arbor: University of Michigan Press, originally published in French 1981).

4) In *The Gulf War Did Not Take Place*, **Baudrillard (1995)** argued that the 1991 Gulf War existed more as images on TV screens than as actual fighting. The Gulf War as media **spectacle** or video game type **simulation** became reality.

5) In the media a piece of information or an image can be **distorted** intentionally in order to **make it appear correct** to viewers. So it's actually **made less true** in order to **appear more true**.

Critics *say Postmodernism's too* Theoretical *and too* Obscure

Postmodernism is criticised for being too theoretical. It's really **hard to find** (or even think of) any kind of **evidence** which would **prove** postmodernism **right** or **wrong**. I mean, if you're starting out from the premise that no idea has a straightforward meaning and individuals create their own reality so that there's no one definition of what's 'real' or 'true' and that reality has been replaced with something that just looks a lot like it — *where on earth do you go from there...*

Critics of Baudrillard say his writing is **deliberately obscure**, and that it **dismisses** the reality of **suffering** and **inequality**.

Practice Questions

Q1 What do sociologists mean when they refer to an audience actively responding to the media content?

Q2 Give an example of a criticism of the uses and gratifications model of audience response.

Q3 Explain the term "preferred reading" in relation to the media.

Q4 What are simulacra?

Exam Question

Q1 'Media audiences actively select and filter the content and messages they receive.' To what extent do the sociological theories and evidence you have studied support this viewpoint?
(33 marks)

Whenever I fancy feeling like I've shoved my head in a blender...

... with an Amazon tree frog and a shot of ouzo, I read some postmodernism. There is kind of a point behind it, though. If you limit it to "people treat media images as if they're real when they're not" and "it's hard to tell images from reality" it's not so bad. Having said that, I dare you to read Baudrillard in the original, or Jacques Lacan or Jacques Derrida. I double dog dare you.

New Media

New technologies like digital TV, the internet, blogging and new fancypants mobile phones are changing how we communicate and how we consume media images and messages. ***This page is for AQA only.***

New Media has Grown Massively — here are some Statistics

1) In 2001/02, **49%** of UK households had a computer. In 2007, it was **70%**.

2) **61%** of **UK households** had **internet access** in 2007 — up from 57% in 2006. In 2007, the proportion of adults who accessed the internet every day or almost every day was 67%. This was up from **59%** since 2006.

3) The proportion of households with a **satellite**, **cable** or other **digital TV** receiver increased from 43% in 2001/02 to 70% in 2006 and to 77% in 2007. By **2012**, **all UK households** will **have** to be digital if they want to watch TV.

4) There is **inequality of access** to the new media. For example, in 2007 **97%** of households in the **highest income group** owned a home computer and 95% had an internet connection. This is in comparison to the **lowest income** group where **35%** of households owned a home computer and 24% had an internet connection.

> *All these lovely stats are from the National Statistics Omnibus Survey.*

New Media appears to offer More Choice

1) **Digital multichannel TV** offers **hundreds** of channels, both UK-based and foreign. Some are subscription-based, others are free to watch. There are channels broadcasting to 'niche' markets — e.g. DIY, motor sport, shopping.

2) However, **Negrine (1994)** suggests that broadcasters fill their channels with cheap imported programmes which are constantly repeated, which actually **reduces** consumer choice.

3) There are hundreds of **news websites** from all over the world. You can get more news than ever before, and you can **compare and contrast** how one story is presented in different places. Some news stories are **exactly the same** on lots of websites, where several news providers have used the **same press release** or the **same news agency feed**.

4) There's tons of **user-generated content** on the internet — photos, blogs, videos, etc. Even user-generated content can be a bit samey, like when you get a link to the same cute kitten video from **everyone on the bloomin' internet**.

> The sheer **amount** of new media content and the **global** nature of new media makes **regulation and control difficult**. It's hard for a state to regulate the content of **foreign digital channels**. Regulation of the internet is extremely hard.

Consumers can become Producers of New Media

1) Anyone can publish their thoughts and opinions on a **blog** (short for web log) for other people to read and comment on. A few popular blogs about celebrity gossip and blogs about politics are very **influential**. Twitter is like a blog but all posts are limited to 140 characters in length. So it's called "microblogging". Cute.

2) **Wikipedia®** is a **user-written**, **user-edited** encyclopedia. **Anyone** can edit Wikipedia® articles — so anyone can insert completely **made-up garbage** into an article. You just have to hope that any rubbish gets **edited out again**.

3) People can submit homemade videos to sites like **YouTube**, for anyone to watch. New **mobile phone technology** makes it easy to take video and upload it straight to YouTube, or email it.

4) In *We Media*, **Bowman and Willis (2003)** describe **citizen journalism** as the public "playing an active role in the process of collecting, reporting, analyzing and disseminating news and information" — this can mean taking **photos** and video and posting them on the internet, or posting **analysis** of news and its coverage on a **blog**.

> **Web 2.0** is a trendy term for the way that web design and development have evolved to make communication and networking easier on the internet. Web 2.0 sites make it easy for users to **search** for content, **add** content and "**tag**" existing content. **Social networking websites** such as **Facebook®** and **photo album sites** are good examples of Web 2.0.

People also socialise on the internet by using **virtual worlds**, e.g. Second Life®, and games like World of Warcraft®. Postmodernist **Turkle (1996)** reckons that individuals can relate to a **simulated virtual world** as easily as they can to **real life**.

Old Media have taken Advantage of New Media — this is called Convergence

1) Producers of **traditional commercial media content** such as **music** and **film** use the internet to advertise and market their products, and **sell** their products online both as "hard copy" and as a digital **download**.

2) Big "old media" companies **form partnerships** with new media companies, e.g. NBC partnered Microsoft® to form the **MSNBC** online news service — or **buy** new media companies, e.g. News Corporation bought **myspace®**

3) **Broadcasters** can interact with their audience through **social networking** and microblogging sites.

4) News organisations make use of **citizen journalism** by asking the public to send in their stories, photos and video. It actually stops being pure citizen journalism then, and becomes **collaborative journalism**.

Globalisation and Popular Culture

The global nature of the media has an effect on society. This all links back to the Culture/Identity AS module. **For AQA only**.

The **Media** is a **Global Industry** and creates a **Global Culture**

1) There has been **concentration of media ownership** — a few media corporations dominate the global market. See p.34-35.

2) **Devereux (2003)** points out that most of the large media corporations are based in the West, so images from **Western** societies **dominate** the global media market.

3) **McBride (1980)** suggests that there is **media imperialism** — Western media products flow into less developed parts of the world and **change local cultures**. This makes a **ready market** for Western

Global mass media has created a "global village"

1) The idea of the **global village** comes from **McLuhan (1962)**. He suggests that new technologies bring people closer together — our neighbours aren't just next door, they're on the **other side of the world**.

2) We hear **news and gossip** about people all over the world, and we can **talk to people** all over the world. Remember — at the time McLuhan was actually writing, this was only on the **phone**, but **new media** technologies like email and blogs are a great example of his ideas.

consumer goods. People in many parts of the world share the **same consumption patterns** as the result of **global advertising** from companies such as Disney, Sony, Coca-Cola® and Virgin. **Klein (2000)** says there's increasing **cultural homogenisation** — everyone's culture is becoming the **same**.

4) Some theorists claim that globalisation is specifically **Americanisation** — it's American culture that gets copied.

5) However **Sreberny-Mohammadi (1996)** suggests that many local cultures have **resisted media imperialism**. She points out the strong and **growing media industry** in Asia and South America which actually **exports media products** back to the West — e.g. **Bollywood** films influence Western culture, and Brazilian soap operas are sold to TV stations all over North America, South America and Europe. Also, it is in the interests of a Western media owner to **promote local cultures** to gain **bigger audiences** and even secure the approval of the local **government**.

Media Culture is Popular Culture — some say the media is "Dumbed Down"

1) Culture can be divided into **high** and **low** culture. High culture is seen as "good" for society — the division of culture is often considered an elitist **binary opposition**. Other theorists refer to **mass culture**, which is passed on by the **media**.

2) **Popular culture** is another way of looking at the culture of the "masses". Some theorists prefer it as it's a more positive term than low culture. Also, the idea of popular culture is based on an **active audience** who can shape their culture, unlike the concept of **mass culture** which relies on a **passive media-controlled audience**.

1) There's a debate about "**dumbing down**" in the media — **simplifying** content and avoiding **intellectually challenging** the audience. For example, the **news** contains more **sensationalism** and **celebrity gossip** than it used to.

2) **Popular classical** artists such as Katherine Jenkins, Il Divo, etc. can be seen as **popularising high culture** and bringing it into mainstream popular culture — or as **replacing** high culture with a **dumbed down** mass culture substitute.

3) The dumbing down argument **isn't new** — back in **1869**, Matthew Arnold feared that high culture was under threat.

4) **Pluralists** argue that audiences get the media they want. So dumbing down **can't be the fault of the media**.

5) **Frank Furedi (2004)** claims that intentionally simplifying cultural content is **itself an elitist activity** — it's not done by the "masses" but done for them, and it **assumes** that they are **too stupid** to understand complex content.

Practice Questions

Q1 Give three examples of new media.
Q2 Roughly what proportion of households have a satellite, cable or other digital receiver?
Q3 What did McLuhan (1962) mean by a global village?
Q4 What do the terms high culture and popular culture mean? Give an example of each.

Exam Questions

Q1 'The developments of new media have led to increased choice for all.'
To what extent do the sociological theories and evidence you have studied support this view? (33 marks)

Q2 Outline and assess the view that media globalisation is damaging indigenous cultures. (50 marks)

There'll be no dumbing down around here...

Hmmm. These arguments about dumbing down sound a lot like the old arguments about high culture versus low culture. I mean, who's to say that people shouldn't watch Britain's Got Talent instead of a performance by the Royal Ballet anyway...

The Nature and Distribution of Power

*Power is a tricky beast. Different theorists think power comes in different varieties. And it's not only governments or states that hold power — businesses, individuals, transnational corporations and the media all do too. These pages are for **AQA** and **OCR**.*

Power is about the ability to Control and Influence

The pluralist **R A Dahl** (**1961** *Who Governs?*, New Haven: Yale University Press) gives this **definition** of power: "**A** has **power** over **B** to the extent that s/he can **get B** to **do something** s/he **wouldn't otherwise have done**".

This is a **useful starting point** for understanding power. From this definition of power, you can see that power relationships can involve processes such as **coercion** (**force**), **manipulation**, **bargaining** or **persuasion**. You also need to think about this definition in terms of **society as a whole** and the way that **some social groups** and **institutions** have **power over others**.

Authority is Legitimate Power

Most sociologists agree that there's a **difference** between **power** and **authority**. **Authority** suggests a sort of power relationship which is **accepted** by the people who are ruled over — they give their **consent**. It's useful to remember the phrase "**authority is legitimate power**".

E.g., most drivers obey **traffic lights**. This isn't because anyone directly **coerces** us — there's no one standing over us with a gun. It's because we know the **law** says we must stop at a red light, and we recognise the authority of the law, and know that the law is sensible, so we obey it. We give our **consent** to the government that makes laws governing the rules of the road.

Max Weber said there are Three Types of Authority

1)	**Charismatic**	People give their **consent** to a **charismatic leader** because of the leader's **exceptional qualities**. The leader inspires great **loyalty** and **devotion**. **Religious** leaders are often charismatic. Examples of charismatic leaders might include: Napoleon, Gandhi, Barack Obama and Fidel Castro.
2)	**Traditional**	People give their **consent** because they **always have**. Established customs and practices are seen as "right" because they've always been that way. For instance, a traditional society might accept their elders as rulers because the elders have always been the rulers of the society.
3)	**Rational legal**	People give their **consent** to an **impersonal legal framework** (a set of rules). The rules are **rational** because they **make sense** and have a particular and **obvious aim**. A modern example would be stopping at a red light to avoid vehicle crashes.

These types are **ideals** — pure theoretical ideas. Weber suggested that in **real life**, authority could be a **mixture** of these "ideal" types. So in our traffic light example, Jim Random might obey them because it's part of a **legal system** of understandable rules (rational legal), because we've **always** obeyed them (traditional), and because he **loves** the Prime Minister (charismatic).

Stephen Lukes has a Radical view — he says there are Three Faces of Power

1)	**Decision-making**	The power to **make** and **implement decisions** which **affect other people**.
2)	**Non decision-making**	The power to **set agendas** — i.e. **limit** what's being **discussed**. If a topic isn't even discussed, **no decision** can be made about it.
3)	**Shaping desires**	The power to manipulate what people **think they want** — powerful groups can make people think they **want** or **consent to** something which actually **harms their interests**.

Lukes suggests that the **third face of power** (shaping desires) is the strongest, because it's never questioned. He suggests that power is exercised **invisibly** by controlling what people **want**. This is related to the idea of **Marcuse** that capitalism creates **false needs** — things that people **don't really need**, but **think** they do.

Karl Marx said only One Group holds power in society — the Bourgeoisie

1)   **Karl Marx (1818-1883)** believed that power in society is **finite** (in other words there's only so much of it), and that it can only be held by **one person** or group at a time. This view of power is called the **Zero Sum Model**.

2)   Marx saw society in terms of social classes **competing** for power. Under capitalism, the **capitalist** class (**bourgeoisie**) hold **all the power** and use it to their advantage and to the detriment of the **working class** (**proletariat**).

3)   Marxists tend to reject the idea of authority as legitimate power, suggesting that the working class are **falsely persuaded** to consent to the rule of the capitalist class. They saw authority as just **disguised power**.

4)   Marxist sociologist **Miliband (1969)** suggests that **political power** is held by the same class who hold **economic power**.

5)   **Neo-Marxists** like **Gramsci (1971)** emphasise the power of **ideas** in perpetuating capitalism. Bourgeois '**hegemony**' (see p. 3) turns bourgeois ideas and values into the 'common sense' of the age. This means the working class **consent** to the **power** of the bourgeoisie over them.

The Nature and Distribution of Power

Elite Theorists *see society as ruled by a small, powerful* Elite

1) **Classical elite theorists** like **Vilfredo Pareto (1848-1923)** and **Gaetano Mosca (1858-1941)** saw society as divided between the rulers (**the elite**) and the ruled. The **elite** take all the **important decisions** in society and these decisions are almost always in their **own interest**. So far, they agreed with the Marxist viewpoint.

2) The big difference between elite theorists and Marxists is that the elite theorists thought **elite domination** was **desirable**, **inevitable** and **natural**. They said the elite become the elite because they are **better** than the rest of us. They saw the **rest of society** as a disorganised and apathetic **rabble**. This is **very different to Marxists** who thought that elite domination was unfair and exploitative.

1) In a more **modern** and **radical** study of the power of elites, **C Wright Mills (1959)** studied three important institutions in American society — the **business community**, the **military** and the **government**.

2) Mills claimed that the elite in all three institutions formed a **single ruling elite**, which he called the **power elite**. Military, industrial and political power were all intertwined in the power elite.

3) He concluded that **unelected elites** sharing the same **social background** dominate American society and run economic and foreign policy in their own interests. Mills argued that the power elite **weren't accountable** to the people. He saw **little difference** between American political parties, so no chance to vote for **alternative** policies.

Statistics show the **majority** of British **MPs**, high ranking **civil servants** and **business leaders** come from the same **social** and **educational** background — this phenomenon has been referred to as the "**Establishment**".

In a study of top decision-makers, **Lupton and Wilson (1973)** found that connections between them were strengthened by close **marital** and **kinship ties**. Strong internal ties within the elite group make it harder for outsiders to break in.

Functionalists *and* Pluralists *see power as* Dispersed *through society*

1) **Pluralist R A Dahl (1961)** found that instead of one elite group dominating society and hogging all the power, there were actually "**multiple centres of power**" — lots of small groups competing for power. Pluralists believe that all sorts of political parties and interest groups can have **power** over political **decision-making**.

2) **Functionalists** believe that the amount of power in society can **increase** or **decrease** depending on how many people see it as legitimate. This is the **Variable Sum Model**. Pluralists mostly believe the amount of power is **constant**.

3) Pluralists are **criticised** for focusing on only the **first** of Lukes' **faces of power** — the power to make decisions.

Postmodernists *like* Foucault *claim that* Power *is related to* Knowledge

1) **Foucault (1967)** argued that power is to be found in all **social relationships**, and is closely linked to **knowledge**. Power and knowledge are linked, with any extension of power involving a corresponding extension of knowledge, and vice versa.

2) Foucault suggests that it's always possible to **resist** power by **questioning** the knowledge it's based on — he gives the example of a psychiatric patient **questioning the validity** of a psychiatrist's diagnosis.

3) Foucault argued that to **understand power** we need to look at its expressions in the **everyday activity** of people, rather than just its relationship to **class** (Marxism) or **politics** (elite theories).

The 'British Ceramics' course Bernard took had had no impact on his personal best.

Lyotard (1984) sees postmodernist politics as being about a **loss of faith** in big political ideologies that say what society should be like (see p.61 for more). Lyotard sees power as belonging to whoever has the most **useful knowledge** — individuals, corporations, governments, etc.

Practice Questions

Q1 What is the difference between power and authority?

Q2 List the three types of authority itemised by Max Weber.

Q3 What are Stephen Lukes' "three faces of power"?

Q4 Explain what is meant by the Zero Sum Model and Variable Sum Model views of power.

Exam Question

Q1 Outline and assess the Marxist view that the bourgeoisie hold power in society. (50 marks)

Three faces of power and five Mighty Morphin Power Rangers.™

... who don't seem to be on the syllabus this year for some reason. Before you can get anywhere with politics and protest, you've got to have an idea of what power is, and who has power in society. Of course, different sociological schools of thought have very different ideas about power. Learn a few names so that you can drop them in your essays — but make sure you keep it relevant.

The Modern State

These pages have definitions and theories about the modern State. For **AQA** and **OCR**.

Most sociologists **Agree** with **Weber's Definition** of the **Modern State**

Weber (1946, 'Politics as a Vocation,' *Essays in Sociology*, New York: Oxford University Press) says the modern State is "a **human community** that (successfully) claims the **monopoly** of the **legitimate use** of **physical force** within a **given territory**".

In other words: ⟹

1) The State is **created by people**.
2) The State can **use force legitimately** — **other** violence in society is **illegitimate**.
3) The State **rules** over a **clear geographical area** — in our case the UK.

The **State** is traditionally made up of **Four Main Institutions**

1) The **government**, who **make laws**.
2) The **Civil Service**, who **implement laws**.

THE STATE

3) The **police**, who **enforce laws**.
4) The **Armed Forces**, who **protect** the **territory** from threats from outside.

Government is often divided into **three branches** — the legislature, the executive and the judiciary:

1) The **legislature passes laws**. In the UK, **Parliament** (the House of Commons and the House of Lords) is the legislature.
2) The **executive** suggests new laws, and **runs the country**. The executive is often called "the **government**". Confusing.
3) The **judiciary interprets laws**. The **courts** are the judiciary.

In modern times, the State has extended its role into **health care**, **education** and **nationalised** (state-run) **industries**.

Pluralists see the **Modern State** as a **Neutral Arena** for debate

1) Pluralists see the power of the modern democratic State as **legitimate** and acting in the interests of society in general. Pluralists see the State as a **neutral arena** where competing interest and pressure groups lobby for **influence**. They say the State **arbitrates** (settles arguments) between competing interest groups, but is neutral itself.

2) Pluralists say the modern State is democratic because of the **multi-party system**, and because of the participation of **interest groups** and **pressure groups**. **Dahl (1961)** looked at the role of interest groups in local politics in the USA, and found that **several groups** had influence. An important study by **Hewitt (1974)** shows the **crucial role** of interest groups and pressure groups in **influencing Parliament**. Hewitt said that no one group got its own way all the time.

3) A study by **Grant and Marsh (1977)** showed that business interests in the form of the CBI (Confederation of British Industry) didn't have massive influence over British government policy. A **plurality** of **other interest groups** influenced policy away from what the CBI wanted.

Critics of pluralism claim that **some interest groups** have **more influence** than others. **Marsh and Locksley (1983)** found that the CBI were successful in getting their own way in key decisions (completely the opposite of what Marsh had found in his earlier study with Grant — Sociology is a funny old thing).

Marxists say the **State Supports** the interests of the **Bourgeoisie**

Marx and Engels said: "The State is but a committee for managing the affairs of the bourgeoisie," (1985, *The Communist Manifesto* Harmondsworth: Penguin, first published 1848).

Marx and **Engels** asserted that the State only became necessary when society became **divided** on grounds of **class**. They said that in primitive society there were no classes and therefore no need for a State.

Marxists claim that the role of the modern State is to **maintain**, **preserve** and **perpetuate** the rule of the **capitalist class** over the **workers**. This is achieved in the following ways:

Engels was Marx's friend and worked with Marx on the Communist Manifesto.

1) **Coercive force** — the **police** are used to contain or suppress **demonstrations** and **riots**.

2) The **illusion of democracy** — universal voting makes it **look** as though everyone has a say and that society is **fair**. This creates the **false consciousness** that the current system is legitimate. However, political parties only represent the interests of **capitalism**, so there's **no real choice**.

3) **Ideology** — a set of ideas by which the State gains approval and consent by persuading people to accept ruling class values. The neo-Marxist **Gramsci (1891-1937)** called this kind of domination **hegemony**. **Gramsci**, **Althusser** and **Poulantzas** all extend the definition of the State to other institutions which pass on values, e.g. **churches**, **mass media**, the **family**.

Althusser called the army, police and courts the Repressive State Apparatus, and the church, family, education and media the Ideological State Apparatus.

Critics say it's **hard to prove** Marxist theory. Concepts like **ideology**, **hegemony** and **false consciousness**, which are key to the Marxist viewpoint, are **difficult to define** and even more **difficult to research**.

The Modern State

Some sociologists argue that the State can act in its Own Interest

Nordlinger (1981) complicates both the pluralist idea that the state reflects the wishes of society and the Marxist idea that the state reflects the views of a minority dominant class, by claiming that a state can act **independently** in three ways:

1) By directly pursuing its **own policies** against the **wishes of the people** — it can do this by using state resources, bribery and secrecy to divide opponents.

2) By **manipulating public opinion** to support its own policies.

3) By asserting control when **public opinion** is either **unsure** or **apathetic** about an issue or policy.

Skocpol (1985) also claims that the state can act autonomously to **increase its own power** and **follow interests** which are not necessarily those of any group in society other than itself.

Neo-liberals are Opposed to State Intervention in the Economy

1) Neo-liberals argue that the keys to lasting economic prosperity are **individual economic enterprise** and a **market** (economy) which is **free** from **state intervention**. Neo-liberal theorists, like **Hayek (1944)**, argue that state intervention in the economy can **stifle capitalism** and make the economy **less efficient**.

2) Neo-liberals therefore believe that **state interference** in the economy such as high taxes, state ownership (nationalisation), or generous welfare benefits should be **rolled back** (i.e. reduced).

3) The influence of neo-liberal thinking can be seen in the **Conservative governments** of Mrs Thatcher (1979-1990) which **privatised** state industries, **lowered taxation** and **reduced universal benefits**.

4) The **traditional challenge** to the neo-liberal view is the **reformist socialist view** — the view that the State **should intervene** in the economy in order to improve **social welfare** and **equality**. The reformist socialist view is associated with Old Labour, e.g. the post-war Labour government which created the Welfare State.

Third Way theorists want a State with Social Welfare and Capitalist Economics

1) The "**Third Way**" was an idea put forward by the sociologist **Anthony Giddens (1998)** and later adopted by Tony Blair's **New Labour Party**. Giddens has described it as "the modernising left."

2) Third Way theorists argue that the **world is changing**, for example through globalisation, and that **political ideologies** need to **change** and **adapt** as well if they are to remain relevant. The Third Way therefore includes **elements** of **both** traditional **left-wing** (socialist) and **right-wing** (neo-liberal capitalist) approaches.

3) Third Way theory suggests that the **traditional Welfare State** should be **reformed** because it **encourages dependency** (a neo-liberal idea). However, it also argues that the State should reform and manage the **global economy** to such an extent that it is able to **intervene** to **invest in its citizens**, e.g. through **education** and **social policy**. They argue this will **empower the population** to lead more prosperous, healthy and fulfilling lives.

Globalisation has changed the role of the State

1) As part of the process of globalisation (see p.66-67) **transnational corporations** (**TNCs**) have developed and become very powerful economically. **Sklair (1995)** claims that there's a **transnational capital class** who have gained power at the expense of nation states — he claims the State just isn't as important any more.

2) There's a trend towards **internationalisation** of politics, which has reduced the influence of nation states. For example, some important decisions are taken by the **European Union** rather than by its **member states**.

Practice Questions

Q1 Traditionally, what four things make up the State?

Q2 Briefly summarise the Pluralist view on the role of the State.

Q3 Briefly summarise the Marxist view on the role of the State.

Exam Question

Q1 Evaluate the view that the people in positions of most power in society have not been directly elected. (33 marks)

No need to get in a State about it...

There are a lot of strong opinions on these two pages. You need to be able to evaluate these different views fairly and objectively, whatever your own personal opinion. And I bet you do have a personal opinion. If you find yourself taking sides and thinking "stupid liberal do-gooders" or "blimmin' Tories" then take some deep breaths and start again.

Political Parties and Participation

*These pages have descriptions of the main parties, and a bit on why party politics in general may be struggling. For **AQA** and **OCR**.*

The UK is a **Representative Democracy**

1) In a representative democracy, the people vote to **elect representatives** to make decisions on their **behalf**. These representatives (**MPs** in the UK) are accountable to the voters at the next election — they can get voted out.

2) **Joseph Schumpeter (1942**, *Capitalism, Socialism and Democracy* New York: Harper and Brothers**)** defined democracy as a system where there is a "competitive struggle for the people's vote". For a government to be a democracy, there must be **more than one candidate** or party standing in an election.

3) **Politics** in modern representative democracies like the UK is where **belief systems** (represented by **political parties**, e.g. the Liberal Democrats, Labour, the Conservatives) **compete** for **power**.

4) Citizens can participate by **supporting** and **voting** for a particular political party that they share beliefs with. They can also join that political party — and help out with **election campaigns**, or become an **activist** (someone who attempts to influence the party's policies or who supports their policies and campaigns on their behalf).

The **Mainstream Political Parties** have a number of **Important Functions**

Garner and Kelly (1993) suggest that political parties carry out a number of **essential functions**:

1) **Governing Function** — British governments are formed out of political parties. The party with an **overall majority** in the House of Commons becomes the government and its leader the Prime Minister.

2) **Electoral Function** — Elections are central to a democratic system, and depend on parties to put up **candidates**.

3) **Policy Function** — By forming distinct policies, parties offer the electorate **choice** — an essential feature of a democracy.

4) **Representative Function** — Political parties represent the views of a wide range of the electorate and therefore allow the views of people to be **heard** and be **influential**. In order to win, parties must represent a **broad base** of opinion.

5) **Participation Function** — Parties are important vehicles through which the people can **participate** in politics.

6) **Ideological Function** — Political parties allow for a debate to occur between **competing principles** and **ideologies**.

The **Conservative Party** is the traditional party of the **Right**

The Conservative Party is the main **right-wing** or **centre-right** party in British politics.

It is made up of three distinct parts — the **Parliamentary Conservative Party** (the elected MPs), the **Constituent Associations** (made up of volunteers) and the paid party professionals (workers at **Conservative Campaign Headquarters**).

All party members elect the **leader**, whose role includes the appointment of the party Chairman, the cabinet (or shadow cabinet) and the deputy leader. The leader has also the **final say** on what goes in the Conservative **manifesto**.

1) The Conservatives were in power from 1979 to 1997 — Margaret Thatcher was the leader through the 1980s.

2) Thatcherism emphasised **low public spending, privatisation, low taxes** and **individual responsibility** and the then government presided over periods of high unemployment and cuts in public services.

3) More recently, the Conservative leader David Cameron has **distanced** himself from traditional Conservative ideas on tax, the environment, NHS spending, gay marriage and public spending. He's used the idea of **'compassionate conservatism'** to rebrand the party as more **centrist** with a new logo, a new style and a softer and more **inclusive image**.

Labour is traditionally the largest mainstream party of the **Left**

1) The main components of the Labour Party are Labour Party **branches, constituency parties** (CLPs), the **Parliamentary Labour Party** (PLP), the **National Executive Committee** (NEC), and the **leader**.

2) The leader of the party is elected by an **electoral college** made up of three parts, each with an equal say — affiliated trade unions, the PLP and the CLPs. The unions and the CLPs ballot their members before casting their votes.

3) On paper, the Labour leader has **less power** than the Conservative leader. In practice, however, modern Labour leaders have been successful in **managing** the party in such a way as to **get what they want**.

4) The Labour Party was created as the party of the **working class**. It's **never** been a **revolutionary** socialist organisation, but from 1945 through to the 1970s it was heavily influenced by **reformist** socialist ideology. Socialism aims to work towards **equality**, and favours a strong and generous **welfare state**, and the **state ownership and control of industries**. Socialism says industry should be run for the **common good**.

5) Since 1979, the Labour Party has gradually changed or removed most of its reformist socialist ideas. During the 1990s, the party redesigned itself as '**New Labour**' under Tony Blair. New Labour talks in terms of a '**Third Way**' between the party's **traditional** ideals and the necessity to **maintain economic growth**. They gained power in 1997.

6) In 1995, Labour reworded Clause Four of its constitution — the clause that committed them to **state ownership** of industry.

Political Parties and Participation

The **Liberal Democrats** are the **Smallest** of the mainstream parties

The Liberal Democrats are the newest of the big three parties, formed in **1988** by a merger of the old **Liberal Party** and the **Social Democratic Party** (SDP). They frequently poll around 20% of the national vote but they rarely get many MPs because of the **'First Past the Post'** electoral system.

1) The Liberal Democrats are a **federal party**, which means local and regional parties have a lot of freedom and autonomy.

2) **Delegates** are sent from every local party to the federal conference. The biannual (twice yearly) federal conference has the **final say** on Liberal Democrat policy issues, **not the leader**.

3) Liberal Democrats are influenced by **progressive liberalism**. This is a move away from **classical liberalism**, which emphasised free markets, individualism and self-help.

4) **Progressive liberalism** calls for **state intervention** to provide services like pensions, hospitals and schools. At the same time it champions **traditional liberal values** of **individual freedom** and **choice**.

The **Influence** of **Political Parties** on the **Political Process** is in **Decline**

1) For many years the UK was seen as the classic model of the **two-party system** — i.e. a system where two **big**, **powerful** and **distinct** political parties compete for power. Other parties exist in a two-party system, but they don't have a **realistic chance** of winning an election and forming a government.

2) Sociologists have been writing about the decline of the influence of the main political parties since the 1960s. In this view, the fact that political parties have **fewer members** and **fewer activists** shows that they're **less likely** to **inspire** people to go and **vote**.

There's some powerful evidence that the influence of political parties is in decline:

1) **Party membership** and **activism** is declining among Britain's three major parties. For instance, **Labour Party** membership peaked at over 400 000 with Tony Blair's victory in 1997, but had fallen to less than half this in 2005. Conservative Party membership is also declining.

2) Young people especially are turning to **New Social Movements** to participate in politics (see p. 61).

3) The differences between political parties appear to be **less pronounced**, resulting in voter "**apathy**", e.g. only **61.3%** of the electorate **voted** in the 2005 **general election**.

However, **Reiter (1989)** is **sceptical** of the claim that political parties are in decline. He says there isn't enough evidence across different countries and over a long enough period of time.

Neo-Marxist **Martin Jacques (1997)** suggests that because of the decline in political parties, British politics should move away from the **"Westminster model"**, which focuses exclusively on the mainstream parties. Jacques suggests that we need to develop new forms of political participation.

Ideologically, British **Political Parties** appear to be becoming **Less Distinct**

1) "**New Labour**" under Tony Blair dropped many of the **traditional**, **left-wing** policies and commitments of the Labour Party, e.g. **democratic socialism**, **nationalisation** and **redistribution of wealth**.

2) New Labour now competes in elections as a party who could **manage the capitalist economy** better than its traditional managers, the Conservative Party.

3) Policies on **taxation**, **foreign affairs** and **economic management** have become very **similar** in the **Conservative Party** and the **Labour Party**. This gives voters less choice, which may make them less bothered to go and vote in elections.

Vote Peter Baffin — your Labervative candidate.

Practice Questions

Q1 Explain the differences between Thatcherism and 'compassionate conservatism'.

Q2 Give three pieces of evidence which suggest that the influence of political parties is in decline.

Exam Question

Q1 Identify and explain two key aspects of the role of political parties. (6 marks)

See if you can spot these guys at the next General Election...

...or on Radio 4 of a morning (if you can face it before your porridge). The fact that a lot of people don't bother with them is what you'll come to know as the decline of the political parties. Make sure you know who the main parties are and what sort of things they believe in. You could always read some of the leaflets they shove through your door.

Voting Behaviour

*This page focuses on the work of psephologists — they're people who study elections. This page is for **AQA** students only.*

Psephologists have identified **Three Main Periods** of post-war voting patterns

1) **1945-1974** — a period of **clear ideological differences** between the parties, with strong **class alignment** (working class Labour and middle class Conservative) and strong **voter identification** with their party — **"partisan alignment"**.

2) **1974-1997** — a period of more **"voter volatility"** with **class** and **party loyalties** seemingly **breaking down**. This period also saw a **big decline** in the **Labour Party vote**, with four successive **Conservative governments**.

3) **1997-2005** — a period marked by the emergence and success of **New Labour** — the Labour Party moved to a more **centrist** position, with **fewer clear differences** from the Conservatives, which won them many **middle class votes**.

Post-war voting patterns have been explained with **Partisan Alignment Theory**

Butler and Stokes (1974) argued that **class alignment** was the main factor influencing voting behaviour. The **working class** supported **Labour** who **represented their interests**, and the **middle class** supported the **Conservatives**, who represented theirs. Voters tended to have **strong identification** with their **particular party** (**partisan alignment**) and the result was a fairly stable **two-party system**. Butler and Stokes argued that such **predictable voting patterns** were caused by **political socialisation** — children **learnt** and **copied** the voting **loyalties** of their **parents**.

Traditional Loyalties have become **Less Important**

If all voters had voted in the way Butler and Stokes suggested there would have been a **permanent** Labour government. The fact that there wasn't led a number of psephologists to investigate the phenomenon of the '**working-class Tory**'.

1) **Bagehot (1867)** first identified the tendency of the working class to be **deferent** to those in authority. The idea of **'deferential' voting** (voting for one's "betters") has been used to explain deviant working class Conservative voters.

2) **Butler and Rose (1960)** used **embourgeoisement theory** to explain working class Conservative voters — they argued that the working class was **changing**, adopting **middle class values** and **aspirations**.

3) **McKenzie and Silver (1968)** suggested that some working class voters were becoming '**secular**', i.e. not voting on established traditional loyalties, but on **policy preference** lines — this idea has been popular in more recent studies.

4) **Sarlvick and Crewe (1983)** argued that during the period of voter volatility, **economic change** and increased **prosperity** weakened the link between class and party — **"class dealignment"**. The **old working class** based in highly unionised **industries** in northern England declined. A **new aspirational home-owning** working class emerged in **south-eastern England**. In this period Labour **maintained** the support of the **shrinking** 'old working class', but **didn't win the loyalty** of the '**new working class**'. This led to the disastrous **election results** for Labour in **1983**.

5) **Denver (2002)** argued that **policy preference** (how much voters like a party's policies) is now **more important** than broader social factors like class, gender, region, age etc. He argues that in recent Labour victories **voters' views** have simply been **closer** to **Labour policies** than Conservative policies.

6) There are **other factors** that shape voting patterns. The **region** people live in can have a big impact — Scotland, Wales and the North have majority Labour support — the South and South East majority Conservative support. **Ethnicity** is also important — **Saggar and Heath (1999)** have shown how Labour has consistently won over 70% of the **ethnic minority vote**. **Norris (1997)** showed that **women voters** are proportionately more likely to vote **Conservative**.

"Voter Apathy" is when people **Don't Bother** to vote

Voter apathy is particularly marked amongst the **young** and amongst **ethnic minority** groups. Several measures have been proposed to tackle this apathy. Some have already been adopted.

Already adopted:

1) Making voting **easier** by making it easier to apply for a **postal vote**. ←

2) Making it easier to **register** to vote — you can register online in some areas.

3) **Educating the voters**, e.g. **Citizenship** is a **National Curriculum** subject in schools.

Not yet adopted:

1) Making **voting** easier by using **new technology**, e.g. internet voting and text message voting.

2) Extending polling day to several days.

3) **Redesigning ballot papers** to make them easier to understand.

4) Giving people the option to register a positive abstention — i.e. a box to tick that says "none of the above" or "abstain".

The postal vote system in the UK has been criticised as open to fraud. Researchers and journalists have shown it's possible to register a postal vote in someone else's name. This accusation has damaged trust in the electoral system.

All the measures seem to focus on **voters** rather than the **decline** and **ideological convergence** of the political parties. Some countries, e.g. Australia, have tackled the problem by making **voting compulsory**. This hasn't yet been proposed in Britain.

The Influence of the Media

*This page is all about what the papers say, and how they control your mind. It's for **AQA** and **OCR**.*

The **UK Mass Media** were **Pro-Conservative** until the **late 1990s**

1) Up until 1997 the only mainstream paper that ever expressed consistent support for the Labour Party was the **Daily Mirror**. The rest tended to support the Conservatives.

2) In the late 1990s "New Labour" made it a **priority** to win the support of **big media owners**, particularly **Rupert Murdoch**. Murdoch's News International controlled the **Times**, the **Sun** and **Sky Television**.

3) The results can be illustrated by the contrasting ways in which Sun headline writers treated two Labour leaders — Neil Kinnock in 1992 and Tony Blair in 1997. The Sun's 1992 election day headline was "**If Kinnock wins today, will the last person to leave Britain turn off the lights**" (Neil Kinnock was the Labour Party leader in 1992). The Sun's 1997 election day headline was "**THE SUN BACKS BLAIR — give change a chance**".

4) The support of significant sections of the **mass media** has been cited as a crucial factor in the **continued electoral success** of New Labour. "**Spin doctors**" are party public relations (PR) officers whose job is to **manipulate** the media and make sure that the party is presented in a sympathetic light, and that the party's opponents are presented negatively.

Marxists suggest that **Media Ownership** makes the media **Pro-Capitalist**

1) Traditional Marxism claims that the media **directly** presents news stories which serve the **interests** of the ruling class, because the media is itself **owned** by the **ruling class**.

2) **Miliband (1969)** said that the mass media was the "new opium of the people" — it keeps the proletariat subdued by showing them nice mindless entertainment. **Marcuse (1964)** said that the media gives people "**false needs**" which keep them consuming the goods that capitalism produces.

3) Neo-Marxists suggest that the world view of the capitalist class is broadcast and reinforced by the mass media through an **indirect approval process**. Editors are from middle class backgrounds, so they tend to select material which reflects their own ideas.

4) **Gramsci**'s idea of **ideological hegemony** (see p. 3) really applies here. Ruling class values are portrayed through the mass media as natural and common sense. Ideas that question capitalism are ridiculed as crazy.

False need or no, Nina just had to have that brass chamber pot.

5) An **example** of this was an attack on the policies of the Liberal Democrats by the Sun in which they superimposed former Liberal Democrat leader **Charles Kennedy's face** on the label of a **bottle of whisky** to illustrate an article about the Liberal Democrats. The headline was "Red Kennedy", suggesting that the Liberal Democrats were **socialists** (red is the colour of socialism), and the subheading was "**Loony left policies of Lib Dems' boozy chief**".

The work of the **GUMG** suggests that **News** is **Politically Weighted**

	The GUMG studied news reports of industrial disputes in the 70s and 80s
Method:	The Glasgow University Media Group studied television news over a long time span to look for evidence of bias. They performed detailed content analysis on television news bulletins.
Finding:	The selection of news and voice-over scripts were biased in favour of dominant class values. During industrial disputes, management had more access to the media than union leaders. Filming and editing were biased in favour of the police.

Practice Questions

Q1 Explain what is meant by political socialisation.

Q2 What does 'policy preference' mean?

Q3 Give three ways in which Marxists say the media promotes the interests of the ruling class.

Exam Question

Q1 "The most important factor affecting voter behaviour is partisan alignment." To what extent do you agree with this statement?

(33 marks)

I vote we all should do some more Sociology revision...

It's worth thinking about just how powerful the media are. The newspapers you read — or the news programmes you catch on TV and the radio — choose what events and whose opinions are worth covering, and how much coverage they deserve. If you get a couple of different papers one day, you'll be able to see how different they are. And you'll also have loads of crosswords to do.

Old and New Social Movements

*These pages are on the different types of social movements — they're for **AQA** and **OCR**.*

Old Social Movements (OSMs) are Pressure Groups or Interest Groups

Bagguley (1995) argues that **Old Social Movements** (OSMs) are influenced by **economic** and **class factors**. They focus their attention on **public policy issues**, attempting to influence **decision-makers** and **law-makers**. Many OSMs are **occupationally based** (e.g. trade unions), whereas others are concerned with **single issues**.

Pressure groups can be either **protective** (also called **sectional**) or **promotional**. **Protective** groups seek to protect the interests of a particular group, e.g. trade unions protect groups of workers, the CBI protects the interests of business, and the British Medical Association looks out for doctors. **Promotional** groups promote causes, e.g. Greenpeace and Friends of the Earth promote environmental causes.

Pluralists argue that pressure group activity is an essential feature of modern democracy.

1) Pressure groups give **valuable input** to government policy and provide expert opinion.

2) Pressure groups provide a vehicle for many **views** to be **represented**.

3) **Pluralists** say pressure groups have **equal access** to government. The State is seen by pluralists as a **neutral arbiter** between **pressure groups** with different opinions.

Marxists suggest that pressure group activity doesn't enhance democracy at all.

1) Pressure groups tend **not** to be **democratic**. Members have little say in the running of the group.

2) Pressure groups are **not equal** — some have more resources and therefore much more influence than others. Marxists claim that the most powerful groups are always the pro-capitalist ones.

3) Marxists think pressure groups shouldn't be powerful as they aren't **accountable** to the people.

4) Marxists think the State **isn't neutral** and can't be a neutral arbiter between pressure groups.

There are Insider and Outsider Pressure Groups

1) **Insider groups** are those which are perceived to be **expert** and **respectable**. They can get close to **government** and **decision-makers**. Governments often need the **help** and support of such groups to plan and implement their programmes.

2) Outsider groups are those who have **little** or **no access** to decision-makers because they're viewed as **extreme** or **not useful** to decision-makers.

3) Pressure groups may **change status** from outsider to insider or vice versa. In the 1970s most **environmental groups** were considered outsider groups with little influence with decision-makers — today they're largely insider groups as the major parties **seek** their advice and support. In the 1970s the trade unions were insider groups with **strong influence** over Labour governments. This changed under the Conservative leader **Thatcher**, who saw them as **dangerous**.

Pressure groups Lobby those in power to Achieve their Aims

1) Pressure groups try to gain **influence** over governments and decision-makers — this is called **lobbying**.

2) Insider groups are able to gain access to decision-makers during the **consultation stage** of legislation and right through the legislative process. Sometimes pressure groups are able to influence Parliament more generally when invited to appear before **select committees**.

3) Pressure groups also lobby politicians through the political parties. An example of this is the **close link** between the **Labour Party** and the **trade unions** which although diminished is still significant — they form a third of the electoral college which elects the party leader (see p. 56).

Select committees are small cross-party committees of MPs who investigate and report on important areas of policy, and who can question anybody important or expert in their field of enquiry.

4) Many pressure groups **don't** have **formal ties** to political parties. They are often **courted** by political parties to gain **endorsement** of their proposed policies.

There are Two Main Types of New Social Movement (NSM)

Hallsworth (1994) defines NSMs as movements which **challenge** the **established political** and **cultural order** in capitalist societies. This includes feminism, environmentalism, the civil rights movement and anti-racist movements. NSMs can either be **defensive** or **offensive** — which has nothing to do with whether they offend people, by the way.

- **Defensive** movements are concerned with **protecting** the environment or people from things they see as a threat, e.g. **nuclear power**, **genetically modified crops**, **global capitalism**, etc.

- **Offensive** movements want to **promote** and widen the **rights** of the groups they represent. Examples of offensive movements are **gay rights groups**, **human rights groups** and **anti-racist groups**.

Old and New Social Movements

The **Young** tend to participate in politics through **NSMs**

1) Hallsworth claims that most members of NSMs tend to be **young** (mainly between 16 and 30) and **middle class,** particularly from the **public sector middle class** (teachers, social workers, etc.).

2) NSMs are **informally organised**, and **non-bureaucratic.** They tend to operate outside of traditional politics. Unlike pressure groups and political parties, NSMs tend to favour **direct action**, such as demonstrations, civil disobedience and sit-ins (see p. 62-63).

This includes young people whose parents are teachers, social workers etc.

Sociologists apply different **Theories** to the phenomenon of **NSMs**

1) **Marcuse (1969)** argues that young people form and join NSMs because they are **alienated** by **capitalism**. Marcuse is a **Marxist** who says that capitalism produces a **shallow**, **superficial** mass **consumer culture** which the NSMs reject. He argues that NSMs have the potential to **liberate** people.

2) **Habermas (1987)** argues that people form and join NSMs as a response to the **intrusion of the State** into private life, and the **failure of the State** to solve problems or control industrial capitalism. He says that NSMs are deliberately non-bureaucratic.

3) **Giddens (1973)** argues that an increase in **risk** has motivated people to start NSMs. Late 20th-century peace movements responded to the increased risk of **war**, especially **nuclear war**. Environmentalist movements have responded to the increased risk of **environmental disasters**.

4) **Melucci (1989)** says that people join NSMs to give them a **sense** of **collective identity**.

Vicky and Chad show off their new social movements.

There's more about identity and protest on p. 64-65.

Some sociologists link NSMs with **Postmodernism**

1) **Crook, Pakulski and Waters (1992)** argue that **postmodernisation** is causing a shift from **old politics** to **new politics**. They define **old politics** as based on **political parties** and **class**, and belonging to a specialised **political sphere**. They define **new politics** as based on **NSMs** and moral issues, and belonging to people's wider lifestyle.

2) Crook, Pakulski and Waters say that a **decline** in the importance of **class** is partly responsible. They claim that class-based party politics is becoming less relevant.

3) The rise in importance of the **media** is another factor. They say that the media **dramatises** potential scenarios such as global warming and nuclear war, which makes people feel that they have to do something about them.

1) **Nancy Fraser (1995)** suggests that what constitutes the "**public sphere**" (where politics goes on) has changed.

2) She argues that it has **fragmented** into **several** public spheres where **special interest groups** can argue issues before trying to get their views onto the **mainstream agenda**.

3) She also claims that the public sphere has **widened**, and that the **personal** and **private** have **become political** — for example, sexual harassment was once seen as private flirting, but feminists have made it political.

1) Postmodernist **Jean-François Lyotard (1984)** claims that in the postmodern era people have lost faith in what he calls "**metanarratives**" — the big sweeping political ideologies of the modern era that say what society should be like.

2) He suggests that politics has become more **localised** and **limited** in scope, and more concerned with **single issues**.

Practice Questions

Q1 What is the difference between protective and promotional pressure groups?

Q2 What is lobbying?

Q3 What does Marcuse say about NSMs?

Exam Question

Q1 Outline and assess the view that new social movements form because people no longer have faith in politics. (50 marks)

No need to get defensive about it — or offensive for that matter...

There's quite a bit of tricky stuff for you to remember here. Make sure you know what it is that makes old social movements old, and new social movements new — and don't you get the two mixed up. Sadly, it's not as simple as new social movements being newer — there's a whole lot more to it than that. Keep scribbling it all down without looking until you're sure you've got it...

Political Action and Protest

*These pages look at forms of direct action engaged in by New Social Movements. They're for **OCR** and **AQA**.*

Direct action happens *Outside* normal *Political Processes*

Direct action is political activity which happens outside the normal political processes. It includes **peaceful demonstrations**, **sit-ins** and **boycotts**, as well as violent action such as **riots**, **vandalism** and **terrorism**.

Some direct action is **large-scale** and **public**, e.g. **demonstrations** and **marches**.
Some is **targeted**, e.g. **letter** and **leaflet campaigns**, **vandalism** and **boycotts**.

1) **New Social Movements** are far more likely to engage in **direct action** than traditional political activity. They don't have a **strong voice** in party political debate. Members of NSMs often feel they **have to take direct action** in order to get their views on the **mainstream agenda**. Getting noticed by the **media** often plays a big part in this.

2) Some say NSMs have **redefined** what is meant by **political action** — taking the political to new areas like the private sphere, e.g. by targeting the issue of domestic violence.

3) The political activity of NSMs is **deliberately** different from that of old social movements.

4) **Cyber-networking** (using e-mail lists, blogs, forums and social networking sites) makes it possible for NSMs to organise large demonstrations **quickly**, making it **difficult** for the authorities to **plan** their **response**.

> Indirect action is the more traditional form of political activity, favoured by old social movements, e.g. lobbying — see p. 60.

Direct Action *is often* Against *the* Law

1) Most illegal direct action is **peaceful**. **Civil disobedience** means direct action which breaks laws. For instance **mass trespass** is a common form of civil disobedience practised by **anti-road protestors** who put themselves physically **in the way** of developers in an attempt to protect woodlands etc. The **Reclaim the Streets** movement causes traffic congestion by organising **street parties** in the middle of busy roads, blocking the road off for the day.

2) Some **direct action** is **violent and criminal** and has been characterised as **terrorism**. Terrorist direct action has been taken against the **USA** and its allies by anti-American Islamist groups, e.g. Al Qaeda. Some Palestinian nationalist groups use terrorist actions, such as **suicide bombs**, against Israel. ETA is another group that takes violent direct action.

3) Terrorism also happens on a smaller scale. For example, the direct action of some **animal rights groups** includes sending **letter bombs** to scientists involved in testing with animals, **threatening** the **families** of scientists involved in animal testing, putting **bricks through windows** and the **firebombing** of shops selling fur goods.

Riots are a *Common* form of *Direct Action*

1) Riots are **violent** outbreaks of **serious urban disorder** on a large scale. Violence can be directed against both property and people.

2) Often riots are understood as the **desperate actions** of people not represented in any other way. In this view, social groups not represented by "Old Politics" (parties and pressure groups) resort to riots to get their **voices heard**. This view **ignores** other kinds of direct action that can be used to attract attention.

3) Riots are not a modern phenomenon, despite the fact that most sociological research has focused on the inner city riots of the **1980s** (Brixton, Toxteth, Tottenham). Throughout the **18th** and **19th centuries** there were frequent riots in the UK in response to problems that came with **industrialisation**.

4) **Peaceful demonstrations** and marches can get **violent** and turn into **riots**.

According to *Benyon (1987)* there are *Four Types* of *Explanation* for *Riots*

1) **Conservative**	Conservatives see rioting as a primarily **criminal** and **unjustifiable** activity. Rioters are seen as selfish, greedy, envious and lacking moral fibre. New Right sociologists like **Murray** suggest the **subculture** of the **underclass** which **embraces criminality** is to blame for rioting. The solution from this perspective is to break the "**dependency culture**" which breeds such **deviant** values.
2) **Liberal**	Liberals identify factors like **unemployment**, **poverty**, **poor housing** and **limited opportunities** as the main causes of riots. When added to **discrimination** (e.g. black youths discriminated against by the police using "stop and search" in Brixton), riots are likely to take place.
3) **Radical**	Radicals like Marxists suggest riots are **conscious legitimate political acts** by groups with **no other way** of expressing their grievances. Marxists see rioting as a reaction by the working class to the injustices and exploitation of the capitalist system. The involvement of black working class people in riots has been seen by Marxists as an expression of **anger** at the way white society has **discriminated** against black people.
4) **Feminist**	**Feminists** have suggested that rioting by **young working class males** is an attempt to **assert masculinity** at a time when **traditional male roles** and male jobs are in **decline**.

Remember also that in large **demonstrations** that have developed into riots, **anti-capitalist NSMs** have played a part in organising and coordinating activity on the internet, e.g. in Genoa at the 2001 G8 Summit.

Political Action and Protest

Riots in Oldham and Bradford have been linked to Ethnic Tension

1) A series of riots occurred in the Northern, mostly working class towns and cities of **Oldham**, **Leeds** and **Bradford** in **2001**. The riots all involved serious clashes between **young Asians** and the police.

2) These riots differed from the inner city riots of the 1980s because they took place in a context of a rapid increase in political activity of **far-right organisations** like the **British National Party** (BNP) and the **National Front** (NF). Both the BNP and NF have concentrated in recent years on Northern towns, especially **Oldham**, to recruit members and mobilise public opinion.

3) The **BNP** is a political party which wants to **end immigration**, and has suggested offering immigrants money to leave the UK. Some people believe the BNP are **racist**, although the BNP **deny** this.

4) Also, **socio-economic deprivation** among both white and Asian groups, housing segregation (the council estates were mainly white), and resulting **educational segregation** have all been put forward as explanations of the riots.

5) The government blamed the riots on the activities of **"thugs"**. Community leaders offered a similar response — blaming the **decline** of **"traditional Muslim values"**. **Kundnani (2001)** argued such responses ignored the deeper social causes of the riots.

Strikes are a form of Direct Action taken by Trade Unions

1) Strikes are where workers deliberately **withdraw their labour**, under the direction of trade union leaders.

2) Strikes are **direct action** by **workers** against their **employer**. Large scale strikes can also be used to influence governments.

3) There were **frequent strikes** in the **1970s**. Trade union law was changed by the Conservative government in the 1980s to make it more difficult for workers to go out on strike, and since then strikes have become much rarer.

Strikes are heavily class-based. The working class (i.e. the workers) are protesting against either their boss, or the state.

A trade union is a pressure group, rather than a New Social Movement. Still, strikes count as a form of direct action.

Direct Action involves issues of Class, Gender, Ethnicity, Disability, etc.

Direct action has been taken by many different groups for many different reasons.

1) Women have participated in "**Reclaim the Night**" rallies against male sexual violence.

2) Disabled people have chained themselves to Downing Street railings in protest against government social policy.

3) Muslim groups have organised **demonstrations** against the Iraq war. **Moderate** groups also engaged with the political process by **voting** for MPs who opposed the war. **Radical** groups **rejected** the traditional political process.

4) **Peaceful direct action** such as **sit-ins** and **marches** characterised civil rights protests in 1960s America. Racist groups sometimes responded with violence. The **civil rights** movement started with **civil disobedience** and a **boycott**.

In **1955**, a **black** woman, Rosa Parks, from Montgomery, Alabama, **refused to give up her seat** on the bus to a **white** person. At that time, black passengers were supposed to sit at the back of the bus and give up their seats to white passengers if the bus was full. She was **arrested**. Local church minister Dr Martin Luther King called for a **boycott** of the bus company by all black people in Montgomery, which lasted until the **bus segregation laws** were **removed**.

Practice Questions

Q1 Give five examples of types of direct action.
Q2 Give two reasons why NSMs use direct action.
Q3 Give four types of explanation for why riots break out.

Exam Question

Q1 Outline and assess the view that riots are caused by economic and social deprivation. (50 marks)

Political action — what a riot...

New Social Movements have all kinds of ways of making their feelings heard. Occasionally they resort to violence (rioting, terrorism, firebombing etc.) but mostly they stick to peaceful methods like demostrations, marches, boycotts or plain old striking. The French are dead keen on all that malarkey. Even their sixth-formers sometimes go on strike. Not at exam time though, alas.

Protest and Identity

*Protest and direct action can be part of the process which constructs a person's identity. This is for **AQA** and **OCR**.*

An individual may create their own *Identity* through *Protest* and *Political Action*

1) Identity is the sense a person has of who they are. A person's identity can have many sources, including their class, gender, sexuality or ethnicity.

2) **Personal identity** is how a person sees themselves, and **social identity** is how an individual is perceived by others. **Personal** identity and **social** identity are not always the **same**.

3) Identities can be influenced by **politics and protest**. Belonging to a political movement based on class is likely to heighten the part of your identity that's based on class. The same goes for **gender**, or **sexuality**, or **ethnicity**.

There are several different kinds of feminism within the broader feminist movement. **Liberal feminism** aims for equality of opportunity for women, and works towards **changing the law** to make things **equal** for men and women. **Radical feminism** stresses women's **identity** as women. They blame **men**, rather than **socialisation**, for women's disadvantaged position.

Ken Plummer (1995) has written about new social movements based on **sexuality**, e.g. the lesbian and gay rights movement. He's also written about **queer theory**, which says that gender and sexual identities are very **fluid**, and can keep **changing**. Queer theory disapproves of the division of the world into **strict categories** of gay and straight. **Stephen Whittle (2000)** has written about **transgender** identities, and transgender rights.

There are NSMs based on **ethnicity**. The **Black Power** movement in 1960s America aimed to find a distinctive identity as black Americans and emphasised the common experience of oppression. The **civil rights** movement aimed to get black people equal opportunities in society.

Identity Politics is politics that comes from a Shared Experience of Injustice

1) Identity politics is based on **differences** between people. Identity politics is the politics of movements which represent the interests and identity of a particular **oppressed group** within a society, rather than society as a whole. Members of the group unite around a **shared identity**. Feminism, Disability Rights, Black Power, and Gay Pride are all varieties of identity politics.

2) Individuals who feel they are **oppressed** or **discriminated** against may create a positive sense of **personal identity** through **protest** and **political activity**. This sense of **positive personal identity** helps to counteract the **negative social identity** that they feel society has given them. In other words, **society** may see an individual as **inferior**, but **protest** and **politics** can give them the sense of being **just as good** as anyone else.

3) For example, LGBT (lesbian, gay, bisexual and transgender) people who feel oppressed by **homophobia** may gain a positive sense of identity by joining a **Gay Pride** group. **Black Power** creates a positive personal identity for black people who have felt oppressed by **racism**.

Some critics **question** the idea of shared experience. Not all women are the **same**, for example — a black woman may have a very different experience of society to a white woman, and a working class woman may have a different experience to a middle class woman. Commenting on **Betty Friedan's (1963)** statement that women should get out of the house and into the workplace, African-American feminist **bell hooks (1981)** pointed out that the **experience** of being a **stay-at-home housewife and mother** was pretty much limited to **white middle class women**. African-American working class women had been doing paid jobs for years.

It can be argued that identity politics **excludes** people who aren't part of the group, e.g. a lesbian activist group would exclude men. Identity politics can also **marginalise** groups — i.e. keep them **away** from **mainstream politics**.

Identity Politics can be linked to patterns of Consumption

1) **Consumption** is spending on goods and services. Some sociologists argue that in the **postmodern era** there's a **link** between **consumption** and **identity**.

2) Identity politics can involve the rejection of **global brands** in favour of products chosen on **moral grounds**, e.g. out of environmental, human rights or animal rights concerns. Examples of such strategies include **boycotts** of environmentally unfriendly products and of products produced in countries with poor human rights records.

There's more on globalisation on p. 66-67.

3) An example of such consumption focused protest is the network of **anti-NIKE websites** which campaign against the employment practices of NIKE in South East Asia. These websites are used to **promote boycotts** of NIKE products and **demonstrations** at NIKE offices.

Protest and Identity

Postmodernists say *Identity Politics* is more important than *Party Politics*

1) Postmodernists like **Lyotard (1984)** argue that people have lost faith in "metanarratives" (see p.61) and party politics.

2) Postmodernists such as **Nancy Fraser (1989)** say that political life has become de-centred — this means people's political goals reflect their personal and social identity, instead of an ideology that applies to all of society.

3) This process has been amplified by **globalisation** and **world travel**. People can consider themselves part of a global social group of say, women, or deaf people, or gay men, or Muslims.

1) **Stuart Hall (1992)** claims that identity is **fragmented**. According to Hall, people no longer have a **single identity** linked to a class or ideology. Instead they possess a **number** of sometimes **contradictory** identities, which he calls "**fragmented identity**".

2) Hall suggests that the increase in number of **New Social Movements** concerned with a huge number of **identities** and **issues** (e.g. feminism, ethnic minority issues, national liberation, environmental concerns, sexuality) have helped to **fragment** people's identity. An individual could be a **Green**, **Welsh Nationalist**, **lesbian feminist** and sometimes identify as **Welsh Nationalist**, other times as **Green**, etc.

Class-based *"Old Politics"* may *Not* be *Quite Dead Yet*

1) Despite massive interest in the growth of **New Social Movements** (**NSMs**), **protest**, and **identity politics** in the last 30 years, it would be **inaccurate** to suggest that the **old politics** represented by the political parties and pressure groups is **dead and buried**.

2) It's true that some rather high profile NSMs have been able to exert significant pressure on governments, e.g. **environmentalism**, but many NSMs have had limited success.

So, not the last resting place of party politics after all...

3) It would also be easy to exaggerate the importance and growth of NSMs. Whilst **most** people **know about NSMs**, very **few** are active **participants** in them. NSMs have recruited well amongst the educated young middle class but they haven't shown much evidence of a more broad-based appeal.

4) People may grumble about party politics, but most people still go out and vote.

Some social movements try to get particular social groups to participate in mainstream politics.

1) The **women's suffrage** movement campaigned to get women the vote in the early 20th century.

2) The **civil rights** movement in America fought for black people's rights, and actively encouraged African-American people to register to vote.

These groups aren't about identity — they're about equality.

3) There are campaigns to increase the number of **women in Parliament**. **Emily's List** was launched in 1993 to raise money to help **women in the Labour Party** stand as MPs. The Labour Party has enforced **all-women shortlists** of candidates for some constituencies to make sure their candidate will be a woman. Some feminists find this **patronising**.

Practice Questions

Q1 What's the difference between personal and social identity?
Q2 Describe three ways people may create their identity through protest and political activity.
Q3 What is identity politics?
Q4 Explain the link between consumption and identity politics.

Exam Question

Q1 Outline and assess the view that falling voter turnout in elections is evidence of the decline of class-based politics and the growth of new social movements.

(50 marks)

She's the only Green Welsh Nationalist Lesbian Feminist in the village...

This identity stuff's a bit complicated. I guess you could sum it up by saying that some people define themselves by what they're protesting about, and the group they protest with. Some criticise identity politics and say it creates inward-looking groups who exclude outsiders. Supporters of identity politics say it gives people a sense of power. I say just learn it.

Globalisation

*It's a whole new world — everything's globalised these days, with companies trading across borders, all sorts of media available worldwide thanks to the web, and all sorts of products, made in all sorts of places, available everywhere. In the spirit of globalisation, these pages are for everyone — **OCR** and **AQA** — heck, even for people not studying sociology.*

Globalisation is the trend of **National Boundaries** becoming **Less Important**

1) Globalisation has been seen to **weaken** the power of nation states to **control** their own **economies**.

2) Because of improvements in communications, consumers are able to purchase goods from all over the world. This has changed a system of national economies into a **global economy**.

3) **Transnational corporations** such as NIKE, McDonald's and Coca-Cola® have tremendous power.

4) Global corporations, with their brands, logos and associations with **lifestyles**, are shaping a global culture.

5) The effects of **global economic activity** such as **pollution** don't respect national boundaries.

6) A highly mobile global population means that **diseases** such as **HIV** are global problems.

7) **Politics** and **political action** have become more globalised, e.g. the anti-capitalist movement.

Economic Globalisation has seen the rise of **Transnational Corporations (TNCs)**

1) **TNCs** are big companies which operate in a **large number** of **countries** and are therefore **beyond** the **direct control** of individual nation states.

2) TNCs like NIKE, Nestlé®, Ford and GM are able to **move production** and **investment** around the world to wherever economic conditions are most favourable. For instance, in the last 30 years much **car production** has been **moved** from **Western Europe**, where **labour costs** are high and **trade unions** strong, to **South East Asia**, where labour costs are relatively low and trade unions aren't so well established.

3) Nation states individually don't have the power to **control** the **activities** of TNCs, and so have lost a significant amount of power over their own **economies**. **Ohmae (1996)** argues that some TNCs are now **more powerful** than many **governments**.

Political Globalisation has **Reduced** the **Power** of the **Individual Nation State**

1) Nation states are increasingly coming together to become members of **transnational organisations** which have a political element to them. For example, the **European Union** (EU), the **United Nations** (UN) and the **North Atlantic Treaty Organisation** (NATO).

2) Membership of such organisations, though beneficial to nation states in many ways, can also result in a partial **transference** of **sovereignty** from the nation state to the organisation. For example, in Britain EU law now has **precedence** over UK law.

Sovereignty is a state's ability to control what goes on within its own borders.

Cultural Globalisation has reduced the state's control over **Culture** and the **Media**

1) The explosion in **internet** and **communications technology** and cable and satellite broadcasting has resulted in consumers worldwide being immersed in **Western values**, culture and lifestyle through advertising and broadcasting.

2) The internet and the large number of TV channels now available globally make it far more **difficult** for nation states to **control access** to **information** or manipulate the media within their own boundaries.

Some sociologists argue that the **Decline** of the **State** has been **Exaggerated**

1) **Hirst and Thompson (1996)** acknowledge that there's been some decline in the power of the nation state due to globalisation, but they argue that it's been overstated. They point out the considerable power nation states continue to have over **foreign policy**, the **military**, the **national territory**, and their citizens' sense of **'national identity'**.

2) They also claim the spread of **economic globalisation** has been **exaggerated**. They point out that many companies labelled as TNCs still operate largely within their **'home regions'** rather than genuinely globally.

Despite globalisation, Millie had managed to work herself up into a right state.

Globalisation

David Held argues that Globalisation has Serious Implications for Democracy

1) **Held (1995)** supports the idea that the power of nation states has **declined** significantly. He points out that this has issues for democracy, with voters voting for governments who **do not** hold the **real power** over economic policy that they used to.

2) Held calls for a new **global approach** to democracy and the setting up of a **world parliament** which could hold powerful TNCs to account and **restore democratic control** over important decisions. Such a world parliament he argues would be able to tackle the **global problems** facing the world — global warming, disease, and food supply and distribution.

The Global Anti-Capitalism movement developed at the end of the 1990s

The two most quoted examples of anti-capitalist political action are the **World Trade Organisation demonstrations** in **Seattle** in **1999** and the **G8 Summit demonstrations** in **2001**. At both there was serious disorder and some rioting. **Reasons** for the development of a **global anti-capitalist movement** include:

1) **International organisations** seem to be running the world — e.g. the G8, the EU, the UN.

2) Improvements in **communications** (especially the **internet**) have allowed activists to **organise** and **network** effectively.

3) The **financial crisis** in East Asia in 1998 rocked many people's faith in the **sustainability** of global capitalism.

4) The politics of liberal democracies tend not to offer **alternatives** to capitalism.

1) Marxist **Callinicos (2003)** suggests that the apparently **diverse** interests of global social movements are linked by the **common source** of their **concerns** — what else but global capitalism (he is a Marxist after all).

2) For instance, he says it's **global capitalism** that causes pollution and therefore creates **environmental protestors**, and it's **global capitalism** which keeps LEDCs (Less Economically Developed Countries) in poverty and therefore creates protesters against **Third World Debt**.

3) It's worth remembering that global social movements cover a **huge political spectrum**. Callinicos may well be **exaggerating** their **revolutionary potential** as an anti-capitalist force.

The Global Anti-Capitalism Movement has attacked Global Branding

1) **Naomi Klein (2001)** argues that young people involved in global social movements are fed up with the global branding of **youth** and **youth culture**.

2) In *No Logo*, Klein argues that people involved in global social movements believe that political parties and "old politics" are powerless to challenge the **dominance** of **global corporations**.

3) **Global branding** gives protesters a **target** for their protests, e.g. producing a spoof advertisement or logo with an anti-capitalist message. This is called **culture jamming**.

4) The **McLibel case** shows the effects of culture jamming. Protesters produced anti-McDonald's leaflets and McDonald's sued for libel. The court case gave the protesters massive **publicity**. The judge agreed with some of their claims.

Practice Questions

Q1 List seven features of globalisation.
Q2 What are TNCs and how have they grown in power?
Q3 Give an example of how political globalisation may reduce the power of nation states.
Q4 What is cultural globalisation?
Q5 Give some evidence to suggest that the nation state is still powerful.
Q6 Explain the ways in which globalisation may be seen as harmful to democracy.

Exam Question

Q1 Assess the view that political activity is becoming globalised. (18 marks)

What do global anti-capitalists like in their sandwiches? Culture jam...

Whether you're a fan of capitalism (yay, go capitalism!) or an anti-capitalist (boo, bad capitalism!) you can't avoid the fact that politics and business are becoming more 'global'. Even issues we can all (just about) agree on, like the need to combat disease and climate change, require a global response. Make sure you know how globalisation is changing the world, and what everyone thinks.

Ideology and Political Action

*These pages are about the different ideologies that motivate political groups. They're for **OCR**, and useful background for **AQA**.*

Conservatism has Three basic Underlying Principles

1) Conservatism emphasises the importance of the **family**, the **nation** and **patriotism** as contributors to **social order** and **harmony**.

2) Conservatism sees people as capable of good and bad — it's suspicious of any ideology which assumes people are either very **rational** or very **moral**. Conservatives therefore believe there is a strong need for a **state** and a **legal system** to **control** people and **protect** them from each other.

3) Conservatives believe that **inequalities** between people **occur naturally** and **resist** any attempts to **impose** equality on people.

Ideology is hard to define but often it's used to mean a set of ideas and beliefs about the way things should be. See p. 2-3 for more.

There are Two Main Strands of Modern Conservatism

One Nation Conservatism (or Paternalistic Conservatism) thinks the government should intervene to help the weak

1) **One Nation Conservatism** was invented in the **19th century** by Conservative Prime Minister **Benjamin Disraeli**.

2) Disraeli's ideas were a response to the **problems** and **inequalities** introduced by the industrial revolution. He described Britain as **"Two Nations"**, the rich and the poor, which could become **one nation** again if the wealthy would fulfil their **duty** of **looking after** the poor with social reforms.

3) This strand of Conservatism sees a need for some **state intervention** in the economy, to make sure the rich do their bit to care for the poor.

One Nation Conservatism doesn't call for <u>equality</u>. It calls for the privileged to <u>look after</u> the underprivileged in one <u>big happy hierarchical family</u>.

Liberal Conservatism (aka Libertarian Conservatism and the New Right) takes ideas from classical liberalism

1) Classical Liberalism believes in:
   - the **free market** and **free enterprise**
   - **minimal state intervention** in the economy
   - the idea that **individuals** should take **responsibility** for themselves

2) Liberal Conservatism has borrowed all of these ideas.

3) Where liberal conservatives differ from liberals is in their belief in **traditional values** and the need for a **strong state** to regulate behaviour and maintain **social order** and **moral standards**.

4) **Neoconservatism** can be seen as a joining of **liberal economics** to moral and social **authoritarianism** and has had a significant impact on modern British conservatism and on the American presidents Reagan and George W Bush.

This type of Conservatism is most readily associated with Margaret Thatcher. It's also referred to as "New Right Conservatism".

Liberalism was at its Highpoint immediately after the end of the Cold War

1) At the end of the 20th century **liberal values** of individual freedom, freedom of thought and conscience, tolerance, rule-based governance and freedom of choice appeared to be **triumphant** almost **all over** the world. **Western-style democracy** was argued to be the best possible political system achievable.

2) But recently liberal democracy has come under **increased criticism** both from Marxist/anarchist inspired **global anti-capitalist movements** and from the emergence of **religious fundamentalism**.

Audrey kept her herd in the valleys below the highpoint of Western liberalism.

Revolutionary Marxism calls for the Violent Overthrow of Capitalism

1) This is the socialism of Marx and Engels which sees society in terms of a **class conflict** between the **bourgeoisie** (owners) and the **proletariat** (workers).

2) Marx and Engels argued that working class oppression would become so **bad** that eventually the workers would become **conscious socialists** and organise a **revolution** to establish a classless society.

Ideology and Political Action

Marxism influences a number of New Social Movements

1) There have been a number of small **revolutionary Marxist** political parties in the West for many years. However, more important perhaps is the **influence** Marxist thinking has come to have on the **global anti-capitalist movement**.

2) **Alex Callinicos (2003)** has suggested that NSMs will become more and more aware that the world's global problems — poverty, famine, disease and the environment — have their common origin in **international capitalism**. Callinicos says that **global social movements** have real potential as a **revolutionary political force**.

> **Anarchism** — which sees the **state** rather than capitalism as the source of repression and exploitation — has also had a big impact on the political activities of NSMs. **Noam Chomsky**, whose political writings are highly influential with global anti-capitalists, works within a recognisably **anarchist tradition**.

The influence of Feminism declined after its peak in the 1960s and 1970s

Heywood (2003) puts the decline in influence of the Women's Movement down to three main factors:

1) The **divisions** between radical, liberal and socialist feminism have weakened the movement.

2) The **anti-feminist backlash** seen in many parts of the world with the rise of **religious fundamentalism** (see below) has promoted a return to **strict patriarchal control** of women.

3) An anti-feminist backlash in Western liberal democratic politics from the 1980s onwards has seen many mainstream political parties focusing on **'family values'** and **traditional** forms of **family life**.

The decline in influence of the Woman's Movement on political action in the UK can also be seen as a sign of its success, as a great many of its **original aims** have been **achieved**. For example, political equality (**the vote**), anti-discrimination legislation, abortion rights, birth control, and equal access to education.

Fundamentalists see certain Religious Ideas as Essential and Unchallengeable

1) The late 20th and early 21st centuries have seen a rise in a new and powerful **religious fundamentalism**.

2) Fundamentalism aims to **turn the clock back** to a mythical time when people lived by the particular **sacred text** and rules they favour. The modern world is seen as **decadent** and **immoral** with its **permissiveness**, homosexuality, available abortion, pornography, etc. Fundamentalism in most of its forms tends to be **deeply conservative**, morally and socially.

3) **Andrew Heywood (2007)** points out that fundamentalists tend to take **political action** which is **militant** and often **violent** in nature, including some shocking acts of **terrorism**. He includes the examples of the **terror attacks** by **Al Qaeda** on 11th September 2001, the **bombings** of **abortion clinics** by American **fundamentalist Christians** which have continued through recent decades, and the **assassination** of the Indian PM **Indira Gandhi** by **Sikh militants** in 1984.

Practice Questions

Q1 Outline two types of modern conservatism.
Q2 Explain what is meant by anarchism.
Q3 Suggest three reasons why the influence of feminism on political action has declined.
Q4 What is fundamentalism?

Exam Question

Q1 Outline and assess the relationship between ideology and protest movements. (50 marks)

Ideology — everyone should have to carry their passport or driver's licence...

This is all about the stuff people believe. And while it would be nice to think that it was merely a private matter, some people end up in positions of power and influence — and when that happens, their ideology becomes kind of important. Make sure you know what everyone thinks and the sort of causes they stand for. Who knows, maybe one day you'll wake up a Marxist feminist.

Defining Crime and Deviance

*This section is for **AQA** and **OCR**. OCR people just have to learn what's in this section. If you're doing AQA, you'll be looking at crime alongside sociological research methods — see Section 8 for all you ever wanted to know about research.*

Here are some **Definitions** of **Crime** and **Deviance**

> Crime = behaviour which breaks laws and is punished by the legal system.

> Deviance = behaviour which goes against the norms, values and expectations of a social group or society.

Crime is mostly deviant, but **not all deviance** is **criminal**. Think about it — it's hard to think of a criminal act which isn't also viewed as deviant but it's easy to make a long list of **non-criminal deviant behaviour** — picking your nose in public and eating it, cross-dressing, barking like a dog during a job interview, swearing at the referee, cheating at poker, etc.

Downes and Rock (**1988** *Understanding Deviance* Oxford: OUP) gave this definition of **deviance**: "Deviance may be considered as **banned** or **controlled** behaviour which is likely to attract **punishment** or **disapproval**."

Crime and *Deviance* are *Socially Constructed*

1)   Both crime and deviance are **culturally determined**. What is considered criminal varies less than what's considered deviant.

2)   **Michel Foucault** wrote about how definitions of **criminal** deviance, **sexual** deviance and **madness** have changed throughout history, e.g. 100 years ago in the UK it was deviant for women to wear trousers, but today it's acceptable. **Deviance changes** with **time** and **place** as values, norms and social expectations change — it's **relative**.

3)   Also, what's **deviant** for some groups in society is **conformity** for others. **Subcultures** have **different norms** to mainstream society.

Plummer (1979) said that the same act can be seen as **deviant** or **non-deviant** depending on the situation:

Societal deviance means acts which are seen by most of society as deviant, in most situations

- **Swearing** at an **authority figure** (it doesn't count if you're watching them on TV!) — even people who do it know it's deviant.
- Random acts of **extreme violence**. ⟵ *Even in manga cartoons, this is the mark of a true nutcase.*
- **Child abuse** — considered universally wrong by society.

Situational deviance means acts which can be defined as deviant or normal, depending on the circumstances

- Being **naked** — OK in your **own home**, deviant on the **high street**. *Social rules can be temporarily rejected.*
- Wearing **fishnet and PVC** from head to toe — OK in a **goth or fetish club**, deviant at **work** in an accountant's office.
- **Killing** someone — OK if you're a **soldier at war** killing enemy soldiers, otherwise deviant.

Social Order and *Social Control* create a *Consensus* of *how to behave*

1)   By definition, **most behaviour** in society isn't **criminal** or **deviant**. **Social order** and **social control** maintain the **status quo** and create a **value consensus** of how to behave. People are **socialised** to follow social norms.

2)   Some norms become **second nature**. For example, when having a **face-to-face conversation**, most people manage to stand the right distance apart, look at each other when they're talking without staring excessively, be polite and tactful, not talk for too long — all **without really thinking** about it.

3)   Other norms are followed because we're **consciously aware** that they're a norm — e.g. stopping at a red traffic light.

4)   **Sanctions** are **rewards** and **punishments** that **reinforce** social norms:

	Positive sanctions — these **reward** people for **conforming** to a norm.	Negative sanctions — these **punish** people for **deviating** from a norm.
Formal sanctions — carried out by an **official agency**.	• A **certificate** for passing an A-level exam. • A **medal** for bravery in the armed forces. • A **cup** for winning a sporting final.	• A **fine** for breaking the law. • **Points** on a driving licence. • A **yellow card** from the referee.
Informal sanctions — carried out by the **public**.	• A **pat on the back**. • Saying **"well done"** for good behaviour.	• Deliberately **ignoring** someone. • A **telling-off** for bad behaviour.

Defining Crime and Deviance

Sociologists are interested in Social Causes of Crime and Deviance

Sociologists are interested in **crime** and **deviance** as a **social phenomenon** — it's part of understanding society.

The key questions about crime are:

Studying deviance is less clear-cut, because there's **deviance** and **social control** in all areas of sociological study.

- • Does crime have a **purpose**?
- • What are the **causes** of crime?
- • **Who** commits crime?
- • What is the **extent** of crime?

This is all discussed on the next few pages.

There are Non-Sociological Theories of why Crime exists

Sociologists are not the only ones interested in understanding crime and deviance in society. The first theories regarding why crime and deviance exist in society were developed in the **19th century** and were based on the **physiological** or **psychological** characteristics of the individual deviant.

Physiological theories say that criminals are physically different

1) 19th century Italian doctor **Cesare Lombroso (1876)** became famous for his theory that criminals were **genetically different**. He stated there were **outward signs** of the criminal personality such as a large jaw or extra fingers or toes.

2) Don't dismiss physiological theories as staying in the 19th century, though. They've moved with the times. **Moir and Jessel** (1995 *A Mind to Crime* London: Michael Joseph) argue **hormonal** and **chemical imbalances** make individuals more likely to be criminal. They say these imbalances affect **men** more than women, explaining why statistics show most crime is committed by men: "The male mind — whether for reasons of evolution or something else — is wired and fuelled to be more criminal."

Psychological theories say that criminals are mentally different

1) Others argue criminals are **psychologically** different from the rest of the population. Again, these theories started in the 19th century but travelled through the 20th century.

2) **Bowlby (1946)** argued that individuals who are **deprived of maternal love** in the first years of life are likely to **develop personality traits** which lead them to commit **crime**.

3) **Eysenck (1964)** concluded from his psychological research that individuals who commit crime have **inherited psychological characteristics** which **predispose** them to crime.

The **21st century** versions of physiological and psychological theories argue there are **genes** which make some people more likely to commit crimes — some individuals **inherit** these genes and others don't. Some theories say that people with **hormonal**, **chemical**, **psychological** or **brain abnormalities** (often caused by experiences when they were young) are more likely to commit crimes.

> For the **non-sociological theories** the cause of crime lies within the **individual**.
> For **sociology** the cause of crime lies in **society**.

Practice Questions

Q1 Give an example of a behaviour which is deviant but not criminal.

Q2 What is situational deviance?

Q3 Give an example of a formal negative sanction and an example of an informal positive sanction.

Q4 Give an example of a psychological theory of crime.

Q5 Give one difference between physiological and psychological theories of crime.

Exam Question

Q1 Outline and assess the view that "the cause of crime lies within the individual." (50 marks)

Naughty, naughty, very naughty...

There's something about the word 'deviance' that conjures up images of men in PVC suits cavorting in vats of custard. Or is that just me... Anyway, point being that deviance isn't limited to weird sexual deviance. It actually covers all behaviour that doesn't conform to social norms. Conformity is rewarded and deviance is punished. Remember, some deviance depends on the situation.

Theories of Crime and Deviance

All sociological theories regarding crime and deviance are trying to say why crime exists. Structural theories of crime all argue the cause of crime lies in the structure of society, but they disagree on a lot more than they have in common. **For AQA and OCR.**

Functionalists argue crime and deviance are **Useful** *and* **Necessary** *in society*

You might well wonder how on earth crime can be useful. Functionalists say it's because it has a **function** in society:

1) Crime and deviance reinforce the **consensus** of values, norms and behaviour of the majority non-deviant population — people can join together in outrage.

2) **Durkheim (1897)** said deviancy allows for **social change** to occur. Durkheim and the **functionalists** who came after him argue that all societies need some change to remain healthy and stable. If society reacts positively to deviant behaviour it starts the process for that behaviour to be seen as non-deviant in the future.

3) **Durkheim** said crime moves from **functional** to **dysfunctional** when the level of crime is either **too high** or **too low**.
   - Too high, and it threatens social order.   • Too low, and there's no social change.

Albert Cohen (1966) identified two ways that deviance maintained **Social Order**

1) He argued forms of deviance such as **prostitution** provide a **safety valve** for releasing tension without threatening social stability.

2) Secondly, he argued deviant behaviour is used as a **warning device** by society to **identify** emerging **social problems**, which can then be dealt with, e.g. civil disobedience, protests and truancy.

Merton said **Crime** *is a* **Response** *to* **Failing** *to* **Achieve** *society's cultural goals*

1) Functionalist **Robert Merton (1968)** concluded from his American study that the vast majority of individuals share the same goals but don't have equal access to the means of achieving these goals.

2) He identified the main cultural goal in American society as **success** and **wealth**. He said that the main (institutionalised) means of achieving that goal was through the education system. When individuals fail or are excluded from this system, this creates **anomie**. ← *anomie = a lack of values, and feeling of normlessness.*

3) Merton argues that individuals who fail at the standard route to success **innovate** to find **alternative** and **deviant** means of reaching success and wealth — e.g. **crime**.

4) Merton says they may also **retreat** from society — e.g. by **dropping out**, **drinking** to excess or taking **drugs**.

5) They may also **rebel** against society, and engage in **protest** and revolution to try and change society.

Subcultural theories say **Cultural Values** *of some groups* **Encourage Deviance**

Some deviance is **conformity** to norms and values — just **different** norms and values to **mainstream society**.

> **Cohen said delinquent gangs provide prestige for adolescents frustrated at their lack of status in society**

Albert Cohen (1955) said that working class boys suffered from a lack of opportunities to succeed in mainstream society, largely due to cultural deprivation. This leads to dissatisfaction with their position in society — which Cohen called **status frustration**.

This tension is **released** by joining or creating groups which have **alternative values** to achieve status. These values tend to be the **reverse** of those of mainstream society — behaviour deviant in society becomes **normal** and **valued** in the subcultural group. For example, **petty crime** or **drug-taking** might be valued by the group.

1) **Cloward and Ohlin (1960) combined** the ideas of **Merton** with the ideas of **Cohen**. They believed there was a **legitimate opportunity structure** (passing exams and getting a job, as Merton said), and an **illegitimate opportunity structure** (being in a gang and committing crime, e.g. theft and vandalism).

2) They also argued that access to the **illegitimate** opportunity structure is **no more equal** than access to the **legitimate** system. In some areas, there are criminal gangs which provide adolescents with a deviant route to success and status, and in some areas there aren't. This explained why **not all** frustrated working class boys turned to **crime**.

3) Cloward and Ohlin said where there's **no access** to criminal gangs, frustrated adolescents form their own **violent gangs**.

4) They also said that adolescents who have **failed** in **both** the legitimate opportunity structure and the illegitimate opportunity structure **retreat** from society and turn to drink or drugs.

The subcultural theories have been criticised for **assuming** that the majority of people aspire to the **mainstream goals** of success and wealth. **Taylor, Walton and Young (1973)** point to deviant groups such as **hippies** who **don't share these goals**.

Theories of Crime and Deviance

Miller thought crime and delinquency come from Working Class Cultural Values

W B Miller (1962) said that general **lower working class culture**, not subcultural gangs, was what encouraged lawbreaking behaviour. According to Miller, values passed from generation to generation encourage **working class men** to break the law. Delinquents are simply conforming to the **focal concerns** of their culture. 'Focal concerns' are the main things that are valued in that culture, e.g. exciting thrills and macho toughness.

Miller was **criticised** right from the beginning. **Bordua (1962)** said that the idea that the working class live their lives **isolated** from the rest of society is **flawed to begin with**.

Miller's ideas have been supported by recent **New Right** sociologists. **Charles Murray (1990, 1993)** believes that there's an underclass in both British and American society with a **distinct culture** and **value system** which **encourages** deviant behaviour.

Marxists see Crime as an Inevitable Consequence of Capitalism

1) Traditional Marxist criminology says that the **rich** and **powerful** decide what is considered deviant and criminal in society to **suit their own interests**. No surprise for Marxists that the most common group convicted of crime is the working class — Marxists say the system is rigged against them.

2) Crime such as robbery and property theft is seen by traditional Marxists like **Bonger (1916)** as an inevitable response to the **extremes** of **wealth** and **poverty** in capitalist society. They see the individual as "**forced**" into crime by the structure of society.

While not out on the beat, Nigel dreamed of the overthrow of the bourgeoisie.

Because Marxists see the 'system' as the cause of crime, much Marxist sociology has looked at the systems of **power**, **control** and **punishment**, i.e. the **police**, the **law** and the **courts**. This is covered on p.85.

Feminist Theories of crime

1) **Heidensohn (1989)** has argued that '**malestream**' sociology — i.e. mainstream sociology, dominated by men — is **gender blind**. She says most studies of crime have been researched by men who have focused on male crime and **ignored the role of women**, either as victims or as criminals.

2) Official statistics suggest women commit **fewer crimes** than men, and commit **different types of crime**. There are a number of different theories trying to explain these differences:

- **Sex-role theory** suggests that women are brought up to be passive and conformist so are less likely to commit crimes.
- **Heidensohn (2002)** argues that in a patriarchal, male-dominated society, women have less 'opportunity' to commit some types of crime. You can't commit, e.g., financial fraud unless you're in control of large sums of money, and more men are found in powerful positions in the workplace. The crimes women do commit tend to relate to their role in the home as a wife or mother, e.g. shoplifting.
- **Westwood (1999)** suggests female identities are changing and women are adopting more typically male behaviour patterns. This could be linked to an increase in female crime.
- **Carol Smart (1995)** has suggested that female crime has to be looked at as part of women's broader experience in society. For example, women are often invisible victims of domestic violence.

Practice Questions

Q1 Why did Merton think people committed crime?
Q2 What is meant by 'status frustration'?
Q3 What did Miller say was the cause of crime?
Q4 What did Heidensohn mean by 'gender blind'?

Exam Question

Q1 "The cause of crime lies in the structure of society, not the nature of the individual." Consider this statement, referring to Marxist and feminist perspectives. (33 marks)

Society made me do it...

Unlikely to stand up in a court of law, that one. I wouldn't recommend defending yourself by quoting Merton and Cohen. It didn't work for me after all that unpleasantness with the goat smuggling. Anyway, I'm not going into all that now. The past is the past. And I was actually doing society a favour — I was acting as a warning device that goats are not fairly distributed in the UK.

Theories of Crime and Deviance

*Social action theorists (interpretivists) say deviance is actually defined by social reaction. Great. **These pages are for AQA and OCR** — but OCR people don't have to learn the stuff about Control Theory and Postmodernists on p.75.*

Interpretivists *say that* Deviant *folk are not that* Different *from everyone else*

Interpretivist (also known as interactionist) study of crime and deviance starts from the standpoint that deviants are **not characteristically different** from the rest of the population. They are deviant because their chosen behaviour is **labelled deviant** by others in society.

Interpretivists are also called social action theorists.

Interpretivists therefore think that there aren't any **universal causes** of deviance or crime to be 'discovered' by sociologists.

Interpretivists stress the view that deviance is **relative** — it varies over time and place because it is defined by each society and by each situation within a society.

Becker (1963) argues deviance is behaviour which has been labelled deviant by the reaction of others

1) This may sound like common sense, but interpretivists like Becker were the first sociologists to **challenge the assumption** that sociologists should focus on what **causes** people to act in deviant and criminal ways.

2) Instead, interpretivists studied how an act or behaviour comes to be **labelled as deviant** by the rest of society, and the consequences of that label or reaction.

3) The **same behaviour** gets **different reactions** depending on the social situation. Becker thought there's therefore nothing intrinsically deviant about the act itself. For example, **nudity** is normal and acceptable in the privacy of your own home but seen as deviant (and criminal) in a public space.

4) The **reaction** of those around you is what makes you **recognise** your behaviour as deviant. Becker said, "Deviance is not a quality that lies in the **behaviour** itself but in the **interaction** between the person who commits an act, and those who respond to it." (1963, *Outsiders: Studies in the Sociology of Deviance* New York: The Free Press)

Being Labelled *as* Deviant *can* Affect Future Behaviour

Interpretivists argue we form our self-identity by **interpreting** how others respond to us and **internalising** the reaction. A **label** can have a **positive** or **negative** effect on the individual and it helps to define them in their **own eyes** as well as in others' eyes. Becker calls this a "**self concept**".

Being labelled 'awesome' had deeply affected Edwin's behaviour.

1) Becker argued that a **self concept** of being deviant can **increase deviant behaviour**. If a person is **shamed** by the reaction of others who know they have been in trouble with the police, they may return to criminal activity or **join a criminal group** to escape the feeling of rejection. This reinforces the label of criminal — it becomes even harder to remove and a bigger part of their identity. Becker called this process the **deviant career**.

2) The **label** of **criminal** is **not easily removed** by society, whatever the actions of the individual — it becomes their **master status** (see glossary). On release from prison many individuals find it hard to obtain work, housing and positions of trust because of the reaction of others to their status as an **ex-offender**.

3) **Jock Young (1971)** used his study of drug users in Notting Hill to demonstrate the process of becoming deviant:

The marijuana users developed a **deviant self concept** because their drug of choice was **illegal**.	The **deviant** element became their **main identity** in society. They were 'hippies' first and foremost.	The **negative response** of those around them and the police made the drug-taking more **significant** to their lives.	Their drug-taking **increased**.

4) **Goffman (1961)** wrote about a deviant career in **mental illness**. He said the **negative label** of being **mad** is **imposed** on the patient by society and psychiatry, and the patient must eventually **conform** to it.

Lemert (1951) *distinguished between* Primary *and* Secondary *deviance*

> **Primary deviance** = the initial deviant act

> **Secondary deviance** = deviant acts committed after the individual has **accepted the label** of deviant

1) Lemert argued **most people** commit some acts of **primary deviance** in their lives but that it was of **little significance**.

2) When there's a **societal reaction** (a reaction from society as a whole or groups within society such as family, peers, police and the media) the individual is **labelled** as **deviant**.

3) Lemert argues that when the individual **feels the weight** of the label 'deviant' or 'criminal', they sometimes commit **more** of the deviant behaviour. For example, once a person is labelled an **alcoholic**, they might drink more because, well, they're an alcoholic, and alcoholics drink. Lemert called this **secondary deviance**.

Public reaction to an individual labelled deviant can be very powerful. Sometimes, individuals **commit suicide** once their deviance has been discovered — e.g. it's not uncommon for suspects in internet child pornography raids to kill themselves.

Theories of Crime and Deviance

Critics argue people are not as Passive as Interpretivists suggest

1) **Ronald Akers (1967)** criticises both Becker and Lemert for presenting individuals as **powerless** to make decisions or take control of their own identity. **Deviance**, according to **Akers**, is not something which **happens** to people but a **choice** that individuals make.

2) **Taylor, Walton and Young (1973)** argue many forms of behaviour are **widely viewed** as deviant — so deviants **know** they are breaking the law or social rules **before** any **societal reaction**, but they **still do it**.

3) Marxist critics accuse interpretivism of **ignoring the role of power** in defining crime and deviance. Certain groups have the **power** to influence what is classified as **criminal** or **socially unacceptable**.

4) **Gouldner (1973)** accused interpretivists of being **fascinated with deviance**, and even suggests they enjoy observing 'cool' deviants, and hanging out with the 'underworld'. He thinks interpretivists aren't interested in changing society.

Control Theory asks Why More People Don't commit crime

Control theory has its origins in Durkheim's belief that all societies need to have shared values. Durkheim called these values the society's '**collective conscience**'.

The sociologist **Hirschi (1969)** looked at reasons why people **don't** commit crime. He suggested that there are **four social bonds** which hold society together:

- **attachment** to society
- **commitment** to society
- **involvement** in society
- **belief** that society's rules must be obeyed

The more strongly an individual feels these bonds, the less likely that individual is to commit a crime.

Wilson and Kelling (1982) put forward the '**broken windows**' thesis. They argued that people who live in well-maintained areas with low crime rates feel like they are **part of society** and are **less likely** to commit crime. When crimes — even minor crimes like breaking windows — go uncorrected and **unpunished**, people start to feel there is no **social control** and lose their sense of belonging. This sense of detachment leads to **increasing crime rates** and a downwards spiral of decay.

Etzioni (1993) suggests that in the past poor communities **policed themselves**. In some communities, this system has broken down and a criminal underclass has taken over. The way to correct this is to create a greater sense of social integration and social responsibility, e.g. by setting up **neighbourhood watch schemes**.

Max and Christine were too hungry and Frankie was just too busy reading the small ads to commit any crime.

Postmodernists put crime down to people's Sense of Identity

1) Postmodernists argue that society is becoming increasingly **fragmented**.

2) In modern society people's **sense of identity** has more to do with what they see in the media and the brands they buy into and less to do with their family, religion or local area. People tend to think of themselves as individuals rather than part of society. Foucault called this trend the **process of individualism**.

3) As this trend continues people feel **less attached to society** and are **more likely to commit crime**.

Practice Questions

Q1 Why are interpretivists less interested in the causes of crime than other sociologists?

Q2 Explain how the reactions of others are significant in the interpretivist understanding of deviance.

Q3 What does Hirschi mean by the 'four social bonds'?

Q4 What is Etzioni's solution to the loss of social control?

Exam Questions

Q1 Assess control theories of crime. (21 marks)

Q2 Outline and assess the view that societal reaction is a major cause of deviance. (50 marks)

Sigh. If you will insist on running naked through the streets...

It's interesting how people react to deviant behaviour. Some people scream and shout, others run away, and others pretend it's not happening. Well, according to Becker and his merry bunch of interpretivists, it's the reaction that people have to deviance that makes it deviant. They even went as far as saying that reaction can make deviants more deviant. Give a dog a bad name...

Theories of Crime and Deviance

Deviance is controlled by society, and kept to a low level. Which is good, as it means you're less likely to be mugged by a naked nose-picker. And nobody likes to be mugged by a naked nose-picker, unless of course they're seriously deviant. **These pages are for AQA and OCR.**

Social Control keeps Order in Society

Functionalist sociologists argue that deviance must be kept to a **low level**. They say that a small amount of deviant activity can actually help maintain social order because it unites the rest of society in disapproval of the deviant behaviour. Functionalists say social control **benefits everyone** in society.

Marxist sociologists agree social control is essential to keep order. They say capitalism is an **exploitative** system which requires systems of social control over the population to **prevent rebellion and revolution**. Marxists say social control **benefits the ruling class** and works against the interests of the majority working class.

Marxists say Social Control is maintained through Hegemony

1) **Informal social control** is achieved through socialisation where individuals are **taught** to accept ideas and norms which support the status quo in society. These ideas are supported by **institutions** of the state such as the **education** and **legal** systems.

2) This ideology (set of ideas and values) is presented as **common sense** and neutral. However, according to neo-Marxists such as **Gramsci**, they're really designed in the interests of those in power.

3) Alternative ideas are overwhelmed by the **dominance** of this **ruling class ideology**.

4) The ability to **informally control** ideas and values in this way is **hegemony**.

5) Part of capitalist class hegemony is the **belief** that the legal system operates in the interests of **everyone** in society. Traditional Marxists argue the legal system is actually a method of **formal social control** over the population. They claim the legal system backs up the ideas and values of the ruling class ideology.

Marxists say the Capitalist State passes Laws which benefit the Ruling Class

1) According to Marxism, laws **aren't the will of the people**. They're a reflection of ruling class interests.

2) Other than the most serious crimes of murder, rape and violence, the vast majority of law in the UK is **property law**. **Chambliss and Mankoff (1976)** wrote that most of this law serves to keep **working class** people **away** from the property and land of the rich. The ruling class uses the law to protect **private property** because **capitalist exploitation** is built upon it.

3) The vast majority of the population have **no power** or **say** in the creation of **laws** and **punishments**.

4) The **lack of legislation** in some areas of life is also a demonstration of the law as an instrument of the ruling class.

5) Canadian sociologist **Laureen Snider (1993)** argues legislation regulating **large companies** is **restricted** in capitalist societies because it could **threaten ruling class interests**. For example, legislation regarding health and safety, pollution and fair trade are passed to a **minimum level** and often **weakly enforced**. **Tobacco companies** have put huge **pressure** on governments **not to pass laws** making them **legally responsible** for the deaths of smokers.

6) **Pearce (1976)** suggested that even the laws which supposedly protect the working class (e.g. health and safety laws, consumer laws) are really in ruling class interests. He said the system needs healthy, safe and loyal workers.

Marxists say Ruling Class lawbreakers are Less Likely to be Punished

Marxists also say the law is not enforced equally in capitalist societies.

1) **Laureen Snider (1993)** argues that working class crimes such as burglary don't cause as much harm in society as corporate crimes such as breaking health and safety law.

2) Marxists suggest that **ruling class ideology** successfully presents the burglars as the 'real criminals' and a threat to society, largely through the media. Meanwhile **corporate lawbreakers** get very **little media condemnation** and are treated more **leniently** by the legal system.

3) Also, if company bosses are charged they have the **money** to buy the **best legal advice**.

4) The work of **Chambliss (1978)** is good evidence for this. He studied crime in the American city of Seattle and found those in power were able to use their power to conduct criminal activity and to avoid prison. He found an organised crime syndicate which included elite businessmen and politicians who used money and influence to bribe officials.

Gordon (1976) argues **selective enforcement** of the law and **selective reporting** in the media gives the impression that criminals are largely working class. He thinks this not only diverts attention from ruling class crime but also **divides the working class** when the working class criminal becomes the target of anger rather than the system itself.

Theories of Crime and Deviance

Traditional Marxists are Criticised for overlooking Other Effects on Crime

1) Traditional Marxists believe that the cause of crime lies within the nature of the **capitalist system**. Their assumption that if you end capitalism you end crime is **rejected** by many. There's **crime** in **socialist societies** like Cuba, and **some capitalist societies** such as Switzerland have very **low crime rates**.

2) Feminists accuse traditional Marxist theory of **ignoring** the role of **patriarchy** in rule creation and social control.

3) More recent Marxist-influenced theory such as left-realism (see glossary) reckons traditional Marxism focuses too much on **corporate crime**. They dispute the argument that other crimes such as burglary are **insignificant**, especially as the **victims** are usually **working class**.

New Criminology argues criminals Choose to break the law

Taylor, Walton and Young's *The New Criminology* (1973) says crime is a choice

Background: *The New Criminology* was an attempt to present a thorough and considered **Marxist analysis** of crime, largely because Taylor, Walton and Young thought other Marxists, including Marx, had **failed** to do so. The main aim of *The New Criminology* was to move the sociology of crime on from the idea that society should be trying to **remove** deviant behaviour to a need to **understand** and **accept** it.

Theory: Taylor, Walton and Young argued that criminals were not **passive** individuals unable to control their economic situation as **traditional Marxists** had stated. Instead, crime was a **conscious**, **meaningful** and **deliberate choice** individuals made to try and **change society**.

Much crime is a **deliberate fight against capitalism**. Taylor, Walton and Young point to political action groups such as the **Black Panther** Movement who use criminal means to **agitate** the system. Robbery is also seen by the new criminologists as a potential means of **redistributing wealth**. (Robin Hood, anyone...)

Conclusion: Sociology needs a "**fully social theory of deviance**". Deviance needs to be explained from **different viewpoints**, which consider how society is **organised** and at the same time **how** and **why** individuals **choose** to be deviant.

Seven Aspects of a Full Social Theory of Deviance, from Taylor, Walton and Young's *The New Criminology*:

1) How **wealth** and **power** are **distributed**.
2) The **unique circumstances** of each **deviant act**.
3) The **nature** of the **deviant act** itself.
4) **Reactions** of the **rest of society** to the deviant act.
5) Who has the **power** to **make rules** about the **treatment** of deviance or **response** to deviance.
6) The **effect** being **labelled deviant** has on an individual.
7) How all these factors **interlink**.

In **1978**, **Hall et al** applied the 'social theory of deviance' to media reports of large numbers of muggings involving black muggers. They analysed the situation in terms of:

- **Social, economic and political conditions** — The country was in **economic crisis**. Unions and militants were **threatening state power**.

- **Motivations of the state** — The government wanted to feel in **control** of the situation.

- **Motivations of the media** — The press and broadcasters wanted a **dramatic story**.

- **What happened** — The police **arrested more people**. The media reported this and presented the muggers as a **threat to society**, creating an unjustified **moral panic**.

Practice Questions

Q1 Give two examples of how traditional Marxists argue capitalism creates crime.

Q2 According to Snider, how does the law protect ruling class crime?

Q3 According to Taylor, Walton and Young, why do people commit crime?

Exam Question

Q1 Outline and assess the view that the law is an instrument of the ruling class. (50 marks)

It's not my fault — capitalism made me do it...

Again, not recommended as a defence in a court of law. It didn't work for me when I insisted on running naked through the streets. Anyway. It's the usual suspects here — functionalists and Marxists. The Marxist theory of criminology is useful to learn. There are a lot of studies, and if you can explain and analyse them in the exam then you'll get plenty of marks.

Theories of Crime and Deviance

Two theories focused on finding a solution to crime have had a big influence on social policy in Britain and America — left realism and right realism. No prizes for guessing which is more right wing and which is more left wing. **For AQA and OCR.**

Left Realists said policy must accept that crime is Real and Rising

In *What Is to Be Done About Law and Order?* **(1984)**, **Lea and Young** launched their **new theory** of crime and how to reduce it. They criticised other leftist writers (especially Marxists) for overlooking the reality of crime in Britain by focusing on the problems within capitalism.

Lea and Young said left wing sociological debate and social policy on crime must start accepting that:
- Crimes **other than white-collar crime** are a **problem**.
- There has been a **rise in crime** in Britain since the Second World War.
- Being a **victim** of crime is a very **significant event** in an individual's life.
- **Fear of crime** is a real factor in shaping modern urban lifestyles, especially for **women**.

Kinsey, Lea and Young (1986) recommend changes in Policing Policy

1) **Kinsey, Lea and Young (1986)** say that British policing policy needs to be centred on **creating** and **maintaining good communication** between the **police** and **local communities**.

   The public **report most crimes** to the police.
   The public **provide most evidence** to solve crimes.   = The police **need** the public.

2) Kinsey, Lea and Young say the public should have a **key role** in deciding **police policy**. They propose setting up **Police Authorities** which are **democratically elected** from the public. These authorities should formulate policing policy and direct police action.

3) This would create **consensus policing** where the police are acting on the instructions of the local community, rather than in isolation from them.

PCs Hillier, Samson, Costa, Armitage, Stevens, Collins and Benjamin slowly came to a consensus on where to lunch.

4) Kinsey, Lea and Young say the key role of the police should then be "**full and proper investigation of crime**" which they reckon has been reduced in recent years.

5) They say the police need to improve their **detection** and **clear-up** rates. At the time they were writing, only 12% of recorded crime was cleared up. This figure has improved since then.

Left realists say Relative Deprivation is a factor causing Crime

1) **Lea and Young (2002)** argue that a sense of **relative deprivation** is a major factor leading to crime. When an individual feels deprived in relation to similar social groups, they can turn to crime to "solve" the problem and acquire the resources to remove the feeling.

2) It's not actual deprivation but the **feeling of being deprived** relative to someone else that triggers this response. This explains why crime occurs in all social strata — the rich can feel deprived next to the super-rich.

3) **Lea and Young** says these feelings of deprivation are compounded by the **consumer culture** of modern Britain — **advertising** and the **media** present individuals with images of what they **could** have and what others have got.

4) Therefore, a rising standard of living can lead to a rising crime rate.

Left realists say Social Inequality must be fought in order to Reduce Crime

Left realists identify **deprivation** and to a lesser extent **marginalisation** as causes of crime. They say that in the long term, order will come from a **fair** and **just** society. **Left realists** stress the need for **all social agencies** to have a direct aim of removing inequality. They include the general public in this — everyone's responsible.

Left realists use the "**square of crime**" to show the **interactions** between **four elements** which affect crime — the state, the public, the offender and the victim. Left realists argue that all four elements should **work together** to understand and reduce crime.

The Left Realist Square of Crime

```
state                 public
(formal     ←→      (informal
control)             control)
    ↕      ↘  CRIME  ↙    ↕
offender    ←→         victim
```

New Left realist work has influenced **Labour** government **social policy** since **1997**. Remember Tony Blair's phrase "tough on crime, tough on the causes of crime" — it sums up the left realism theory pretty well.

Theories of Crime and Deviance

Critics say that if *Left Realism* was **Correct** there'd be **More Crime**

1) **Hughes (1991)** says the left realists haven't explained why **some people** who experience **relative deprivation** see **crime** as a **solution** and others don't. He argues there would be a lot **more crime** if **relative deprivation** was the main cause.

2) Critics also say that Kinsey, Lea and Young didn't collect enough data to develop a full theory of crime. Their theory only focuses on **property crime**.

No one wants to end up here

Right Realists have influenced **American Social Policy**

1) **Wilson (1975)** believes individuals commit crime because the **gains outweigh** the chances of being **caught and punished**. In order to reduce crime, Wilson says it's necessary to issue **harsh punishments** for the smallest crimes — so the benefits won't outweigh the punishment any more. Punishment should be a **deterrent** to future offenders.

Wilson was a social policy advisor to the Reagan government of the USA in the 1980s.

2) This has been put into action in the social policy of **Zero Tolerance**, first in America and now in parts of the UK (e.g. Middlesborough).

3) **Wilson and Kelling (1982)** say that damage to a neighbourhood has to be put right straight away, or problems of crime and delinquency quickly get out of hand. This is called the "One Broken Window" idea — their article says that tolerating just one broken window sends the message that you can get away with crime.

4) Wilson and Kelling actually advocate **taking resources and police supervision away** from areas where law and order has **broken down** — this sounds wrong, but Wilson says that once social order has gone it's almost impossible to regain it, so it's not worth **wasting resources** on trying. He recommends **diverting police** to areas which **aren't too far gone**, to **prevent breakdown** of social order in those areas.

> **Wilson and Herrnstein (1985)** claim there's a **biological predisposition** to crime in some individuals — but with the right **socialisation** they can be trained away from it. They argue that **single-parent families** are more likely to have "criminal children" because their socialisation hasn't been complete.

Murray (1997) claims that the higher the **risk** of going to **prison**, the less likely people are to commit crime.

Right Realism has been **Criticised**

1) **Critics** of right realism have been many and varied. The argument that criminals are **biologically different** is **rejected** by many as coming from theories that have already been discredited.

2) **Jones (1998)** questions the assertion that resources put into run-down areas are wasted. He argues that investment in these areas makes a positive difference to the communities who live there.

3) **Matthews (1992)** didn't find any evidence that tolerating broken windows leads to crime.

4) Critics also say that Zero Tolerance policies have led to a big rise in the **US prison population** — e.g. the "**three strikes and you're out**" policy which means three serious offences automatically result in **life imprisonment**.

Practice Questions

Q1 Give an example of a sociological theory being used in social policy.
Q2 How does left realism differ from Marxist criminology?
Q3 What do left realists say causes crime?
Q4 Give two examples of things that right realists say would reduce crime.

Exam Questions

Q1 Outline and assess the left realist argument that different policing strategies would reduce crime. (50 marks)

Q2 Outline and assess the view that relative deprivation can trigger a criminal response. (50 marks)

A kid broke my window playing football last week — give him life in prison, I say...

Both these new approaches are quite different to the old sociological theories, which just tend to blame society. The left realists are quite harsh on Marxism, and say that it ignores the effect of crime on ordinary people. Right wing politicians and right realists have been quite firm in their claim that prison works, but just like everything in sociology, there's no broad agreement.

SECTION FIVE — CRIME AND DEVIANCE

Measuring Crime

Measuring crime isn't straightforward. Different statisticians use different techniques and reach different, conflicting conclusions.
These pages are for AQA and OCR.

Police *crime figures* Don't *reflect the* Full Extent *of* Crime *in Britain*

Police crime figures are official statistics that have been recorded and published **annually** in Britain since **1857**. They're useful because they're easy to **access**, can be used to **identify trends** and show the **social background** of criminals. For 100 years, they were largely taken as an **accurate** record of all crime, but then sociologists began to **question** how reliable police stats are.

(1) **Firstly**, official police records only report crimes **known to the police**. Not all crime is **reported** to the police.

1) Individuals don't report crime if they **don't have faith in the police** to investigate and solve it.

2) Crime won't be reported to the police if the victim is **intimidated** by the perpetrator. Many communities have **gangs** of criminals who **threaten** anyone who reports their crimes, including witnesses as well as victims.

3) Much sexual crime is not reported because of the embarrassment, fear and shock of the victim.

4) Some victims see the crime against them as trivial — or fear the police will see it as trivial.

(2) **Secondly**, the police **don't record all crime** that's reported to them. Police officers use their own discretion to decide whether an incident is **worth reporting** — if there's enough evidence to say a crime has been committed, if the incident is serious enough to be a crime, etc. This makes crime reporting unreliable — some officers will record an incident, but others may consider it too **trivial** or lacking in evidence, especially as there's a lot of **paperwork** involved.

(3) **Thirdly**, not all offences **count** as crimes to be recorded by the police. For example, police weren't required to record all common assaults until 1989. **Official rules** and definitions **change**. In **1998**, **new guidelines** allowed police to record a lot more incidents as crime. This alone increased the level of crime recorded by 15%.

Trends in police recorded crime statistics 1981-2003 (Home Office)

old rules
new rules post 1998

Official recorded crime figures show crime increased by two thirds between 1981 and 1995, with a very sharp peak between 1989 and 1992. The highest number of crimes recorded by the police was 6 million in 2003/4.

Victim Surveys *include crime* Not Reported *to the* Police

A **victimisation** (or victim) **survey** is an **anonymous** survey of individuals asking for details of crimes committed **against them** (even if **not reported** to the police) within a set time period, usually the last year. Because they include figures for reported and unreported crimes, they're more **representative** than police crime figures. Other advantages of victim surveys are that they use a **large sample size** and have a **high response rate**.

1) The most significant victim survey in Britain is the **British Crime Survey** (**BCS**), which interviews a **sample** of the population (approx 14 000), and asks them about their experiences of being a victim of crime over the previous year. Answers are confidential and can't be passed on to the police. The survey results are applied to the whole UK population.

Trends in crime: BCS 1981-2003

2) In the past the BCS has indicated a significant level of **unrecorded** crime. In recent years BCS and police figures have been much closer. In 2007/8 the BCS showed **27%** of crimes were **vandalism**, with the police figures showing **21%**. The BCS showed **burglary** as **7%** of all crime, compared to **12%** of police-recorded crime.

3) Victim surveys and police figures reveal the same **broad trends**. Crime **rose** in the **1980s** and early **1990s**. Since **2002** there's been a **small drop** in crime. In 2007/8 BCS levels of crime were the lowest since 1981 when the survey began.

4) There are **problems** with the reliability of victim surveys:

- Even the largest **victim surveys** only interview a **small sample** of the population.
- BCS doesn't survey all crime, e.g. it doesn't include crimes committed against businesses.
- **No under-16s** are interviewed for the BCS.

Sociologist **Jock Young (1988)** questioned the validity of victim surveys by pointing out that **each respondent's definition** of what's criminal is **different**, so the same incident would be mentioned by one person and not by another. Also, some people are **more willing** to **reveal their experiences** than others. Young accepts that victim surveys have a place in research, but maintains they **don't** give a **true, full picture** of crime.

Measuring Crime

Self-Report Studies ask people about Crime They've Committed

1) **Self-report studies** ask respondents to **reveal crime** they've committed. They're **less widely used** than victim surveys.

2) Self-report studies are **anonymous** and representative of the population, like victim surveys.

3) The obvious drawback is that respondents may not believe that their crimes won't be reported to others, including the police.

4) However, they have been important in researching **who commits crime**.

> An analysis of 40 self-report studies by **Steve Box (1981)** indicated that **juvenile crime** was not a **working class** problem as had been widely argued. **Middle class** juveniles committed crime too but were less likely to get caught.
>
> Similar results have been found in the **adult** population. **Maguire (1997)** concluded **most respondents** admitted committing **some crime** at some point in their life. This is evidence against the argument that certain social groups are more likely to commit crime than others (there's more about this idea on pages 82-83).

Official Statistics show Fear of Crime is Rising

1) Statistics show that public **fear** of being a victim of crime is rising.

2) Public assessment consistently **overestimates** the actual amount of crime in Britain. People believe that the crime rate is going up faster than it really is. Also, far more people fear becoming a victim of crime than ever will become a victim of crime.

3) This stark difference between the level of crime and fear of crime has been attributed to the way crime is reported in the media. **Tabloid** papers often use **alarmist headlines** about crime and deviance to grab the attention of readers. It's been argued that these **exaggerate** the chances of being a victim of crime — which creates fear or panic in the population.

4) The **Home Office Statistical Bulletin** (2003) revealed that those individuals who read **tabloid newspapers** were twice as likely to be worried about crime compared to those who read broadsheets or didn't read any newspapers.

5) **Fletcher and Allen (2003)** identify several factors which affect the fear of crime, including locality, health, age, perception of disorder and whether a person has previously been a victim of crime.

Pantazis and Gordon found the poor are most likely to fear crime

Pantazis and Gordon (1999)* analysed household surveys and found households with the **lowest incomes** were most likely to **fear** crime, but households with the **highest incomes** were actually the most likely to become **victims** of crime.

This is due to the consequences of crime being **more severe** for people who are **too poor** to **insure** their property, or buy **replacements**.

* Pantazis and Gordon (1999) 'Is Crime and Fear of Crime More Likely to be Experienced by the 'Poor'?' in Dorling and Simpson (eds) *Statistics in Society* (London, Arnold)

Practice Questions

Q1 Name two types of statistics published each year on levels of crime in Britain.

Q2 What crimes are not covered by the British Crime Survey?

Q3 What's a self-report survey?

Q4 Which social groups are most likely to fear crime?

Exam Questions

Q1 Identify and explain two ways in which official statistics may underestimate the level of crime in the UK. (6 marks)

Q2 Examine the problems faced by sociologists trying to measure the level of crime in the UK. (12 marks)

What's that old saying about lies, damned lies and that other thing...

There are quite a lot of statistics just on these pages. Once you scratch the surface of various government statistics it's amazing just how many figures there are out there. Try not to get too bogged down in detail, but do learn the central trends and which type of study they come from. Each type of study has its own supporters and its critics — make sure you can say why that is.

Patterns of Crime

Some groups of people seem to commit more crime than others — or at least to get caught out more than other people.
These pages are for OCR and AQA.

Young people are Convicted of More Crime than Older People

Most crime is committed by teenagers. The peak age for criminal activity is 18 for men and 15 for women (Social Trends, 33).

1) It's argued that young people commit more crime because their **lifestyles** take them to **environments** where **crime takes place**. The vast majority of crime is **property theft** — young people are more likely to be on the **streets** or in **clubs**, which is where **pickpocketing** and **mugging** often happens.

2) This is supported by the evidence that **young people** are most likely to be **victims** of crime too — if you're aged 16-25 you're six times more likely to be a victim of crime than those aged 75 and older. It's not age itself, but the **likelihood** of being in areas where **opportunities for crime** arise which is the significant factor.

3) Young people may actually commit more crime, or it may be that they get **caught more** than older people. Crime committed by the **young** is typically more **visible**, e.g. vandalism, so it's likely to be witnessed, and the perpetrator is more likely to be caught. 'White-collar crimes' such as **fraud** are more likely to be committed by **older people**, but these offences are more **hidden** and don't take place in the public arena.

4) **Social stereotypes** that young people commit crime lead to police **suspecting** and **monitoring** young people more than older social groups — increasing their chances of being caught.

5) Young people are more likely to be **convicted** once in court — partly because they can't afford expensive **lawyer's fees**.

Men are Convicted of More Crime than Women

Women make up only **6%** of the prison population. (HM Prison Service)

58% of male prisoners released from prison are **re-convicted within 2 years**. (Social Trends, 1998)

In 2001, **167 per 10 000** of the **male** population were **found guilty** or **cautioned** for an offence, compared to **3.7 per 10 000** of the female population.

1) Men are **suspected**, **charged** and **convicted** of crime of all types more than women. This pattern crosses **all other social factors** such as **age**, **class**, **ethnicity** and **region**.

2) The subcultural theories of **Miller (1962)** and **Merton (1968)** argue that the **culture** and **lifestyles** of **young men** encourage and lead to crime (remember, most crime is committed by the young.)

3) **Heidensohn (1986)** is a feminist who says gender socialisation prompts men to be more **aggressive**, which makes them more likely than women to commit violent crime. She also says that **women** are **socialised** into **not being criminal** in the same way as men are socialised into seeing criminal activity as acceptable. **Abbott and Wallace (1990)** argue young women are more closely watched by their families and given **less freedom** outside the home, reducing their **opportunities** for crime. Criminal behaviour would be seen as highly **deviant** as well as criminal for women.

4) **Ian Marsh (1986)** reckons that men commit more crime because they have more opportunities to do so. He said that where females have similar opportunities to males they seem as likely to break laws. An example of this is handling stolen goods — women have more opportunity to sell, buy or use stolen property than to steal goods in the first place.

5) There may be an **underestimation** of female crime because the police and courts are **less likely** to **suspect** women or give women a **custodial sentence**. The stereotypes of men as criminal work as a form of **sexism** against men, which allows female criminal activity to go **unchecked**. **Campbell (1981)** did a **self-report survey** which unearthed a lot **more female crime** than the official statistics. However, she did include more trivial crimes than the official statistics do.

Urban areas have much More Crime than Rural ones

According to the Home Office report ***Crime in England and Wales 2003/2004***, in 2003-2004, **metropolitan (urban) police** forces recorded **43% of all crime**. In 2002, less than 2% of people living in rural areas became victims of burglary. And, in 2003-2004, **60% of all robbery** in the UK took place in **three urban areas** (London, Manchester and West Midlands).

This table shows the percentage of households which have been **victims** (at least once) of **vehicle theft**, **burglary** and **violent crime**. The data's from the British Crime Survey, 2004.

Area type	All vehicle theft	All burglary	All violent crime
Inner city	15.3	5.3	5.8
Urban (towns and outer part of city)	10.3	3.3	4.4
All non-rural (cities, towns, suburbs)	10.8	3.6	4.6
Rural	6.5	1.9	2.7
All households/all adults	9.7	3.2	4.1

There's **more crime** in **cities**.

Sociologists argue most crime takes place in cities because there are more **opportunities** to be involved in crime in cities. Higher density populations mean more chances for **robbery** and **property crime**. Most young people live in urban areas and they are the most likely to commit crime. It's hard for criminals to remain anonymous in close-knit rural **communities**.

Patterns of Crime

Most criminal convictions are of people with a **Working Class Background**

There are more **working class** people in **prison** than any other social class. Home Office figures also show that the majority of people who appear in **court** are working class, regardless of whether they're found guilty or not.

The idea of an upper class person in prison is so rare and contrary to cultural norms that a Lord convicted of fraud can find himself on a 'celebrity' reality TV show.

1) **Subcultural theorists** such as **Miller** argue this reflects the working class subcultures which often have crime as an accepted or rewarded activity.

2) **Marxists** argue the system of law and order is run by the **ruling class**, against the interests of the working class. They say parts of the working class are criminalised by a biased system — see p.76-77.

3) Middle class crime is treated more leniently by society. Fraud and white collar crime is often undetected and seen as 'victimless crime' by the public. Consider the public response to benefit fraud compared to tax or insurance fraud. There's more about **Marxist** opinions of why this is on p.76-77.

An **Ethnic Minority Background** increases your chances of arrest and conviction

	Population of the UK	Police "stop and search", England and Wales	Arrests for serious offences, England and Wales	Male prison population	Female prison population
White	92%	74.3%	84.3%	75.7%	69.1%
Asian	4%	7.3%	4.8%	3.4%	0.8%
Black	2%	14.6%	8.8%	16%	25.3%
Mixed and Other	2%	3.7%	2.1%	4.8%	4.7%

2001 census, and the Home Office "Statistics on Race and the Criminal Justice System" (2004)

1) Some have argued that **police racism** results in higher suspicion against black people in general. The **Macpherson Report** (1999) concluded that the police were **institutionally racist**. The court system has also been accused of automatically favouring white middle class defendants. There are relatively few black people in the police or the legal system.

The stop and search, arrest and prison figures are based on <u>what a person looks like</u>. The census records what a person <u>identifies themself</u> as.

2) **Hall et al (1978)** and **Gilroy (1987)** argue that young black people have been labelled as criminal by modern British society and have become a **scapegoat** for social problems in society.

3) Hall also says that high levels of **unemployment** among young black men leads some young black men to **opt out** of **mainstream society** and turn to **crime**.

Similar in some ways, but Hall blames the system and right realists blame the person.

4) Right realist sociologists favour a **subcultural** explanation for the differences.

5) **Ethnic minority** households are **more at risk of crime** than other households — e.g. the British Crime Survey says they're more likely to be mugged than white groups, and slightly more likely to be victims of vehicle theft. Pakistanis and Bangladeshis were more likely to be **burgled**. The survey found ethnic minority respondents were **more worried about crime** in 2000 than white respondents.

Only **23% of reported crimes** in 2003 were **solved** — i.e. someone was convicted for the offence in 2003 (2004 Social Trends). The social profile of who committed the **unsolved** and **undetected** crimes could change these patterns considerably.

Practice Questions

Q1 Which social groups are most likely to be convicted of crime in Britain?

Q2 What evidence is there that crime is more prevalent in urban areas?

Q3 Briefly state the two explanations that Hall gives for increased arrest and criminality among the black population.

Exam Question

Q1 Referring to sociological theories, suggest why 76% of the UK male prison population is white. (12 marks)

Avoid committing crime — be an old woman and live in the countryside...

Of course, that's easier said than done for many of us, particularly young men. But just because a task is difficult does not mean you shouldn't strive to achieve it. Being young, male, working class, black and living in an urban area puts you at the highest risk of being convicted, or of being a victim, of crime. There are loads of possible reasons for this — make sure you understand them.

Victims, Prevention and Punishment

This fine pair of pages opens with some thrilling theories about how people become victims of crime, ramps up the fun with a look at ways of preventing crime, then concludes with a spectacular grand finale on punishment. **For AQA and OCR**.

Victimology Theories try to explain How people become Victims

There are two main sociological theories to explain how people become victims of crime — '**positivist victimology**' and '**radical victimology**'.

1) Positivist victimology is interested in how some people are **more likely** to become victims than others — either because their **actions** (e.g. leaving valuables on display in a car) lead them to becoming a victim of crime or because of their **lifestyle**. This approach has been criticised for '**blaming the victim**'. Positivist victimologists have tended to focus on '**visible**' crime, such as **reported robberies** and **assaults** — they've been criticised for ignoring issues such as **state crime** (see p. 86).

2) Radical victimology is more **left wing**. It argues that in a structurally unequal capitalist society, **poor people** are more likely to be the **victims** of crime, as part of a wider pattern of **inequality** and **disadvantage**. Radical victimologists have used the concept of '**human rights**' as a more universal yardstick for measuring victimisation rather than using official statistics. This has allowed them to focus on state and corporate crimes that often go **unrecorded**.

Some Facts and Figures about Victims *

* from 'Crime in England and Wales 2002/03' and 'Crime in England and Wales 2005/06,' published by the Home Office.

- **Men** are almost twice as likely to become **victims of violence** as women.
  More **women** are **afraid** of becoming victims of crime.
- Young **men aged 16-24** experience the most violence — 13% in this survey.
- Men are most likely to experience violence from **strangers** and **acquaintances**.
- Women are more likely than men to be victims of **domestic violence** — 0.6% of women were affected but only 0.2% of men. People who suffer domestic violence are likely to experience **repeat attacks**.
- The 2002/03 report said that, of **mixed race** adults, 46% had been victims of crime — much higher than other groups. Just 30% of Asian and 27% of black, white and 'Chinese or other' adults experienced crime.

Feminists say Women become Victims because of Patriarchal Attitudes

1) Feminists argue that **domestic violence** is the result of an **unequal power relationship** between men and women. **Radical feminists** see domestic violence as a form of **patriarchal power and control**.

2) Some feminists argue that **fear of crime** is used to **constrain women** from taking a more active part in social life. **Stanko (2000)** suggests that women have to restrict their behaviour by taking care not to be too provocative in their behaviour and appearance.

3) **Marxist feminists** say domestic violence can be explained by the frustration and **lack of control** that men experience in the **capitalist work place**.

4) Many feminists believe the **law is biased against women** and crimes against women have been ignored. **Heidensohn (2002)** says crimes against women often go unreported and calls this 'gendered crime'.

5) Feminists have **campaigned** to widen the definition of what behaviour is criminal, e.g. campaigning for **legislation** against **sexual harassment** in the **workplace**.

There are Three Main Approaches to Crime Prevention

1) **Structuralists** argue that crime is caused by **inequalities** in wealth and income. They say the only way to reduce or prevent crime is to address these inequalities. **Subcultural**, **Marxist** and **left realism** theorists are structuralists.

2) The **individualist** or **interventionist** approaches argue that some groups of people are more likely to commit crime than others. They say the best way to prevent crime is to **change the behaviour** of these 'criminal types', e.g. by targeting children from a disadvantaged background. **Prison** and **community** sentences can also be seen as interventionist approaches, with the aim of discouraging other people from committing crimes.

3) The **situational approach** says society can use **changes to the physical environment** to make it harder for people to commit crimes. Changes could include creating **gated communities**, putting up more **surveillance cameras** or improving **lighting** in streets and car parks. **Zero tolerance policing** — where anti-social behaviour is tackled swiftly and strictly — is another situational approach. **Right realism** theorists favour the situational approach, advocating the development of 'community-minded' areas where there is a sense of social responsibility. Situational approaches can be effective but evidence suggests they don't always reduce crime, just move it to a less well-protected area.

Victims, Prevention and Punishment

Society tries to Control Crime through Formal and Informal Agents

1) The **police** are a **formal** agent of social control, responsible for **enforcing the law**.

2) Other formal **agents** include **Parliament**, which passes laws to say what behaviour is criminal, the **Crown Prosecution Service**, which decides who should be taken to court for a particular crime, the **courts**, which determine any punishment, and the **Prison Service** which imposes any punishment.

3) There are also agents of **informal social control**. These include the **family** unit, the **education** system, **religion** and the **media**. All these channels help to reinforce a general sense of what behaviour is considered acceptable.

In theory the **police** should be **impartial**, but have sometimes been accused of **institutional racism** and **sexism**:

- The **Macpherson Report (1999)** into the Stephen Lawrence case said the way the police handled the case showed clear signs of **racism**.
- A report by the **Metropolitan Police Authority** (2004) found **black men** are four times more likely to be **stopped and searched** than white people.
- **Graef (1989)** said the police have a '**canteen culture**'. He thought the majority of police officers, who tend to be white males, adopt racist and sexist attitudes as a way of fitting in.

Criminals are Punished for a number of Reasons

Most societies around the world have systems for **punishing crime**.
Sociologists (unsurprisingly) have different views on the **purpose** and **importance** of punishment.

1) **Functionalists** argue that punishment **keeps society going**. If crimes went unpunished the result would be anarchy and society would collapse. Durkheim said that **public punishment** of criminals was good for society. He thought it helped create **unity** and **consensus** as people came together to condemn the criminal — in other words, a public hanging was good for society.

2) **Marxists** say punishment serves the needs of capitalism by **keeping the workers under control**. They argue that the police are used to **enforce social control** in **poorer areas** whilst the rich get way with crime unchallenged.

3) The **interventionist** camp see prison as a deterrent — the very fact it exists should put people off committing crimes. The evidence suggests that this theory does not work in practice.

Labour and the Conservatives have different Attitudes to Crime

The **Labour Party** used to favour the **structuralist** approach to crime. Their main policy was to **reduce inequalities** in society.

The **Conservative Party** has tended to favour **individual** and **situational** approaches. During the most recent period that the Conservatives were in government (1979-1997) they put **more police** on the streets and more criminals were sent to **prison** — so many that Britain had the highest rate of imprisonment in Europe.

When **New Labour** came to power in 1997, Prime Minister Tony Blair promised to be **"tough on crime and tough on the causes of crime"**. The party continued to focus on reducing inequalities of opportunity (by tackling unemployment, poverty and social exclusion), while giving more emphasis to punishment.

Practice Questions

Q1 What percentage of women in England and Wales experience domestic violence, and what percentage of men?

Q2 Which sociologist said women face restrictions to their behaviour thanks to fear of crime?

Q3 Give two examples of situations in which the police were found to have behaved in a racist way.

Q4 Which political party has favoured the structural approach? Which favoured the individual approach?

Exam Question

Q1 Outline and assess the arguments for and against a situational approach to crime prevention. (50 marks)

Prevention is better than cure, they say...

Unfortunately, by the time all the sociological theorists have finished debating how we become victims and the best ways of preventing and punishing crime we'll all be... no, what am I thinking — sociologists will never stop debating. The best policy for you as a conscientious sociology student is to learn what the main arguments say, and draw your own conclusions.

Recent Issues in Crime and Deviance

*A global crime is one which affects national and international economies, politics or security. Globalisation (see p.18-19) has meant that different societies have become connected economically, culturally and environmentally, and has had a big impact on the nature of crime. These pages are for **AQA** students — **OCR** students just need to learn the section on the media on p.87.*

Trading in illegal **Drugs** and **Arms** causes huge social problems

1) According the UN's *World Drug Report*, in **2005** the **global trade** in **illegal drugs** was worth around **$320 billion**, supplying around **200 million drug users** worldwide. This amounts to around **one eighth** of all **world trade**.

2) **Karofi and Mwanza (2006)** have outlined the **negative impact** of the trade in illegal drugs. They pointed to the consequences for **health**, the changes in **social behaviours** and the **funding** of **terrorism** and **war** with the profits.

3) The **Transnational Institute** in **Amsterdam** reported that the majority of **armed conflicts** across the globe are **funded** or **part funded** by the **illegal drugs trade**.

4) Global communications and relatively unregulated financial markets have made the illegal trade in **arms** easier to carry out and harder to trace. **Karofi and Mwanza** highlight its role in **destabilising societies** (violent crime) and making existing conflicts worse.

5) The trade in **small arms** (firearms carried and used by one person) is particularly problematic, causing an estimated 80% of conflict deaths each year. Former UN Secretary-General **Kofi Annan** called small arms **"weapons of mass destruction in slow motion"** because of their **deadly impact** in the **developing world**.

Human Trafficking creates modern day Slavery

1) **Human trafficking** is the **illegal movement** of **people** for **exploitation**. Victims are taken either with **force** or **deception**.

2) According the UNDP's 2007 report *Human Trafficking and HIV*, the **illegal global trafficking** of people is an industry worth between **$5 billion** and **$7 billion** a year. Human trafficking is one of the **fastest growing global crimes**.

3) According to the UN's Global Initiative to Fight Human Trafficking, an estimated **2.5 million people** are in **forced labour** as a result of trafficking. People trafficking is a global problem — it involves criminal groups from across the globe and has a **devastating effect** on its victims.

Cybercrime is crime that uses the Internet

1) Globalisation has seen a massive increase in computer use and internet use, giving rise to **'cybercrimes'** such as **data theft**, **fraud**, **credit scams**, **email scams** and **illegal pornography**. Because cybercrime breaches **national borders**, existing criminal law is often **powerless** to tackle it.

2) The extent of cybercrime is difficult to assess accurately, but some observers have suggested that it will soon **rival** the **drugs trade** in terms of **profits**.

> The **globalisation** of **communications** and the media has also aided the growth of **international terrorism**. Terrorists can now access a global audience for their **propaganda**, and are able to create **online networks** for their organisations.

Environmental or Green Crimes are those which Harm the Environment

1) Green crime might be something as small-scale as **fly-tipping**, but on a global scale it includes the illegal trade in **environmentally sensitive substances** (e.g. refrigerator CFCs), the illegal trade in **protected animals** and products derived from them, and illegal and unregulated **logging** and **fishing**.

2) The environmental impact of green crimes can be huge — e.g. illegally traded **CFCs** significantly contribute to ozone depletion. There are also severe **financial costs** — the World Bank estimated that **illegal logging** costs timber-producing countries around **10-15 billion euros** per year in **lost revenue**.

State Crimes are commited by Governments

1) State crimes are where governments break **national** or **international criminal law**.

2) State crimes include the funding of **terrorism**, **war crimes**, **genocide**, links with **organised crime**, **corruption**, use of **torture**, and **other crimes against human rights**.

3) State crime is often a controversial topic as it's states themselves that define what is **"justifiable"** and what is **illegal**.

Recent Issues in Crime and Deviance

The *Media* plays a powerful role in *Amplifying Deviance* in society

Interpretivists (also known as interactionists) such as **Stanley Cohen (1972)** argue the media helps to **create** the deviance it predicts or anticipates.

> **The Amplification of Deviance:**
> 1) The media presents a **distorted view** of the level of crime.
> 2) This distorted view creates **public concern**.
> 3) Related incidents of crime and deviance are **over-reported** and given more prominence than they'd otherwise have.
> 4) This keeps the issue or problem **high** on the **public agenda**.
> 5) The public want **something done** about the problem.
> 6) The police are more **aware** or sensitive to the problem, so they **discover more crime**.
> 7) Police records **reinforce** the idea that there is **more crime** and **deviance**.

LOCAL RABBIT RANSACKS VEGETABLE BASKET

1) The risk of being a victim of crime is **amplified** by **over-reporting** by the **media**. This creates a public response of **panic** or **outrage**. Cohen refers to this as a **moral panic** (see p.45).

2) Cohen developed his idea about moral panics from a study of conflicts between **Mods and Rockers** in 1964, but there are plenty of **new** examples, especially with the increased power of the media — e.g. gun crime, "bogus asylum seekers" and benefit fraud.

3) The state response to a moral panic in society is often to introduce **stricter** forms of **social control** through legislation.

4) **Hall et al (1978)** claim that the national concern about **mugging** in the early 1970s was a **moral panic**. The media claimed that mugging was a new kind of crime, but Hall et al point out that violent street robbery had been going on for a long time, and wasn't rising particularly fast at the time of the moral panic. (See p. 77 for more on this.)

5) Some sociologists have suggested that the **fear** of **global terrorism** following the attacks on New York on September 11th 2001 is another example of a current moral panic, and that the terrorist threat has been exaggerated.

Ian Taylor argued *Economic Liberalisation* has caused an *Increase* in *Crime*

1) **Taylor (1997, 1998)** argued that **economic deregulation** had given some people more **opportunity** to commit crimes like **fraud**, **money laundering** and **tax evasion**.

2) He also argued that **globalisation** and **deregulation** have made employment less secure and increased economic instability by **reducing** the **control** states have over their economies. **Increased unemployment** and **cuts** in **welfare** have led to a **rise in crime** as people don't believe they will be able to secure a **reliable income**.

3) According to Taylor, **globalisation** is partly to blame for the growth of the **drugs trade** in **poverty-affected areas**.

4) Taylor also blamed **marketization** for rising crime. This is where **economic considerations** begin to **dominate** in the way people think of social life. Success becomes equated to owning **expensive consumer goods** — some people turn to crime as a way to achieve this, e.g. by stealing an expensive car.

5) Taylor argued that it's **too late** to turn the economic clock back completely, but believed that attempts should be made to **recreate** shared **values** of community and civility to **counteract** the process of marketization.

Practice Questions

Q1   What is meant by the term 'global crime'?
Q2   What is cybercrime and why is it difficult to police?
Q3   Give three examples of moral panics.

Exam Question

Q1   Assess the view that globalisation is a significant cause of crime.   (21 marks)

Can't we all just agree to play by the rules...

Of course not — especially when those who set the rules break the law themselves. State crime's like a referee who goes around kicking all the players at a football match. Another rather unhappy page for you to learn — make a cup of tea and get cracking.

Suicide

There's an awful lot of sociology on suicide, for two reasons. Firstly, it's a totally individual act, so it's a big task for sociology to explain. Secondly, it's been a focus for exploring issues of sociological methodology since Durkheim used his study of suicide to explain the "rules" of sociological research and enquiry. These two pages are just for AQA.

Durkheim's study of Suicide is one of the most Important Sociological Works

Durkheim wrote in the **1890s**, and was one of the very **first sociologists** — right at the forefront of establishing and defining sociology as a scientific discipline. Durkheim argued that it was not only **possible** to apply **scientific principles** to **social phenomena** but that it was **essential** to do so in order to produce **useful sociology**. His 1897 book *Suicide: a study in sociology*, uses his scientific methods to explore suicide.

1) Durkheim chose suicide **deliberately**, because as the most **individual**, **private** and **psychologically driven** act it was considered by most **not** to be a **social** phenomenon.

2) If sociology could identify **social** factors and **causes** of suicide, this would demonstrate the power and impact of **society** on **individual behaviour**.

3) Durkheim followed the **methodology** laid down in his earlier book, *The Rules of Sociological Method*, in his suicide study. This methodology produced a **rigorous**, **systematic**, **detailed** and **scientific** analysis.

4) Durkheim said that if this **scientific methodology** is followed then "**social facts**" can be discovered in the same way as **scientific** research reveals laws or facts of the **natural world**.

Analysis of Statistics found some groups were More Likely to Commit Suicide

1) Durkheim's analysis of the **official statistics** on suicide revealed some **social groups** were **more likely** to commit suicide than others. He looked at a large amount of data from **different societies** and from **different cultural** and **social groups** within the same society.

2) Social **patterns** of suicide rates demonstrate suicide is **not a random individual act**. **Social factors** play a part.

> **Correlation between suicide and other "social facts".**
> - Suicide rates were higher in predominantly **Protestant** countries than in **Catholic** ones.
> - **Jews** were the religious group with the **lowest suicide rate**.
> - **Married** people were **less likely** to commit suicide.
> - **Low suicide rates** were found in some countries after a **national upheaval** or **crisis**. This might be because people feel better **socially integrated**.
> - Those with more **education** had a **higher suicide rate**.

Durkheim used "social facts" as his raw data and then analysed the data to draw conclusions on the cause of suicide. He didn't question the reliability or accuracy of the statistics — that all came later...

Durkheim concluded there were Four Forms of Suicide

Durkheim said different forms of suicide were related to how much **integration** and **regulation** there was in a society.
Social integration means **socialisation** into the **norms**, **values** and **lifestyles** of social groups and society.
Moral regulation means the **control** that society and social groups have over an **individual's behaviour**.
Durkheim's **four types of suicide** relate to **dysfunctional** integration or regulation.

Form of suicide	Cause	Example
Egoistic	**Not enough integration**. The individual isn't successfully integrated into groups or society.	More suicide in Protestants compared to Catholics because Protestants had a **looser social network/belief system**.
Anomic	**Not enough regulation**. Society has insufficient control over individuals.	Often in periods of **economic depression** or **very rapid expansion**, the suicide rate rises. People find it hard to adapt.
Altruistic	**Too much integration**. An over-integrated individual sacrifices their life for the group.	**Followers** who commit suicide after the death of their **leader**. Terrorist **suicide bombers** are a modern example.
Fatalistic	**Too much regulation**. The individual is too highly controlled by society.	Suicides of **prisoners** or **slaves**.

Durkheim has been Criticised by some Positivist Sociologists

Positivists try to use scientific methods. See p. 123.

Halbwachs (1930) largely supported Durkheim's conclusions but he pointed out that the impact of **rural** versus **urban** lifestyles on suicide rates hadn't been considered.

Gibbs and Martin (1964) argued that Durkheim hadn't used vigorous enough scientific methods even though he'd stressed how important they were. The key concepts of **integration** and **regulation** weren't **defined** closely enough to be **measured statistically**. Gibbs and Martin query how anyone can **know** what "**normal**" levels of integration and regulation are.

Suicide

Interpretivist sociologists have devised Alternative Theories of Suicide

Interpretivist sociologists say social reality isn't a series of "social facts" for sociologists to discover, but a series of different **meanings** and **interpretations** that each person brings to and takes from each situation.

Durkheim's work is **fatally flawed** from this perspective because he relies on the **unquestioning** use of official **statistics**. According to interpretivists, **statistics aren't fact** — they're a **social construction** based on the definitions of the people who compile them. In other words, statistics give you **one picture** of society, not the **only picture**.

Douglas (1967) said there was a need to categorise suicides according to their **social meanings** because the **triggers** and **response** to suicide are **different** in **different cultures**.

Douglas identified **four social meanings** for suicides in modern industrial societies.

1) **Transformation** of the **soul** (e.g. a way of getting to heaven).

2) **Transformation** of the **self** (e.g. a way of getting people to view you differently).

3) Achieving **sympathy**.

4) Achieving **revenge**.

Baechler (1979) used **case studies** for his research into the meanings behind suicides. He concluded suicide was an action **chosen** by individuals to **solve a problem** when all other solutions had **failed**. Suicide is one response to the social circumstances an individual is in.

Atkinson asked, "How do deaths get Categorised as suicide?"

There is a **social process** involved in a death becoming **labelled** as a **suicide**.

1) **Atkinson (1978)** studied coroners' courts and suggested that coroners use their own **interpretations** and **definitions** in order to define a death as **suicide**.

2) He thought that coroners had a **"typical biography"** of a suicide victim to compare the case against — the more factors **fitted**, the more likely they'd record the death as suicide. For example, the deaths of **young single men** were more likely to be labelled suicide than those of **middle-aged married men**.

Coroners don't have to record a death as suicide, murder or accident. They can record an open verdict if they aren't 100% sure.

3) Atkinson concludes suicide statistics are **not facts** but reflections of **coroners' interpretations**.

Critics of Atkinson have said that, although the suicide statistics are **socially constructed**, they follow a **clear set of criteria** which are **shared**, and therefore there will be **consistency** in the figures.

Taylor identified a number of Factors that influence Inquests

1) Over a twelve-month period, **Steve Taylor (1990)** studied **32 cases** where people had been struck and killed by London tube trains, **without** having left **suicide notes**.

2) The inquests into the **32 deaths** recorded **17 suicides**, **5 accidental deaths** and **10 open verdicts** (i.e. the cause of death isn't given). In cases without suicide notes, Taylor concluded that a suicide verdict was far **more likely** if the victim had a **history of mental illness** or had suffered a **recent setback** or **humiliation**. A coroner was also more likely to record a suicide verdict if it was found that the person concerned had **no clear reason** to have been **at the underground station** at the time.

3) Like Atkinson, Taylor believed that suicide **statistics** were **unreliable**.

Practice Questions

Q1 What are the two reasons why the study of suicide is so important to sociology as a discipline?

Q2 What did Durkheim mean by "regulation" and "integration" in society?

Q3 What does Atkinson suggest about the social construction of suicide?

Exam Question

Q1 Assess the view that suicide statistics tell us more about the values and interpretations of coroners than they reveal about the causes of suicide.

(21 marks)

On a more cheerful note, section five has just ended...

This all ties in with the stuff on sociological methods in section eight. Suicide, although a terrible downer, is something that sociologists find deeply fascinating. Never let it be said that sociologists aren't an odd bunch. The key is to understand Durkheim's theory, where he got his data from, and why he's criticised by positivists and interpretivists.

Stratification

This section is for **AQA** and **OCR**. These two pages are technically only for AQA, but they're useful background for OCR. This section is related to the Section 8 sociological methods stuff — there's tons there about applying research methods to this topic.

Societies are Stratified — divided into Layers

This topic is called 'Exploring Social Inequality and Difference' in the OCR specification.

Stratification means the way societies are divided into **layers**. The **richest** and **most powerful** are at the **top**, the **poorest** and **most powerless** are at the **bottom**. In between are lots of **strata** (layers, like the layers in rock) organised in a **hierarchy**.

A **stratified** society can contain inequalities of **status**, **income**, **class**, **religion**, **ethnicity**, **gender** and **age**.

Social class is the main stratification system in **modern**, **Western capitalist societies** like the **UK**. Social class is partly based on **economic** factors — **jobs**, **income** and **wealth**. Social class also has elements of **power** and **prestige**.

Other stratification systems include the caste system used in India, and the feudal system used in medieval Britain.

Sociologists often talk about Four Social Classes in the UK

1) The **upper class** are **wealthy** and **powerful**. The original upper class was the **landowning aristocracy**. Their wealth is **passed on from generation to generation**. People who have made a lot of money from business or from the entertainment industry are also sometimes considered to be upper class.

2) The **middle class** earn their money from **non-manual work**. Teachers, doctors, managers and pretty much anyone who **earns their living sitting in an office** are middle class. The middle class is **getting bigger** because there are **more non-manual jobs** these days, and fewer manual jobs.

3) The **working class** make their money from **manual work**. Farm labourers and factory workers are working class. The working class have **poorer life chances** than the middle class.

4) The **underclass** get their money from **state benefits**. They include the long-term unemployed and the homeless. The underclass have **the poorest life chances**.

Sociologists have most often focused on the division between the middle class and the working class.

Marx divided society into just Two Social Classes

1) The **proletariat** (workers) produce goods of economic value. According to Marx, they don't own the means of production — all they own and control is their own labour power.

2) The **bourgeoisie** (bosses) own the means of production. Marx said they exploit workers in order to generate profit.

3) There wasn't a clearly defined **middle class** at the time when Marx was writing his economic theories.

See p.94 for more on Marxist stratification.

Relating Class to Occupation poses Problems

1) Occupation does bring **status** and **prestige** with it. People **judge** each other by the jobs they do.

2) Two individuals in the **same occupational class** can have very different **income** and **prestige** status — e.g. a highly paid consultant neurologist compared to a low paid junior doctor.

3) Basing class entirely on occupation misses out most of the **upper class** — a lot of them **don't have jobs** as such, but live off **rental income** from property, and income from **share ownership**.

'A job? I'm far too wealthy for one of those...'

A good social class scheme must **represent** what people in society **really think** about the **status** that goes with each occupational class — it must be **devised** and **tested** by **research**. There are far **too many occupations** for a research sample to say what they think of them **all**, so sociologists usually ask individuals about 20 or so **common** and **representative occupations**. They make inferences about the rest of the occupations in society — which is the tricky bit.

The Government used to use a scale of Five Classes called the RG scale

1) This scale is called the **Registrar General's Scale** (RG scale), and was used until 2000.

2) The **never employed** aren't included, and **unemployed** people are classified according to their **last job**.

3) The RG scale is based on the **head of household's** occupation (usually the man).

4) **Married women** were classified according to their **husband's job** — this was **sexist**.

5) Also, because the RG scale only considered the head of household's job, it didn't matter what kind of job **other people in the home** had. For example, it **wouldn't distinguish** between a household made up of **two lawyers** and a household made up of a **lawyer** and a **cleaner**.

6) There can be **huge variations** in **income** and **life chances** between different occupations within a class.

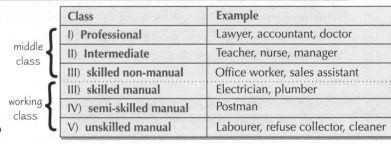

	Class	Example
middle class {	I) **Professional**	Lawyer, accountant, doctor
	II) **Intermediate**	Teacher, nurse, manager
	III) **skilled non-manual**	Office worker, sales assistant
working class {	III) **skilled manual**	Electrician, plumber
	IV) **semi-skilled manual**	Postman
	V) **unskilled manual**	Labourer, refuse collector, cleaner

"Head of household" meant highest male earner, or if no male, highest female earner.

Stratification

The *Government* now uses a scale of *Eight Classes* called the *NS-SEC*

Since 2000, the **government** has used a new scale — the **National Statistics Socio-Economic Classification** (NS-SEC). The NS-SEC has **eight classes** based on type of **employment**, rather than **skill level**:

1) **higher managerial and professional**	Lawyer, doctor, company director
2) **lower managerial and professional**	Nurse, social worker, police officer
3) **intermediate**	Secretary, personal assistant, paramedic
4) **small employers and self-employed**	Owner of a restaurant, self-employed plumber
5) **lower supervisory and technical**	Builder's foreman, sales floor supervisor in a shop
6) **semi-routine**	Postman, receptionist, sales assistant in a shop
7) **routine**	Waitress, van driver, farm labourer, cleaner
8) **never worked and long-term unemployed**	Last worked more than a year ago

Class 1 can be divided into a) large employers and managers, and b) higher professional.

1) The NS-SEC is based on three areas:

- **Employment relations** — whether someone is an **employer**, **self-employed** or **employed**, whether they're **salaried** or paid a **weekly wage**, and how large an organisation they work in. *This is Weberian — see p.95.*
- **Labour market situation** — income, benefits and job security, promotion prospects.
- **Work situation** — where the person is in the **workplace hierarchy**, and how much **control** they have at work.

2) The RG scale was replaced by the NS-SEC because of the recent changes in **employment patterns**. There were fewer **manual** workers and far more workers in **service industries**, so **skill level** was no longer a good way to classify workers.

3) The NS-SEC takes into account changes in social position of some occupations (e.g. shop assistants).

4) Each **individual worker** is classified, rather than classifying a whole **household** by one person's job.

5) The NS-SEC still doesn't account for the "idle rich" — wealthy **upper class** people who don't need jobs.

Class can be defined both *Objectively* and *Subjectively*

1) An **objective** definition of social class is based on something **definite** which can be **measured** or **classified**, e.g. income or occupation — the NS-SEC is an **objective** way of defining social class.

2) A **subjective** definition relies on factors which **can't be measured** — e.g. what an individual feels their social class position is. For instance a **self-made millionaire** may be **middle class** by all **objective** standards of wealth and income, but may still **perceive** themselves to be **working class**, have working class friends and share a working class culture.

Traditional Class Analysis tended to Ignore Women

The old RG scale classified the social class of all members of a family by reference to the occupation of the **head of the household** (usually the **man**). **Michelle Stanworth (1984)** suggested that by using this sociologists miss some important issues, saying that often the social class experience of women within a household is very different to that of the men.

Stanworth's ideas have been backed up by research into social mobility by **Abbott and Payne (1990)**. They concluded that women were far **less likely** to be **upwardly mobile** than their husbands and partners and that those very few women who were upwardly mobile didn't get much further than social class 3. There's more about women and social mobility on p105.

Practice Questions

Q1 Give one problem of using occupation to measure class.

Q2 What class was missing from the Registrar General's scale?

Q3 Give an example of a semi-routine occupation from the NS-SEC scheme.

Q4 What's the difference between subjective and objective definitions of social class?

Exam Question

Q1 Assess the validity of judging social class solely on occupation. (40 marks)

Oh how I wish this was a classless society — there'd be less to learn...

What a lot of class schemes. For the bare basics, learn the NS-SEC, the RG scale, and the differences between them. If you want to look like you're really on the ball, you can mention that class/occupation schemes can be Marxist (based on economics and income) or Weberian (based on labour market position and employment relations). The NS-SEC is well Weberian. Innit.

Class Inequality and Stratification

*Pages 92-102 are for **both OCR and AQA**. So, there's no dispute that power, status and economic assets aren't equally distributed within society. There is an awful lot of debate about why, though. A sociologist's answer depends on their fundamental beliefs about the nature of society. Off we go again...*

The **Higher** an individual's **Social Class**, the **Better Chances** they have in life

This is almost **common knowledge** — but in sociology you have to give **evidence** to go along with common knowledge stuff.

1) Class affects an individual's chances from birth. The chances of a child dying before their first birthday are much higher if they're born into a lower social class.

Infant Mortality Rates in the UK (per 1000 live births)	1991	2001
Professional class	5.1	3.6
Unskilled Manual Class	8.2	7.2
Overall rate	5.3	4.6

Social Trends 33, (2003)

2) When a child goes to school, their chances of achieving **good results** are better if they're in a higher social class.

3) When they go on to work they're more likely to become unemployed if they're from a working class background — **Goldthorpe and Payne (1986)**.

% achieving 5 or more A-C GCSE grades	2002
Higher professional	77%
Routine workers	32%

Social Trends 34, (2004)

4) If they stay in work they're more likely to be paid less in a lower class occupation than in a middle class occupation.

5) An individual is more likely to suffer ill health and poor medical resources if they're working class. The **Black Report (1980)** and **Acheson Report (1998)** document this in detail.

Average Gross Weekly Incomes 2002	
Non-manual (men)	£608
Manual (men)	£366

Social Trends 33, references 2002 New Earnings Survey

6) Finally, social class affects how long a person lives.

Average Age at Death 1997-99	Men	Women
Professional class	78.5	82.8
Unskilled manual class	71.1	77.1
Overall	75.0	79.7

There's more on health inequalities according to class, gender, and ethnicity in the AS course.

Functionalists say the **Class System** helps society to **Run Smoothly**

1) Functionalism says that society is a **meritocracy** — the most able people rise to the top.

2) Fundamental to **functionalism** (try saying that quickly...) is the **strong belief** that the class system enables each individual to find their **right place** and **role** in society.

3) Functionalists say that the **most important** positions in society must be filled by the brightest and most able people.

4) According to **functionalism**, the people who do well in terms of the common values of society will be at the top of the stratification system. High **status**, **power** and high income are **rewards** for conforming to society's values.

5) Most people **don't object** to people in powerful positions getting **extra status** and **rewards**. According to functionalists, this shows that they support the values which underpin the system.

Talcott Parsons was an influential functionalist

1) Parsons established the functionalist position that stratification is **inevitable** and **useful** in all societies.

2) He argued that stratification systems **evaluate** individuals in terms of **common social values** — high status is a reward for **conforming** to society's values.

3) In Parsons' view, stratification **reinforces** the **collective goals** of society and establishes **order**.

I know my place

Me too. Comforting, isn't it.

I doubt Parsons was thinking about strata in rock...

Davis and Moore (1945) argue that without a stratification system, society would break down

1) According to Davis and Moore, stratification has the function of **role allocation**. It makes sure the most able and talented do the most important jobs.

2) **Inequality in reward** (pay) and **status** are essential to **motivate** the best individuals to take on the most important roles and jobs. These roles usually require long periods of training. High rewards compensate people for spending a long time in education and training.

This argument may sound familiar — it's often used to justify high rewards given to company directors and even famous sports stars.

Class Inequality and Stratification

The New Right argue that the Social Stratification system is Unequal but Fair

New Right thinking became popular in the 1980s. It's based on **19th century liberalism**, which saw the **free market** as the **best** way of sorting out everything in society from boredom to backache. The New Right say **governments shouldn't intervene in the market** or promote equality as this takes away motivation for people to **pull themselves up by their bootstraps**.

New Right thinking is sometimes known as **neo-functionalism** (or **political functionalism**) because it pursues similar themes.

1) **Peter Saunders (1990)** is a key British New Right sociologist. **Saunders** argues that societies with stratification systems based on economic differences aren't inevitable (as Parsons thought), but they are a good idea.

2) Saunders says **stratification** is a good idea because **unequal rewards motivate** people to **work hard**. He says that in a society with equal rewards, some people wouldn't pull their weight. He sees physical force as the only alternative to unequal rewards — and obviously prefers unequal rewards.

3) Saunders says that **inequality** promotes **economic growth**. Individuals are motivated to **start businesses** so that they can make money, which **benefits society** by creating **jobs** and **wealth**. He points to the rise in small businesses and entrepreneurs in modern society to demonstrate how anyone can do well if they work hard enough.

4) New Right thinkers like Saunders believe in legal equality and **equality of opportunity**, rather than **equality of outcome**. Saunders says that it's more important for society to be a **meritocracy** than for society to be **equal**.

5) In a **free market**, market forces control who earns what, according to the **supply of talent** and **demand for talent**. People whose skills are highly **demanded**, but in short **supply**, can earn a lot of money. A system based on the free market is **unequal** (some people earn a lot more than others), but it's **fair** according to New Right thinkers.

1) **Saunders (1996)** sees Britain as pretty **close** to being a **meritocracy**. He thinks that **economic rewards** match up with **merit** and **ability**.

2) He argues that what **looks** like **inequality of opportunity** between middle class and working class is actually caused by **inequality of ability** and **effort**. In other words, he thinks that middle class children **deserve** better jobs because they're more able, and they work harder.

Not surprisingly, this view is highly controversial...

Critics of Functionalism and New Right theory claim it Isn't Fair At All

1) **Tumin (1953)** criticised functionalism, and claimed that there's actually **inequality of opportunity** in society.

2) He also criticised Davis and Moore's ideas that some jobs are more **functionally important** than others. In any case, the usefulness and importance of a job doesn't seem to match up to the rate of **pay**. Tumin pointed out that **pay inequality** between groups may be to do with differences in **bargaining power**, rather than differences in usefulness.

3) Tumin argued that instead of **motivating** people, stratification could actually be a **barrier to motivation**.

4) Critics of functionalism also point out that the functionalist view of stratification **ignores the negatives**. Stratification is a system of haves and have-nots, and people in the bottom strata can feel **excluded** from society.

5) **Gordon Marshall** and **Adam Swift (1993)** say that capitalist societies are not as **meritocratic** as the New Right claim. They argue the **free market** does not guarantee a **fair chance** for all. Opportunities vary according to which class you are born into — for example, inherited wealth makes it easier to start a business. **Luck** can play a part in success, too.

6) Evidence shows that people from **working class** backgrounds are **less likely** than middle class people to get top jobs — even when they have the **same educational qualifications**. **Class** plays a part even when people have **equal ability**.

Practice Questions

Q1 In what way did Parsons say that stratification was useful for society?

Q2 Explain what Davis and Moore mean by role allocation.

Q3 Why does Saunders say stratification is a good idea?

Q4 Give one criticism of New Right thinking on stratification.

Exam Question

Q1 Examine the view that social inequality is an inevitable product of a successful society. (12 marks)

New Wrong thinking had even more critics than usual...

There's a pattern to Sociology teaching at A-level: you study the main theories about each topic and then evaluate and compare them... It's a good approach because it teaches you to look at topics from different points of view. It can get a bit repetitive though. Functionalist, Marxist and interpretivist views come up over and over again. What about Zoroastrian views? Huh?

Class Inequality and Stratification

Surprise — some more theories of stratification! Sorry, I should have warned you on the last page. That was a cruel trick.

Marxists *see stratification as a* Deliberately Divisive *tool for* Exploiting *workers*

1) For Marx, **class** was the key to understanding **absolutely everything** in society. And I mean e-v-e-r-y-t-h-i-n-g.

2) Marx argued there are **only two classes** (strata) in society — the **proletariat** and the **bourgeoisie**.
For Marx, a class is a **social group** who share the **same relationship** to the means of **production**.

Producers	Proletariat or subject class	Majority	Only own their labour	Poor
Non-producers	Bourgeoisie or ruling class	Minority	Own the means of production	Wealthy

The ruling class own the means of production

1) Those who own the means of production can control both the **price** at which they **sell** the goods produced, and the **wages** they pay those who produce the goods.

2) It's only by paying the workers **less** than they **sell** the goods for that they can make a **profit**. It is this profit which gives them the **wealth** and **power** to **control** the rest of society in their own interests.

The subject class are the producers

1) They **don't own** the means of production. They only own their **labour**. Because they only own their labour power they have **very little control** in society.

2) They're **completely dependent** on the **ruling class** for **wages** to live on.

1) Marx argued that all other forms of power come from **economic** power.

2) Marxism says the **education** system, **legal** system, **police** and **media** are all instruments of ruling class power. This is because those with **economic power** also have the power to **shape** and **control** the institutions in society. According to Marxism, all these institutions serve to keep the subject class in its place — powerless.

3) The ruling class also use **institutions** in society to **control ideas** and **values** in society — via the **dominant ideology**. For example, the notion that capitalist society is meritocratic and anyone can get to the top is a "false truth" according to Marxism. **Institutions** in society such as education spread this idea, and everyone's happy in the belief that society is fair. This is **useful to the ruling class** — it prevents workers from rising up and starting a revolution.

Marx *thought that* Workers *should have a* Revolution *and bring in* Communism

Marx thought society could be **equal** if the **means of production** were owned by **everyone**, so everyone benefited rather than a few. He was certain this would be the end result of capitalism — workers would eventually realise their power and strength, and overthrow the ruling class in a **revolution**, creating a new equal society which Marx called **communism**.

The 20th century saw the **start** and **end** of some large-scale communist societies such as the USSR. The **failure** of these communist societies, and the high levels of both **corruption** and **inequality in communist societies** have caused many sociologists to say that Marx was wrong and **egalitarian societies aren't possible**.
Modern Marxists argue that the USSR and China **weren't true communism**.

China is still officially communist, but it's adopted "capitalism with Chinese characteristics", a mixture of both ideologies.

Neo-Marxist *theories of stratification try to explain the* Middle Class

Traditional Marxism didn't predict the growth of a large **middle class** such as the UK experienced over the twentieth century. Modern Marxists have grappled with different ways of explaining this.

1) **Erik Olin Wright (1978, 1989)** developed a Marxist analysis of class which explained the middle class of salaried professionals which grew in the late 20th century. This group have some control over the means of production, and may own bits of it, but they don't control large sections of labour power. This group is called the **petty bourgeoisie**.

2) Wright says these individuals may experience **"contradictory class locations"** — they have **things in common** with **both** classes at **different** times. For example, they may own shares (part-ownership of modern means of production) but may also lose their livelihood at the will of the ruling class (e.g. if they lose their job, or the share price falls).

3) Wright concludes that **class conflict** and **exploitation** are more **complicated** in the late 20th (and now 21st) century than Marx predicted but **class** is **still** the basis of **power** and **wealth** in society.

4) **Edgell (1993)** accuses Wright of leaving Marx behind and having more in common with **Weber**.

The **key message** from neo-Marxists is: **don't dismiss Marx's theory completely** just because he didn't focus on the middle class.

Class Inequality and Stratification

Weber argued Class is "Unequal Access to Material Resources"

Weber considered many of the same issues as Marx. Like Marx, he argued class and stratification come from an **economic** basis. Unlike Marx, he didn't go into any detailed predictions about the future, or analysis of the past.

Weber said that there are **three distinct areas** or forms of **stratification** in modern society.

Class power	Economic power to access material goods and resources in society.
Social power	Status and prestige, and being respected by others.
Party power	Political power and ability to influence decision-making.

These tend to be **interlinked** in real life — a person with **social power** is also likely to have **political** and **economic** power.

1) **Weber** concentrated on class power. He argued that an individual's **class power** and **class position** derives from their market position — i.e. their **economic chances**, and their ability to **control** their **wages** and **working conditions**.

2) An individual's **market position** varies partly depending on how in **demand** their skills and talents are — i.e. how much an employer is willing to pay for their services. Be careful though — market position isn't just an individual's ability to get a job. It also covers their **ownership** of **property** and **assets** (e.g. shares).

3) For Weberians, stratification isn't a case of **two classes** opposed to each other (Marx) or a **competitive meritocracy** (Functionalism and New Right) but a **complex** hierarchy of layers, each with their own class or market position.

Neo-Weberian Theory influences modern Class Schemes

The NS-SEC system (see p91) was developed from Goldthorpe's own classification system.

The big name in neo-Weberian theory of class is John **Goldthorpe**. For his 1972 study of social mobility (see p104), Goldthorpe categorised **seven classes** based on occupation, with **three main classes** — service class ("white collar" professionals), intermediate class and working class.

An individual's **class position** is the **market position** he or she has in the **labour market**.

When the labour market **changes**, it may be necessary to **re-categorise** the classes.

Goldthorpe has been criticised for **neglecting** the position of **women** in the labour market — e.g. by **Arber**, **Dale** and **Gilbert (1986)**.

Pete was so professional he didn't even need a collar...

Postmodern theory argues that Class isn't as Important as it used to be

1) Postmodernists claim that **other differences** such as gender, age and ethnicity are **at least** as important.

2) **Pakulski and Waters (1996)** say that **cultural differences** (values, lifestyles and beliefs) are what classify individuals into particular groups or strata in current society — not economic position.

3) Crucially, they say individuals can **define themselves** as belonging to social groups or social strata and **freely move** from one to another by choosing their **lifestyle** and **identity**.

4) Pakulski and Waters **criticise** the rest of sociology for still focusing so much on **class** when they feel that other forms of **inequality** and **identity** are more relevant.

Practice Questions

Q1   What are the two classes described by Marx?
Q2   What is the "petty bourgeoisie"?
Q3   What three types of power does Weber acknowledge?
Q4   What do postmodernists say about class?

Exam Question

Q1   Assess the importance of class in British society from different sociological perspectives.   (40 marks)

You should have guessed when there were no Marxists on the last page...

You knew deep inside it was too good to be true. Marx ignores the middle class, mainly because there wasn't really a middle class in the 1840s. Neo-Marxists acknowledge that society today is more complex. Weberians base everything on labour market position. And postmodernists pop up to say that class doesn't exist in a postmodern world, and that identities are all self-built anyway.

Changes in the Class Structure

The British stratification system underwent considerable change in the 20th century — alongside changes in society.

There have been Changes in Work Patterns and Wealth/Income Distribution

1) There are **fewer** people in **manual** jobs and **more** people in **non-manual** jobs compared to the early 20th century.

2) Service industries such as **leisure** have grown, and primary and manufacturing industry has decreased.

3) A higher percentage of **women** now work — this has risen from 56% of working-age women in 1971 to nearer 70% now.

4) Between 1945 and 1980 income and wealth became more **evenly distributed**.
   However, from 1980 onwards, the wealth/income gap has actually started to **widen** again.

5) Many state controlled industries were **privatised** in the 1980s and 1990s.

This made private business more powerful and also increased share ownership.

6) One thing hasn't changed massively — most **wealth** is still owned by a small **minority**.

The Ruling Class has Changed — opinions differ on just How Much

The New Right say that the ruling class has disintegrated.

Peter Saunders (1990) argues that the increase in the number of people **owning shares** in the UK has led to power being spread more widely. The small minority in power has been replaced with a **nation of stakeholders**.

Marxists insist the ruling class is alive and kicking.

1) **John Scott (1982, 1991)** agrees with Saunders that **more and more people own shares** in the UK but argues this hasn't led to a break-up of the ruling class. Most individuals own a **few** shares but hold **very little** real **power**.

2) Scott, and **Westergaard and Resler (1976)** say there's still a **power elite** who control business and the economy.

The Middle Class has Grown, but may be Breaking Up into Several Classes

1) Functionalist and Weberian sociologists cite the rise of the **professions** (e.g. teachers, doctors, lawyers) as evidence of an expanding middle class.

2) **Embourgeoisement** means working class people **becoming middle class** in lifestyle and values as their incomes increase. It was a popular idea with sociologists in the 1950s and 1960s.

3) **Goldthorpe et al (1968)** tested the embourgeoisement thesis by interviewing car workers in Luton. They concluded that affluence had **not** made the workers middle class, and clear differences remained between them and the non-manual middle class workers — e.g. their attitudes to work and possibility of future promotion.

Some say the middle class is fragmenting into several middle classes with different life-chances and experiences.

1) **Goldthorpe** says there's an **Intermediate Class** of low grade non-manual workers who have little in common with middle class professionals. In terms of wages, perks, and relationship with employers, these groups are totally distinct.

2) Marxist **Harry Braverman (1974)** says many non-manual workers have been de-skilled by technology, so that they now have more in common with the working class in terms of job security and wealth. This is **proletarianisation**.

3) **Roberts et al (1977)** interviewed "middle class" workers about their view of their own class position and found wide variations in how groups saw themselves. They concluded the middle class is being fragmented into smaller strata.

4) Influential sociologist **Giddens (1973)** disagrees — he says there's a **distinct middle class**. The middle class is distinct from the working class because its members can sell their "**brain power**" as well as, or **instead** of, their **labour power**.

Postmodernists Pakulski and Waters (1996) have declared that Class is Dead

Pakulski and Waters give the following evidence to suggest that **class** and therefore **class analysis** in social science is **dead**:

1) **Wealth** became more **equally distributed** during the 20th century. This means not only that economic class differences are less pronounced, but that more people have more **spare cash** to spend on consumer goods. Pakulski and Waters argue that people **define themselves** and **judge each other** based on what kind of things they buy.

2) **Educational status** has become **more important** in deciding life chances, and class background less important.

3) There's a **new postmodern politics** based on non-economic issues such as ethnicity, identity, and the environment.

4) People are **less likely** to **vote along class lines** — e.g. manual workers no longer vote for left-wing parties (see p.58).

5) Pakulski and Waters claim that **globalisation** has lessened the importance of class inequality within countries.

Pakulski and Waters argue society changed from an **economic class society** in the 19th century, to a **hierarchical class society** in the first half of the 20th century, to a **status society** in the late 20th century.

However, Marxist sociologist **John Westergaard (1995)** suggests that because gaps between rich and poor are widening and big business is more powerful, class is becoming **more** significant in the late 20th and early 21st century — not less significant.

Changes in the Class Structure

The 20th Century has Weakened and Divided the British Working Class

The decline in the **traditional working class** sectors of **manufacturing** and **heavy industry** in the 20th century has **reduced** the **size** of the British **working class**.

1) **Ralph Dahrendorf (1959)** argues that instead of uniting, the working class has disintegrated.

2) He said that the working class has been divided into groups of **skilled**, **semi-skilled** and **unskilled** workers, and that this is because of changes in technology.

3) Dahrendorf is criticised by **Penn (1983)**, whose research into cotton mills in Rochdale suggests that the working class has been divided into skilled, semi-skilled and unskilled since at least the **1850s**.

4) **Crewe (1983)** argues that the working class is splitting into groups with different concerns and interests, so it can no longer be considered a "real" class. He says that there's a **"new working class"** who live mainly in the South, work in the private sector and own their own homes. They have very different life experiences to the "old working class" who live mainly in the North, in council houses, and work in the public sector.

The idea that the working class is on its way out has been criticised, particularly by Marxist sociologists.

1) Marxist sociologists say that the working class can change its occupation and still be working class.

2) **Beynon (1992)** points out that the old working class jobs have been replaced by new occupations which are **equally badly paid** with poor conditions and rights — e.g. call centres, fast-food outlets and hotels. Beynon says that **cooking burgers** is **manual**, **repetitive labour**, just like working on an assembly line in a factory.

3) Marxists argue what hasn't changed is the **status**, **rights** and **power** that go with the employment — the lack of these things is what makes it working class.

Remember the connection to **globalisation** (see glossary) — part of the reason that manufacturing working class jobs have vanished in the UK is because they've **moved abroad** to cheaper labour markets. There's an **"international division of labour"**. Globally, the **working class** includes workers in **South East Asia** and **China** who have few rights and low pay.

Some Sociologists say there is a growing Underclass below the working class

The idea that the most **disadvantaged** groups in society are a **separate group** from the working class isn't **new**. Marx referred to the "lumpenproletariat" (beggars, pickpockets) and the "relative surplus" (people who aren't part of the regular labour market, but who do casual labour when needed). The idea of an underclass has gained support in the late 20th century.

1) The New Right see the underclass as dangerous to society. American sociologist **Charles Murray (1989)** defines the underclass by **behaviour** — **uneducated**, **delinquent** and **work-shy**.

2) **Runciman (1990)** defines the underclass as people who are **permanently dependent** on **welfare benefits**.

3) **Giddens (1973)** defines the underclass as the **most disadvantaged** in the job market — e.g. illegal immigrants. He says there's a **secondary job market** of **low-paid** jobs with **low job security**, which are the best the underclass can get.

4) **Dahrendorf (1987)** argued that the underclass is **growing rapidly**. This may be because of globalisation — as manual work now goes overseas, there is less demand for manual workers. Also as the labour market becomes more **flexible**, there's much more **insecure**, **temporary** or **casual** low-paid work.

Practice Questions

Q1 Identify two long-term trends which have affected the British class structure in the 20th century.
Q2 Explain Saunders' argument that the ruling class is no longer relevant in modern Britain.
Q3 Explain what sociologists mean by the terms embourgeoisement and proletarianisation.

Exam Questions

Q1 Examine the argument put forward by some sociologists that the working class has become so divided in the 20th century that it can no longer be considered a "real" class. (12 marks)

Q2 Evaluate the reasons put forward by sociologists for changes in the British class structure in the 20th century. (40 marks)

Breaking up is so very hard to do...

There are a ridiculous number of sociologists on this page. I know it's a Sociology book, but still. I mean, for heaven's sake. It starts off OK until we reach Peter Saunders, and then they just start closing in on you. Scott starts agreeing and Goldthorpe starts testing and then Giddens disagrees and Penn criticises Dahrendorf... please, sociologists, just give it a rest. Seriously.

Inequality, Stratification and Gender

Traditionally gender and stratification was a neglected area of sociology.
Feminist sociologists however have identified it as an important area which should be studied in its own right.

Sociologists say that **Sex** and **Gender** are different things

1) Sex refers to the **physical** and **biological** differences between men and women.

2) Gender refers to the **socially constructed roles** of what's considered "**masculine**" and what's considered "**feminine**".

3) Sociologists don't see gender roles as fixed. Because they're created by society and don't depend purely on a person's sex, gender roles can therefore **change over time** and can be very **different** in different **cultures**. Sociologists like to try to understand the reasons for the construction of gender roles.

Women experience **Inequalities** in the **Stratification System**

1) In the UK, women **earn less** than men and are **less likely** to be in the **top jobs**. There's still a "**glass ceiling**". In sociology-speak, the labour market is "**vertically** segregated in terms of gender" (men on one level, women on another).

'In my day, the only glass ceiling was the one in the conservatory...'

- In 1996, **23%** of board members of **British government bodies** were women.
- After the labour election win of 1997 there were many **new women MPs** (they were known at the time as "Blair's babes") but even with this increase only **18% of MPs** were women
- In 1994-5 **93%** of all **professors** in English universities were **men**.

(Office for National Statistics, 2000)

2) Some **occupations** are almost exclusively **female** — e.g. primary school teaching. There are **more women** than men in **clerical** jobs, in **retail**, and in **catering**. There are more **male** than female **building site foremen**. In sociology-speak, the labour market is "**horizontally** segregated in terms of gender" (men on one side and women on another, on the same level of the class hierarchy). Some of these "feminine" jobs may be lower paid than equivalent masculine jobs.

3) There are also **health inequalities** between women and men

- On average **women live** five years **longer** than men, but because the chances of disability increase with age there are many **more** elderly **women** living with **disabilities** than there are men.
- In 2001, it was estimated that **women** aged **15-24** had a **higher risk** of being infected with **HIV** than men of the same age.
- Women are more likely to be **diagnosed** with mental health problems. Some sociologists say this is because of more stressful lives, while others say it's to do with sexism within the medical profession.

Liberal Feminists blame gender inequality on **Discrimination** and **Stereotypes**

1) The first liberal feminists, e.g. J S Mill and Harriet Taylor, were heavily influenced by the ideas of **political liberalism**, specifically **equal rights**, **individualism** and **liberty**. They suggest that once genuine **equal rights** have been established, 'accidents of birth' like sex will become irrelevant in society.

2) To promote equal opportunity, liberal feminists believe in campaigning to change **laws** — from votes for women in the 1920s to the more modern **anti-discrimination** legislation such as the Sex Discrimination Act (1975).

3) Liberal feminists also believe in changing **attitudes**, and overcoming **prejudice** about the roles of men and women.

4) Liberal feminists say **sexism harms everyone**, men as well as women.

Evidence suggests **Anti-Discrimination** laws have **Narrowed** gender inequalities

1) The **1970 Equal Pay Act** and its **1984** "**equal pay for equal work**" amendment helped to narrow the pay gap. The **1975 Sex Discrimination Act** made it illegal to advertise a job for specifically a man or specifically a woman.

2) Between 1970 and 1999 the pay gap between men and women narrowed. In 1970 women in full-time work earned around **63%** of average male earnings and by 2005 this had gone up to around **82%**.

3) However in **2008** the Annual Survey of Hours and Earnings reported that the gap was beginning to **widen** again. The difference in earnings of women and men in full-time employment rose slightly by 0.1% over the year.

4) Women still seem to be disadvantaged in the workplace, holding relatively **few top positions** and being over-represented in relatively **low-paid areas** of employment — administration, services, clerical and secretarial work.

5) The 1984 "equal pay for equal work" amendment says a woman should be paid the same as a man in a job of **equal worth** — but it can be very difficult to decide which jobs are equivalent to each other.

Inequality, Stratification and Gender

Radical Feminists say there is Conflict between All Men and All Women

1) **Patriarchy theory** is favoured by radical feminists. Radical feminists suggest that society is run in the interests of patriarchy — male power. According to this view, men take most of society's rewards and privileges for themselves. Men are the ruling class and women are oppressed.

2) Radical feminists argue that men also use their control of culture to create the belief that **gender inequality** and **patriarchy** are "natural".

3) Sexual oppression is seen as the most fundamental form of inequality, with all others such as class and ethnicity being seen as secondary.

4) Radical feminists want to **free women** from what they see as patriarchal control. Some radical feminists put forward the idea of **separatism**.

It had a lovely big moat to keep all the men out.

5) **Female biology** and the way it's treated by society are seen by radical feminism as a cause of gender inequality.

> **Sherry B Ortner (1974)** says that because women give birth they are seen as **closer to nature** and further from culture than men — and they're therefore seen as **inferior** in society.
>
> **Shulamith Firestone (1970)** asserts that gender inequalities are the direct result of **biology**. She says pregnancy and childbirth lead to physical, psychological and social disadvantages. She claims that gender inequality can only be put right when women take **control** of the **reproduction process**. She advocates **abortion** and **contraception** and ultimately calls for a future where human reproduction takes place in **artificial wombs**.

Marxist feminists blame gender inequality on Capitalism as well as Patriarchy

1) Marxist feminism says that gender inequality can only be understood in a **social and economic** context.

2) From this perspective, it **suits capitalism** that women are exploited by men on many levels. Engels even went as far as to suggest that the emergence of capitalism had resulted in 'the world historical defeat of the female sex'.

3) Marxist feminists say that **capitalism exploits women's work** in specific ways:

- Employers treat women as a **"reserve army of labour"** to be hired and fired as needed.
- Male workers try to **exclude females** from their **trades** and **crafts**.
- Husbands **exploit** their wives' **unpaid housework**.

4) Marxist feminists see the **bourgeois family** in capitalist society as **patriarchical** and **unequal**. They say that this is because it is set up by men in order to pass **property** on from fathers to sons. Women are seen as working for the benefit of this system, rather than for their own benefit. The logic of this argument suggests that **without private property** there would be no need to do this.

5) For Marxist feminists the solution to gender inequalities is therefore the **end of capitalism** through socialist revolution.

Black Feminism and Three Systems theory say Ethnicity is also important

In *Ain't I a Woman?* **(1981) bell hooks** (yes, she does spell her name without capital letters) argues that because they benefit indirectly from living in a racist society, white feminists are not enthusiastic about tackling racism. She says that mainstream white feminism makes the **false claim** that black and white women face **exactly** the **same problems**.

Sylvia Walby (1990) said women are oppressed in three systems: **gender** (through patriarchy), **social class** (through capitalism) and **ethnicity** (through racism). This is known as a **"triple-systems theory"** of patriarchy.

Practice Questions

Q1 What is the difference between sex and gender?

Q2 Give three pieces of evidence that there is gender inequality in society today.

Q3 Briefly outline the similarities and differences between liberal, Marxist and radical feminism.

Exam Question

Q1 Assess sociological explanations of gender difference and gender inequality in society. (40 marks)

Ah, more sociological disagreement — always fun...

If you were just flicking through, and not really bothering to revise, you probably wouldn't realise that there are so many different kinds of feminism. So make sure you learn this lot properly. Remember that you can apply these ideas to many other topics that you've studied — e.g. the family, gender inequality in health, religion as patriarchal, representations of women in culture.

Inequality, Stratification and Ethnicity

Lots of evidence suggests that different ethnic groups have different chances in society.

Sociologists make a distinction between **Ethnicity** and **Race**

1) **"Race"** as a word is usually used to refer to groups sharing a particular physical or biological set of characteristics (usually skin colour). Sociologists however **reject** the concept of "race" for two very important reasons:

   - There's **no scientific basis** to ideas of race — the genetic differences between groups of humans are tiny.
   - Ideas of race were largely **discredited** in the early to mid-20th century with pseudo-scientific ideas such as Social Darwinism being used to justify horrendous persecution in places such as Nazi Germany.

2) Instead, sociologists prefer the concept of **ethnicity**, which places emphasis on **culture** (shared norms and values) rather than on spurious biological differences. **Ethnicity** is therefore something which is **socially constructed**.

3) There are still **difficulties** in using the concept of ethnicity, though. Many ethnic groups are **huge** and subdivided into very different subgroups, e.g. "Asian" covers an enormous range of different cultural experiences.

Ethnic Minorities are more likely to experience **Discrimination** and **Inequality**

1) **8%** of the current UK population belong to an **ethnic minority** — Social Trends 33 (2003).

2) People in households headed by someone from an **ethnic minority** are more likely to be at the **bottom** of the **income scale** than those where the head of household is **white** — Social Trends 33 (2003). *It's important to distinguish between different ethnic minority groups.*

3) **Bangladeshi** and **Pakistani** groups have the **highest unemployment** rates in the UK.

> In the UK in 2001-2002, **21%** of working-age **Bangladeshis** were unemployed and **16%** of **Pakistanis**, compared with **4%** of the **white** population, **6%** of the **Chinese** population and **7%** of the **Indian** population.

(Annual Labour Force Survey, reported in Social Trends 33, 2003)

4) **Bangladeshis**, **Pakistanis** and **Black Caribbeans** were **least likely** to be in the **highest socio-economic group** (higher managers and professionals).

> In 2001-2002, of people in employment, **3% Bangladeshis**, **4% Pakistanis** and **5% Black Caribbeans** were in the highest social economic group, compared to **11% Chinese** and **34% White** (made up of **8% White British**, **10% White Irish** and **16% Other White**).

(Annual Labour Force Survey, reported in Social Trends 34, 2004)

5) People of **Bangladeshi**, **Black African** and **Other Black** origin were **most likely** to live in housing in the **social rented sector** (rented from the council and housing associations). Whites and Indians were most likely to own their home.

> In 2001, **48%** of **Bangladeshis**, **50%** of **Black Africans** and **50%** of **Other Black** were in social rented housing, compared to **8% Indian** and **17% White British**. **79%** of **Indians** and **71%** of **White British** were owner-occupiers.

(2001 census)

Important **public inquiries** have found evidence of **racism** in modern Britain, in many areas of life. The **Gifford Report (1989)** found evidence of **widespread racism** in the police force. The post-Brixton riot **Scarman Report (1981)** said Britain wasn't institutionally racist, but public policy often had **unintended consequences** that **disadvantaged ethnic minorities**. The **Macpherson Report (1999)** into the investigation of the Stephen Lawrence murder said that the police force was **institutionally racist**, and said the recommendations of the Scarman Report had been ignored.

You can use **Examples** of ethnic inequality from **Other Units** you have studied

Education	According to research by **Modood et al (1997)**, Black Caribbean boys are the group most likely to be excluded from school, and Chinese and Indian pupils are the least likely to be excluded. The same research shows Black Caribbean boys are the lowest achievers, and Chinese and Indian pupils the highest achievers.
Health	Pakistani and Bangladeshi people report the **highest** levels of ill health, and Chinese and Indian people the lowest. Government statistics from 1999 show **Bangladeshi men** are more likely to **smoke** than other groups.
Crime	The **British Crime Survey (2000)** shows ethnic minorities are more likely to be **victims** of crime than the majority population, and also more likely to be **arrested** or **imprisoned**.

Patterns of ethnic disadvantage are **Changing** and in many cases **Decreasing**

Andrew Pilkington (1999) gives the following as evidence:

1) Large numbers of people from ethnic minorities have **high status jobs** in non-manual/professional occupations.

2) The **labour market position** of all ethnic minority groups has improved at a faster rate than whites.

3) The **continuing disadvantage** of some ethnic groups (e.g. Bangladeshis) has a lot to do with **cultural** factors — e.g. attitudes to women working outside the home, and linguistic deprivation (not having fluent English) in new immigrants.

Inequality, Stratification and Ethnicity

Functionalists believe Ethnic Inequality is only Temporary

Functionalist **Sheila Patterson (1965)** suggests that disadvantages will gradually melt away as the immigrant communities and the host communities **adjust to each other** and the meritocratic principles of society start to take effect. Patterson says racism and disadvantage are therefore only **temporary** — eventually and inevitably the immigrants take on the values of the host culture and **assimilate** into the host society, and the hosts **accept** the immigrants.

Functionalists cite as evidence the successful assimilation of minority groups in the UK and USA. They have been **criticised** for assuming that assimilation is somehow inevitable and **ignoring** the obstacles of **racism** and **class conflict**.

Marxists suggest that Capitalism Benefits from Ethnic Inequalities

1) **Castles and Kosack (1973)** say that capitalism benefits from having a working class **divided** by ethnic inequality and racial tension — a divided class is easier to rule.

2) They argue that ethnic differences are used to **distract** the working class from the real cause of their problems. For instance, ethnic minorities get the blame for problems such as **unemployment** and **housing shortages**. The power of the working class is diminished so long as some ethnic groups see themselves as **superior** to others. Instead of uniting to start a revolution, the working class **fights amongst itself**.

3) Castles and Kosack say that ethnic division also creates a **reserve army** of **relatively cheap ethnic minority labour**. Capitalism therefore encourages ethnic division and disadvantage.

Weberians see Ethnic Inequalities in terms of Labour Market Position

1) Weberians like **John Rex (1970)** use the term "**underclass**" to mean people who have the lowest social class and lowest social status. They say the underclass are **beneath** the rest of the working class, and **alienated** (cut off) from the rest of the working class. They feel this describes Britain's **ethnic minorities**.

2) **Rex and Tomlinson (1979)** state that there are **two types of job** and **two types of worker**. In the **primary labour market**, workers have secure jobs, good wages, opportunites for training and high status. In the **secondary labour market**, jobs are less secure, wages are low, there are few opportunities for training, and workers are not valued by employers. Their evidence shows a disproportionate number of people from ethnic minorities are in the secondary labour market.

New Right sociologists use Cultural Explanations of ethnic disadvantage

1) New Right theorists like **Charles Murray (1984)** and **Peter Saunders (1996)** believe that most of Western society is meritocratic — in other words, individual ability is rewarded, and lack of ability means lack of rewards.

2) The New Right agree that the **underclass** is disproportionately made up of people from **ethnic minorities**. Because they believe society is a **meritocracy**, they blame ethnic minority groups rather than society, or racism.

3) Murray suggests that the distinct **subculture** of some ethnic minorities causes their disadvantage. He believes that this subculture contains an **unwillingness to work**, a tendency to value criminal activity and a tendency for **single-parent families**. He says this leads to dependency on State welfare benefits and ultimately leads to poverty.

4) New Right ideas have been challenged by sociologists who argue that in "blaming the victim" they **ignore** both the damaging influence of **racism** and the **structural causes** of poverty. **Giddens (1973)** says that **poor access to education** means people from ethnic minorities are often **underskilled** and **underqualified**.

Practice Questions

Q1 Why do sociologists use the term ethnicity and not race?

Q2 Give three pieces of evidence that there are differences in life chances between different ethnic groups.

Q3 Briefly outline the Marxist explanation for ethnic inequality.

Q4 What does Charles Murray blame for ethnic disadvantage?

Exam Questions

Q1 Outline the evidence that some ethnic minorities are disadvantaged in society (20 marks)

Q2 Assess New Right explanations of ethnic inequality. (40 marks)

Sociologists blame the usual suspects...

In other words, it's the fault of the labour market, capitalism or the victim. Functionalists even suggest that ethnic inequalities serve some purpose in society, although I must admit their definition of "purpose" seems to be stretching it a bit. Remember that not all ethnic minorities are poor, or trapped in low-paid work. One of the richest people in Europe is an Indian steel baron.

Inequality, Stratification and Age

*This page is for **OCR** and **AQA**, but page 103 is for **AQA** only.*

Age Categories *are Socially Constructed*

Views about age **aren't fixed** or **universal** — they can change with **time** and vary between different **societies** and cultures.

For example, in traditional societies which venerated age, older people had **high status** due to their accumulated experience. **Modern** societies have such a fast pace of change that this is no longer the case. The elderly are sometimes stereotyped as **out of touch** and their knowledge and experience seen as **irrelevant** to the technological age.

There is *Stratification* by *Age* — both the *Young* and the *Old* face *Inequality*

Older people face disadvantages in society

1) Retirement is frequently accompanied by a **loss of status**, self-respect and influence. Old people may become **socially isolated**, because of the decline of the **extended family**.

2) After retirement, old people are vulnerable to money problems which can lead to **poverty** — particularly for old people who rely on the **state pension**.

3) Historically, older people have faced inequality in the workplace — being **forced to retire** before they want to, or being passed over for promotion or training opportunities due to **stereotyped** views of their **capability**. The **Employment Equality (Age) Regulations 2006** makes it **illegal** to discriminate on the grounds of age.

The law says employers can still discriminate if they really need to in order to meet a "legitimate aim"...

Children and young people also face inequality

1) In work, young people are **paid less** than older workers — this is partly to be expected, as they lack job experience. The **minimum wage** is **lower** for workers under 22 than workers over 22, and lower still for workers under 18.

2) Students in higher education face large **debts** after they graduate. **Student loans** have to be paid back once you're in full-time work and earning over a certain amount.

3) Young people in work often experience **low pay**, low responsibility, and **low status** work. In 2001 around a quarter of a million young people were being paid no more than the **minimum wage**.

4) State benefits such as **Income Support** and **Housing Benefit** are paid at a lower rate to the under 25s.

5) Children and young people experience **discrimination** in society. They are often **stereotyped** as **irresponsible** and lacking the knowledge and experience to make judgements and choices.

6) There are **changes** to patterns of stratification by age. Young people today stay **dependent** for far longer than in earlier generations. Before 1944, people could leave school and start a full-time job at the age of **14**. Recently there's been a big increase in the number of people going on to **further or higher education** rather than straight into full-time work.

There are *Different Sociological Explanations* of *Age Inequality*

Functionalists see age inequality as useful to society

1) Functionalists like **Parsons (1977)** say that passing through age groups has the important function of **integrating people** into society. The **role sets** of the different age groups allow a person to develop **full functioning** in society.

2) There's a criticism — functionalism doesn't explain the role of the **elderly**, who tend to **disengage** from society.

Marxists see age inequality as helping capitalism by providing cheap labour

1) Capitalism benefits from treating young workers differently because they can be **paid less**, and **hired and fired** more easily than more mature workers — and society tends not to object. Paying young people less means more profits can be made. Also the low pay of the young can help to **keep general wages lower**.

2) From a Marxist standpoint the elderly become **irrelevant** and **marginalised**, especially if they are poor. Richer old people who have been able to plan a relatively **affluent retirement** can maintain status in a capitalist society. Once again, Marxist sociologists see **class inequality** as the inequality that takes precedence over all the others.

Weberians explain age inequality by reference to labour market position

1) Both the young and the old have a **poor labour market position** compared to people in middle age.

2) For Weberians, social status and political power are also important in social stratification. Both the old and the young have relatively low **social status**, and may find it difficult to influence **political decision making**.

Inequality, Stratification and Disability

*This page on disability is for the **AQA** exam only.*

Disability affects Life Chances and Social Position

Despite being **overlooked** by sociology for many years, **disability** has a serious impact on a person's life chances.

1) Registered disabled people are around **seven times more likely to be unemployed** than able-bodied people. This is despite recent anti-discrimination legislation which **in theory** makes it **illegal to discriminate** against disabled people. The result is that large numbers of disabled people suffer poverty and live on state benefits.

2) Disabled people in work are more likely to be in **low-paid**, low-skill, **low-status** jobs than the general population.

3) The Low Pay Commission Report (2007) says **disabled women** are more likely to be **unemployed** than disabled men.

People with disabilities have Unequal Access to Education and Leisure

1) Traditionally, disabled people went to **special schools** instead of mainstream schools. At these schools, opportunities and facilities were sometimes limited.

2) Nowadays, many people with disabilities do attend mainstream schools. However, in some cases disabled pupils can't get the **support** they need to get the best out of mainstream education.

3) **Attainment levels** amongst disabled people are considerably **lower** than for able-bodied people, and less than 50% of disabled people continue their education after the school leaving age.

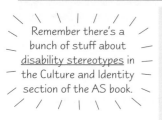
Remember there's a bunch of stuff about <u>disability stereotypes</u> in the Culture and Identity section of the AS book.

1) Despite the Disability Discrimination Act of 1995 making discrimination **illegal**, disabled people still encounter **practical difficulties** in accessing cultural and leisure amenities — e.g. lack of wheelchair ramps, signs that aren't clear enough for the visually impaired etc.

2) They may also experience social **stereotyping** and **social exclusion** from clubs and activities — due to able-bodied people's prejudices about their abilities.

3) Some children and teenagers with disabilities don't have the opportunity to **socialise with other kids** without **adult** carers being present.

Recent Sociology of Disability focuses on Disability as a Social Construct

Traditionally, a **medical model** of disability has shaped society's attitudes towards disabled people.

1) The medical model focuses on the physical impairment and tries to "fix" it.

2) Treatment is **interventionist** — it's something that's done to the disabled person.

3) The medical model can **label** disabled people as **dependent** and **weak**, or "faulty".

More recently, sociologists in the disability movement have suggested that disability discrimination and disadvantage doesn't actually have much to do with actual impairments and is more to do with disabling **social** and **environmental factors** — e.g. attitudes, **stereotypes**, lack of access, and lack of rights. They suggest disability is a **social construct**.

1) This **social model** of disability suggests that it's **society** that needs to be fixed, not people with disabilities.

2) It has prompted changes in **social policy**. The most important is the **Disability Discrimination Act** 1995, which makes **equal access** a legal requirement for employers, shops, schools, bus and train stations etc.

Practice Questions

Q1 Give two ways in which the elderly may face disadvantage in society.

Q2 Give three ways in which children and the young may face disadvantage in society.

Q3 Give two examples of how disability impacts on life chances.

Q4 Explain the difference between the medical and social models of disability.

Exam Question

Q1 Assess sociological explanations of age inequality in society (40 marks)

Not to be ageist or anything, but it's the same "old" story...

Just like with gender inequality and ethnic inequality, there are now laws to make age and disability discrimination illegal. It's not as simple as passing a law and *boom* the inequalities instantly vanish, though. People try to find loopholes in the law to let them carry on doing things the old way. And you still have to change attitudes and stereotypes, which can be a toughie.

Social Mobility

Social mobility is about how easy it is for people to change class, e.g. if you just go next door and start A2 history. **For AQA only.**

But might also be useful for OCR.

Learn these Definitions of Mobility

Social mobility = the movement from one stratum (class) to another.

Intra-generational mobility = social mobility of the same person within their **lifetime**.

Inter-generational mobility = social mobility **between generations** (i.e. does a person stay in the same class as their parents).

Absolute Mobility = how much social mobility there is in the society as a whole.

Relative Mobility = how much social mobility different social groups have relative to each other.

Ascribed status = status given to a person at birth either through family (e.g. being a prince) or through gender or ethnicity.

Achieved status = status resulting from hard work, merit and effort.

Societies which allow for **achieved status** are called **open systems of stratification.** *Open systems have a lot of social mobility, and they're meritocratic.*

Societies where social position is **ascribed** are called **closed systems of stratification.**

The First major study of Social Mobility in Britain was in 1949

Glass (1954) compared social class of fathers and sons

David Glass used statistical data and analysis to compare the class of fathers and sons. He found there was a high level of social mobility — two thirds of sons were in a different social class from their father. This mobility was equally split — one third upward and one third downward.

But, the social mobility was mostly short-range. Most sons moved to the next class up or the next class down. (Glass categorised seven classes.) The study also found that the upper class had fewer people moving in or out of it than the other classes.

Conclusion: The evidence was Britain was a society with unequal opportunities for individuals of all classes to reach the top.

This study was done in 1949, but not published until 1954. Yes, that's a long time ago, but it's a classic study — and a springboard for all the research that's happened since.

The Oxford Mobility Study found Higher rates of Social Mobility in 1972

This study was conducted by **Goldthorpe et al** and used Goldthorpe's seven-class scheme (see p.95). You'll see this referred to as the **Oxford Study**, the Goldthorpe Study or the Nuffield study. Whatever the name, it's the same study.

Goldthorpe et al. (1980) also compared social class of fathers and sons

	This study was done in 1972, but not published until 1980.
Results:	There were higher rates of social mobility than in 1949 — half of all sons were in a different social class from their fathers. More of this movement was to a **higher social class** than down to a **lower** one.
Conclusion:	Opportunities for working class individuals had improved in the second half of the 20th century. This has been used by functionalist sociologists to show that Britain has become a more open and meritocratic society.
However:	Closer analysis showed that the chances of getting into the higher classes were much greater for those whose fathers were already there. There was some movement but relatively those born upper class were still better off.

A neat summary of the probabilities of upward mobility and downward mobility is given by **Kellner and Wilby (1980)**. The data revealed a **1:2:4** rule of "relative hope" — whatever the chance of a **working class** son being in the **professional class** as an adult, it was **twice** as much for an **intermediate class** son and four times as much for an **upper class** son.

So, this study has also been used by sociologists to show Britain is an unfair society.

Upper class people tend to be Born Upper Class

There's a much greater chance of **higher class** individuals **staying** in that class than **working class** individuals **moving up**. The top classes in the UK remain very **static** — the majority of members come from families who have been in the upper class for **generations**. The elite recruit the sons of those already in the elite (**elite self-recruitment**).

1) **Stanworth and Giddens (1974)** found that of the top company positions in over 400 British companies, only 1% were occupied by individuals with working class origins.

2) **Goldthorpe and Payne (1986)** did a follow-up to the Oxford study, looking at mobility rates during the **economic recession** of the 1970s. They concluded that mobility rates had **increased generally** but the chances of reaching **top classes** remained **unequal** in favour of those whose parents were upper class.

3) The **Essex study** of social mobility by **Marshall et al (1988)** looked at 1984 data and found that social mobility was increasing, but it was mainly short-range. Working class children are less likely to get top jobs. The **Essex study** also showed that working class people who got upper class jobs were less likely to retain them than upper class people.

Social Mobility

Other sociologists say the Social Mobility Data shows Britain is Meritocratic

There **aren't many** sociologists who interpret the data as evidence of **equality of opportunity**, but there are some.

1) The main man is the New Right thinker, **Peter Saunders**. He uses the Essex study and the National Development Survey to conclude that the **opportunities** are there for social mobility but the **individual** has to get off their backside and take them.

2) Saunders argues the inequality that exists results from differences in the **talent** and **hard work** of the individual — not their class of origin.

> "Class destinations reflect **individual merit** much more than class background."
> **Saunders** (1996, *Unequal but Fair? A Study of Class Barriers in Britain* London: IEA)

3) Saunders has been **criticised** by many sociologists. His **methodology** is criticised — he **doesn't include** the **unemployed** and **part-time employees** in his analysis.

4) Saunders' views have also been criticised because **class bias** at school could mean that school achievement reflects class background rather than ability. **Labelling** and **stereotypes** at school might discourage **working class** pupils from applying themselves to their studies.

See the AS course, or the OCR section on education, p.109.

Savage and Egerton (1997) analysed the **same** development survey as Saunders, but came to a very different conclusion. They found that those with the same ability didn't all have the same chances of ending up in the higher classes. Other factors such as **social networks**, **confidence** and **cultural advantages** helped upper class children get to the top — e.g. Savage and Egerton argue that educational qualifications and tests are based on middle and upper class culture and values.

What about the girls — Women's Social Mobility wasn't studied until 1981

1) One of the biggest problems with the usefulness of the study of social mobility is that almost all major studies failed to take any account whatsoever of the class position of **girls** and **women**.

2) The first time women were included in a study was in 1981. **Heath (1981)** went back and looked at the statistics for 1971 and 1975 and compared **fathers'** and **daughters'** social class positions (still no mothers). He found that in classes one and two, **daughters** were much more likely to be **downwardly mobile** than sons.

3) **Goldthorpe and Payne (1986)** concluded that women's mobility rates varied according to which class they were in — just the **same as men**. They argued from this that the non-inclusion of women in previous studies didn't affect the overall results. Class overrode gender.

4) The **Essex study (1988)** looked at male and female mobility and found that women moved both up and down into the **routine non-manual** group — most routine non-manual work was done by women regardless of their class of origin.

5) **Savage and Egerton (1997)** looked at male and female mobility and found that class affected opportunity less for daughters than it did for sons. This may be because middle class sons can access an "**old boys' network**", or because of sexism in traditional upper middle class jobs.

Upward mobility is fun.

A woman's class used to be defined by the class of the **male** she lived with (see p.90-91). **Feminist sociologists** used to argue that as long as that was the case, social mobility studies **couldn't reveal much** about the impact of gender on social mobility. In **2000**, government statistics switched from a scheme that measured women by the **man's job** to a scheme which measured women by their **own job**. So, some **more useful studies** might come along soon.

Practice Questions

Q1 Explain the different types of social mobility sociologists have studied.

Q2 What did the Oxford mobility study find out about social mobility?

Q3 What's meant by saying that the upper class is "static"?

Exam Question

Q1 Identify and explain two difficulties faced by sociologists when attempting to accurately measure social mobility. (6 marks)

I'm upper class — I have to go up three flights of stairs...

This may not be your favourite topic. You may be pining for the heady days of 'Section One: Beliefs in Society'. Thing is, you've got an exam coming up, and this could be a good opportunity to get some marks squared away. Learn the studies — the Oxford study, Goldthorpe and Payne's follow-up, and Savage and Egerton are three good ones to learn and remember.

The Role of the Education System

*This section is for **OCR only**. AQA people have already covered Education in the AS course. We won't be seeing them again until section 8. Tchuh. Slackers.*

Education Socialises children by passing on Knowledge

1) Socialisation **transmits culture** — it **teaches** children **knowledge**, **skills**, **roles**, **norms** and **values**. Socialisation also **reproduces culture** — it makes children **copy** knowledge, skills, roles, norms and values.

2) There's only one **agent** of **primary** socialisation — the **family**. In early childhood, individuals learn the **skills**, **knowledge**, **norms** and **values** of society. Children **internalise** norms and values by **imitating** their parents or guardians. Children are **rewarded** for socially **acceptable** behaviour and **punished** for socially **"deviant"** behaviour.

3) **Secondary socialisation** comes after primary socialisation and **builds on it**. It's carried out by **various institutions**, including **education**, **peer groups**, **religion** and the **mass media**.

The education system aims to pass on **knowledge and skills** such as reading, numeracy and basic science, and skills which pupils will need in the world of **work**.

Learning these skills is a part of socialisation, but sociologists suggest that **education socialises individuals** in **other ways** as well. Education passes on **core values** such as working hard to succeed, respect for authority, and cooperating with others.

Behold the tools of socialisation!

Durkheim said education Integrates Society by passing on Norms and Values

1) The functionalist **Durkheim (1925)** said education helps **create social order** based on **cohesion** and value **consensus**.

2) He said that children must learn to **identify** with society. Education teaches children to identify with wider society by teaching them the **history** of their society — e.g. children in the **United States** learn about the Founding Fathers, about the Constitution, and about American values as personified by the life story of **Abraham Lincoln** (who was raised in a humble log cabin and yet went on to be President). They even start each day by **swearing allegiance** to the American flag.

3) Durkheim said that school teaches children to **interact** with each other, and with adults, by **following rules**. He said school rules should be enforced **strictly**, because pupils should be **rewarded** for acceptable behaviour and **punished** for deviant behaviour. He also thought that children had to learn that **rules benefit society**.

4) Durkheim saw school as **society in miniature** — in other words, it's an agent of **cultural reproduction**.

Parsons saw education as the Main Agent of Secondary Socialisation

1) The functionalist **Parsons (1959)** saw education as a **bridge** between **family** and **society**, preparing children for their role in society.

2) Families treat their children as individuals and love them unconditionally, but in society people are judged by **universal standards**. Schools start to judge children by universal standards — e.g. **good behaviour**, following school **rules**, and doing well in **exams**.

3) Parsons said that schools pass on **universal values** — **achievement**, **hard work**, and **equality of opportunity**.

4) Parsons says that school is **meritocratic** — the best students rise to the top. This means that education can **allocate** people to **roles** in society. Schools test pupils' talents, and see which pupils are suited to which kind of job.

Davis and Moore said education allocates roles based on achievement

1) **Davis and Moore (1945)** say that every society sorts its members into different positions. They think that there are **rules** for this — called **"principles of stratification"**.

2) They believe that education **sorts people out** according to their **talents** and **abilities**. According to Davis and Moore, those who do **best at school** will do **best in society**.

There's more about this on p.92-93, if you want to read more around it.

Functionalist views of Education have been Criticised

1) Functionalism is deterministic — it assumes that all pupils get the **"message"** of shared values. Critics like **Hargreaves (1975)** say education **doesn't succeed** in transmitting **shared values**. Children ignore rules, or feel they **don't belong**.

2) Evidence of **differential achievement**, in terms of class, gender and ethnicity, suggests that education **isn't meritocratic**.

3) There **isn't** a close relationship between academic **achievement** at school, and **earnings** at work.

4) There's even **doubt** that the education system grades people according to ability. Some say **intelligence** doesn't have much impact on academic achievement.

5) Functionalism doesn't consider that education might transmit **ruling class** values. It **doesn't explain conflict**.

The Role of the Education System

Marxism Says Education Legitimises Inequality through Ideology

1) The neo-Marxist **Althusser** sees education as part of the "**ideological state apparatus**".
In other words, it's a tool of capitalism which is used to justify, maintain and reproduce class inequalities.
According to Althusser, education transmits and reproduces an **ideology** about what it **means** to be
working class, what it means to be middle class, and what everyone's **place in society** ought to be.

2) Marxists say education makes sure that the **ruling class** continue to get the most **powerful**
positions in society, and makes sure that the **working class** continue to do **poorly paid** manual jobs.

3) Marxists also say that education is used to pass on the **belief** that society is **fair**.
This means that pupils **accept their lot** and aren't ever motivated to change society.

4) The belief that education is a fair **meritocracy** is also used to **blame** pupils for not succeeding.
Children at the bottom feel they only have themselves to blame — that they must be "thick".

5) Marxists agree with functionalists that education passes on culture — but Marxists say this culture is ruling class
culture. Education is a tool of cultural **hegemony**. **Bourdieu** used the concept of **cultural capital** (language, skills,
knowledge and attitudes) to explain how the middle class get into the top positions. There's **plenty** on this on p.111.

6) Marxists think education produces the **docile** and **obedient** workforce that capitalism needs.
Bowles and Gintis (1976) say this happens through something called the **hidden curriculum**.

The **hidden curriculum** means things that pupils learn at school that aren't part of the **formal curriculum** of school subjects.

1) Pupils learn to **sit down** and **be quiet**, even when they're bored. In their study of an American high school, Bowles
and Gintis found that kids who **kept their heads down** and didn't cause trouble got **better grades** than students who
showed **independence of character**. The students who conformed tended to be middle class.

2) **Accepting** the **authority** of teachers is part of the hidden curriculum.
Bowles and Gintis say this prepares kids to be **obedient workers**.

There's more about what
Marxists think about the link
between school and work on p116.

3) The hidden curriculum teaches pupils to be **motivated by external rewards**
such as **good grades**, rather than the fun of learning. Yes, the fun. Of learning.

4) The hidden curriculum is taught partly by the way **school** is **organised**. Pupils sit and face the teacher who stands at
the front, which helps teach children that the teacher is an **authority figure**, and that they should sit and be **passive**.

5) The hidden curriculum is also taught by the way that **subjects** are organised. In school, knowledge is
compartmentalised into lots of different subjects which are taught separately — "**knowledge is fragmented**" if you
want to be fancy. Marxists connect this to the way that work is **broken up** into **separate jobs**.

Marxist views of Education have also been Criticised

1) Marxist views of education are **deterministic** — they assume that all pupils get the "message" of ruling
class ideology, and that all working class pupils learn to be good little workers. They ignore pupils who
disagree with or **ignore** everything their teachers say.

2) Even some **Marxists** and neo-Marxists **disagree** with the traditional view of education as a tool to create
an obedient workforce. Neo-Marxist **Paul Willis (1977)** found that some kids aren't obedient. They form
an **anti-school subculture** and cope with school and then adult work by mucking about. See p.116.

Practice Questions

Q1 According to Durkheim, what is the function of education?

Q2 According to Davis and Moore, what is the function of education?

Q3 Give two examples of Marxist criticisms of the idea that education is meritocratic and fair.

Q4 Give three examples of things the hidden curriculum teaches pupils.

Exam Questions

Q1	Outline and assess contrasting views of the role of education in socialisation.	(50 marks)
Q2	Outline and assess the view that education is meritocratic.	(50 marks)

So, what norms were you socialised into today...?

*Sociologists sometimes over-analyse. Take education — so far on this page it has been the means of passing on core values,
a way of creating social order, the main agent of secondary socialisation, a tool of capitalism and various other things. I mean, it's
just school. Still, thinking is a well-paid indoor job with no heavy lifting, and if you learn all this stuff you could do it too.*

The Role of the Education System

Functionalists and Marxists are only part of the story. You also need to know the New Right, social democrat and interactionist (also called interpretivist) views of what education is for and what effects the education system has on society.

The New Right saw education as Failing and Inefficient

The **New Right** believe that the job of education is to prepare children for the **world of work** and give them the skills and qualifications needed in the workplace. Unlike functionalists and Marxists, they believe that education is **failing** at its job.

1) New Right theorists argued that the education system was partly to blame for the **economic downturn** that Britain experienced during the **1970s**. They argued that a **well-educated** and **highly skilled workforce** would have driven the economy, but that there wasn't such a workforce because education had failed to produce one.

2) Educational policy in the 1960s and 1970s had focused on trying to smooth out inequality. The policies of the time promoted **mixed ability teaching**. The New Right think this was a **failure** — they argue that weaker and less motivated students had disadvantaged the more able and motivated students and actually **lowered** their attainment.

3) In the 1970s, parents had little choice about where to send their children, unless they could afford private school. The New Right thought this was wrong for **two reasons** — firstly because **choice** and free will were **good** things by themselves, and secondly because letting parents choose would give schools a **reason to improve**.

4) The New Right thought that **politicians**, **bureaucrats** and **special interest groups** had far too much influence on the education system. They said that education should be primarily for the benefit of the **consumers** — parents and pupils, in other words. The New Right argument was that the education system was actually run more for the benefit of the **producers** — teachers and bureaucrats and politicians.

1) The New Right argued that raising standards would mean a **better education system for all** and would allow more able, motivated students to develop their talents. They thought this was a better idea than trying to reduce inequality.

2) The New Right favoured **standardised testing**, and school **league tables**. This would help parents **decide** which schools to send their children to.

3) The Conservative government of **1979-1997** was influenced by New Right ideas. See p120 for more on this.

Chubb and Moe (1988, 1997) thought the Market Principle was the answer

New Right theorists **Chubb and Moe (1988, 1997)** argued that declining educational standards could only be solved by introducing the **market principle** into education — in other words **letting parents choose** their children's school, and **rewarding popular schools** with more funding. They said that parents didn't have **much choice** where to send their children to school and schools didn't have the **incentive** or the **freedom** to improve and meet the needs of employers and parents.

Chubb and Moe compared state schools and private schools in America. They found that **private** schools were more responsive to the needs of **consumers** — parents of school pupils, in other words. They suggested this was for two reasons:

1) **State** schools were under the control of **politicians** and **administrators**. Politicians had to please lots of different groups of people in order to get elected. They had to please **teachers' unions** and other groups who represented **special interests** — e.g. lobby groups, exam boards and even book publishers. Administrators just did what they found easiest and what would **keep them in a job**.

2) **Private** schools depended on **school fees**. They had to please **parents**, otherwise parents would take their children away from the school and send them to a different school. No pupils = no fees = no school.

This is all the opinion of the New Right — the way they see it, everyone acts in their own interests.

Chubb and Moe suggested a **voucher system** — parents would be given a voucher which would allow them to "buy" education for their kids of a value which the government would decide. They said this would **improve standards**, as schools would have to improve their grades to **attract students** and the funding which came with each student. They also suggested that this would make the education system **more efficient** and **reduce costs**.

Social Democrats think education should try to make society More Equal

1) Social democrats believe in **equality of opportunity**, and a more **equal society**. They think education should provide **equal opportunities** for everyone to **fulfil their potential**, and they think schools should **develop** the potential of pupils.

2) Some social democratic theorists think that if education provided real equality of opportunity, it could make society **more equal** by increasing **social mobility**. They think that if everyone got the **same benefits** out of education no matter what their **social class**, then they'd carry those benefits on into **adult life** and could end up in a **better-off class**.

3) Social democrats **Halsey, Floud and Anderson (1961)** criticised the education system of the time, which sent people to different secondary schools depending on whether they passed or failed an academic test in the final year of primary school called the 11+ exam (see p.118 for more on the 11+). They claimed that children who failed the 11+ were sent to schools which **didn't develop their potential**. Over 75% of pupils failed the 11+ exam.

The Role of the Education System

Interactionists stress the importance of Labelling pupils as good or bad

Interactionists (also called interpretivists) focus on **teacher-pupil relationships** at school. For example, **Hargreaves**, **Becker**, **Rist** and **Keddie** have looked at the way that teachers judge pupils and **label** them as "good", "lazy", "troublemaker" etc.

Children who are **positively labelled** get more out of school than children who are **negatively labelled**. This is called the **self-fulfilling prophecy** theory.

1) Teachers spend more time on pupils labelled "**bright**", and expect **higher quality work** from them. Teachers **don't expect much** from pupils who they've labelled as "**thick**".

2) The pupils' **ideas about themselves** and their work are **affected** by the **teachers' behaviour**. Pupils labelled as "**thick**" believe that they **can't achieve much**, and **don't bother trying**. So, they end up **not achieving much**.

Hargreaves et al (1975) looked at how teachers classify pupils

Speculation: Teachers **guess** what **type** of pupil a child is, according to the following criteria: **appearance**, whether they **do as they're told**, apparent **ability**, **enthusiasm**, how they **get on** with other kids, their **personality**, whether they're **deviant** (naughty).

Elaboration: Teachers refine their initial impressions of pupils based on more data.

Stabilisation: After a few weeks, teachers feel they know the pupils. The pupils' actions are seen in terms of the type of pupil the teacher thinks they are.

Becker and **Rist** found that labelling isn't as **gradual** as Hargreaves suggests.

1) **Rist (1970)** found that children in a kindergarten were **permanently** labelled on the **eighth day** of school. Children were sat at three separate tables — supposedly on grounds of ability.

2) In Rist's opinion, the children had actually been labelled on the basis of **class**. Children with a **neat appearance** and a "nice" **middle class background** got onto the "fast learners" table.

3) **Becker (1971)** found that teachers tend to evaluate pupils in terms of an **ideal student**. This included ideas of **ideal work**, **ideal conduct** and **ideal appearance**.

'So...what do your mummy and daddy do?'

Streaming puts children into Classes depending on Ability — or on Labelling

Streaming puts children into different classes, depending on how well they're perceived to do at school. The **top stream** are given the most **academic** education. The bottom stream are given a more **basic** education. Top stream kids are prepared for **university** education, while bottom stream pupils are prepared to go straight into **employment** — usually low-paid employment.

1) **Ball (1981)** found that pupils' **behaviour** changed according to what stream or band they were in. He thought this was because teachers had stereotypical views of different bands — the top band were supposed to be best behaved, the bottom band were least able, but supposedly quiet, and the middle band were supposed to be **worst behaved**.

2) **Keddie (1973)** studied a humanities course for pupils of all abilities. She found that teachers' attitudes depended on the stream that pupils were in. Teachers also transmitted more knowledge to A stream pupils than C stream pupils.

3) Keddie also looked at the **pupils' experience** of the class. She thought A stream pupils were more likely to take the teacher's word on trust. C stream pupils objected when teachers said things that didn't match their own experience. It appeared to Keddie that A stream pupils were more willing to **play the game**, and were rewarded for this.

Practice Questions

Q1 Why did the New Right think that a voucher system would improve standards?

Q2 How do social democrats think that education could increase social mobility?

Q3 What is the self-fulfilling prophecy effect?

Q4 According to Keddie, which stream contained pupils who didn't question what they were taught?

Exam Question

Q1 Outline and assess the view that teachers' stereotypes of pupils affect pupil experiences of education. (50 marks)

Kids are taught to sit quietly and work? I think my teachers would disagree...

There must be more to school than learning facts — otherwise we could all stay at home and read books instead. Interactionists are very big on the interaction between pupils and teachers in the classroom. They think this explains a lot about social inequalities in education. Learn all this lot, and then you can start applying it to the stuff on the next six pages.

Class and Differential Educational Achievement

Sociologists have investigated how social class affects how well people do at school. The middle classes do better than the working classes, but the upper classes don't seem to get a mention. Probably posh schools refuse to let grubby sociologists in.

Social Class *tends to affect* Educational Achievement

1) Pupils from **professional** backgrounds are significantly **more likely** to enter **higher education** than those from unskilled backgrounds.

2) Pupils from **middle** and **upper class** backgrounds are more likely to study **A-levels**, whereas **working class** pupils are more likely to take **vocational** subjects.

3) Pupils from disadvantaged backgrounds are **more likely** to **leave school at 16** and **less likely** to start school being able to **read**.

4) Pupils from **unskilled backgrounds** on average achieve **lower scores** on SATs and in GCSEs and are more likely to be placed in **lower streams** or **bands**.

I wonder if class affects how well you do in a school of fish...

Eysenck (1971) and Saunders (1996) have suggested the relative intelligence levels of different social groups account for differences in educational attainment. But it's very **difficult** to isolate whether IQ or social factors are the key to achievement. Some sociologists think that IQ tests are **culturally biased**, and measure things that **middle class** kids are more likely to know.

Processes Inside School — *Labelling*, *Streaming* and *Subcultures* are factors

1) **Negative labelling** of students can lead to a **self-fulfilling prophecy of failure**. Interactionists **Becker (1971)** and **Keddie (1973)** say that teachers tend to evaluate pupils in terms of an **ideal student**, by looking at appearance, personality, speech and social class.

2) Negative labelling can mean students get put into **lower streams or bands**. **Ball (1981)** found that the pupils in the top bands were from **higher social classes**. Teachers had **higher expectations** of them and they were **taught in different ways**. Keddie found that pupils from middle class backgrounds tended to be in the top stream, and get access to higher levels of knowledge.

3) As a response to negative labelling and frustration with low status, pupils may form **anti-school subcultures**. **Hargreaves (1975)** found that those in the **bottom streams** were more likely to be non-conformist. **Woods (1983)** responded by saying that there are lots of different reactions to school, but **non-conformist** reactions were more likely to come from **working class** students.

These explanations are useful when looking at day to day experiences in schools. The problem is that they don't explain how **factors outside of school** (e.g. poverty, cultural deprivation) can influence achievement.

Labelling theory is also too **deterministic** — it says that once you're negatively labelled, that's it — you'll fail. This isn't always the case. Pupils can **resist negative labelling**, and work extra hard to **prove the teacher wrong**.

Material Deprivation Outside School *can affect achievement*

The theory of **material deprivation** says that **economic poverty** is a big factor in low achievement at school.

1) In 1997, the **Joseph Rowntree Foundation** classified **one in ten** children as **poor** — which was defined as being in a family that couldn't afford at least three things other families took for granted.

2) **Halsey (1980)** found that the **most important factor** preventing working class students staying on at school was **lack of financial support**.

3) **Douglas (1964)** found that children in **unsatisfactory living conditions** (poor housing, lack of nutritious food, overcrowding) didn't do very well in ability tests compared to kids from comfortable backgrounds.

4) **Unemployment** or **low income** means less money for books, the internet and school trips. Low income families can't afford **nurseries** and **private schools** and they can't afford to support their kids through **uni**.

5) Poverty and unsatisfactory living standards may cause **health problems** and **absence from school**.

Cultural Deprivation Outside School *can affect achievement*

The theory of **cultural deprivation** says that **working class culture** and **parenting** aren't aimed at educational success.

1) **Douglas (1964)** thought the **level of parental interest** was the most important factor affecting achievement. Middle class parents are more likely to visit schools for open evenings. Bear in mind that **working class parents** may not go to open evenings because they work **inconvenient shifts** — not because they aren't interested.

2) Some sociologists say that working class kids don't have the **knowledge** and **values** that help achievement. **Museum visits**, **books** and **parental knowledge of education** may help middle class pupils to succeed.

3) Some **styles of parenting** emphasise the importance of education more than others.

Class and Differential Educational Achievement

Some sociologists say **Class Affects Attitudes** to **Education**

1) **Sugarman (1970)** said that pupils from non-manual backgrounds and manual backgrounds have **different outlooks**. The pupils from **manual** backgrounds lived for **immediate gratification**. The pupils from **non-manual backgrounds** were **ambitious** and **deferred their gratification** — they invested time in studying and planned for the future.

2) **Hyman (1967)** said that the **values** of the working class are a **self-imposed barrier** to improving their position. He said that the working class tend to place a **lower value** on education.

> **But...**
>
> Material and cultural deprivation theories **don't** explain how **factors inside school** affect achievement.
>
> **Cultural** deprivation theory **generalises a lot** about differences between middle class and working class life. It **ignores** working class families who **do** place a high value on education, and tends to **assume** that working class families have **no culture** at all, or that working class culture can't be **relevant** to school.
>
> The **method** may be **unsound**, e.g. attending parents' evenings might not be a good measure of parental interest.

Bernstein found **Working Class** pupils were **Linguistically Deprived**

1) **Basil Bernstein (1970)** found that working class pupils in the East End of London weren't comfortable with the style of language required by school. They used a **restricted code** — short forms of speech.

2) **Middle class students** knew how to use the same **elaborated code** as the **teachers** — a much more wordy style of speech with everything made very explicit. In terms of **language**, the working class kids were at a disadvantage.

Bernstein's theory is **criticised** for painting with a very broad brush.
There are **linguistic variations** within the middle class and within the working class.

Cultural deprivation theorists have developed Bernstein's ideas to say working class speech patterns are **wrong**. **Labov (1973)** disagrees, arguing that the elaborated speech code is just **different**, not better.

Marxist **Bourdieu** said schools require **Middle Class Cultural Capital**

1) **Bourdieu (1967, 1974)** reckons middle class students are at an advantage because they have the right kind of "**cultural capital**" — the right **language**, **skills**, **knowledge** and **attitudes**.

2) He thought that the **more cultural capital** you have, the **more successful** you'll be in education — and he believed that working class pupils don't have **access** to cultural capital.

3) **Middle class** families **pass on cultural capital** and **expectations** from parents to children. This is **cultural reproduction**.

4) Bourdieu said that working class pupils **knew** the system was **biased** against them, so they **left school** rather than staying on in further and higher education.

Bourdieu was criticised for being too **deterministic** — not all working class students fail, even if they lack cultural capital.

Also, **Halsey (1980)** found that **material factors** are **more important** than cultural factors. Pupils may feel they have to get a job as soon as possible after leaving school. Nowadays, tuition fees may discourage pupils from going on to university.

Practice Questions

Q1   Give two facts about social class and educational achievement.

Q2   Name two factors inside school that help explain the links between social class and achievement.

Q3   For Halsey, what was the most important factor preventing working class students staying on at school?

Q4   Briefly outline the findings of Sugarman's 1970 research into class attitudes to education.

Q5   Who used the term "cultural capital"?

Exam Question

Q1   Outline and assess the view that the education system is biased against working class pupils.   (50 marks)

Immediate gratification sounds good to me...

Just a quick word of warning. In the exam you could get a question like "Assess how factors inside and outside school affect levels of achievement". This is a very broad question. You'd need to look at home and school factors for ethnicity, gender AND class. This means you'd need to have revised pages 112-115 as well as these two pages. So get on with it.

Gender and Differential Educational Achievement

Gender is another factor that can influence how well people do at school. Since the 1980s, things have changed. Sociologists used to talk about female underachievement. Now there are worries that boys are falling behind.

Here are **Six Facts** about **Gender** and **Differential Educational Achievement**

1) Girls get **better results** at all levels in National Curriculum tests.
2) Girls get **better results** in **most subjects** at **GCSE**.
3) Girls are **more likely** to **pass** their **A-levels**.
4) Women are **more likely** to go on to **university**.
5) **Men** seem to have most success at the **highest levels** of university. A higher proportion of male students get **first class degrees** and **PhDs**.
6) **Girls** tend to go for **communication based subjects** like English and sociology and **boys** tend to go for **technical** ones like maths and physics.

it's so BORING...

Statistics are all very well, thought Jodie, but it doesn't mean I have to like school.

Factors Inside School explain why **Females Now Do Better**

1) **Mitsos and Browne (1998)** say teaching has been **feminised**. Women are **more likely to be classroom teachers**, especially in primary schools. This gives girls **positive role models**.
2) **Textbooks** and **teaching resources** have changed and are less likely to include sexist **stereotypes**.
3) The National Curriculum **forced** girls to do **traditionally** "**male**" subjects. For example, more girls started to do **science**. Other Local Education Authority and government initiatives tried to encourage girls to do science, technology and maths, e.g. WISE (Women Into Science, Engineering and Construction) and GIST (Girls Into Science and Technology).
4) **GCSEs** include more **coursework** than earlier qualifications. **Mitsos and Browne** argue that coursework suits girls better because they put in **more effort**, are **better organised** and can **concentrate** for longer than boys (that's quite a sweeping generalisation though...)

Factors Outside School explain why **Females Now Do Better**

1) Liberal feminists have promoted policies such as the **Equal Pay Act** and **Sex Discrimination Act**, which have helped to create **more equal opportunities** in wider society. This has **changed values** of society and attitudes in school.

   The Equal Pay Act (1971) makes it illegal to pay men and women different money for the same work. The Sex Discrimination Act 1975 means employers can't discriminate on the basis of gender.

2) **Sue Sharpe (1994)** found that girls' priorities have changed. They now want **careers** — and qualifications. More women go out to work, so girls see lots of **positive role models** in work. Girls nowadays often want to be **financially independent** — they don't just want to marry a rich man any more.
3) **Boys** tend to spend their leisure time being **physically active**. **Girls** are more likely to spend their leisure time **reading** and **communicating**. This means girls develop **language skills** that are useful for most subjects.
4) The **feminist** movement caused a **change in female expectations**, and made more people **aware of inequality**. People are now more careful about negative stereotyping, sex discrimination and patriarchy.
5) The **New Right** claim that having a **single mother** has a negative impact on a boy's educational achievement. They argue that these boys lack strong **male role modes** and **discipline**.

Here are some **Reasons** why **Boys Underachieve**

1) Boys may be having an **identity crisis**. The rise of **female independence**, the decline of the **breadwinner** role for men and the rise in **male unemployment** might mean that boys don't see the point of education. This may lead to anti-school subcultures.
2) **Interactionists** (also called **interpretivists**) say that teachers have **lower expectations of boys**. This may lead to a **self-fulfilling prophecy** of poor behaviour. **Negative labelling** may explain why they're more disruptive. Boys are more likely to be sent out of class or **excluded** from school — which cuts the time they spend learning.
3) The **feminisation** of **teaching** means that boys don't have as many **role models** in school.
4) **Reading** is often seen as "uncool" or "girly". Boys who **avoid books** don't develop **communication skills**.
5) Boys may **overestimate** their ability, which means they don't work as **hard** as they need to to get good grades.

Some sociologists say that there's been a bit of a **moral panic** about males underperforming.

Weiner et al (1997) say that there's a **backlash** against female achievement. They also say that the concern about **male underachievement** is more specifically about **underqualified working class males** turning to **crime**.

Gender and Differential Educational Achievement

Subcultures help to explain Gender and Achievement

Negative labelling and putting students into different **streams** or bands can cause some pupils to rebel against school's values. They form **subcultures**. These can be either **pro-** or **anti-school** subcultures.

1) Marxist **Willis (1977)** studied a group of boys who **rejected school** and formed an **anti-school subculture**. They **coped** with their own underachievement by having a **subculture where it didn't matter**, and where having a laugh was more important. See p116 for more on Willis.

2) **Mac an Ghaill (1994)** says that **subcultures are complicated**. There are **lots of different types**. Boys may join a **macho lad subculture** because of a crisis of masculinity. But boys could also join **pro-school subcultures** and be proud of academic achievement.

There are different ways to Explain links between Gender and Subject Choice

Girls tend to go for **arts and humanities**. Boys tend to go for **science and technology**.

1) **Subject choice** may still be influenced by **gender socialisation**. The ideas of **femininity** and **masculinity** create different **expectations** and **stereotypes** of what to study. Kids often see biology as "the science that it's OK for girls to do" — as opposed to physics and chemistry.

2) **Kelly (1987)** found that **science** is seen as a **masculine subject**. Boys dominate the science classroom, and Kelly claims this puts girls off studying science.

3) **Parental expectations** and **teacher expectations** may encourage girls to follow what they see as the traditional "**normal**" choice for their gender. There's a pressure to **conform** to a social norm.

4) **Abraham (1995)** studied a comprehensive school and found that some pupils formed **subcultures** that **rejected** school expectations of **masculinity**, **femininity** and **gendered subject choice**. Boys in the mixed "**gothic punk**" subculture rejected ideas about "boys' subjects" and "girls' subjects", and preferred art and music to science and technology.

Gender, Class and Ethnicity all Interact and Influence Achievement

1) According to National Statistics for 2004, young **Afro-Caribbean** boys as a group have poor educational attainment. Only **27%** of Afro-Caribbean boys gained five A*-C grades at GCSE — compared to **52%** of all boys. Quite a big difference. Factors contributing to this are discussed on p.114-115.

2) However, according to **Mirza (1992)** young black girls have a **positive attitude** to education and are more likely to achieve. According to the same official National Statistics, in 2004 **44%** of Afro-Caribbean girls achieved 5 A*-C grades at GCSE, compared to **62%** of all girls.

3) **Mac an Ghaill (1992)** found that pupils felt their teachers saw **Asian girls** as having more academic potential than black girls. **Negative labelling** can affect pupils' levels of achievement in school (see p.110 and p.114).

4) **Class** and **gender** interact, too. **Working class girls** don't do as well as middle class girls. A recent **Equal Opportunities Commission survey (2001)** found that working class pupils had more "traditional" views about gender roles than middle class kids — this could mean working class girls had **lower expectations** for their own achievement than middle class girls.

Practice Questions

Q1 Give two facts about gender and educational achievement.
Q2 Which sociologists studied how classroom interaction disadvantaged girls?
Q3 Name one inside of school factor that explains why girls now do better than boys.
Q4 Who found that girls' priorities have changed?
Q5 Give one reason why boys and girls choose different subjects.

Exam Question

Q1 Outline and assess the view that the education system is institutionally sexist against boys. (50 marks)

Girls are DOOMED... no wait, boys are DOOMED... no wait... ah, forget it...

Obviously a lot of boys do really well in school. These pages are just talking about overall trends (which seem to change every decade or so anyway). So don't give up hope, you readers with Y chromosomes out there — you can still get an 'A' grade in your Sociology A2 exams no matter what Mitsos and Browne say...

Ethnicity and Differential Educational Achievement

Ethnicity is another factor that can influence how well people do at school. Quick reminder — ethnicity means the shared cultural traditions and history which are distinct from other groups in society.

Some *Ethnic Groups* do *Better* than *Others*

These figures are from **Modood et al (1997)** — the Policy Studies Institute's fourth survey of ethnic minorities in Britain:

All these statistics are averages. If you look at someone and say, "she does well cos she's Chinese," you might be wrong.

Higher levels of achievement

1) The survey found that **Chinese, African Asians** and **Indians** were more qualified than whites. **Afro-Caribbean women** were more likely to have **A-levels** than white women.

2) Ethnic minorities were **more likely than white pupils** to continue into **further education** (from ages 16-19).

3) People from ethnic minorities who were **born in the UK** had much **higher qualifications** than people who moved to the UK from abroad.

Lower levels of achievement

1) **Bangladeshi** and **Pakistani women** were least well qualified. **Afro-Caribbean, Pakistani** and **Bangladeshi men** were least qualified.

2) **Pakistani** and **Afro-Caribbean** groups were **less likely** to get onto **university** courses, and **more likely** to get into **less prestigious universities**.

3) **Afro-Caribbean boys** are **more likely** to be **excluded from school**, more likely to be put in **lower streams** and more likely to do **vocational** courses.

African Asians means people of Indian origin who lived in Kenya and Uganda and then moved to Britain in the 1970s.

There are big **variations** between the **average achievement level** of different ethnic minority groups. There must be something behind it all — probably more than one factor, and probably some **social** and **economic** factors.

Some people say that **intelligence is inherited** and that people underachieve because they've inherited low IQ. HOWEVER... **IQ tests** can be **biased**. Sometimes they ask things that aren't really a test of brains, but really a test of **cultural knowledge**. The **Swann Report (1985)** found that if you took into account social and economic factors there were **no significant differences in IQ** whatsoever between different **ethnic groups**.

Processes Inside School — *Labelling, Curriculum and Prejudice* are factors

Labelling theory says that teachers have **different expectations** of **different ethnic minority groups**. **Gillborn** (1990 *Race, Ethnicity and Education* London: Routledge). found that teachers **negatively label black students**. Afro-Caribbean students were seen as a **challenge to authority** — and are more likely to be excluded from school. Gillborn calls this the "myth of the black challenge". Teachers had high expectations of Asian students. Negative labelling could result in a **self-fulfilling prophecy of failure**. **Mac an Ghaill (1992)** also found that teachers saw Afro-Caribbean boys as a threat, and saw Asian girls as having more potential than Afro-Caribbean girls. Black girls were encouraged to do non-academic subjects.

There's also an issue about whether the school curriculum is **ethnocentric** — i.e. that it might fit the mainstream, white, middle class culture better than other ethnicities. It could be **Europe-centred** too. Languages in the National Curriculum are mainly **European** — kids usually learn French and German, not Gujarati or Chinese. **Assemblies**, **school holidays** and even **history lessons** may not fit with the culture and history of particular groups.

Some sociologists see British education as **"institutionally racist"**. This is where **policies** and **attitudes** unintentionally discriminate against ethnic minority groups. **Wright (1992)** found that even though members of staff said they were **committed to equal opportunities**, Asian girls got **less attention** from teachers and felt their cultural traditions were disapproved of (e.g. staff assumed Asian girls' parents wouldn't allow them to come on a school trip). **Afro-Caribbean boys** were more likely to be punished and **sent out of class**.

Some sociologists say that these factors may lead to a **low self-esteem** for ethnic minorities. **Coard (1971)** said that black students are made to feel inferior in British schools.

Low Self-esteem exists — but it *Isn't Really All That Widespread*

1) **Mirza (1992)** found that black girls had **positive self-esteem** and **high aspirations**. The girls experienced discrimination but had **strategies** to minimise the effects. It **wasn't low self-esteem** that affected their achievement — it was being **unwilling to ask for help**. Mirza found that teachers often tried to help in **counterproductive** ways, e.g. by not letting a girl enter an exam because the teacher thought the girl was overworked at home.

2) **Fuller (1980)** found Afro-Caribbean girls in London **resisted negative labelling** and **worked hard** to gain **success**.

3) Negative labelling and racism can affect pupils' reactions to school. Pupils may join either a **pro-school subculture** or an **anti-school subculture** to maintain their self-esteem, depending on their experience of school.

Ethnicity and Differential Educational Achievement

Factors Outside School — *Language Difference* affects achievement

1) **Language** was a barrier for kids from **Asian** and **Afro-Caribbean immigrant families** when they **first arrived** in the UK.

2) The **Swann Report** found that **language didn't affect progress** for **later generations**.

3) **Driver and Ballard (1981)** also found that Asian children whose **first language** was **not English** were **as good at English** as their **classmates** by the age of 16.

4) **Interactionists** would say that language might not be a barrier, but **dialects** or having an **accent** might **influence teacher expectations** and lead to **negative labelling**. For example, a teacher might **assume** that a child isn't good at English because they have a foreign accent and put them in a lower set.

Factors Outside School — *Family Difference* affects achievement

Some studies say that **family life varies** for different groups and this can influence achievement.

1) **Driver and Ballard (1981)** say that the **close-knit extended families** and **high parental expectations** increase levels of achievement in **Asian communities**.

2) Some sociologists say that the underachievement of Afro-Caribbean boys is connected to high levels of **single-parenthood** in Afro-Caribbean households, and a lack of male role models.

3) **Pilkington (1997)** found that although there are high levels of **divorce** and **single-parenthood** in Afro-Caribbean households, and very low levels of single parenthood in **Asian** families, **both** had more children staying on at school after 16 than **white working class** families. He also said that **economic** factors and **racism** were as important as cultural factors.

4) **Mac an Ghaill (1992)** found that a group of Afro-Caribbean and Asian pupils saw their **parents** as their main source of **inspiration**.

Ethnicity Combines with *Social Class* to affect achievement

On their own, the inside school factors and outside of school factors may not seem all that convincing. If you bring **social class** and **material factors** into the equation you get a more complex explanation.

1) The Swann Report found that **socio-economic** factors affected the lower levels of achievement of **Afro-Caribbean** pupils.

2) **Pakistani**, **Bangladeshi** and **Afro-Caribbean** groups are more likely to be in **lower class positions** such as routine occupations (assembly line workers, factory workers) and elementary occupations (cleaners, labourers). This may result in poor housing, periods of unemployment, poverty and **material deprivation**.

3) **Chinese**, **African Asian** and **Indian** groups are more likely to be in **higher class** positions and **less likely** to experience material deprivation.

 If you were answering an exam question on this, you'd need to bring in stuff from p110-111 about class and achievement.

Practice Questions

Q1   Give two facts about ethnicity and educational achievement.

Q2   Why do sociologists dislike genetic explanations about intelligence and educational success?

Q3   Name one inside of school factor that explains the underachievement of some ethnic minority groups.

Q4   How does language affect educational achievement?

Q5   Give an example of how social class combines with ethnicity to affect achievement.

Exam Question

Q1   Outline and assess the significance of inside of school factors in explaining the educational achievement of different ethnic minority groups.

(50 marks)

The Swan Report found that waterfowl tended to underachieve in schools...

Remember that not all ethnic minorities underachieve — so don't go storming into your exam answer with a pre-prepared rant that it's all about white / black racism. There are always several different factors that affect each ethnic group. Also, remember that other factors like class and gender (see page 112) also influence how someone does at school.

Education and the Economy

After leaving education, pupils enter the world of work. Sociologists have various theories about this transition from school to work, and various theories on what the relationship between education and the economy ought to be.

Functionalists say that education must *Teach Skills* required by the Economy

1) The functionalist view of education says that employers use qualifications to **sort** school leavers into jobs that suit their level of **ability**. According to **Davis and Moore (1945)**, school is the place where people's ability is **tested** and **graded**. Remember, functionalists think education is a **meritocracy**.

2) Functionalists also think that the job of education is to teach the **skills** that are needed by the economy.

But...

This view has been criticised, especially by Marxist sociologists such as **Harry Braverman (1974)**. Braverman said that work had become more and more **deskilled** and **automated**. This would mean that education was actually teaching people **far more skills** than they **needed** in order to work in the economy. There is, after all, not a great deal of skill required to work in a **fast food** outlet. However, the economy also requires computer database analysts, electricians and accountants — which all require skill. The question isn't just **how much skill** the economy needs, but **what skills** the economy needs.

There's more about teaching **job skills** on p.119.

Marxists say education *Prepares Working Class* children for *Work*

1) Marxists believe that education is an **apparatus of the state**, which has the purpose of providing an **obedient workforce**. According to Marxism, the capitalist system **demands** a willing and obedient workforce to do low-paid jobs in order that the capitalist class can maximise profits.

2) In the Marxist view, education is more about **transmitting the right sort of attitudes** towards work than about transmitting actual measurable **skills**.

Marxists **Bowles and Gintis (1976)** say there's a close link between school and work, and a **correspondence** between **pupil experiences of school** and **adult experiences of work**. This link is called the **correspondence principle**.

1) Pupils have to accept the **hierarchy** at school. Work also has a hierarchy.

2) Pupils are **motivated by exam success** to do **boring work**. Workers are **rewarded with pay** to do **boring work**.

3) The **school day** is broken into **small units**. So is the **work day**.

4) At school and work, **subservience** (following the rules) is **rewarded**.

Bowles and Gintis say that the **hidden curriculum prepares people for work** — see p.107.

Paul Willis (1977) says school *Doesn't* prepare children to *Work Hard*

Willis's study "Learning to Labour" researched working class pupils

Background:	Willis (1977, *Learning to Labour*, London: Saxon House) studied a school on a working class housing estate in a small town in the Midlands. He focused on a group of **12 white working class boys**. His aim was to find out how the pupils **interacted** with school, and what their **attitudes** to **school** and **work** were. He wanted to find out "**why working class kids get working class jobs**". Willis was a **neo-Marxist** who was also influenced by interactionism (interpretivism).
Methods:	Willis used **observation, participant observation, group discussions, informal interviews** and **diaries**.
Findings:	The lads had an **anti-school subculture**. They were deliberately opposed to the values of hard work and conformity that the school was trying to transmit. The lads felt **superior** to **conformist** pupils, and to the teachers. They aimed to do as **little work** as possible, to **skive off lessons** as much as possible, and to **muck about** as much as possible. They didn't often confront teachers' authority head on, but tried to see how much they could **get away with**. The lads' subculture was **sexist** and **homophobic** — they saw boys who worked hard in lessons as effeminate. They were also **racist** towards ethnic minorities.
Conclusion:	Willis thought that the lads were **nothing like** the **obedient worker** that Bowles and Gintis wrote about. However, Willis thought the lads' **experience of school** and **attitude** towards schoolwork actually **prepared them very well** for work as adults. They went on to **unskilled** or **semiskilled manual jobs**, which they saw as "real work" (as opposed to office jobs). The **anti-work, having-a-laugh subculture** was carried on to the lads' **first jobs**. Just like in school, they didn't challenge the boss head on, but tried to **get away with** as little work as possible **without getting the sack**. The work culture was **sexist, homophobic**, and somewhat **racist**.

Education and the Economy

Social Democrats *think* Equality *of* Opportunity *will* Help *the* Economy

1) Social democrats promote **equality of opportunity** in education, and believe this will make society fairer and more meritocratic.

2) They argue that if everyone fulfils their **potential**, then everyone can make the best contribution to **society** and the **economy** that they possibly can. Therefore the economy will grow and thrive better than if people had unfulfilled potential.

This outlook has been criticised. Even social democrats themselves such as **Halsey, Heath and Ridge (1980)** admitted that education hadn't managed to bring about equality of opportunity. New Right thinkers argued that equality of opportunity was the wrong thing to focus on in the first place...

The best contribution to the economy I can possibly make...

New Right Sociologists *blame* Skills Shortages *on* Schools

1) **New Right** theorists **agree** with **functionalists** that the job of education should be to teach people the skills that are **needed by the economy**. However, New Right thinkers accuse education of **failing** to do this.

2) New Right sociologists blame a **skills shortage** on the **education system**. They say that education in the 1980s was teaching pupils an **outdated curriculum** which didn't serve the **needs of industry** — e.g. not enough computer skills, and not enough stress on learning the right businesslike, professional **attitude**.

Industrialists tend to complain that many school-leavers and graduates enter the world of work without basic job skills and IT skills.

3) The New Right suggest teaching children a more **business-oriented** curriculum. The 1988 Education Reform Act introduced **City Technology Colleges**. These were inner city schools for 11-18 year olds, sponsored by private industry. They were set up to teach technology, to meet the needs of industry. In 2000, the New Labour government launched a very similar policy of **City Academies**, again sponsored by businesses.

Conservative governments were influenced by New Right ideas.

Feminists *say* Education *prepares pupils for* Gendered Job Choices

Subject choice in school tends to be **gendered** (see p.112-113). According to feminists, this prepares boys for stereotypically male jobs, and girls for both stereotypically female jobs and for the housewife/mother role.

This gendering of subjects and skills was pretty darn **explicit** back in the 1950s, 1960s and 1970s. **Girls** did **home economics** (cooking), and **needlework** classes, while **boys** did **woodwork** and **metalwork** — almost entirely without exception. Today, this gendering is less explicit. Resistant Materials is still seen as more male, while Food Technology is seen as more female.

Feminist sociologists think that boys and girls are **encouraged** towards **gendered work experience** and **career choices**.

A survey of pupils in Scotland by the **Employment Research Institute at Napier University (2004)** found that pupils held **stereotyped** views about career choices and gender, especially when it came to what job they **themselves** would be suited to. Only 11% of boys felt they were suitable for nursing compared with 57% of girls, and only 10% of girls felt they were suitable for engineering, compared with 63% of boys.

Practice Questions

Q1 In what way did Braverman criticise the functionalist view of education and the economy?

Q2 What is meant by the correspondence principle?

Q3 Why does Willis disagree with Bowles and Gintis?

Q4 What did the New Right blame the education system for?

Exam Question

Q1 Outline and assess the view that the role of education is to prepare pupils to contribute to the economy. (50 marks)

At my school, the girls did the Waitress Race on sports day...

In the 'Waitress Race', the girls had to run while carrying trays of drinks. The winner was the first girl to finish without spilling all her drinks. We were clearly being prepared by a patriarchal hidden curriculum to grow up to be very fast waitresses. The boys meanwhile got to do the sack race and have fun. Not that I'm bitter or anything.

The Education System and State Policy

For your course, the focus is on what's happened in education policy since 1988. But to have a decent idea why any of those post-1988 changes were made, you need to know a bit of the historical background. This page is background, but p119 covers vocational stuff that mainly happened after 1988.

Between 1944 and 1965 there was the Tripartite System and the 11+

In the tripartite system, you took the **11+ exam** (like an IQ test) at the end of primary school and then went to one of three types of school:

1) **Grammar schools** were for the able kids who passed the 11+. Pupils were taught traditional subjects ready for **university**. About **20% of kids** got in to grammar school.

2) **Secondary modern schools** were for the **75-80%** of pupils **who failed** the 11+. Secondary moderns offered **basic education**.

3) **Technical schools** were meant to provide a more **vocationally-minded** education for those pupils with aptitude for **practical subjects**.

The tripartite (three-part) system was set up to provide good education for everyone, but there were several problems with it:

1) The **11+ didn't necessarily measure your intelligence**. It was **culturally biased**, and suited the middle class more than the working class.

2) **Few technical schools were built**, so the vocational part of the plan didn't work especially well.

3) Most children ended up either at grammar or secondary modern schools. These schools were supposed to have "**parity of esteem**" — they were supposed to be considered as having **equal value**. The problem was that grammar schools were seen as the best. Not a surprise since which school you went to was decided by how well you did in an exam.

4) Kids who failed the 11+ were **labelled as failures**, which sometimes turned them off education completely.

5) When kids from well-off families failed the 11+, their parents could still afford to send them to **private schools**.

6) **Grammar** schools and **secondary modern** schools taught traditional **academic** subjects — maths, science, history, geography, etc. **Grammar schools** taught **Latin** (and sometimes Greek) as well. Critics said that this didn't give pupils relevant **job-related skills**.

Social democratic theorists such as **Halsey (1980)** were very **critical** of the tripartite system. Halsey said that secondary modern schools didn't develop potential, and didn't produce a highly educated and skilled workforce either.

In 1965 the Labour Government made Schools Comprehensive

Comprehensive education replaced the three-tier system with a **one-tier system** where all state-educated pupils in an area went to **one secondary school**. They did this to try and make sure that everyone had **equality of opportunity**. "**Comprehensive school**" means it's universal — everyone's meant to get the same deal.

Positive aspects of the comprehensive system	Criticisms of the comprehensive education system
There's no 11+, so **80%** of the school population don't get labelled as **failures**.	Comprehensive schools still **stream** pupils into sets depending on test scores. (So it's still possible to feel like a failure without the 11+.)
High-ability pupils generally still do well with this system. Lower ability pupils do better in comprehensive schools than in the old secondary moderns.	Schools in **working class** areas have **lower pass rates** than those in middle class areas.

The comprehensive system has **not** achieved equality of opportunity. Schools tend to be '**single-class**', depending on the local area — a school in a very **middle class area** where **all the pupils** are **middle class** ends up quite different to a school in an area with a lot of social deprivation. Class still has an effect on educational attainment (see p110-111).

Because of the **variation** in educational achievement between comprehensive schools, where people can **afford to live** (and whether there are good state comprehensive schools nearby) is important in educational attainment.

Cultural deprivation theory (p110) influenced **compensatory education** in the 1960s. The idea is that if cultural deprivation affected educational achievement, then **equality of opportunity** wouldn't be enough to give you **equality of outcome** — working class kids would **still fail**. Compensatory education tried to give **more resources** to schools in deprived areas.

In the 1960s and 1970s there was a trend for Liberal, Progressive Education

Liberal theorists believe that education should develop children as **individual human beings**. They want children to learn by experience and have the opportunity for individual **creative** work. This view influenced liberal, **progressive**, child-centred education in the 1960s and 1970s. Schools which took this approach were **less strict** than traditional schools.

Functionalists and the New Right criticise progressive education for **failing** to teach either **skills** or **cultural norms**. Some sociologists argue that the focus on individual development is at odds with the aim of providing a **skilled workforce**.

The Education System and State Policy

In 1976 the Push for Vocational Education Started

In a **1976** speech, **Labour** Prime Minister **James Callaghan** said he thought British education and industry was in decline because schools didn't teach people the **skills they needed in work**.

Conservative governments between **1979** and **1997** developed this idea, and introduced policies to create a closer link between school and work. This is called **new vocationalism**.

Youth Training Programmes were introduced from 1978 onwards

1) The **Youth Opportunities Programme** (YOP) was introduced in **1978**, and run by the Manpower Services Commission (responsible to the Department of Employment). It provided one day a week **off-the-job training**, which included teaching **good attitudes to work**, punctuality and discipline.

2) **Youth Training Schemes** (**YTS**) replaced YOP in 1983. YTS started as a year-long job-training scheme for 16-17 year old kids leaving school. In 1986 it was extended to a two year scheme.

3) YTS was rebranded **Youth Training** in 1989. Youth Training was a lot less **time-consuming** than YTS.

4) The introduction of the **New Deal** in 1997 means unemployed young people must attend courses aimed at getting them **into work**, or **back into education**. They're offered various options — a subsidised job, full-time education, or a job in the voluntary sector. If they don't take one of those options, they **lose their right to benefits**.

Standard Vocational Qualifications were introduced from 1986

In the early 1980s there was a variety of vocational training schemes and qualifications, some of them specific to **particular jobs**. In 1986, a **National Council for Voluntary Qualifications** was set up to **standardise** vocational qualifications.

1) In 1986, the first **National Vocational Qualifications** (**NVQs**) were introduced. They have four levels, from basic GCSE standard to specialist post-A-level standard, and they cover specific job knowledge and skills.

2) In 1993, **GNVQs** were introduced — they're a **vocational alternative** to GCSE and A-level qualifications, aimed at broad job fields, e.g. catering. They're designed to make the transition from school to work easier.

3) In 2000, new **Key Skills** qualifications started. These are supposed to be useful for **all jobs**, and for **life in general**. There are six key skills — communication, application of number, ICT, working with others, improving your own learning, performance and problem solving. The courses have the same four skill/difficulty levels as NVQs. Key Skills qualifications can be taken by **pupils in school** or by **adults** in job-related training or adult education.

4) The **National Apprenticeship Service** (NAS) was launched in 2009 to run **apprenticeships**. These are mostly spent learning on-the-job, but around one day a week is spent in college working towards a qualification.

New Vocationalism has been Criticised

1) Marxist sociologist **Phil Cohen (1984)** argues that vocational education aims to teach **good work discipline**, not skills. Other people say that this isn't necessarily a problem if it results in equality of opportunity, or economic growth.

2) Some sociologists such as **Dan Finn (1987)** say that vocational training provides **cheap labour** and that governments encourage people to go into training schemes (instead of signing on as unemployed) to **lower unemployment statistics**.

3) **Finn** also points out that a lot of **young people** have **part-time jobs** so they already have work skills, and don't need vocational education schemes.

4) **Marxists** also argue that vocational education **legitimises class inequality** — they say it perpetuates the idea that middle class kids get educated and working class kids get trained.

5) **Traditionalists** favour a strong **academic** curriculum instead of vocational qualifications.

6) Some theorists say that work is becoming more **flexible**. They say that because the demands of the global economy change rapidly, it's better to have a **broad general education** than to be taught specific skills.

Practice Questions

Q1 Briefly explain two problems with comprehensive schools.

Q2 Give two examples of vocational qualifications introduced since 1988.

Exam Question

Q1 Outline and assess the changes in vocational education since 1988. (50 marks)

They've been trying to "sort it out for good" for donkey's years...

Cavemen probably argued about whether it was better to teach kids to count with rocks or with woolly mammoth bones...

The Education System and State Policy

These two pages are very much <u>not background</u> — this is the meaty stuff that you need for your course.

The **Conservative** government were influenced by the **New Right**

1) The **New Right** believe in the introduction of **market principles** to all aspects of social and economic life. This includes **less central control** from the government, and encouraging **more competition**. They argue that this makes services **more efficient** while **reducing dependence** on the state (see p.108).

2) New Right ideas influenced the **education policy** of the **Conservative government** which was in power 1979-1997.

The **1988 Education Reform Act** — *Choice, Inspections and More Tests*

In 1988, the **Conservative** government introduced some **major reforms** in education.

Education should link to the economy

The government introduced **more vocational courses** and more **work placement schemes**.

There should be better standards in education

1) The government introduced a **National Curriculum** of **compulsory subjects** for all **5 to 16 year olds**.

2) **OFSTED** (Office for Standards in Education) was set up to **inspect** schools and make sure they were doing a **decent job**. You might have seen **teachers** getting somewhat **frantic** before an inspection.

3) Schools could **opt out** of their local education authority and become **grant-maintained schools**. This means that they got money **straight from the government** and could **spend it how they liked**. The government believed this would **improve standards**.

There should be a system of choice and competition

1) Parents could **choose** which school to send their child to — if the school had **space**.

2) Parents could use **league tables** to help them choose. **League tables** show **how many** kids at each school **pass their exams**, and how many get **good grades**.

3) Schools worked like **businesses** and **advertised** for students.

There should be more testing and more exams

Pupils had to sit **SATs** at **7, 11 and 14**, and **GCSEs** at **16**.

A meeting of the League of Tables...

Brown (1990) *says these changes are a move towards* **Parentocracy**

parentocracy = rule by parents

Phillip Brown (1990) argues that the changes in the 1988 Education Act are shifting the focus of the education system from what **pupils** can **achieve**, to what their **parents want** and **can afford**.

He talks about a change from the "ideology of meritocracy" to an "ideology of parentocracy".

1) The **marketisation** of education gives parents a lot of **choice** and **power**. Parents are like **customers**, and schools are like businesses — and in business, it's a good idea to give your customers **what they want**.

2) Schools publish glossy **brochures** and prospectuses. These are aimed at **convincing parents** that they will provide good exam results, strong standards of discipline, good ICT facilities, modern sports facilities, a caring environment, a learning-oriented environment, a good preparation for university or work, etc.

3) Brown says that **parental wealth** has an effect. Even with **free education**, the wealth of parents affects the **choices** they can make. Parents who can **afford** to move to a house in the **catchment area** of a school with **good exam results** and OFSTED inspection reports will often choose to do so. Parents who can't afford that kind of house don't get as much choice about where to send their children to school.

4) Parents can also "play the system" in other ways. For example, they may start **going to church** in order to give their children a better chance of getting into a church school.

5) In some cases, parents have power to **influence** how subjects (especially potentially controversial ones like PSHE) are taught in school, or what kind of religious assemblies take place. Schools may choose to go along with what parents want in order to **avoid bad press**.

New Right theorists **Chubb and Moe (1988, 1997)** believe that parentocracy is a **good thing**. They argue that it's better for schools to follow what parents want than it is for schools for follow what **politicians** and **special interest groups** want.

The Education System and State Policy

New Labour Try to Mix Some of the Old Ideas Together

In 1997, New Labour took over. They wanted to do something about **inequality**, but they also said there should be **choice** and **diversity** in education. It's a bit like the old Labour policies and the Conservative policies **mixed up together** — it's called "**third way politics**".

The government has made some changes since 1997:

1) They've **reduced infant class sizes** to a maximum of **30**.

2) They've introduced **numeracy hour** and **literacy hour** in **primary schools**.

3) New Labour have allowed **faith schools** and **specialist status schools**.

4) New Labour have set up **Academies** — state secondary schools partly funded by businesses.
   These are very similar to the **City Technology Colleges** that the Conservatives introduced in 1988.

5) They've set up **Education Action Zones** in areas with **high deprivation** and **low educational achievement**.
   These zones get money from the government and the **private sector** — it's used to **pay teachers** more, and set up **homework clubs** to provide children with a quiet place to do homework, with access to books.

6) They've tried to **increase** the **number of people going to university**.

7) In 2000, policy changed to make A-level education broader.
   Students now have to do **AS/A2s** and **key skills**, and there are more **vocational courses**.

Since 1997 there have also been some changes to the **National Curriculum**.
The New Labour government are keen on **citizenship education** to make pupils more **aware of politics** and social issues.

New Labour Policies Follow Third Way ideas

1) The '**Third Way**' is a **middle ground** between New Right ideas on **marketisation** and the left wing policies of **government intervention**.

2) New Labour have continued the process of **market reforms** begun by the previous Conservative government. For example, they've allowed schools to **specialise** in certain subjects — e.g. by becoming Music Colleges or Science Colleges — to try to **create diversity** and **increase choice for parents**.

3) They've also pursued some interventionist policies, such as setting up **Education Action Zones**.

New Labour have been criticised

1) **New Right** thinkers have **criticised** New Labour for not giving parents **greater choice** in which schools they send their children to.

2) **Left wing** sociologists such as **Geoff Whitty** have argued that market-oriented educational reforms **create greater social divisions** by benefiting middle class families more than working class families.

3) **Beckett (2007)** criticises Academies. He argues that private sector businesses get too much **control** over what's taught in academies, compared to the amount of money they actually put in.

Practice Questions

Q1 Briefly describe two changes brought about by the 1988 Education Reform Act.

Q2 Outline one way in which New Right ideas have influenced public education policy since 1988.

Q3 Give one example of parentocracy in education.

Q4 Name three changes in education brought about by New Labour since 1997.

Exam Questions

Q1	Outline and assess the view that changes to educational policy since 1988 have improved equality of opportunity.	(50 marks)
Q2	Outline and assess the view that changes in education since 1988 have resulted in an "ideology of parentocracy".	(50 marks)

Some day you'll move out and escape the parentocracy...

Heh, you thought it was bad enough that your parents try to run your life — now it turns out that they're the shadowy force behind the whole post-1988 education system. It sounds good that your course only wants you to focus on changes since 1988, but when you look at the sheer amount of changes that have been packed in since then, you just want to say, "STOP! ENOUGH!"

Research and Sociological Theory

*Depending on who you believe, sociology may or may not be a science. Of course whether sociology's a science or not comes down in large part to what science actually is. Page **122** is for **AQA only**, but is also useful background for people doing **OCR**. Page **123** is for **AQA** and **OCR**.*

Science uses Experiments and Observation to Test Theories

1) Scientists collect data through **experiments**, **observation** and **measurement** in order to **test hypotheses** (a hypothesis is an unproved theory).

2) Science values **objectivity** (an unbiased viewpoint). Scientific statements are **based on evidence** which has been collected using **systematic**, **logical methods**.

There are Different Philosophies of Science

Obviously, it couldn't all be that simple. There are **different views** about **what science is all about**.

The Logical Positivists believe that scientists go off in search of scientific laws

1) The researcher **observes** something, and decides it needs to be **explained**.

2) The researcher thinks up a **hypothesis** to **explain** the observed phenomenon.

3) The hypothesis is **tested** by **experiments**.

4) If the experiments **agree** with the hypothesis, then the hypothesis becomes a **scientific law**. Scientific laws are **universal** — they explain all phenomena which are similar to the one which was observed in the first place.

This process is called verification, which means checking that something is true.

Rudolf Carnap (1936, 1966) and Carl Hempel (1966) are examples of logical positivist philosophers.

Popper (1959, 1963) argued that experiments should try to prove the hypothesis wrong — this is called "falsification"

1) The idea is that you can't ever **prove** a hypothesis **100% correct**, no matter how much evidence you've got — but you can prove it **wrong** with just **one** piece of evidence that **contradicts** it.

2) For example, the hypothesis "all swans are white" isn't proved correct by seeing one flock of white swans. You'd have to look at **every single swan in the universe** and see that they were all white to do that. But if you see just **one black swan**, that proves that "all swans are white" **isn't true**.

3) Popper believed that it wasn't possible to know **absolute truth**, because you can't prove things are correct.

Popper's view has been **criticised** by later philosophers of science who point out that an experimental result that disagrees with a hypothesis may be because of **experimental error** and **silly mistakes**. In Chemistry practicals, you may not get the **predicted result**, but that doesn't mean you've **proved chemistry wrong** — it usually means you've made a **mistake**.

Thomas Kuhn (1962) disagreed with both the logical positivists and Popper

1) Kuhn believed that science uses an **accepted body of knowledge** to solve puzzles. He called this "normal science". He was pretty critical of it...

2) He thought that scientists took a lot of **assumptions** about the world **for granted**. This assumed **way of looking at the world** is called a "paradigm". He said that what scientists do is **constrained** by the **paradigm** they take for granted. For example, for hundreds of years people thought that the Sun went around the Earth, and astronomical observations were interpreted according to the paradigm that the Sun went around the Earth.

3) Kuhn argues that **big leaps** of scientific progress come about when **evidence** which **doesn't fit the paradigm** builds up to the point where it **can't be ignored**. Then, scientists come up with a **new paradigm**. This process is called **scientific revolution**.

Paul Feyerabend (1975) went even further, and claimed that there **weren't** any **hard and fast rules** of scientific method. He argued that scientists make all kinds of **tweaks** to theories to make them work. He also disagreed with the idea that science tests hypotheses according to whether they fit observed facts, claiming that already-accepted theories **influence** the way scientists actually **observe** facts.

There's Disagreement about whether Sociology is Scientific

1) **Auguste Comte** (lived 1798-1857) was one of the founders of sociology, and he thought of it as a science. He thought sociology should be used to develop a **rational theory** of **society**.

2) **Popper** (see above) said that some sociological concepts **weren't scientific** as they couldn't possibly be **proved wrong**. Sociology could only be a science if it made **hypotheses** which could be **falsified**.

3) **Kuhn** argues that sociology **doesn't have a paradigm** — there isn't a consensus as to what it's about and how it's done. So in his view, it doesn't count as a science.

Research and Sociological Theory

Sociology is More Subjective than Traditional Science

1) **Objective knowledge** is the **same** no matter what your **point of view**. **Objective** methods provide **facts** that can be easily **verified** or **falsified**. Objective research is also **value-free** (see below), and doesn't have any bias.

2) **Subjective knowledge** depends on your **point of view**. **Subjective** methods give data that **can't** be easily tested. Subjective research requires **interpretation**.

AQA people should see p.126 for social action theory and subjectivity.

3) Sociology is **more subjective** than the physical **sciences**, but it aims to be at least partly objective.

4) Some **postmodernists** like **Lyotard (1984)** claim that it's **impossible** to be objective at all. Lyotard sees **knowledge** as something that people **construct**, not something that people **discover**.

Positivist Sociology tries to be as Objective as Possible

1) **Positivists** think sociology should be **scientific** and **analyse social facts**. Positivists define social facts as things that can be **directly observed and measured**, e.g. the number of followers of Christianity in Britain. Positivists claim that social facts are **external** to individuals, and constrain their behaviour.

2) Positivists look for **correlations in data**, and **cause and effect relationships**. To do this, they use **quantitative** methods like **questionnaires** (see p.138) and **official statistics**, which are **objective** and **reliable**.

1) **Interpretivist sociologists** (also called **interactionists**) reckon **sociology doesn't suit scientific methods**. They try to understand human behaviour from the point of view of the **individual**, so they use methods that let them discover the **meanings**, **motives** and **reasons** behind **human behaviour** and **social interaction**.

2) **Weber** (see p.169) said it's important to use **empathy** to figure out **why** an individual is doing what they're doing. He called this "**Verstehen**". Interpretivists take this idea very seriously — they're big on empathy.

There's Debate over whether Research can be Value-Free

1) **Value-free research** doesn't make **judgements** about whether the things that are researched are **good** or **bad**.

2) Value-free research doesn't let the **researcher's own beliefs** get in the way. For example, questionnaires mustn't ask questions that **lead** the respondent towards a particular answer.

3) In order for this idea of **value freedom** to work, the researcher must **interpret** all data **objectively**.

4) Value freedom means that the **end use** of the research **shouldn't matter**. Research should come up with **knowledge**, and how that knowledge is **used** isn't up to the researcher.

5) Positivists argue that **quantitative** research methods are, in general, **more value-free** than **qualitative** methods. Qualitative methods, such as unstructured interviews, mean the researcher is **more involved** and so there's **more risk** their attitudes and feelings will **influence** the respondents. Quantitative methods, such as closed questionnaires, allow the researcher **less opportunity** to influence their respondents. They allow the researcher to **keep their distance**.

Some sociologists say **sociology can't be value-free**.

1) The decision to research in the first place is **value-laden** — someone has to decide that the research is worth spending money on. Some say that research which the **state** or **businesses** want to see is most likely to get funding.

2) It's difficult to **completely avoid bias** and interviewer effects (see p.142). Researcher bias may interfere with structured questionnaires as it's still the researcher who chooses the questions respondents answer.

3) Some Marxist and feminist sociologists **deliberately choose research** with an **end use** that they **approve** of. They believe that sociology **should** make **value judgements** about society and **suggest** ways it could be **better**.

Practice Questions

Q1   What is a hypothesis?
Q2   Why do some sociologists say sociology can't be value-free?

Exam Question

Q1   Explain why some sociologists say that the study of sociology is scientific.   (15 marks)

Don't even get them started on "What is art?"...

*If you're flagging, remember that Sociology can lead to all sorts of **good jobs** — researcher, writer, lecturer, civil servant, NHS manager, housing officer, social worker... If you want to be a lion-tamer though, you're in the wrong book.*

Consensus Structuralism

*Structural perspectives analyse society as a whole system made up of different parts that mesh together. Structural approaches can be either consensus or conflict based. Consensus structuralism is pretty much the same thing as **functionalism** (which you already know and love). It stresses the harmonious nature of society, something Durkheim called "social solidarity".* **For AQA and OCR.**

Functionalists *use the* "Organic Analogy" *to describe the* Nature *of* Society

1) The **organic analogy** is used by **Talcott Parsons (1951)** to show how society acts like a **living organism**. An organism has a series of **organs** that are **interconnected** and **interdependent**, and Parsons says that likewise **society** is a set of parts that are all **interconnected**, and all **interdependent**.

2) Functionalists describe change as **"evolutionary"**, which means that if there's a change in one part of society, other parts will **slowly evolve** to adapt to this change.

3) **Social ills** (such as excessive crime) have a **disabling** effect on certain parts of the organism (society), and they can gradually "infect" other parts.

> According to functionalism, interrelations between the various parts of society can only happen because all members of society **agree** on values and norms. In other words, **society functions by value consensus**. These agreed values and norms are passed down from generation to generation through the process of **"socialisation"**.

Functionalism *says* Society's Needs *are met by* Four Major Subsystems

1) **Functionalism** says all members of society have **needs** and **desires** that the **social system** must cater for. These needs can be broken down into **instrumental** needs and **expressive** needs.

2) **Instrumental needs** are **material** — e.g. the need to be fed, the need to have a home. These needs are supported by the **economic subsystem** (**industries**) and the **political subsystem** (**political parties** and **trade unions**).

3) **Expressive** needs are **emotional** — e.g. the need to **belong**. They're looked after by a **kinship subsystem** (marriage and family) and a **cultural subsystem** (which includes schools and churches).

Functionalism tries to Explain Everything

1) Functionalism, through the work of **Comte, Durkheim and Parsons**, was the first real attempt to create a theory to explain the operation of the **whole of society**. This kind of theory is called a **macro-theory** — i.e. a **large-scale theory**, as opposed to a **micro-theory** or **small-scale theory**.

2) It's useful in showing how all the main institutions of society, such as the **education** system and the **family**, are **linked** to each other.

3) It helps to explain activities and actions that superficially seem **unusual** or strange. An example of this is **Durkheim's** study of **suicide (1897)**. In this study, Durkheim argues that **social structure** and problems in the modern world cause people to commit suicide. In this case, what seems to be an **individual act** is actually part of a **wider social picture**.

There's plenty more about suicide on p.88-89. Go and read it — it's relevant to this section.

Functionalism is Criticised for Ignoring Conflict and Maintaining Inequality

1) Functionalism is criticised for its focus on **harmony** and **cooperation**. It fails to take into account the **differences** and conflicts between groups in society.

2) It tries to see a **positive purpose** in **all aspects of society** — even aspects which many people would view as harmful and negative. Durkheim claimed that if a **social phenomenon** didn't fulfil a **function**, it wouldn't **exist**.

3) Functionalism has been seen by critics as a **conservative** approach to society that **upholds inequality** and injustice. Critics say the problems suffered by the working classes, women and ethnic minorities have not been adequately explained and justified by functionalism.

4) Functionalism has an almost **fatalistic** approach to the nature of **inequality** in society — it's seen as **inevitable**. Functionalists such as Parsons talk about **"meritocracy"**, which is the idea that people succeed or fail based on their own merits. This suggests that society is **already fair**, so it's pointless to make things more equal.

5) According to functionalists, **conflict** in society is **minimal** because people **accept** the **inevitability** of inequality. **Conflict theorists** (see p.125) definitely disagree on this.

Functionalism says that this hairstyle has a purpose in society.

Conflict Structuralism

Marxism is conflict structuralism. Marxists acknowledge that society is made up of institutions that work together. However, they believe that there is a conflict of interests between two different groups in society: the bourgeoisie and the proletariat.

Marxism says **Capitalist** society has created **Two Classes** with **Different Needs**

1) According to **Marx (1867)**, the ruling class owns and controls the means of production, and the working class work for the ruling class.

2) Marx explained change in society as the result of a **conflict of interests** between the **classes**.

3) According to Marx, the ruling class owns the **infrastructure** (the means of production) and sustain their control over it by utilising the **superstructure** (the **institutions** within society, e.g. religion, the education system).

4) In Marxist thought, the job of the superstructure is to legitimise the position of the ruling class through **ideological messages** within the institutions of society — i.e. society's institutions are set up to stop the working class gaining power, and also to make it seem okay for the ruling class to own and control everything.

5) Marx claimed that the proletariat (working class) are lulled into a **false consciousness**, which means they aren't fully aware of the **oppression** they suffer and how to **break free** from it. Marxists argue that only through **revolution** will the proletariat see how they have been oppressed, and then a socialist/communist society will emerge.

Neo-Marxism focuses on Ideology

1) Neo-Marxists such as **Althusser (1969)** and **Gramsci (1971)** redefined the focus of Marxism by developing the theory of **ideology**.

2) For example, Gramsci argued that the ruling class can only maintain power through **gaining the consent** of the working class by manipulative use of **ideology**. Althusser talks about **ideological state apparatuses** — e.g. the education system. See page 3.

Marxism is criticised for its Structural Focus and Determinism

1) Marxism is **deterministic** — it assumes that oppression is inevitable for the working class, until a revolution happens.

2) Marxism fails to see everyday life in any other terms than "**class conflict**". **Ethnicity** and **gender** are largely **sidelined**.

3) Additionally, the fall of Communism in Eastern Europe has been used as evidence for flaws in Marxist theory. However many people argue that Eastern Europe didn't have **true Communism** anyway.

4) The increased affluence and consensual nature of many Western societies highlights the **lack of conflict**.

Weber was Critical of Marxism

Weber said that there could be **conflict** between **all kinds of groups** in society. He **rejected Marx's idea** that the division between **owners** and **workers** was the **only important division**.

Weber claimed that people were divided by **class**, **status** and **political** grouping. Weberian conflict theorists such as **Dahrendorf (1959)** argue that conflict is **much more complicated** than Marx had claimed. Dahrendorf argues that conflict is based on **power** and **authority**, not **economics**.

Practice Questions

Q1 What are the four subsystems in society, according to functionalists?
Q2 What is the main difference between neo-Marxism and traditional Marxism?
Q3 Why are Marxist methodologies likely to be similar to functionalist ones?

Exam Question

Q1 Compare and contrast functionalist and Marxist theories on the nature of society. (33 marks)

I'm barely functional before my first cup of tea...

You'll probably be at least a little bit familiar with these theories from other sections. It helps to have it all here, so that you can revise what you need to know for the sociological theory and methods questions without getting it mixed up with other stuff. Make sure you know the differences between consensus and conflict structuralism — and the main criticisms of both.

Social Action Theory

*Social action theorists focus on the interaction between individuals and small groups, rather than on the big structures of society. Social action theory is pretty much the same thing as **interpretivism** (which you already know and love...).* **For AQA only.**

Social Action *sees individuals as "Social Actors" who* Act *rather than* React

1) Social action theorists see people as **making their own choices**, and taking their own **action**, rather than being **controlled** by **social structure** or **reacting** to social structure. They see people's actions as key to studying society.

2) Social action theory claims society is **constructed** from people's meanings, interpretations, behaviours and negotiations.

The process of **labelling** is important for understanding how people interact on a daily basis. People observe the behaviour of others and **classify** that behaviour into various **categories** — e.g. responsible, or delinquent, or deviant. Social action theorists see labelling **everywhere** — in the family, in education, in health care, in the sociology of deviance, etc.

Social Action Theory *sees* Social Order *as a* Social Construction

1) Social action theorists argue that social order isn't something generated by **institutions**, either through consensus or conflict. Social order is **part of everyday life**, and they see everyday life as a series of **interpretations**.

2) They say social order is a social construction — a **product** of individuals' minds. They say people want to believe that there's order in society so they behave towards others in a way that **convinces** them that there **is** order. For example, they **follow social norms**, e.g. being **polite** to each other, **not stealing** from each other.

Social Action Theory *rejects the idea that* Sociology *is* Objective

1) The idea is that if you believe that people put their own meanings and labels on the world, you also have to accept that they can all put **different labels** and **meanings** on the **same action**. Every person will interpret an action (e.g. drinking alcohol regularly) slightly differently to others depending on the meaning they attach to it, e.g. one person might think it's a normal part of relaxing after work, and another person might think it's the first sign of alcoholism.

2) This means that sociologists **can't predict** people's behaviour as easily as structural approaches would suggest. People don't passively react to external stimulation in exactly the **same way** every single time. They act differently according to the **circumstances**, and according to their own **personal opinions**.

3) In other words, social action theory says sociology **isn't an objective science**. It's all very, very subjective.

Social Action Theory *is* Criticised *for being so* Subjective

1) Social action theory is **criticised** for its **subjective** and **relativist** nature. Critics worry that if the world is seen as subjective and based on assumptions and interpretations, then **nothing is true or false** — this would reduce sociology to a **mess of individual opinions**.

2) Structuralists argue that social action theory fails to properly address the **large-scale structure** of society. They accuse social action theorists of concentrating too much on the **small scale**, and ignoring the **wider social context** that individuals act (or react) in.

3) Critics of social action theory also point out that social action theory doesn't really **explain social norms**. They're taken-for-granted as something we believe in, maybe because we want there to be some kind of social order.

This is a simplified version of Giddens' theory. The real thing is pretty abstract.

Structuration *combines* Structuralism *and* Social Action

1) Structuration theorists such as **Anthony Giddens (1984, 1987)** believe that there's a place for a strand of sociological theory and research that looks at both the **relationship between individuals** and their **social setting**.

2) Structuration theorists say that individuals are subject to **restrictions** and **pressures** generated by **social structures** and **social systems**, e.g. laws. But... they also argue that individuals **respond** to these in **different ways**. Individuals have an **awareness** of the social rules and structures and have **some level of choice** about how to react to them.

3) Structuration theorists say social structures are **open to change** — they can be **changed** by the actions of individuals.

Critics of structuration theory point out that institutions can **severely restrict** people's actions — not just affect them a little bit. Structuration theory assumes that if people want to change the world, they can manage it fairly easily. This is something that Marxists and feminists would disagree with.

Modernity and Postmodernity

Modernity refers to the Modern, Industrial, Ordered world

1) Modernity refers to the industrial world. It's linked to **urbanisation**.

2) It's also linked to the rise of **state bureaucracy**.

3) Modernity refers to a period of time when studies of the world were guided by **ordered**, **rational scientific** thinking. **Science** was seen as the answer, rather than the **traditional** sources of knowledge, such as religion.

4) Modernist sociological theories aim to **investigate** the world **scientifically**. They explain why societies have **evolved** to be the way they are, and explain why they're **arranged** in the way they are.

5) The modernist theories are the **structuralist** theories of **Marxism** and **functionalism**. These are also called "**grand narratives**", which is a fancy way of saying "**big stories**", and "**metanarratives**", which is a fancy word for "stories that **make sense** of **other stories**". They're **big**, **all-encompassing stories** that explain **how** the world got to be the way it is.

6) Modernist theories like Marxism claim a **monopoly of truth** — they claim that they're **objectively right** about the way the world is.

Postmodernism argues that Society has Progressed from Modernity

Postmodernists say that society today has **moved on** from the ordered industrial world of modernity. They point to various **changes** in society:

1) **Work** has become more **flexible**, and service industries have partly taken over from manufacturing industries.

2) **Globalisation** has affected both **production** and **communication**. There's been globalisation of **consumption** and **culture**.

3) There's an emphasis on **consumption of cultural products**.

4) There's **pluralism of culture**, and **pluralism of roles**. People **interpret** society, and their own identities, in **different ways** according to the **circumstances** they're in (i.e. the same woman could have labels and roles of "mother", "wife", "friend" and "employer").

Work had become increasingly flexible for Jeffrey

Postmodernists argue that sociology has moved into a time when "**metanarratives**" don't answer all the problems of the social world. Postmodernists say that there's a whole range of **competing theories** out there, which all have **something** to say about society. They argue that no one theory can claim a monopoly of the truth.

Postmodernism is Criticised by Structuralists and Social Action Theorists

1) Postmodernists emphasise the role of **culture** and the **media** in driving the creation of **identities**, **norms** and **values**. People no longer seek one answer to life but are happy to **pick** and **choose** values and identities.

2) This approach largely ignores the interactions between **individuals**, which **upsets social action theorists**. It also ignores the relationships between **social institutions**, which **upsets structuralists**.

3) Some sociologists **disagree** with the claim that we're living in a postmodern society. **Giddens (1990, 1991)** argues that we're actually in a state of "**high modernity**", with **high risk** of war, economic collapse or environmental disaster. He sees high modernity as like a **juggernaut** — a massive force which we can collectively try to direct, but which could go **out of control**.

Practice Questions

Q1 Which is more important to social action theory — social structure or personal circumstance?

Q2 How does structuration theory combine both structuralism and social action theory?

Q3 What is meant by the term "metanarrative"?

Exam Question

Q1 Evaluate the usefulness of structural and social action theories in a study of society. (33 marks)

When crossing the road, look both ways for the juggernaut of modernity...

Postmodernism is a lot easier to understand when you look at modernism. Modernism has all these ideas about how the world should be, and how sociology should be, and postmodernism decides to do the opposite. Remember that you can be asked about the usefulness of social theories in general to explain society, and that includes all the theories on these pages and on p.124-125.

Feminism

*These pages cover the main schools of feminism, and also have a little section on realism. For **AQA** and **OCR**.*

Feminist Theory aims to explain the causes of Gender Inequalities

1) Feminists believe that society is **patriarchal** — institutions are run by, and in the **interests** of, **men**.

2) Feminist theory aims to **unmask** patriarchy and to **empower** people to campaign against it.

3) Feminists also believe that traditional sociology and its theories and methods are often patriarchal and male-orientated. They are often interested in studying issues which have been **ignored** in **traditional sociology**, for example **domestic violence**, power relationships within the **family**, and gender inequalities in **education**.

4) There are many **different strands** of feminism, including **liberal** feminism, **radical** feminism, **black** feminism, **Marxist** feminism and **socialist** feminism.

Liberal Feminists want Equal Rights for Women

After completing her degree in engineering, Phyllis was delighted to find work within existing power structures.

1) **Liberal feminists** believe that the **main cause** of inequality is a lack of legitimate **opportunities** for women in **education**, **employment** and **politics**.

2) Liberal feminists believe the most effective way to bring about greater gender equality is to work within **existing power structures** to create **equal opportunities**.

3) An example of this is the introduction of laws that prevent sex discrimination, such as the **Equal Pay Act (1970)**.

4) Liberal feminists have been criticised by radical feminists for failing to recognise that **patriarchal values** are rooted in other areas of social life such as the **family**, as well as in formal institutions.

Radical Feminists want to Change Society Itself

1) **Radical feminists** argue that the very **structure** of **society** is based on the **oppression of women**. **Revolutionary change** is needed to bring about new **'gender roles'** and **real equality**.

2) **Kate Millett (1970)** argued that **patriarchy** was the **first** and is the **most fundamental** form of **inequality**. She argued that, **regardless of class**, **all women** are expected to be **subservient** to **all men**. While it may be **difficult** to **change** your **class**, historically at least, it has been all but **impossible** to **change** your **sex**.

3) Millett argued that there's a form of **politics** in all **relationships** featuring an **imbalance** of **power** — such as **at work** and **in the home**. Sexual politics for Millett was the **working** of that **power** to keep **women** in a **subordinate role**.

4) Millett saw the **ideology** of **patriarchy manifest** and **maintain** itself in:

   the family — where women are brought up to **expect** and **assume subordinate roles**.

   education — where women **aren't expected** to **study subjects** which **lead** to **high powered** or **highly paid jobs**.

   religion — which uses its **authority** to **strengthen patriarchy**.

5) Millett believed that women largely **internalise patriarchy** and come to **see themselves** as **inferior** — but that the **final guarantee** of **male dominance** is **force** and the **threat of violence**.

6) Millett **analysed** well-known **literary texts** by **D H Lawrence**, **Norman Mailer** and **Henry Miller** to show how they promote **sexist patriarchal ideology**.

Friedan blamed the Feminine Mystique

1) Influential feminist **Betty Friedan (1963** *The Feminine Mystique* New York: Norton**)** argued that women were limited by ideas of **'femininity'**, and that women were victims of an ideology she called the **'feminine mystique'**.

2) This promoted the idea that a **'good woman'** gloried in her own femininity, and focused her life on trying to "catch" a **man**, please her **husband**, and be a **good mother**.

3) Friedan argued that this limited the possibilities in spheres outside of the home, and that women brought up only to be **wives** and **mothers** often ended up feeling **unfulfilled** with no real **identity** of their own.

4) Friedan believed women were **ashamed** of these **feelings**, and so **didn't talk** about them. This led Friedan to describe this **unhappiness** as **"the problem with no name"** — something she discovered after sending out an **in-depth questionnaire** to her classmates at Smith College, 15 years after graduation.

Feminism and Realism

Feminist Sociology doesn't try to be Value Free

1) Generally, feminist sociologists **don't believe** in **value-free research** — they want their work to help **combat patriarchy** and the oppression of women.

2) Feminists would argue that much sociology in the past that claimed to be value-free was in effect **biased** against women. Feminist sociology has countered **"malestream"** sociology, which largely ignored the situation of women, by focusing on previously ignored topics — such as **domestic violence**.

3) In her **1983** essay **"Do her answers fit his questions?"**, Hilary Graham suggested that surveys are often designed around the experiences and assumptions of men — even when they're specifically for women — and so women's experiences haven't really been captured. Many feminists feel that their research should be **designed** and directed to take into consideration their **respondents' needs** as much as the needs of their research.

4) Much feminist sociology has been qualitative and interpretivist in nature. **Oakley (1981)** argued that a feminist interviewing women should aim at a **more friendly**, **less hierarchical** relationship with interviewees. When researching the experiences of pregnant women she felt obliged to answer any questions they had about her work and their pregnancies — which fundamentally **changed** the normal **interviewer-interviewee** relationship.

5) Feminists also use **quantitative data and analysis**, for example for studying the **disparity** in average **wage levels** between the genders.

Realist Sociology argues that Sociology can be Scientific

1) **Realists** believe that sociology can be **scientific** — but they define science in a different way to positivists (see p.123). They divide science into two kinds:

   - The study of **closed systems** — subjects like chemistry where the **variables** can be **closely controlled** and laboratory experiments can be done.
   - The study of **open systems** — subjects such as meteorology where the variables are **difficult** or impossible to **control**. Scientists can't make very accurate predictions and can't easily test them experimentally.

2) **Sayer (1984)**, a realist, argued that sociology is the scientific study of an **open system**. Society, like the weather, is **too complex** a system to lend itself to accurate predictions and experiments, but that doesn't mean sociology's not a science.

3) Realists use **qualitative** as well as **quantitative** methods. Individual human motivations — which are investigated by qualitative methods — can't be **directly observed** or **measured**. But realists argue that science has a long and **successful history** of **researching** things that can't (or couldn't at the time) be **directly observed**, e.g. **black holes** in space.

4) Realists argue that science isn't fundamentally defined by the **collection** and **recording** of **observable data** — for them it's the **search** for the **underlying causes** of **things**, even if those causes aren't directly observable. Realists believe that the **mechanisms** behind social trends and phenomena are **real** and can be **scientifically studied**.

5) They argue that sociology **can't** be entirely **value-free**, but researchers must try to **collect** and **present data** in a **clear** and **neutral** way.

Realism is a tricky concept. It's used in lots of different ways in all sorts of contexts — politics, international relations, criminology. Here we're just talking about sociology and different realists from the right and left realists you study in the Crime and Deviance topic.

Practice Questions

Q1 Name three schools of feminism.

Q2 Why don't most feminists believe in value-free research?

Q3 What, for realists, is the difference between an open and a closed system?

Exam Question

Q1 Outline and explain the concept of patriarchy.   (15 marks)

It's a real headache...

I like feminism — although it has many different varieties, it's stacked around central concepts that basically make sense. It's a school of sociology that has clear ideas about the kind of things to be researched (women, gender, etc...), and has a long history of campaigning and getting things done. Now realists, on the other hand, can't even get a monopoly on their own name.

Sociology and Social Policy

Social policy focuses on social problems and how social institutions respond to them. Social policy analysts use sociological research to inform governments and other organisations, and influence their response to social problems. **For AQA only.**

Giddens claims the study of sociology gives Four Practical Benefits

Anthony Giddens (2001) believes that sociological research has four practical purposes:

> 1) An **understanding** of the world.
> 2) A heightened awareness of the needs of **individual groups**.
> 3) An assessment of **"what works"** — **evidence-based policy**.
> 4) An increased **personal knowledge** of ourselves and others.

Social Policy is the area of Government that tries to Help People

1) **Social policies** are those parts of **government** policy that deal with the **well-being** of their **citizens** — pensions, unemployment benefits, education, health, etc. **Social Policy** has also come to be the name of the **academic subject** that **studies** this area of government.

2) New ideas for social policy are generated by **governments**, **political parties** and **pressure groups**. Social policy **varies** with the **party** in power — i.e. in the UK most likely either **Labour** or the **Conservatives**.

3) Most **research** into social policy issues is carried out by **government agencies** such as the departments for **education** and **health**, but some is done by **charities**, such as the **Joseph Rowntree Foundation**, and **university departments**.

4) Governments use **quantitative statistical social research** to **discover** basic **social trends** such as the levels of **population growth**, **unemployment**, **income** and **inequality**. More in-depth, **qualitative social research** can give governments an **insight** into the **causes** of **social problems** such as **poverty** and **crime** — and can **help** in the **search** for **policies** to deal with them.

Sociological Research gives Policy Makers insight into Poverty and Inequality

1) The creation of the **Welfare State** after the Second World War gave many the **impression** in the late 1960s that **poverty** had been largely **eradicated** from the UK.

Empirical evidence means data that's from observation and experience.

2) However, **empirical evidence** from **Peter Townsend (1979)** and **Mack and Lansley (1985)** showed that poverty was a hidden problem. Later research by the **Child Poverty Action Group** reported that some groups experienced poverty more than others.

3) Sociologists then did more research to come up with theories of **why** certain groups were more vulnerable to poverty. **Social Democrats** blamed an **inadequate** welfare system, the **New Right** (e.g. **Marsland (1989)**) blamed **reliance** on an over-generous welfare system, and **Third Way** thinkers emphasised **citizenship** (two-way responsibility between the citizen and the state).

4) These theories, plus **empirical data**, guided **social policy** about welfare, poverty and inequality.

This link between sociology and social policy was particularly close in the case of **Frank Field (1989, 1996)**, who wrote about the underclass as a group denied citizenship rights, and suggested **social policy changes** to improve the living standards of the elderly and unemployed, and to get the unemployed back into work. Between 1997 and 1998, as a **Minister** in the Labour government, he actually **was** a **social policy maker**.

Weber believed Sociology shouldn't tell decision-makers How to Fix Society

1) Weber believed that sociology **shouldn't make value judgements** — it shouldn't tell policy makers **how to fix society**.

2) Weber argued that sociological research can tell decision makers whether a particular policy is likely to have the **desired result**, and what **social costs** the policy will incur. Weber thought that the policy maker should come up with the **policy first**, and **then** the researchers should go away and find evidence to work out the best way of doing it.

3) Weber thought it was important to have **good methodology** to give the most **useful information** to policy makers.

4) Critics of this view say policy should come **after evidence gathering**, not before. There's a danger that only evidence which **backs up** the policy will be found. Evidence which might suggest a **much better policy** might be ignored.

Postmodernists have Diverse Views on the link between research and policy

1) Postmodernist **Zygmunt Bauman (1990)** believes that sociology **should** inform social research, and worries that society may **get worse** if sociological theories about **poverty** and **welfare** aren't listened to. He argues that **postmodern consumer society** is **marginalising** the Welfare State, and believes this to be a bad thing.

2) On the other hand, Lyotard is worried that **"scientific"** methods of sociological research could be used to construct **oppressive metanarratives**. **Lyotard** sees **modernist metanarratives** (see p.127) as leading to **strict doctrine** and **oppression**. (Go back and read about metanarratives on p.127 if you're getting confused...).

Sociology and Social Policy

Marxists think sociology is **Too Close** to the **Capitalist System**

1) Marxists believe that sociology is too closely intertwined with the **capitalist system** to make a difference to society. Since Marxists believe that capitalism is inherently flawed and oppressive, they suggest that sociological study is a **tool** used to **justify unjust social policy**.

2) Marxists believe that research is **controlled** by **ruling class interests**, which prevents it from being used to change the system to socialism. They point to the amount of **funding** for sociological research which comes from the **state** and from **industry** — they claim sociology is being **bought**.

3) An example would be the use of empirical data to show that the poorest in society are over-represented in prison. Marxist commentators argue that sociology is being used here to **justify social policy** designed to **further oppress** and **marginalise** the working classes by focusing on crimes committed by the poor rather than looking at the underlying reasons for crime (i.e. the nature of capitalism, according to Marxist theory).

Some Feminists believe Sociology **Can't** affect **Gender Inequality**

Feminists are in **disagreement** over whether or not sociological research can actually improve the lives of women in a patriarchal society.

1) **Liberal feminists** believe that sociological research and analysis has influenced governments and had **beneficial results** for women's lives. For example, the UK has developed social policy designed to improve the status of women and make them equal in all spheres of social life including employment and benefits.

2) However, **radical feminists** argue that liberal feminist sociology can't **make much difference** to the lives of women because society is **inherently patriarchal**. Radical feminists such as **Shulamith Firestone (1971)** believe that patriarchal society must be dismantled before women's lives can ever be improved.

3) **Socialist feminists** claim that social policy oppresses women in particular. They argue it **undervalues women's labour** (e.g. in the voluntary and informal welfare sectors) and assumes they will bear a double burden of work and housework. Socialist feminists propose changes to social policy based on their own research and ideology.

Some believe the **Link** between **Sociology** and **Social Policy** isn't all that strong

Governments take account of research, but they're **constrained** by **other factors**.

1) Firstly, governments often seek to implement social policy that's **popular** with the **electorate**. It's argued that policies which aren't clear vote winners don't get implemented.

2) Some groups in society may be marginalised because they **don't vote** in **large numbers**. Even if sociology focuses on these groups, they may still find themselves neglected if they don't have electoral power.

3) Governments must consider the **financial implications** of any policies they introduce. If a policy is **too expensive**, then no matter how persuasive the sociological research behind it is, it **isn't going to happen**. Also, **expensive policies** tend to make **voters worry** that **taxes** might have to **increase** to pay for them.

Practice Questions

Q1 What four practical benefits does sociology have for society, according to Giddens?

Q2 What role did Weber think sociology should have in relation to social policy?

Q3 How do Marxists criticise the link between sociology and social policy?

Q4 What other factors affect government decisions on social policy, other than sociology?

Exam Question

Q1 "Sociology has no effect on social policy." How far do the sociological perspectives and evidence you have studied agree or disagree with this statement?

(33 marks)

Sociology, eh — what's it all for...

In an exam, remember that all arguments in this topic are broken into three camps: 1) sociology should actively try and influence policy, 2) sociology should try to change and replace the system, and 3) sociology shouldn't influence social policy. Some people criticise sociologists such as Giddens for overplaying the ability of sociology to influence government decisions and actions.

Stages in the Research Process

*The first step in sociological research is figuring out what you're going to research. The second step is condensing your topic down into a single question, or a single hypothesis. These pages are for **OCR** and **AQA**.*

Sociologists pick a **Topic** based on their own **Preference** and **Knowledge**

Well, obviously. But there's slightly more to it than the obvious, so here you go.

1) Sociologists often **specialise** in different fields of the subject and therefore will often choose a topic that they have experience or knowledge of — for example, **Steve Bruce** specialises in **religion**.

2) Sociologists try to pick a topic that they think they'll find **enjoyable** and **interesting** to research. It's best not to try a piece of research that you won't enjoy — it only leads to a poorly constructed report that may be either flawed or just plain boring.

3) Also, certain topics become popular in sociology at different times. For example, research in the **mid-twentieth century** often focused on **stratification** and the **class system**. **Nowadays**, the focus of sociologists has moved on to other topics such as **World Sociology**. To gain **prestige**, **funding** and public or academic **interest**, sociologists are more likely to focus their research on topics that are currently **in vogue**.

4) Sociologists and other academics who want to make a **change** in society prefer research that could help develop **solutions** to **social problems**.

5) Sociologists may feel that a particular issue is **neglected** by other researchers, so they'll research the issue to try and "**plug the gap**" — and encourage others to embrace the issue as well.

People often asked Francis what it was that first made him focus on the sociology of coastal leisure in the Caribbean.

Funding and **Cooperation** for **Research** have an impact on the choice of **Topic**

1) There are a wide range of potential **sources of funding**. Some research is funded by **charities**, e.g. the Joseph Rowntree Foundation. Some is funded by **industry**. Some are funded by the **government**. A lot of quantitative studies are done **directly** by **government agencies**.

2) The organisation which funds the research is sometimes called a **gatekeeper**, because it often has the final say in the **choice of topic**, the **way** that the topic is **researched** or whether a topic gets researched at all. Government agencies often do research into areas covered by current or proposed **government policy**. **Industrial** grant providers tend to fund research that gives their industry some **practical benefit**.

3) Additionally, a researcher needs to decide whether or not they will be able to get the **cooperation** of the groups they'll be studying if they choose a particular topic. If potential subjects refuse to give their help for the research, then the topic may not be viable.

The researcher's **Career** in **Sociology** is another factor in selecting a topic

1) Sociologists have their eye on their **careers**, just like everyone else. Researchers would jump at the chance to conduct a study that improves their **employability**. Interesting, original or popular topics that are well researched, with good clear results, improve an academic's chance of having their work **published**. Getting work published, particularly in one of the **big sociological journals**, really **improves a researcher's standing** in academia.

2) A quick way for a sociologist to progress in their career is to respond to another sociologist's work. The aim can be either to **prove** the other sociologist **wrong**, or to **add something** to their research. Practically speaking, this could mean investigating the same topic, but using slightly different methods, or investigating a different group of people.

3) This can mean that particular social groups are researched a lot. For example, **routine office workers** are frequently researched in order to test out **theories of stratification** — some systems classify them as working class and some as middle class. Each sociologist who wants to **disprove** or **add to** earlier research on classification has to research **yet another** bunch of routine office workers. Beekeepers **never** get this level of interest from sociologists.

Reviewing the **Field** is crucial to a good research topic

1) **Reviewing** and **critiquing** existing **data** and **literature** is an important feature in any sociological report. It requires the researcher to spend time reading **articles**, **publications** and other sources of information already produced on the subject.

2) The researcher then needs to **analyse** this material to help clarify the issues around the subject.

3) Reviewing the field gives the researcher useful information on the types of **methodology** used in **previous studies**. They can see whether specific methods, e.g. structured interviews, worked in the past. They can see if research samples were big enough, and form ideas about how big their own sample should be.

"Lush, undulating, 4/5"

See p.134-145 for more on methodology.

Stages in the Research Process

Research Questions give Focus to sociological research

1) Once the researcher has chosen a broad topic area, they need to **narrow down** the focus of their research so they don't spread their work out too thinly and end up with not enough detail. They do this by coming up with a **single research question** that their research aims to **answer**.

2) A good research question should focus on **one part** of the topic, and it should be **clear** and **easy** to **research**.

3) Questions should be as **value-free** as possible. In other words they shouldn't be **biased**, or **suggest potential social changes**. So, "Should governments provide vocational education to 14-year-olds?" isn't a good research question because it asks for a **value judgement** on social policy. "What are the attitudes of employers, parents and teachers towards vocational education for 14-year-olds?" is **better**.

Hypotheses are Statements that make Predictions that can be Tested

1) A hypothesis is a **statement** that makes a **prediction**. A hypothesis acts as a **starting point** for research. The research will aim to either **show that the hypothesis is true**, or **show that it's false**. Having an idea and then testing against the evidence is the traditional view of scientific research. Having a hypothesis and trying to prove it wrong is called the falsification model (see p.122).

2) A hypothesis states a **relationship** between **two factors** — e.g. "sociology teachers wear corduroy trousers" or "material deprivation causes educational underachievement".

Terms like "democracy" need to be Operationalised — i.e. Made Measurable

1) Sociology prides itself on giving names to **concepts** and **ideas** that aren't **easily explained** or measured. For example, it's **tricky** to measure things like "democracy", "development" and "culture".

2) You end up measuring these concepts by measuring **something else** that's **linked** to the tricky concept — sociologists call this an **indicator**. This is called "**operationalising**" a concept. It means making it operational, or workable, by finding a way to measure it.

3) Researchers do this **every time** they conduct a piece of research, because you **can't research** something if you **can't measure** it. Each difficult concept needs an **indicator**, e.g. electoral participation or diversity of electoral results for democracy.

4) There's a **series of steps** that a researcher needs to go through in order to **operationalise** a concept properly:

Operationalising a concept	Example — "democracy"
1) Clearly **define** the concept.	Rule by the people
2) Define its **dimensions** — i.e. say what **other ideas** it's **made up of**.	Voting, freedom of speech
3) Define **potential indicators** to test the various **dimensions** of the concept.	Electoral **turnout, voting patterns**
4) Select the **most useful** indicators.	**Voting patterns**
5) Create **data collection techniques** for each indicator.	Compare successive **general election results**

5) Researchers need to be able to **justify** how they **operationalised** their concepts in their final report. This is often a **subjective** process and the way a researcher operationalises may be **criticised** by other sociologists.

Practice Questions

Q1 Give three factors to consider when choosing a topic for research.

Q2 Why is reviewing the field useful?

Q3 What is the "operationalisation of concepts"?

Exam Question

Q1 Explain the importance of operationalisation in sociology. (15 marks)

Isn't operationalising setting terms to music?

Not only is it vital you learn these pages for your exams, it's worth knowing about this stuff if you're thinking of becoming a sociologist. That's a frightening thought, isn't it. One day you too could find your name in a revision guide, with your life's work condensed into a nice maroon box. And then the following box will explain why everyone else thinks you're an idiot.

Research Design

*This page is a spot of revision of AS material for **AQA** and **OCR**. There is some new stuff here too though, so don't skip over it.*

Remember the **Difference** between **Reliability** and **Validity**

1) Reliable research can be **repeated** to get the **same results**. Reliable data means data that **another researcher** would be able to get by using the **exact same methods**.

2) **Sociological research** isn't generally as reliable as research in the **natural sciences** (physics, biology, chemistry, etc.).

1) Valid data is a **true picture** of what the researcher is trying to measure.

2) Even **reliable** data isn't always valid. For example, you could measure democracy by measuring voter turnout. This wouldn't always give a true picture, because it's possible to have **high voter turnout**, but **completely fixed elections** (e.g. under a dictatorship).

Research can be **Primary** or **Secondary** and **Quantitative** or **Qualitative**

Primary Data	Secondary Data
Information gathered by the **researcher themselves** — it's new, **original** and not taken from any existing data set.	Information gathered from **existing data sets** or **documents** — e.g. official statistics, diaries etc.
Primary data is as **valid** and **reliable** as the researcher's method makes it.	The researcher has to **trust** that the data is **valid** and **reliable** — this is easier if the researcher can find out the **original methodology**.
Collecting primary data can be **time-consuming** and **expensive**.	Using secondary data can **save** the researcher **time and money**.

Quantitative methods	Qualitative methods
These produce **numbers** and **statistics**.	These produce **stories**, and include people's **motivations**, and the **meanings** they give to what they do and think.
Can be **very reliable** — studies are easily repeated.	Qualitative methods **aren't reliable**.
May not be valid. Doesn't include anything subjective.	Can be **very valid**.
They allow the use of **large samples** (see p.135) so they can be **highly representative** of the population.	They're **time-consuming**, so they only use **small samples**. This means they're **less representative** than quantitative methods.

Theoretical considerations **Influence** choice of **Method**

1) **Structural** theories like **functionalism** and **Marxism** favour a **positivist** approach and **quantitative** methods.

2) **Functionalists** argue that the social world acts similarly to the **natural world** and therefore all study should be similar to that of "natural science" — i.e. using **objective** and **quantitative techniques**.

3) **Marxists** explain the nature of society in **economic** terms which also tend towards "scientific" techniques of data collection — i.e. quantitative methods.

4) **Social action** theories are interpretivist — they favour **qualitative** methods, because social action theory is **subjective**.

5) For a social action approach, methods of data collection are more **small-scale** and **in-depth**. In order to analyse **why** people make the assumptions they make and act in the way they do, researchers **observe** and **question** them **at length**.

6) Social action theorists prefer techniques that give detailed **stories** and **meanings** — e.g. ethnographic studies, unstructured interviews (see p.139) and observation (see p.140).

Practical considerations **Influence** choice of **Method**

1) Some methods take a lot of **time** — **qualitative** methods tend to **take longer** than quantitative methods. Participant observation takes a very long time both to plan and to complete. But quantitative methods can also be time-consuming — social surveys take a relatively short time to **complete**, but a **long time** to **interpret**.

2) **Funding** affects choice of method. The **researcher's time** costs money, **resources** such as computers cost money, and it costs money to send out **postal questionnaires** to large samples.

3) **Lack of access** to primary sources would mean that the researcher has to use **secondary** sources.

Research Design

Before you can Start — you Need a Sample

1) All researchers have a **target population** in mind before conducting research, which might be anything from **everyone** in a **country** or **region**, to a select group with **specific characteristics**, such as 'all women over 50' or 'all pupils in one school'.

2) It's **too expensive** and **time-consuming** for sociologists to survey the **whole population**. They select a **sample**.

3) If the **characteristics** of the **sample** reflect the **characteristics** of the **target population** — with similar proportions of people in terms of age, class, ethnicity and gender — then the sample can be said to be **representative** of that target population. The extent to which a sample represents the target population is known as its **representativeness**.

4) If the sample is sufficiently **large** and **representative**, then it should be possible to make **generalisations** from it about the **wider target population**. The extent to which you can accurately do this is the sample's **generalisability**.

5) Some target populations may be **difficult** to **access** — e.g. criminals, the very young or very old. In these cases you can use **non-probability sampling** methods such as **snowball sampling** — see the section on non-probability sampling below.

Probability Sampling involves Random Selection

Probability sampling involves picking names out of a "sampling frame" at **random**. A sampling frame is a **complete list** of the population being sampled, which needs to be **accurate**, **complete** and without any **duplicate** entries — easier said than done. **Random**, **systematic** and **stratified random** are all kinds of probability sampling.

1) In simple **random sampling**, names are taken completely at random, e.g. randomly selected from a list by a person or a computer, so each member of the population has an **equal chance** of being selected.

2) **Systematic** sampling involves choosing a **starting point** in the sampling frame and selecting every *n*th value, e.g. every fifth name. There may be bias, if there's an underlying pattern in the sampling frame.

3) In **stratified random sampling** the population is put into **segments** called "strata" based on things like age, gender or income — e.g. age 18-24, 25-34, 35-44, 45-54, 55-64, 65+. Names are selected at random from within each segment.

Non-Probability Sampling involves Human Choice

The following are different types of **non-probability sampling**.

1) In **quota sampling**, the selection is made by the **interviewer**, who'll have a quota to meet — e.g. "interview 20 women between 25 and 34". It's a bit like stratified random sampling, but it's not random — interviewers tend to pick people who look "nice", which introduces bias. It's quick and useful, though.

2) **Multi-stage sampling** means selecting a sample from **within another sample**. It's often used to select samples for opinion polls to measure voting intention. First, a selection of constituencies is chosen to represent the whole country, then postcodes within that constituency are selected, then houses from those postcodes.

3) **Snowball sampling** means finding **initial contacts** and getting them to **give you more names** for your research.

4) **Purposive sampling** is when researchers select non-representative samples that will yield information-rich cases for in-depth study. There are many different ways of doing this. **Extreme** or **deviant sampling** means selecting the most extreme or unusual individuals for study. **Typical case sampling** involves studying those who are average or typical of a particular group.

5) Sociologists sometimes **deliberately** pick a sample who **aren't representative**, in order to try to **falsify** a hypothesis about social behaviour. E.g. feminist sociologists trying to disprove the idea that gender roles are determined by biological difference deliberately looked for samples where women's roles **weren't different from men's roles**, or weren't traditionally "feminine".

A Pilot Study is a Small-Scale Practice Run before the Real Research

A **pilot study** lets you test the **accuracy** of your questions, and check if there are any **problems** in your **research design**. You can use them to make studies **more valid** and **reliable**, test how **long** the research will take, and **train** your interviewers. Though they're **time-consuming**, **expensive** and create lots of **work**, they show that the project is **feasible**, and can help you secure **research funding**.

Practice Questions

Q1 What does it mean to say that a study is: a) reliable, b) valid?

Q2 What is a sampling frame?

Exam Question

Q1 Identify and explain two methods of sampling that you could use for a postal questionnaire. (6 marks)

I did a pilot study once — I made notes while golfing with a Wing Commander...

These pages cover the real nuts and bolts of sociological research. Every study at some point involves someone sitting down and having a good think about these things — what population to study, what methods to use, what kind of sample to select...

Ethics in Research

*Ethics is concerned with appropriate behaviours and procedures that sociologists must adhere to when conducting research. The British Sociological Association publish guidelines to help researchers to conduct ethical research. For **AQA** and **OCR**.*

Ethical Considerations can be grouped into Four Main Areas

1) **Consent** — all participants must have openly agreed to take part.
2) **Confidentiality** — the details of all participants and their actions must remain confidential and private.
3) **Avoidance** of **harm** — participants should not be physically or psychologically harmed by the research process.
4) **Avoidance** of **deception** — researchers should be open and honest about the study and its implications.

Participants should give Free, Informed Consent to their role in the study

1) The researcher should get participants' **consent** before they conduct their study. Sociologists should be **open** and **honest** about the work they wish to carry out. It's important that the respondent knows what they're signing up for.
2) **Children** or people with **learning difficulties** may **not fully understand** what participation would entail. This is problematic. It can be argued that **uninformed consent** isn't really consent at all.
3) Consent can be **difficult to obtain**, especially from **secretive** groups (e.g. Scientologists, the Freemasons, gangs) or when the research is about a **sensitive** topic (e.g. crime, sexuality).

But... studies can be **endangered** if the person studied is aware of the **real purpose** of the work.

Milgram (1974) was not honest with participants in his experiments on obedience

Background:	Milgram conducted a series of experiments in which volunteers were ordered to administer electric shocks to another person on the other side of a glass screen, when that person failed to give the correct answers in a memory test. Many volunteers kept on giving punishment shocks until the actor pretended to pass out.
Deception:	• Milgram lied about the purpose of the experiment. He told the volunteers that they were doing an experiment about **memory**. • The electric shocks **weren't real**. The person who the volunteers were "shocking" was an actor, pretending.
Results:	The results of the experiment were **very useful**. The experiment showed how people are ready to **obey** authority without **question**. This helped people understand how **ordinary people** take part in war crimes and genocide.

The experiment **wouldn't have worked** if the volunteers **knew** the real purpose of the experiment. If they knew that their **obedience** was being tested, they might have deliberately been less obedient. If they knew the shocks weren't real, they wouldn't have behaved in the same way. Milgram **had to be dishonest** for the experiment to work at all.

The general opinion is that this experiment **wouldn't be allowed to go ahead today** — partly because of the **deception**, but mostly because of the risk of **psychological harm**. Some participants were disturbed at how **easily** Milgram had **manipulated** them. However, Milgram **debriefed** all the participants afterwards so they all **understood** the study, and did **follow-up work** to check that they weren't psychologically harmed. He found that some participants saw it as a **valuable learning experience**.

Covert Studies are Criticised for not getting Informed Consent

1) Covert methods (e.g. **covert participant observation**, see p.140) **don't tell** the group being studied that they actually are being studied. They're often criticised for their **lack of honesty** and the absence of **true informed consent**.
2) Covert participant observers argue that to **negotiate access** into **sensitive** or **dangerous** groups such as criminals, the researcher often has to either **pretend to be part of the group**, or not inform the group of the **true purpose** of the study.

Laud Humphreys' "Tearoom Trade" (1970) was a covert observation of secretive homosexual activity

The group:	The group Humphreys wished to study were men who engaged in homosexual activities in **public places** (especially public toilets). They were **secretive** about their activities for three main reasons — homosexuality was **taboo** in mainstream society, sexual activity in public is **against the law**, and some of the men may have been married men leading a **"secret life"**.
Covert study:	Humphreys probably wouldn't have gained access to this group if he'd openly and honestly informed them about the nature of the research and then sought their permission. Even if he did gain their permission, it's likely that they'd have **acted very differently** if they were aware that they were being observed. Humphreys therefore posed as someone who watches homosexual acts for a sexual thrill. This enabled him to gain the **trust** of the group and for him to observe **genuine actions**.

Not that sort of tearoom...

Other sociologists argue that work like Humphreys' shouldn't be conducted, even if they give valuable insights to sociology.

Ethics in Research

Respondents have Rights to Privacy and Anonymity

1) All respondents taking part in a piece of research must have their **basic right to privacy** valued and **upheld**. The **data** gathered from them and their **personal details** must not be distributed to anyone **outside** the **research process**.

2) When the report is finally produced, respondents must be made **anonymous**. Any descriptions of people, geographical locations and institutions have to be written in a way that prevents readers from easily recognising the participants. **False names** may be used — in which case the researcher should **clearly state** that false names have been used, in case someone who **shares** the name is **mistakenly identified** as having taken part in the research.

3) Of course, if a researcher **breaches** trust and confidentiality, potential participants will be **put off** taking part in future studies. Research participants must feel they can **trust** the researcher, especially if the research is of a sensitive nature — e.g. a self-reported crime study, or a sexual health survey.

Researchers must make sure that Nobody is Harmed by Taking Part in a study

1) Emotional and physical harm is **never acceptable** in sociological research, and work is actively criticised and rejected if it has allowed harm to come to those involved.

2) For example a study into street prostitution could potentially be carried out through observation. It could be argued that the researcher is putting the prostitute into a **dangerous situation** just to gain useful data.

3) Researchers studying topics such as **mental health** or **geriatric care** may stumble across **situations** and **experiences** that cause individuals **harm** — e.g. inappropriate living conditions, or abuse by carers. There is an ethical question as to whether they should **stop** or **suspend** the research in order to **remove** the individual from the dangerous situation.

4) Some topics that are discussed may be **traumatic** for the respondents — they would need to be **informed** of the possible temporary mental and emotional harm before starting the study. Remember, it's important to make sure that all consent is **informed consent** (i.e. that the person fully understands all the implications and aspects of the research before they agree to take part).

Some Sociologists can justify Bending or Breaking ethical rules

There's a lot of **good** that can come from sociological research. Many sociologists can **justify** breaking or slightly bending some of the **ethical rules** — if the data that they'll gather is likely to make a beneficial contribution to society. This justification becomes even stronger if potential ethical problems are minimised — e.g. if there's **minimal harm** and **full confidentiality**, but just a **wee bit of deception** (the basis of covert participant observation).

1) For example, **Nigel Fielding (1981)**, in a study of the **National Front** (an extreme right-wing political party with a secretive hierarchy) argues that he needed to conduct covert research otherwise he wouldn't have been able to gain access to the group and gather information.

2) **"James Patrick" (1973)** was a false name given to a researcher conducting a study on **violent gangs** in Glasgow — to ensure his **own safety** and protection.

3) **Roy Wallis (1977)** wasn't entirely **honest** when researching Scientology. He didn't say he was a sociologist when he signed up to a Scientology course. If he had been honest, the Scientologists may have told him to go away. Wallis was also forced to **name** some of his sources, during a **legal battle** between the Church of Scientology and another researcher. This broke the rule on **privacy** and **anonymity**, but in this case Wallis had **no choice**.

Practice Questions

Q1 What are the four main ethical considerations a sociologist needs to assess in their study?

Q2 Why is covert participant observation seen as unethical?

Q3 Give two reasons that sociologists give to justify breaking ethical rules.

Exam Question

Q1 Assess the importance of ethics when conducting sociological research. (40 marks)

Danger, sociologists at work...

Well, obviously you wouldn't decide to do a covert observation into how people react to being hit over the head. Because that would be wrong. The key point here is that sometimes there are justifications, but only when the research is likely to provide such useful information that it's worth bending the rules a bit. More than nine times out of ten the best option is to stick to the rules.

Quantitative and Qualitative Methods

*Quantitative data is the kind you get from things like questionnaires — it can be turned into numbers, and put in graphs easily. Qualitative data comes from things like unstructured interviews — it's in-depth data. Although most of this was covered in the AS syllabus, it's on the A2 syllabus as well. These pages are for both **AQA** and **OCR**.*

Questionnaires *mainly provide* Quantitative Data

1) When planning a questionnaire, the researcher must first operationalise their concepts (see p.133). Once they've come up with a bunch of indicators, they can plan questions which accurately test for those indicators.

2) **Closed questions** and standardised **multiple-choice answers** give **quantitative** data. They're appropriate for **positivist** research (see p.123).

3) You can do a questionnaire with **open-ended questions** but it's harder to quantify the data into nice neat numbers. It's not impossible though — you have to classify the answers into **categories**. This is called coding (see p.144).

4) Questionnaires should use **clear**, **simple questions** which are **easy to understand**.

5) They should give **clear instructions** and have a clear layout.

6) **Multiple-choice** questions must give an appropriate number of responses. The researcher doesn't want too many respondents to answer "none of the above" or "other".

Questionnaires have several advantages

1) Questionnaires are **easy to administer**, and they can collect a **lot of data** in a **short time**. Closed questions provide quantitative data which can be **quickly** analysed too.

2) Questionnaires are **reliable**.

3) Questionnaires are **anonymous** and don't require the respondent to sit **face-to-face with an interviewer**. This makes them suitable for **sensitive topics**. For example, the National Survey of Sexual Attitudes and Lifestyles was a **postal questionnaire** rather than a face-to-face structured interview.

4) A **large sample** can be given a questionnaire, so they produce **representative data** that can be used to make generalisations.

Questionnaires have limitations — they aren't very valid

1) Respondents **may not tell the truth**. They may lie, or they may be mistaken.

2) Questions may be **misleading** or **mean different things** to **different people**. This means they may not accurately measure what you **want to measure**.

3) Respondents can't give any **extra information**, even if it would be really helpful to the researcher.

4) Because the respondent fills in the questionnaire on their own, there's no one there to **explain** the questions if the respondent doesn't understand them.

5) Postal questionnaires have a **low response rate**. If it's **too low** it won't be a **representative** sample.

Pilot studies (see p.135) are useful for questionnaires. Researchers can test if the questions make sense to the respondents.

Structured Interviews *are* Questionnaires *given* Face to Face

1) **Structured interviews** are **questionnaires** given to **individuals** or **groups**, face to face.

2) The main plus point over a postal questionnaire is that the interviewer can **explain** and **clarify** the questions.

3) Also, most structured interviews get a much **higher response rate** than questionnaires. People tend to agree to be interviewed — unless the research topic is **sensitive** or **taboo**.

4) However, they're **more expensive** than questionnaires — you need to **pay for the interviewer**.

5) In a structured interview, the interviewer has to **follow the list of questions** so they **can't ask for more detail** if the respondent says something **particularly interesting**.

Social Surveys *use* Questionnaires *and* Structured Interviews

1) **Social surveys** collect information about a **large population**, using **questionnaires** or **structured interviews**.

2) There are three main types — **factual**, **attitude** and **explanatory**. Some surveys are a **mixture** of more than one type.

Type of survey	What it's for	Who conducts it
Factual	Collects descriptive **information**	**Government agencies** and sociologists
Attitude	Collects **opinions**	**Opinion poll organisations** and sociologists
Explanatory	Looks for **reasons** and tests out hypotheses	Sociologists

Quantitative and Qualitative Methods

Unstructured Interviews give Qualitative Data

1) **Unstructured interviews** are **informal**, without a **rigid structure**. They use **open-ended questions** and give **qualitative** data, so they're quite **valid**. Interviews are **flexible** — they can be used to find out facts or attitudes.

2) In a **fully unstructured** interview, the conversation just develops **naturally**. Interviews can be **partly structured** and partly **unstructured** — i.e. the interviewer has to follow the questions in a set order, but they can let the respondent **elaborate** on any interesting points, and they can **ask** the respondent for **more information.**

3) Interviews can be done with **individuals** or small **groups**. Group interviews let the researcher observe **interaction**.

4) Because they're used with **smaller samples than questionnaires**, they're **not as representative**. However, they're **more representative** than **participant observation**.

5) Unstructured interviews are good for researching **sensitive issues** where the interviewer has to gain the respondent's **trust** — for example sexuality, domestic violence, crime. They're appropriate for **interpretivist** research (see p.123).

6) The interviewer needs to have **skill** so they can **probe** to **find out more detail** about the interviewee's **beliefs** and **opinions**.

7) There are a lot of **interviewer effects** in an unstructured interview. The interviewee may say what they **think** the **researcher wants to hear**.

See p.142 for more about interviewer effects.

8) It takes a **long time** to write up an **unstructured interview**. You have to write down a **whole conversation**, not just the **codes** for **multiple-choice answers** (see p.144). It's possible to do some **limited coding** of responses — the researcher could code for a particular category of opinion expressed, for example the respondent saying, "I'm worried about crime".

1) Interviewers usually use a **non-directive** style — they keep their own opinions to themselves, and they don't show any approval or disapproval of what the respondent says.

2) However, some sociologists choose to be more **aggressive** and **argumentative** in their questioning — more like a journalist. **Becker (1970)** took this approach when interviewing teachers, and claimed he'd got more useful information out of them than if he'd used the traditional non-confrontational approach.

3) **Ann Oakley (1981)** included unstructured interviews in her description of a "**feminist methodology**", and contrasted them with structured interviews, which she saw as masculine. She liked the respondent to get **involved** in the research process, and sought to get more from them by becoming **close** to them.

Pilot studies allow the researcher to find out what kind of question gets a **substantial response**. They let the researcher find out whether they need to **warm up** with a gentle **chat** to gain **rapport** with the respondent before asking more meaty questions.

Longitudinal Surveys are done over a Long Period of Time

Longitudinal studies are done at **regular intervals** over a **long period of time**, with the same people. They're often **large-scale quantitative** surveys. Some are more **qualitative** — e.g. the TV programme *Seven Up*.

1) You can **analyse changes** and **make comparisons** over time.

2) You can study how the **attitudes** of the sample **change** with time.

3) It's **hard** to recruit a **committed sample** who'll want to **stay** with the study.

4) You need **long-term funding** and you need to **keep the research team together**, which may be problematic.

Seven Up was a TV documentary that asked 14 kids aged 7 what they thought about life, and what they wanted to be when they grew up. The programme makers came back to interview them every seven years.

Practice Questions

Q1 Give two advantages and two disadvantages of questionnaires.

Q2 Give two advantages of unstructured interviews compared to questionnaires.

Q3 What is a longitudinal survey?

Exam Question

Q1 Outline and explain the advantages and disadvantages of interviews as a method of data collection. (15 marks)

Top tip: never subcontract your interviews to Trappist monks...

It's worth giving these methods a good going over, even if you think you remember them from the AS course. There's a little bit more detail here, and you're supposed to take a more critical approach at A2 level. That means you don't just learn what each method is, you have to be aware of pros and cons, and how to figure out if it might be appropriate for a particular topic.

Quantitative and Qualitative Methods

*Sociologists can do experiments on people, or they can observe them — with or without the subjects knowing about it. Or, they can take the opposite approach and just read about people through secondary data. This is for **AQA** and **OCR**.*

Experiments provide Quantitative Data

1) **Lab experiments** are done in a **controlled environment**. They analyse **one variable** in terms of **another** (see p.144). This method is often used by **psychologists**. Experiments can be very **reliable** and give **quantitative data**, but on the other hand they may not be valid because it's **hard** to **reproduce real social situations** in a lab.

2) **Field experiments** are a response to the criticisms of lab experiments. They take place outside of the lab in **real social settings** and those involved are often **unaware**, which poses **ethical problems**. This method is used by **interpretivist** sociologists. They're highly valid, but much less controllable and reliable than lab experiments.

Observation provides Qualitative data about Behaviour in Real-Life Settings

1) In **covert observation**, the researcher **doesn't tell the group** they're being observed. The BSA advise that you should only use covert observation when there's **no other way** of obtaining the data.

2) **Overt observation** (direct observation) is when the group is aware of the research and they know who the researcher is.

3) **Participant observation** is when the researcher **actively involves themselves in the group**.

> 1) Participant observation gets the researcher **right to where the action is** — so they can **check out the dynamics of a group** from **close up**. The researcher gets **first-hand insight** into people in **natural real-life settings**.
>
> 2) **Participant observation** allows you to research the workings of deviant groups (see **Humphreys**, p.136).
>
> 3) The researcher may get too involved and find it **hard to objectively observe** the group. **Whyte (1955)** became so involved with the gang members he studied that he started to see himself as **one of them** — even though his research was **overt**. The researcher in a **covert observation** may be pressurised to join in with illegal acts if they're in a **deviant** group.
>
> 4) Participant research is extremely **flexible**. The researcher can change their ideas based on what they see.
>
> 5) Participant research **lacks reliability** — it can't be repeated. A covert observer may find it difficult to **record** the study accurately, and without imposing their own subjective values on it. However, interpretivists say observation can be used to assist more objective methods. **Becker (1970)** used observation to collect information that he used to formulate a **hypothesis**, which could then be checked out in further research.
>
> 6) There are **ethical** and **practical** problems in **getting in, staying in** and **getting out** of the group.
>
> 7) The research usually includes a **small group** so it's not **representative** of the population. **Goffman (1968)** studied just **one** mental asylum.
>
> 8) It's **hard work, time-consuming** and **expensive**.

Overt researchers may have a "sponsor" who gets them into the group. Covert researchers must pretend to be just like the group members.

4) **Non-participant observation** is when the researcher **observes** the group but isn't actively a part of the group.

Ethnography Studies the Way of Life of a Group

Anthropology is the study of humans.

1) **Ethnography** is the scientific description of a specific culture by someone with first-hand experience of observing that culture. It was first used by **anthropologists** to study **traditional societies**. They joined the community, learnt the language and noted their observations.

2) Ethnography is **in-depth research** which gives **inside knowledge** about a community. You get a **valid** picture from ethnography, but it relies on the **researcher's interpretations** of what people do and say. It's **difficult** to **make generalisations** from small-scale research.

3) It is based on small-scale fieldwork that tends to produce **qualitative** data. It's **valid** because you can study behaviour in **natural settings**. You can use all sorts of methods to get **primary data**. You can use **unstructured interviews**. You can **observe** a community and see what they get up to.

Focus Groups are a Type of Semi-structured Observation

1) A **focus group** is a **small sample**, perhaps fewer than ten people. The sample are **put in a room together**, and asked to talk about a particular issue or to try to answer a specific set of questions. The discussion is **observed by a researcher**.

2) Because this is more like a **natural conversation**, the subjects may feel **more able to express themselves** than if they were speaking **directly to an interviewer**. Sometimes the focus group is **left alone** and a **video camera** or **audio recorder** is used to **record the discussion for later analysis**. Sometimes researchers **stay with the group** and **take part in the discussion** — they use the focus group to conduct a **group interview**.

Quantitative and Qualitative Methods

Case Studies *focus on just* **One Thing**

1) Case studies are **detailed investigations** of **a specific thing** — e.g. one person, one group, one institution or one event.

2) One particular kind of case study is the **life history**, which studies one person's whole life.

3) Examples of case studies include **Willis's (1977)** study of one group of boys in a school (p.156) and **Venkatesh's (2008)** study on the organisation and impact of one criminal gang (see p.150).

4) **Interpretivists** like case studies because they can provide very **detailed data**, and they can give the researcher great **insight** into the subject under investigation.

5) Positivists dislike case studies as they **aren't representative** of wider populations, and so they can't be used to make accurate generalisations because of the **small sample size**.

Statistics *are a Source of* **Secondary Data**

Official statistics are a source of secondary data. They're produced by local governments, central government and government agencies.

Kenny found all statistics hard.

1) **Hard statistics** are **objective**. Politicians can't fiddle with them. Statistics on births and marriages are hard statistics.

2) **Soft statistics** are more **subjective**. Politicians can fiddle with them. Statistics on **crime**, **poverty** and **unemployment** are soft statistics. In the 1980s and 1990s, the government **changed the method** used to **measure unemployment** over 20 times.

3) **Social Trends** is a collection of **regular government surveys** published every year. It's a **great source** of **secondary data**.

4) The **census** is a survey of every household every 10 years. Every household has to fill in the form **by law**.

5) The **British Crime Survey** looks at victims of crime. The data is collected by a questionnaire.

Non-official statistics are statistics collected by organisations other than the government. For example:

1) **TV ratings** collected by the **British Audience Research Bureau**.

2) **Surveys** carried out by **special interest groups**, such as charities.

3) **Surveys** carried out by **sociologists**.

Documents *and* Mass Media *are a Source of* **Secondary Data**

1) A document is **written text**. Documents can be **personal** — like **letters**, **diaries**, **autobiographies**, **memoirs** and **suicide notes**. Documents can also be **official**, like **school records**, **health** records, **church** records and **social work** records.

2) Documents can be **expressive** — more to do with **meanings**, like a **suicide note**. Documents can be **formal** — like **official documents**. Interpretivists prefer **expressive** documents because they're a big source of **qualitative data**.

3) **Max Weber** used **historical documents** when he was studying how the **religious** beliefs of Calvinism brought about a **social change**. **Michel Foucault** used **historical documents** to analyse changes in **social control** and **punishment**.

4) **Content analysis** is a method of **systematically** analysing a communication (e.g. a speech, film or letter) to understand its **meanings**. It is often used to study the mass media, e.g. research by the Glasgow University Media Group.

5) There are **problems** with documents. They can be **difficult to understand** if they're old. They might be **fakes**. They might contain **lies** — especially personal documents.

Practice Questions

Q1 What is the difference between covert and overt observation?

Q2 What is ethnography?

Q3 Give three examples of official statistics.

Exam Question

Q1 Identify and briefly explain three problems of using participant observation in sociological research. (9 marks)

Plenty of quantity and quality on these pages...

Data is to the sociologist what clay is to the sculptor, or what pigeon liver and celeriac are to the chef — you can't do great work without the best raw materials. Studying methodology may not have the Hollywood glamour of criminology or the rustic charm of politics — but without data sociologists have nothing to do. So you'd best learn where and how to find it.

Issues About Validity

*The way in which data is collected can seriously affect its validity. These pages are for **AQA** and **OCR**.*

Data must be **Valid** — the **Collection Process** can make it **Less Valid**

1) Respondents in an interview may **forget** things, **exaggerate**, or just plain **lie**.

2) They may try to show themselves in the **best possible light**. They may say they **wouldn't commit crime** when **really they would**. They may say they **recycle all their rubbish** when **really they don't**.

3) **Criminals** interviewed by **Laurie Taylor (1984)** later claimed that they'd **made up lies** to see if Taylor **believed** them.

Asking people about their **attitudes** to an event a **long time afterwards** often isn't valid. People **change their views** over time, and may **alter their description** of the past in the light of their **current beliefs**. For example, a middle-aged person may **falsely claim** to have been law-abiding as a youth when really they were a teenage delinquent.

There is a danger in **participant observation**, particularly **covert** participant observation, that the researcher will "**go native**". This means they get **too involved** and find it **hard to stand back** and **observe** the group **objectively**.

The **Research Process** can **Alter** the way **Respondents Behave**

1) Respondents in interviews may give the sort of answer they **think** the **interviewer wants to hear** — or the **exact opposite**, if they're feeling contrary.

2) Interviewers can give **subtle direction** towards certain responses — often **without realising** they're doing it.

3) These are known as **'interviewer effects'** (or 'researcher effects').

1) Participants in experiments may try harder at what they're doing to get a **positive response** from the researchers.

2) This is called the **Hawthorne effect** — first observed in an experiment at the **Hawthorne** electricity plant in Chicago, analysed by **Elton Mayo (1933)** in his work on motivation. The experiment was **meant** to test worker responses to **changes in variables** such as **workplace lighting**, but in fact **productivity increased** with **each variable change**, positive or negative. The workers seemed to be responding to the fact that they **knew an experiment was going on**.

3) These effects mean data from experiments may not be **valid**.

1) Even relatively unbiased researchers have to make **decisions** about how to **present** and **interpret** the **data** they've collected. They will tend to do so in line with their own **ideas** and **values** — this is known as **researcher imposition**.

Cultural Issues have an Impact on Validity

1) **Labov (1973)** found that **black American children** were much **more forthcoming** with a **black interviewer** than a **white** interviewer. He suggested that this could lead white researchers to think that the children had poor linguistic ability.

2) Ethnicity wasn't the only factor — the children were most forthcoming in an **informal setting**, where they could bring a **friend** with them.

3) Labov's explanation was that the children didn't speak up and show their abilities when they perceived the situation as alien, or **hostile**.

4) **Oakley (1981)** thought that **women** responded to a **friendly** interview style.

The **acceptability** of some sensitive issues **varies** between **social groups**. Some social groups may be less keen on **admitting embarrassing** or **socially undesirable** things, e.g. deviant behaviour, or mental health symptoms.

Publication must be Honest and allow Criticism and Comment

1) In the quest for objectivity, researchers should be open and public when they **conduct** research and when they **publish** their findings. Being open and public enables the researcher to **avoid accusations** of **falsifying data**, **over-emphasising insignificant findings** or using **dodgy methodology**.

2) Researchers should present their data and allow other researchers to build on it, criticise it or compare it to other work. This means that results get analysed in terms of **objectivity**, **validity** and **reliability**, and it allows others to **check** the researcher's **interpretations** to see if they are correct.

3) **Accountability to participants** is **crucial**. All participants should be given **access** to the final report.

4) The report should be **fair** and **representative** of their meanings, actions and beliefs.

5) The report must not **identify** the participants without their consent.

Issues About Validity

Many people question how valid or reliable a piece of research is if the presence of the researcher has affected the results. Reflexive researchers acknowledge that their opinions affect their work, and take this into account.

Research can be affected by the **Background** or **Opinions** of the **Researcher**

1) An individual's **social background**, their **perspectives** on life, their **sociological viewpoint**, and their **culture** will all affect how they **perceive** the world around them.

2) This counts for **sociologists** in exactly the same way as it does for us **regular folk**. Sociologists **are** regular folk.

3) What the **researcher** observes or notes as relevant depends on **their idea** of what's useful, true and accurate.

Reflexive Research takes the *Researcher's Opinions* into *Account*

1) Reflexivity refers to the **understanding** that a researcher has that their research **will be affected** by their own **opinions** and **standpoints**.

2) Reflexivity forces the sociologist to see **social structures** and **norms** and ways of **interpreting** them as something they have **in common** with the people they study.

3) Sociologists aren't magically free of the effects of the social world. They can't necessarily be **value-free** or **impartial**, but they **can** keep a **sense of self-awareness** about their preconceptions.

4) **Bourdieu and Wacquant (1992)** saw reflexive sociology as a way of giving a **deeper** and more **meaningful** understanding of the social world. They thought that if the sociologist saw themselves as in the **same boat** as the people they studied, they'd understand them better.

5) Bourdieu and Wacquant argued that **reflexivity** could **help Sociology** to be **more objective** — they thought it was very important to **keep an eye** on the way that researchers **actually obtain knowledge**, as it could help researchers avoid settling for poor methods.

6) Reflexivity rejects the **certainty** of **functionalist** approaches, and rejects the "**there's no truth**" attitude of some **postmodern** approaches.

The **Reflexive Researcher** will try to **Guarantee Valid Research**

1) A researcher who's **aware** of **potential bias** can take steps to **avoid** it.

2) Reflexive work can often be found in **social action/interpretivist sociology** (see p.123 and 126). Social action researchers use subjective methods that involve **interpretation**. Reflexivity techniques require the researcher to put themselves **in the place** of their participants for long periods of time to seek a **fuller understanding** of the **meanings** that participants put on their actions.

3) For example, **Barker (1984)**, in her study of the Unification Church (the Moonies), spent significant periods of time with **Moonie families** to gain their **trust** and understand their lives **from their point of view**. This allowed her to understand Moonie lifestyle without excessively imposing her **own interpretations** (which may have been different to theirs).

4) **Cicourel (1968)** actually spent time as an **unpaid probation officer** which enabled him to interpret the meanings attached to the definition of "delinquency" from the perspective of the probation officers.

1) **Respondent validation** is asking respondents for their **opinions** on the research — checking that the researcher's findings are **fair**, **accurate** and **reflect** their views. Interpretivists argue that this is a good way of **assessing** the **validity** of data collected.

2) Research may still be **valid** even if respondents **disagree** with it. Respondents might **not understand** how their experiences have been **analysed**, or may be more concerned with presenting themselves in a **good light** than with accuracy.

Practice Questions

Q1 What is the Hawthorne effect?

Q2 What are the benefits of making research open and public?

Q3 What is meant by "reflexivity" in sociological research?

Exam Question

Q1 Outline and assess the importance of openness and honesty in sociological research. (15 marks)

If you tap my knee, I'll do an interview — the reflexive researcher...

These pages are all about how researchers can have an unwanted impact on their research — and the steps they can take to reduce it, such as using respondent validation. This is really important to interpretivist sociologists, as they want their research to be as valid as possible — even if it means joining the Moonies or becoming a probation officer for a stretch.

Quantitative and Qualitative Analysis

*Once a researcher has gathered their data, they need to analyse it. The way data is analysed depends on whether it's quantitative or qualitative. These pages are for **OCR** — but **AQA** students need to learn the stuff about triangulation.*

All *Quantitative* data needs to be *Coded* and *Collated*

1) Coding means the creation of a numbered category for a series of similar responses.

2) The responses to **closed questions** are **pre-coded**. The data merely needs to be **counted** and **grouped** according to the answer given.

3) Open questions require more work. Data from open questions and observations needs to be grouped into **categories** of **similar answers**.

4) Once all of the responses have been given a numerical code, the figures should be collated and transferred onto a **coding sheet**.

> Yes = 1 and No = 0 are the answer codes
>
> Do you like worms? Yes ☐ Yes = 1
> Please tick one box only No ☐ No = 0

All *Quantitative* data can be presented in *Graph* and *Chart* form

1) Presenting complex data in a **table** or **chart** allows non-experts to **understand** the results fairly easily.

2) **Other sociologists** and **policy analysts** can confidently **use** the data in reports without having to do **too much work** themselves.

3) On the other hand, charts and graphs can **mislead** people over the significance of findings. With a **small sample**, freak results can look quite significant on the chart.

1) **Correlation** is a measure of how **closely** two variables are **related**, for example household income and number of children. Correlation may be **strong** (high), **weak**, or there may be no apparent correlation at all.

2) Correlation is **useful**, but it **doesn't prove** cause and effect by itself. Correlation could be coincidence or there could be a third variable affecting the results.

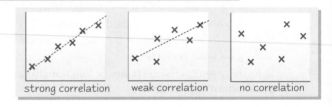
strong correlation   weak correlation   no correlation

3) **Trends** are the long-term movement of a variable, for example household income over a number of years. Trends may be **upward**, **constant** or **downward**, but there are usually **fluctuations** around the trend.

4) The pattern revealed by data can be **extrapolated** into the **future**, meaning you can identify the **trend**, and **assume** it will carry on. All you do is draw a line of best fit to show the trend, and continue the line to project the trend into the future.

Qualitative data needs to be *Collated* but *Not All* the data gathered is *Useful*

1) Qualitative data needs to be collated in a way that makes it **useful** and **relevant** to the topic of research. The nature of qualitative data means that a great deal of the information gathered may be **irrelevant** and useless for the research. Care must be taken when deciding what to include in the final data to be analysed.

2) A researcher can gather the data through **audio recording** — that way they don't need to **remember** exactly what was said, or rely on **notes** from the interview or observation, which might have missed something out. The only problem is a practical one — it means that the research process is more expensive.

3) Data can be categorised according to patterns and similarity. Some sociologists **make notes** as they're going along on what seems to be **useful**, and what's **linked** with what. Useful data can then be **coded** and **included** in the final report.

4) A **full original data set** should be kept so the researcher can **refer back** to see **exactly** what was said or written.

Qualitative analysis involves looking for *Themes* and *Interpretations*

Qualitative content analysis of an interview or document looks at the **symbols** and **meanings** in the text. Qualitative analysis can suffer from **interpretive bias**. The researcher may see what they **want to see**, instead of what the respondent **actually meant**.

Differences and similarities in the ways that different social groups **interpret** and **respond** to a situation are key to **social action** research (see p.126).

Qualitative Data is usually presented as an *Essay*

1) Qualitative data can't be presented as charts and graphs, so qualitative researchers present their data in the form of a **written discussion** or **essay**.

2) **Quotes** from respondents are often included to highlight particular points of interest.

3) Researchers detail **similarities** and **differences** between respondents — e.g. their **gender**, **class** and occupation.

Mixed Methods

Triangulation *is when you* Combine Methods *or* Data

1) Triangulation is when sociologists combine different methods or data to **get the best out of all of them**.

2) Triangulation can **combine** quantitative methods and qualitative methods, e.g. questionnaires and unstructured interviews.

3) **Triangulation** gives a more **detailed picture** than when you only use **one method**, so it's more **valid**.

4) When you triangulate, you can **check different sets of data against each other**, so it's more **reliable**. You can even triangulate between data produced by **different researchers**.

5) Triangulation combines the **strengths** and the **weaknesses** of different types of data.

6) It can be **expensive** and **time-consuming** to do the same research with lots of methods.

7) Sometimes, it's **not possible** to use triangulation — e.g. you might only be able to use **one method**, or there might not be very many **different kinds of data** for what you're studying.

Harvey and MacDonald (1993) list **three kinds of triangulation:**

1) **One researcher** uses **two or more methods** — so the results from one method can be checked against the results from another.

2) **Two or more researchers** use **the same method** — so the results obtained by one researcher can be checked against the results obtained by the other.

3) **Two or more researchers** use **two or more methods** — so researchers and methods can be checked against each other.

Eileen Barker (1984) studied the Moonies

The Moonies are a religious organisation, also known as the Unification Church. Barker used **in-depth interviews**, **overt participant observation** and **questionnaires**. She used questionnaires to test out hypotheses that she'd thought of after doing the interviews and observations.

Mac an Ghaill (1994) studied masculinity

He used **overt participant observation** and **interviews** with young straight men and young gay men. He **discussed ideas** about what made a man masculine. He didn't just observe the young men and try to figure out what they thought.

Mixing Methods *makes it* More Likely *that some are* Fit for Purpose...

1) A method is **'fit for purpose'** if it's capable of giving useful results. For example, if you were studying people's experiences of crime, a **questionnaire** given to a **large sample** should produce useful results. So for that study, a questionnaire is **fit for purpose**. It wouldn't make sense to try to do **participant observation** — you'd have to follow people for a **very long time** and the act of observing would probably **decrease the probability of them becoming a victim** of crime. So for this study, participant observation is **not fit for purpose**.

2) It's not always obvious which methods are going to be fit for purpose **before a study begins**. Using **mixed methods** can be an advantage — if one of your methods turns out to be **not fit for purpose** during your study then you could still be able to collect useful results from **the other methods**.

3) Trying to find patterns is more difficult when you have to simultaneously analyse lots of **different kinds of data**. Sometimes it isn't clear how the results of different tests **relate to one another** and sometimes it's just difficult to **think about all the results at once**.

4) But successful use of mixed methods usually leads to **increased validity** and **increased reliability** because each set of data is **checked** against all the others. It's very unlikely that all the methods will be **invalid** in the same way. If any one is **unreliable** then it won't **affect the outcome** of the study as strongly as if it was the **only method** used.

Paul Feyerabend (1975) argued that sociologists should pick the **most appropriate method** for their study — whether **quantitative** or **qualitative** — and should even **change methods** if the study calls for it. This approach has come to be known as **methodological pluralism** — studying society using a **mixture** of **methods** instead of having to declare one in advance.

Practice Questions

Q1 What is a correlation?

Q2 What is meant by 'fit for purpose'?

Exam Question

Q1 Outline and assess the view that sociologists should always use triangulation. (40 marks)

You can mix methods — but don't get your methods mixed up...

You've got to hand it to him. You spend a whole book learning about how positivists with their quantitative methods don't get on with interpretivists, with their qualitative methods. Then Feyerabend chips in — "Hey guys, don't worry about it."

Sociological Research: Crime and Deviance

*The following pages are about applying sociological methods to the topic of crime and deviance. They are for **AQA** students who are studying the **Crime and Deviance** topic (see section 5) only.*

Crime can be looked at in a number of Different Ways

1) A sociologist's **theoretical perspective** influences both their **research topic** and the **methods** they use.

2) **Structuralist** sociologists prefer **positivist** methods. **Social action** theorists prefer **interpretivist** methods.

3) **Consensus** structuralists (e.g. functionalists) focus on the **background** of criminals, while **conflict** structuralists (e.g. Marxists) are more **critical**, focusing on the role of **elites** and **agents of social control** in the criminalisation process.

Positivists use Quantitative Data to study Crime and Deviance

1) The positivist view is that an individual is **shaped** by **society** and by their position in the **social structure**. The point of doing research is to uncover the **underlying laws** that govern human behaviour.

2) Positivists work with **official statistics** and other sources of **quantitative data** such as **police-recorded crime**, the **British Crime Survey** and the **Youth Lifestyles Survey** to gain an overview of how the crime rate varies across regions and social groups. They use this data to look for **correlations** and to try and establish what the **causes** of higher crime rates might be.

3) Official statistics show that high crime rate areas are often characterised by:
   - **poverty**
   - high levels of **social disorder**
   - high levels of **rented accommodation**

Cyndi didn't know why she loved stealing German police cars — maybe it was because they had great sandwiches in them.

4) Official statistics **(Crime in England and Wales 2008)** reveal that offenders are more likely:
   - to be **male**
   - to be aged between **16 and 24**
   - to have **parents** who have **committed crime**
   - to have had an **absent father**
   - to have a history of **truancy** and **drug abuse**

5) Positivists prefer to use **official statistics** in understanding crime and deviance because they are **reliable** — they provide us with an **overview** of crime in society, and they make it easy to **compare** crime rates across regions.

Interpretivists prefer Qualitative Data

Interpretivists criticise the use of official statistics, arguing that they give us a **false impression** of the nature and extent of crime in British society. Interpretivists argue that —

> 1) Both **official police statistics** and the **British Crime Survey** are **socially constructed**. The public **selectively** report crimes and the police **selectively** record them — e.g. a member of the public might not bother to report low-level vandalism.
>
> 2) The crime statistics may reflect the **bias** of the police — e.g. if the police think **young people** are more likely to commit crime, they may **over-police** the young and uncover more of their criminal behaviour as a result.

Interpretivists prefer to use **qualitative**, often small-scale research methods such as **unstructured interviews** and **participant observation**, for the following reasons:

> 1) They can provide **in-depth insight** into the **lives** of criminals and deviants.
>
> 2) They allow for **empathetic understanding** between researcher and respondents. They enable the researcher to see how criminals **perceive their own crimes**, and what reasons they **themselves** give for their behaviour.
>
> 3) This approach has also led to the establishment of **labelling theory**. This focuses on the **agents of social control**, by looking at how **labelling** can affect the **self concept** and **behaviour** of those labelled 'criminal' (see p. 74).

Interpretivist methods are often used by **social action theorists** such as **Howard Becker (1963)**. They are often **sympathetic** to criminals and **'take the side of the underdog'**. This is not value-free and can involve **'turning a blind eye'** to criminal acts while conducting research — which creates ethical problems.

Sociological Research: Crime and Deviance

Consensus Sociologists believe some people suffer Anomie in Society

1) **Consensus theories** include **functionalism, strain theory, subcultural theory** and **social control theory**.

2) They argue that the social system is **generally good** and functions well for the majority of people.

3) Consensus sociologists see institutions such as **education** and the **family** as being crucial to **maintaining social order**.

4) They argue that **crime** and **deviance** are a result of individuals becoming **detached** from **mainstream institutions**. They blame the specific failings of the **institutions**, or **peer groups** for encouraging deviance, rather than the system.

5) Consensus-based research tends to be **positivist** in nature, i.e.

> • Research is usually **quantitative** and **comparative**, seeking to understand and establish **correlations** between **social conditions** and **criminal behaviour**.
>
> • Research focuses on what it is about criminals' **backgrounds** that lead them to commit crime.

Conflict Sociologists argue that Injustices in the Social System cause crime

1) **Conflict theories** include traditional **Marxism** and **feminism**.

2) Conflict theorists argue that institutions of **formal social control** maintain the power of the elite groups (i.e. the bourgeoisie or men) over oppressed groups.

3) They argue that it's the **oppressive system** and **prejudiced agents of social control** that marginalise and selectively criminalise powerless sectors of the population.

4) Conflict theorists use a mixture of **quantitative** and **qualitative** research methods focusing on —

> • How the **injustices** of the social system generate criminal behaviour.
>
> • How **institutions** work in the interests of **elite groups**.

5) Research is **sympathetic** to criminals, seeking to understand how deviant action can be **rational** for the **marginalised**.

Sociologists' Theoretical Perspectives shape their ideas about Social Policy

Theoretical perspective influences ideas about what policies should be put in place to **combat crime**:

Positivists and Consensus theorists	They believe in **'early intervention'** to stop **'high risk'** individuals from committing crime, such as putting policies in place to encourage **strong families** and **higher school attendance**.
Conflict and Action theorists	They may work with the police to **reduce prejudice** and **labelling**. They aim to **reduce inequalities** within the society. They may believe that a **complete change** of system is necessary to reduce crime.

Practice Questions

Q1 Suggest two reasons why positivists prefer to use quantitative methods when researching crime and deviance.

Q2 Suggest two criticisms an interpretivist might make of the positivist approach to crime.

Q3 Identify two things that conflict criminologists might research that consensus-based criminologists wouldn't.

Exam Question

Q1 Identify and explain one problem of using official statistics, such as the British Crime Survey, in researching crime and deviance.

(3 marks)

Someone's only gone and nicked my clipboard...

Quite a bit there for you to get your teeth into — again it comes down to what questions sociologists ask and how they get their answers. Just remember, if there are sociologists turning a blind eye while you're busy embezzling, they're most probably interpretivists of some sort. Unless they're undercover Interpol officers disguised as sociologists. It's all so confusing.

Sociological Research: Crime and Deviance

*In their choice of research methods sociologists are influenced by ethical considerations, practical constraints, and their theoretical perspective. These pages are mainly on positivist/quantitative approaches. For **AQA** students studying **Crime and Deviance**.*

Different Factors influence the choice of Research Topic and Method

1) **Theoretical factors** are important. **Positivists** tend to prefer **quantitative methods** because they're more representative, reliable and objective. **Interpretivists** tend to prefer the greater validity of **qualitative** methods (see p. 146).

2) **Practical constraints** include:

- **Time and money** — the easiest data on crime to use is *Crime in England and Wales* which is available for free. If a criminologist wants data that's **nationally representative** they must use **quantitative** methods. Qualitative research will always **take longer** and **cost more** for the same number of respondents.

- **Funding** — by far the largest source of funding for criminology is the **government**, which favours quantitative research as it's more **representative** and **objective**. The government's also more likely to fund research that fits in with its **current aims**.

- **Access** — it may be difficult to gain access to some groups. Elite cadres and corporate criminals, for example, would take years of personal networking to infiltrate. **Covert participant observation** (p. 140) may be the **only method available** to research criminal and deviant groups.

3) There are also **ethical considerations**. Researchers need to think about how those involved are **impacted** by the research process. Some topics need to be researched with **sensitivity** — researching victims usually requires unstructured interviews to ensure the setting is not too intimidating.

4) The **interests** and **values** of the **researcher** may influence what is seen as **worthwhile** or **ethical** to study in the first place. Some **feminist researchers** in the 1980s, for example, studied the victims of **domestic violence**, a group who were extremely marginalised in society. This fitted in with their theoretical perspective and concerns.

Positivists value Representativeness, Reliability and Objectivity

1) Positivists use **quantitative data** from **police-recorded crime** and large-scale surveys such as the *British Crime Survey* in order to uncover **society-wide** patterns of offending, such as the relationship between crime and locality. They believe this is necessary to ensure that data is **representative of society as a whole**.

2) Positivists believe that statistical data is **more objective** than data obtained by qualitative methods. There are three major sources of data on crime that positivists rely on —

- **Police-recorded crime** includes all crimes reported to and recorded by the police. These are collected by police forces across England, Wales and Scotland.

- The **British Crime Survey** asks ordinary people if they have been a **victim of crime** in the previous 12 months and whether they **reported the incident** to the police. This is carried out every other year, using a sample of over 40 000 people living in private households.

- **Self-report studies** are surveys of a cross-section of the population which ask what **offences** they've committed.

The government publishes crime data in the yearly publication *Crime in England and Wales*, which contains both information on **police-recorded crime** and data from the **British Crime Survey**. This is freely available and can be used to compare the differences between police-recorded crime and the BCS data on crime.

Police-recorded Crime (PRC) figures are Easy to get hold of...

1) It's easy to make **comparisons** across regions because all police forces use the **same categories** to record crime.

2) They are **readily available**, easy and cheap to use.

3) They allow the **efficiency** of the police to be **assessed**.

...but they need to be handled with Care

1) **New counting rules**, which increased the number of different offences that are counted, were introduced in **1998** and **2002**, which makes it **difficult** to make **comparisons over time** — although these new counting rules should improve the **validity** of police-recorded crime statistics.

2) The number of offences recorded will vary with **police initiatives**. If more resources are put into tackling knife crime, the police will uncover more of it. An increase in police-recorded crime may mean the police are getting **more efficient** at detecting crime, **rather** than indicating an increase in the actual rate of crime.

3) Most importantly, **not all crimes** are recorded by the police. Before a crime is officially recorded someone has to **notice** a crime has occurred and **report** it to the police, and then the police have to **record** it. At each stage, certain crimes **disappear**. This results in what criminologists refer to as the **"dark figure of crime"** — crimes that do not appear in the PRC statistics.

Sociological Research: Crime and Deviance

The **British Crime Survey** reveals the extent of the **Dark Figure of Crime**

The **British Crime Survey** shows the chance of a crime being reported to the police depends greatly on the **type of offence**. Based on the **2007/08 BCS**:

- **42%** of incidents were **reported** to the police.
- **Thefts of vehicles** were **most likely** to be reported (93%).
- **Vandalism** (35%), **assault without injury** (34%) and **theft from the person** (32%) were the **least likely**.

The **British Crime Survey** has its own **Weaknesses**

Despite providing criminologists with a more valid measurement of crime, there are still limitations to BCS data.

1) The data is based on a **household** survey which means it will not detect crimes against the **homeless** or **prisoners**.
2) Some types of crime are **excluded** from the *BCS*, such as **corporate crime** and **fraud**.
3) Despite the survey being **anonymous**, people appear to **under-report** sexual offences.
4) Crimes against **children** are excluded, as only those **aged over 16** are interviewed.

Self-report Studies uncover **Hidden Crime...**

1) They **reveal information** about the kind of offenders who **aren't caught** or processed by the **criminal justice system**.
2) It is possible to find out about these **'hidden offenders"** ages, gender, social class and even their location.
3) It is also the most useful way to find out about **'victimless' crimes**, such as illegal drug use.

...but tend to miss **Serious Offences**

1) Self-report studies are only useful for finding out about relatively **minor offences** — serious offenders would probably lie.
2) They also create the **ethical problem** of **knowing about crimes** committed, but not being able to report them due to the necessity of keeping information **confidential**.

Interpretivists deny that official statistics are **Objective**

1) Interpretivists argue that despite claims of objectivity, police statistics and the *British Crime Survey* are very much reliant on **'social processes'**. They are reliant on a series of decisions made by individuals, each with their own **motivations**, **values** and **views**.
2) Interpretivists say official statistics such as police-recorded crime are **'socially constructed'**. Before a crime is **officially recorded** a number of things must happen (it must get **noticed**, **reported** and then **recorded**), and at each stage certain crimes disappear — speeding offences **go unnoticed** on country roads, people **don't bother** to report vandalism, or may be **too scared** or **ashamed** to report domestic violence. Sometimes the police may fail to record crimes for the **sake of their statistics**.
3) Interpretivists argue against **quantitative macro-style sociology**, saying it treats human beings as though they are puppets, merely **reacting to social forces**. They believe that to fully understand why some people commit crime, you need to take an **in-depth look** at their lives. Interpretivist methods are covered on p.150-151.

Practice Questions

Q1 Suggest two practical constraints on a sociologist's choice of research method.
Q2 Why might some crimes not make it to the police records?
Q3 What do interpretivists mean when they call official crime statistics 'socially constructed'?

Exam Question

Q1 Assess the strengths and limitations of using victim surveys such as the British Crime Survey to understand the nature and extent of crime and deviance.
(15 marks)

Admit it — you love criminological research methods...

Though some sociologists don't think they're great, official crime statistics are at least free to look at and easy to get hold of. Interpretivists claim the whole enterprise is riddled with socially-constructed nonsense. But at least it gives you solid numbers to play with. Make sure you know the pros and cons of police-recorded crime, the British Crime Survey and self-report studies.

Sociological Research: Crime and Deviance

*These pages are mainly about qualitative/interpretivist methods. They are only for students studying the **Crime and Deviance** topic on the **AQA** syllabus.*

Interpretivists prefer Qualitative Methods

1) Interpretivists value **validity** — research is valid if it provides a **true picture** of what is really **'out there'** in the world.

2) Generally speaking, the more **in-depth** the research, the fuller picture we get of the **thoughts** and **feelings** of the individuals involved. Data becomes more valid when the researcher **stands back** and allows the respondents to **'speak for themselves'**. Methods such as **participant observation** and **unstructured interviews** aim to gain valid data.

Unstructured Interviews have helped in researching Victims of Violence

1) Unstructured interviews allow researchers to deal sensitively with difficult topics, as **Dobash and Dobash (1983)** did with their research into the **victims of domestic violence**.

2) Unstructured interviews with **victims of crime** also have the advantage of giving the **powerless a voice**.

Winlow and Hall used Unstructured Interviews to research Street Violence

1) **Winlow and Hall (2006)** used unstructured interviews to understand more about **young people's attitudes** to the culture of **drink** and **violence** in the 'night-time economy' of clubs and pubs.

2) This method allowed the young people to talk to the researchers **as naturally as possible** about their **everyday lives**, and about what violence **meant to them**.

- They **interviewed** 43 working class youths mainly aged between **18-25** in the North East of England who were in **temporary** or **casual employment**.

- They found that the main leisure activity was **drinking alcohol** with friends in the many city centre bars and pubs. **Drunkenness** allowed normal rules and expectations to be **flouted** in a situation where there was **little policing**.

- **Violence** seemed to be accepted as **inevitable** because of the high **alcohol consumption**. It did not put young people off going out, rather it provided an **'edge'** that was part of the **attraction** of night life.

- Based on their findings, Winlow and Hall were able to **reject previous theories** about night-time violence being a form of **'resistance to oppression'**.

Participant Observation means building relationships with Respondents

1) **Participant observation** allows the researcher to gain an **empathetic understanding** with a group.

Paul Willis (1977) used participant observation to research the attitude to school of 12 rebellious working class boys. He found they **rejected school** because they saw it as **irrelevant** to their future work plans. Messing around was a strategy that helped them **pass the time** and **regain power** by getting their own back on those in positions of authority.

2) Participant observation allows the researcher to **'follow their nose'** and **discover the unexpected**.

Sudhir Venkatesh (2008) spent **10 years** with a gang of crack dealers in Chicago. He found that they **structured themselves** much like any normal regional sales business.

3) **Covert participant observation** may be the **only way** to gain access to some groups.

Donal MacIntyre conducted research for the BBC by **infiltrating** the hooligan 'firm' the Chelsea Headhunters. He uncovered how they **organised** their football violence and their links to **right-wing groups**. It's unlikely they would have **opened up** to MacIntyre if they had known he was a researcher.

Participant Observation has its Problems

1) It's often very **difficult** and **time-consuming** to gain **access** to the group being studied — it took both Willis and MacIntyre **months**.

2) Both Willis and Venkatesh could be accused of **'going native'** as both appeared sympathetic to their key respondents. This implies a **loss** of **objectivity**.

3) The data is **unrepresentative** of wider groups. Venkatesh was especially **reliant** on JT, the leader of the crack gang, for much of his information. His findings may not be relevant to other criminal gangs — it's all specific to this one group.

4) There can be **ethical problems** with participant observation. Venkatesh **witnessed** drug dealing and several beatings during his research but decided **not to inform the police**.

Sociological Research: Crime and Deviance

Secondary Documents *can be useful in research into* **Crime** *and* **Deviance**

1) **Autobiographies** such as **Charles Bronson's (2000)** give us a valid, **in-depth insight** into the **viewpoint** of a criminal.

2) **Diaries** have been used by researchers to encourage respondents to **express themselves**. One example is the 'Freedom Writers'. **Erin Gruwell**, an idealistic English teacher at a high school in California, encouraged a class of **"unteachable, at-risk"** students to write diaries about their **day-to-day experiences**. Their diaries eventually got turned into a book. It presented the students' lives from their own **point of view** and in their **own words**.

3) Writers may be **selective with the truth** — especially where details of **criminal acts** are concerned.

4) Those documents selected for publication are likely to be the **more sensational** and **exciting** ones. Mundane crimes will be missed, giving an **exaggerated picture** of the nature and extent of crime in a society.

Qualitative Methods *present their own* **Problems**

1) Methods such as **participant observation** — where the researcher can spend **several months** or even **years** with a small group of respondents — are **not very reliable** as it's **impossible to replicate** the original research exactly.

2) These methods are also open to researcher, or interviewer **bias**. The more **involved** the researcher, the more they may **bias the results**.

3) In **extreme** cases, the researcher may **'go native'** and start to **sympathise** with the respondents — to **share** in their point of view rather than just to **understand** it — even if they're criminals. This means the research would no longer be **value-free**.

After a decade undercover studying the links between crime and mime, Andrei struggled to communicate his findings.

Positivists *argue that* **Laboratory Experiments** *can provide* **Useful Data**

1) **Experiment-based research** can **isolate** the effects of one variable on another.

2) Positivists argue that the method is **reliable** because the conditions of the experiment are easily **repeated**.

- One classic example of a laboratory experiment is the **Bobo doll** experiment, by **Bandura, Ross and Ross (1963)**.

- In the experiment, children were split into two groups. One group was shown a **film** of a person beating an inflatable plastic **Bobo doll** with a mallet. When the two groups of children were then put in a room with a Bobo doll and a mallet, the group which had watched the video acted more **aggressively** towards the doll.

- One of the conclusions drawn was that children who **witness violent images** are more likely to be **aggressive** than those not exposed to such images.

3) Interpretivists would argue that the experiment lacks **ecological validity** as the conditions are **not true to real life**.

4) In the real world, **media violence** does not have an isolated, independent effect on children, because they rarely watch television alone.

5) The experiment does not distinguish between the effects of **different types** of violence in the media.

Practice Questions

Q1 Suggest two advantages of using unstructured interviews in researching crime and deviance.

Q2 Identify two limitations of using secondary documents in social research.

Q3 Suggest two limitations of using laboratory experiments to understand deviant behaviour.

Exam Question

Q1 Assess the strengths and limitations of using participant observation to understand the nature and extent of crime and deviance.

(15 marks)

Studying research methods? Infiltrate a gang of sociologists...

Only kidding — I was in the group that didn't get to see the video. Some sociologists seem to just love getting as close as possible to their respondents — either by joining their gang (like the interpretivists) or by bringing them back to the lab (like some positivists). The interpretivists in particular seem mad for going out 'into the real world' — make sure you know why.

Sociological Research: Stratification and Difference

*The following pages are about applying sociological methods to the topic of stratification and difference. They are for **OCR** students, and **AQA** students who are studying the **Stratification and Differentiation** topic.*

There are Different Approaches to researching Stratification and Differentiation

1) The choice of research topic and the methods employed are often linked to the particular sociologist's **theoretical perspective**.

2) **Structuralist** sociologists prefer **positivist** methods. **Social action** theorists prefer **interpretivist** methods.

3) **Consensus structuralists** (e.g. functionalists) focus on the **benefits** of **stratification**, while **conflict structuralists** (e.g. Marxists and feminists) are more **critical**, focusing on the role of **elites** and **agents of social control** in creating stratification.

Positivists use Quantitative Data to look at the Big Picture

1) The **positivist view** is that an individual is **shaped by society** and by their position in the **social structure**. Research can uncover how factors such as an individual's **class**, **gender** and **ethnicity** can shape their **life chances**.

2) Positivists work with sources of quantitative data such as **Census data**, the **British Social Attitudes Survey** and **official statistics** from **government departments** that use **objective measurements** of class, gender and ethnicity.

3) Official statistics show that there is often a **link** between an individual's social class, ethnicity and gender and their life chances. Some examples taken from *Social Trends 38* **(2008)** are given below:

- In 2005/2006 there were **1.5 million women enrolments** in **higher education** compared to **1.1 million men**.
- **Black African, Caribbean, Bangladeshi and Pakistani households** are **roughly twice as likely** to be **non-working** households than **white** and **Indian households** (roughly 20% compared to 10%).
- In English state schools the **rate of truancy** among pupils **eligible for free school meals** was almost **three times** that of the other pupils.

4) Positivists prefer to use **official statistics** in understanding stratification as they provide **objective data** that is **reliable** and can be **compared** easily.

Interpretivists prefer Qualitative Data

Interpretivists prefer to use **qualitative**, often small-scale research methods such as **unstructured interviews** and **participant observation** to explore the **complex nature** of class, gender and ethnic identities in modern Britain.

Interpretivists **criticise** the use of **official statistics**, arguing that their reliance on **clear-cut definitions** of **class**, **gender** and **ethnicity** is **flawed**. For example, **gender identity** and **sexuality** are **more complex** than the simple **male-female distinction**.

Savage *et al.* (2001) discovered that people don't have simple ideas about class

Savage *et al.* carried out **in-depth interviews** with **178 people** living around Manchester and discovered that most people had an **ambivalent attitude** towards their **own class**. Many of the people he interviewed thought their area **contained** a particular **class**, but that they themselves **weren't defined** by it.

Connell (1995) investigated different forms of masculinity

Connell researched the **life histories** of men through **in-depth interviews**. Connell identified **different forms** of **masculinity**, such as an idealised 'hegemonic' masculinity involving **toughness** and **authority**, which **subordinates** other masculinities, including **homosexual** masculinity.

Theoretical Perspectives also shape ideas about Social Policy

Theoretical perspective influences sociologists' ideas about what social policies should be put in place to combat inequality.

1) **Consensus theorists** believe sociologists should work within the **existing system** to reduce inequalities. Consensus theorists believe that **some inequality** in society can be **beneficial** (see p.92).

2) **Conflict sociologists** generally have a more critical view of inequality, and believe we need more **radical changes**, for example to the **taxation system** or even to the **system of government** itself, to bring about greater equality.

Sociological Research: Stratification and Difference

The choice of *Research Topic* and *Method* is influenced by *Several Factors*

1) **Theoretical factors** are important. Positivists tend to prefer **quantitative methods** because they are more representative, reliable and objective. Interpretivists tend to prefer the greater validity of **qualitative methods**.

2) **Practical constraints** influence the choice of method. These include such things as how much **time** and **money** are available.

> • **Time and Money** — the easiest data for the sociologist to use is produced by the **Office for National Statistics**, which is available for **free**. If a sociologist wants data that is **nationally representative** they must use **quantitative methods**. **Qualitative research** will always **take longer** and **cost more** for the same number of respondents.
>
> • **Funding** — by far the largest source of funding for sociology is the **government**, which favours quantitative research as it's more **representative** and **objective**. The government's also more likely to fund research that fits in with its **current aims**.
>
> • **Access** — it may be difficult to gain access to some groups — **elite cadres**, for example, may be difficult to access as they would take years of personal networking to infiltrate. On the other hand **marginal groups** such as some **ethnic minorities** and the **lower classes** may not allow access, if they think they have little to gain from being researched.

3) Research must also take into account **ethical considerations**. This involves thinking about how the research **impacts** on those **involved** with the **research process**.

4) The **interests and values** of researchers may influence what is seen as **'worthwhile'** or **ethical** to **study** in the **first place**. **Marxist** and **feminist** researchers might see the **role** of **social research** as **political** — about **understanding** the **plight** of the **oppressed** and giving them a **voice**, for example.

Ethics and *Access* are Important Factors

1) Many sociologists would like to do **more research** on **elite groups**. Powerful elite groups tend to remain **under-researched** as they are **hard to infiltrate**. This means that there is an **imbalance of data** available about members of **different social strata**.

2) Trying to do research on **unwilling groups** raises many **ethical problems** — it's generally accepted that wherever possible sociologists should get the **consent** of the participants in their research, and **shouldn't deceive** them about the **aims** of the research. This can make some groups **incredibly difficult** to research. See p. 136 for more on **ethics**.

At last Dr Miriam Elstree, Professor of Sociology and Social Policy at Beanthwaite University, had found a group willing to talk to her.

Practice Questions

Q1   Suggest two reasons why positivists prefer to use quantitative methods when researching stratification.

Q2   Give a criticism the interpretivists make of the positivist approach to stratification.

Q3   Briefly describe the method used by Savage in his study of attitudes about class in the Manchester area.

Exam Question

Q1   Assess the strengths and limitations of using official statistics to understand the nature and extent of stratification in British society.

(15 marks)

Quantitative data — research that counts...

More for you here on all the little battles that keep sociology interesting — heck yes. Some of this stuff may be pretty familiar to you by now, but it's worth thinking about how people with different perspectives will end up asking different questions in different ways. Even within perspectives — like feminism — there's plenty of room for disagreements. It's never simple or straightforward.

Sociological Research: Stratification and Difference

Sociologists' theoretical perspectives have a big impact on what they research and how they do it. These pages focus on the positivist approach to researching stratification and differentiation. For AQA students studying the Stratification and Differentiation topic, and all OCR students.

Positivists value Representativeness, Reliability and Objectivity

1) Positivists believe that statistical data is **more objective** than data obtained by qualitative methods.

2) Positivists use **quantitative data** from **official statistics** and **large-scale surveys** such as the **English Longitudinal Study of Ageing (ELSA)** to uncover **society-wide** patterns of stratification. They believe this is necessary to ensure that data **represents society as a whole**.

It had the reliability Penny was after — but did it have the objectivity?

Positivists like to use Objective Social Class Scales in their research

1) **Social classes** are groups of people who share a similar amount of **wealth**, a similar level of **income**, type of **job** and **education**.

2) There are different '**class scales**' that group people in **different ways**.

- The **Registrar General's scale** ranks people according to the **occupational skill** of the head of the household.
- The **Hope-Goldthorpe scale** classifies people according to **market position**, or how **in-demand** a particular type of job is by employers.

3) The advantage of **objective class scales** is that they enable comparisons to be made.

These comparisons can be within the same **period**...

Data from the **Office for National Statistics** tells us that there are still variations in life expectancy across social classes. In the period 2002-05:

- **Males** in the **professional class** had a life expectancy at birth of **80.0 years**, compared with **72.7 years** for those in the **manual unskilled class**.
- **Females** in the **professional class** had a life expectancy at birth of **85.1 years**, compared with **78.1 years** for the unskilled manual class.

...or **over time**.

A recent example of a study on intergenerational social mobility carried out by the Sutton Trust in 2005 compared the mobility of people born in 1970 to those born in 1958.

- The study found that intergenerational mobility had **fallen** markedly over time in Britain.
- The **difference** between the **proportion** of people from the **poorest 20%** of households who had been to **university** compared with the proportion of people from the **richest 20%** had **increased** between these years.
- One of the explanations given for the **decline in mobility** is the growth in the relationship between **family income** and **educational achievement**. **Extra opportunities** to stay in education at age 16 and 18 **disproportionately benefitted** those from more **wealthy backgrounds**.

There are Disadvantages to using Objective Class Scales

1) Different studies use **different social class scales**, so it's **difficult** to **compare** the results across the studies.

2) Some of the **old social class scales** do not work today, as the nature of social class has **changed**.

3) Social class is a **complex mix** of education, occupation, income and value — so it's not surprising that many people don't feel as if they '**fit**' their **objective social class**. People who are objectively working class may feel that they are middle class.

4) Some argue that **ethnicity** and **gender** are more important sources of stratification.

Sociological Research: Stratification and Difference

Large-Scale Surveys provide reliable quantitative data on *Stratification Issues*

1) A good example of a large-scale survey is the **English Longitudinal Study of Ageing (ELSA)**, which was set up by **Michael Marmot**. It follows a group of **over 8500** people from all social classes who were **born before 1952**.

2) The ELSA is partially funded by **central government**.

3) The subjects have had to fill in a questionnaire **every two years** since **2002** about their health, work, experience of healthcare, cognitive abilities and income. In 2004, the questionnaire was combined with **a visit from a nurse** to measure things such as **blood pressure** and **lung function**.

4) A new report on the study is **published** after every set of questionnaires.

5) In 2006 the study showed that over **ten times** more participants aged 50-59 from the **poorest 20%** of the population had died than those in the **richest 20%**.

6) It also showed that there is a **strong relationship** between levels of wealth and **mortality and morbidity**.

Longitudinal studies are ones that follow the same group of subjects over a long period of time.

Advantages of Marmot's research method

1) Marmot has generated a **huge amount** of **quantitative data**, which is helpful for **scientific** and **positivist** research.

2) **Longitudinal studies** are the most **reliable** way to analyse **changes over time** as they eliminate the possibility of **different sample groups** each being **unrepresentative** in **different ways**.

Disadvantages of Marmot's research method

1) Longitudinal studies are **very expensive** and **time-consuming** — long-term funding is essential.

2) Some of the original group inevitably **leave the study** as time progresses — either **by choice** or just because they **die** or become **impossible to contact**. This affects the **reliability** of the research.

Many sociologists use *Mixed Methods*

Sociologists researching **stratification** and **differentiation** will often **use a combination of methods** — both quantitative and qualitative (see p.145). This gives a **more detailed picture** than you'd get with one method — so it's more **valid**.

1) **Connor and Dewson (2001)** used **focus groups**, **interviews** over the phone (both qualitative methods), and **postal questionnaires** (a quantitative method) to research the factors that influence whether school leavers from lower social class backgrounds enter higher education.

2) They identified who was from the lower classes using the **Registrar General's scale** (see p.154).

3) They discovered a number of important factors that discouraged qualified **working class** candidates from entering **higher education**:

- **Candidates from lower-class backgrounds** were more likely to want to **earn money** and be **independent** as soon as possible.
- They were **more concerned** about the **cost** of funding their studies.
- They had **less confidence** in their **ability to succeed** in higher education.

Practice Questions

Q1 Name two social class scales.
Q2 Briefly describe two criticisms made of objective class scales.
Q3 What is the name of the large-scale survey set up by Michael Marmot?
Q4 Name the different methods used for gathering data by Connor and Dewson (2001).

Exam Question

Q1 Identify and explain one disadvantage of using longitudinal surveys to research stratification. (3 marks)

These pages are pure class...

Positivists want representativeness, reliability and objectivity — and they're prepared to go to great lengths to get data that fills those criteria. Just imagine all the data that ELSA's generated — filing cabinet after filing cabinet of the stuff. It makes a mockery of all those interpretivists, with their cassette-taped chats. You could bury all the interpretivists in ELSA generated data. All of them.

Sociological Research: Stratification and Difference

These pages focus on the use of qualitative methods in researching stratification and difference.
*They're for **OCR** students, and **AQA** students studying the **Stratification and Differentiation** topic.*

Interpretivists prefer *Qualitative Methods*

1) Interpretivists value **validity** — research is valid if it provides a **true picture** of what is really **'out there'** in the world.

2) Generally speaking, the more **in-depth** the research, the fuller the picture we get of the **thoughts** and **feelings** of the individuals involved. Data becomes more valid when the researcher **stands back** and allows the respondents to **'speak for themselves'**. Methods such as **participant observation** and **unstructured interviews** aim to gain valid data.

Qualitative Methods have *Advantages* for researching *Stratification*

1) Qualitative methods give the researcher **insight** into the **lived experience** of **marginalised groups**.

2) Qualitative methods allow the respondents to **speak for themselves**, which could provide them with a **sense of empowerment**.

3) The researcher may find out **unexpected things** that enable **policy makers** to more effectively **tackle poverty** and **marginalisation**.

Qualitative Methods present their own *Problems*

1) Methods such as **participant observation** — where the researcher can spend **several months** or even **years** with a small group of respondents — are **not very reliable**, as it's **impossible to replicate** the original research exactly.

2) These methods are also open to researcher or interviewer **bias**. The more **involved** the researcher, the more they may **bias the results**.

3) In **extreme** cases, the researcher may **'go native'** and start to **sympathise** with the respondents — to **share** in their point of view rather than just to **understand** it. This means the research would no longer be **value-free**.

Qualitative Methods are appropriate for researching *Marginalised Groups*

1) A good example of research into marginalised social groups is **Paul Willis's (1977)** study of a group of 12 working class boys as they made their **transition from school to the workplace**. He used a mixture of **observation**, **group interviews** and **individual interviews**.

2) He found that the group had formed an **anti-school culture** that **rejected trying hard** in favour of **disruptive behaviour**. The group had decided not to try to **achieve qualifications**, even if they were **intellectually capable**.

3) Willis found that they transferred the same **anti-authority culture** to their **workplace**. Most of them found work as shop-floor staff in factories.

4) Willis claimed that their anti-authority nature was something they **created themselves** and not something that was **transmitted to them** by school or society.

Advantages of Willis's research method

1) Most human interactions are **instinctive** and best studied in **real situations**. Willis used **direct observation** to see how the group acted in school and in their workplace, **group interviews** to see how they acted in each other's company, and **individual interviews** so that he could get an idea of what each subject was like on their own.

2) Individual interviews gave Willis a chance to **build a rapport** with the boys, allowing him to gain an **in-depth understanding** of their behaviour.

Willis's work is an example of a mixed method study (see page 145).

Disadvantages of Willis's research method

1) A sample of just 12 working class boys is **unlikely** to be **representative**. It would be misleading to generalise about all working class boys from these results.

2) However, performing the same study with a larger group of boys would be **very expensive**.

Sociological Research: Stratification and Difference

Unstructured Interviews give insight into Personal Experiences of Stratification

1) **Simon Charlesworth (1999)** conducted **unstructured interviews** with a **mixed** male and female group of 43 **working class** people in Rotherham, Yorkshire.

2) He focused on how **unemployment** has affected the lives of many of these people, finding that they had lost their **sense of identity** and **belonging** as a result of the decline of **traditional manual labour**.

3) One of the reasons Charlesworth was successful in gaining **access** was that he was from a **working class family** from **Rotherham**.

---

1) **Winlow and Hall (2006)** interviewed **43 young people** who were in **temporary jobs** in the **North East of England** about their attitude to **violence**. As well as the interviews, the researchers also carried out observation work.

2) They discovered that **violence** at the weekend was an **ordinary** and **anticipated** part of their **social life**. The researchers theorised that this was because of **frustration** caused by the sense of **'going nowhere'** in temporary employment, fuelled by **cheap alcohol** in **densely packed city centres**.

3) **Winlow** came from a **working class background** in **Sunderland** — which helped in finding **contacts** in the area for the study.

"Kid, you're the best, you're number one, you're an animal. Now go get 'em."

---

1) An important study by **Diane Reay (1988)** based on the 33 mothers of children at two London primary schools found that the **cultural capital** of the **middle class mothers** gave their children an **advantage** at school.

2) Middle class mothers were found to be **more likely** to do such things as **help** their children with **homework**, **bolster** their **confidence**, and **sort** out their **problems** with **teachers**.

---

1) **William Labov (1972)** used **informal, unstructured interviews** to test the theory that **"linguistic deprivation"** was a cause of **underachievement** of **working class** and **ethnic minority children**. Linguistic deprivation — a lack of ability with **Standard English** and a tendency to use **slang** — was believed to cause them to underachieve despite the fact that they may **express** the **same ideas** as high achievers.

2) He discovered that when **working class African-American children** were interviewed by a **white person** in a **formal interview**, they became **tense** and **spoke nervously**, appearing to be **linguistically deprived**. When they were interviewed by a **black person** in an **informal setting**, they became much more **articulate**. So the **apparent linguistic deprivation** seemed to be a reaction to a **perceived hostile environment** rather than a genuine feature of the children's **communication methods**.

Practice Questions

Q1 What does participant observation mean?

Q2 Why can we not treat Paul Willis's 1977 research as representative?

Q3 According to Reay's research, what things did middle class mothers do which gave their children an advantage?

Q4 What criticism of formal interviews does Labov's research suggest?

Exam Question

Q1 Examine the advantages and limitations of using qualitative methods when researching marginalised groups in society.

(15 marks)

It's no use sitting on your class — get these pages learnt...

So, what's your favourite approach? I think I'd go with using quantitative data. That way you can stay at your desk all day, making the odd cup of tea, periodically checking what's in the biscuit tin. That's clearly the way to do sociology. You won't end up bumping into crack dealers that way either. But both methods have their pluses and minuses, so learn them well.

Do Well in Your AQA Exam

*These two pages are all about how to do well in AQA exams. So don't bother reading them if you're not doing **AQA** — go straight to p.162. For your A2 you'll get **two exams** — one on Unit 3, and one on Unit 4. **Unit 3** is worth **60 marks**, **20%** of the whole A-Level. **Unit 4** carries **90 marks**, which is **30%** of the A-Level.*

> These pages show how the AQA exam papers are likely to be formatted — though there may be a few changes. So it's important that when you take the exams, you **read the instructions and questions really carefully**. Don't assume they'll always follow the same pattern.

You'll have a *1½ Hour Exam* on Unit Three

1) In Unit 3 you have four topics to choose from: **Beliefs in Society**, **Global Development**, **Mass Media**, and **Power and Politics**. You should **only** answer questions from **one section**.

2) You might have been taught **more than one topic** — it's probably a good idea to revise **two** of them and then choose the **best questions** on the day. **Read** all the questions on the topics you've studied **before** making your choice.

3) In this unit you will usually have to answer **three questions**:
   • The first **two questions** are compulsory. They're likely to be **data response questions**.
   • For your **next question** in Unit 3 you'll probably get a choice of **essay questions**.

You'll have a *2 Hour Exam* on Unit Four

1) There are two sections in this exam — one on **Crime and Deviance** and the other on **Stratification and Differentiation**. Pick the section on the topic you've studied and answer all the questions.

2) There will probably be **four questions** you need to answer:
   • two data response questions on your **chosen topic**
   • a data response question on **sociological research methods** in the context of your chosen topic
   • an essay question on **sociological theory** and **methods**.

3) The exam paper should give clear **guidelines** on **how much time** you should spend on each question — make sure you stick to the advice they give you.

You Get Marks For...

In A-Level Sociology you'll be given marks for two Assessment Objectives — **AO1** and **AO2**:

AO1   **Knowledge** and **understanding** of the **theories**, **methods** and **concepts** in sociology and the **links between them**. Also included in AO1 are marks for **communicating knowledge** in a **clear** and **effective** manner.

AO2   The demonstration of the skills of **application**, **analysis**, **interpretation** and **evaluation**.

1) There are **more AO2 marks** available in the **A2 exams** than there were for the AS exams.

2) This is significant. You must be able to draw on a wide range of studies and theories and **analyse** them in detail. However much knowledge you display, if you don't **analyse** and **evaluate** it you won't get high marks.

Take a concept and *Make It Work* for you

A way to build up those AO2 marks is to master the art of **writing about sociological concepts**. There are key concepts in every topic — here's how to **wring the marks out of them**:

1) **Define** the concept.
2) Give **examples** of it in practice.
3) Present **different viewpoints** on the same concept.
4) Present **evidence** for each viewpoint.

Kit really felt the concept "sailor" worked for him.

Do Well in Your AQA Exam

Use what you learnt in your AS-Level

Don't make the mistake of **forgetting** all the Sociology you learnt to get your stunning AS grade. The key research and theories will be relevant to these exam questions, too. The A2 units are **synoptic** — this means you need to show awareness and understanding of how topics interlink and the subject as a whole.

Oh... and don't forget **the basics**.

The AQA examiners really care about stuff like being able to read your handwriting — they're always going on about it in their examiners' reports.

- Write as **neatly** as you can.
- Use good **grammar** and **punctuation**.
- Check your **spelling** — especially of words to do with sociology.
- Make sure you **answer the question**.

It's important to be **disciplined** about **time** in the exam. Practise answering past papers under timed conditions. Candidates often lose marks by spending too much time on questions worth relatively few marks.

Here's an example of the **Source Material** for the **Unit 3** paper

Item A

In the UK, the number of people turning out to vote is in decline. Recent election statistics prove alarming reading for politicians. When New Labour first got elected in 1997 they did so with a turnout of around 71%. By 2001 this figure had dropped to about 59% — a staggering decrease.

The issues of voter absenteeism and voter apathy undermine the UK's democracy. A democracy without legitimacy is no democracy at all. Without a high turnout of voters in general elections it is difficult for the winning party to claim meaningful legitimacy or mandate from the people.

5

Here's an example of a **Short-Answer Question** for **Unit 3**

| 13 | Identify and explain some evidence which supports the view that the ideological differences between the main political parties are no longer significant. | (9 marks) |

There has been a significant shift in the ideological positions held by the mainstream British political parties in recent years, with Labour continuing to move to the right, and the Conservatives moving left away from the Thatcherism of the 1980s and 1990s.

Address the question straight away.

Before its recent shift rightwards, Labour was a recognisably democratic-socialist party seeking to transform society to a more socialist model. For instance, the Labour Party favoured a strong welfare state and state ownership of key industries. In contrast, the Conservatives under Margaret Thatcher were committed to free-market economics, privatisation, low taxes and a New Right approach to social policy.

Show off relevant background knowledge.

Today the situation is different. Labour, following the reforms of Tony Blair, has become 'New Labour' — adopting a new set of ideas called 'The Third Way' which seek to fuse a pro-business, free-market approach to economic management with some of the caring aspects of 'Old Labour' such as a continued commitment to the Welfare State. The Conservatives under David Cameron have moved away from Thatcherism to a more 'compassionate conservatism' which attempts to be more inclusive.

Keep your evidence relevant to the question.

This shows that the two main political parties now occupy similar ideological ground, which suggests that the old class-based, left-right ideological division is now less important.

Do Well in Your AQA Exam

*Here are some more sample questions and answers for the **AQA exams** to show you the kind of thing to aim for.*

Here's another **Example Question** based on the **Source Material** on p.159

14 Using material from Item A and elsewhere, examine the view that voters have become apathetic about participating in politics.

(18 marks)

It is clear from Item A that voter turnout in elections is falling, with a turnout of only 59% in 2001 compared to 71% in 1997. This suggests that people are less interested in participating in politics.

Make sure you refer to the source material if it's mentioned in the question.

As well as a fall in voter turnout, there has also been a decline in membership of the main three political parties. For example, Labour's membership has fallen below 200 000 (compared to around 400 000 in 1997). This suggests that people no longer feel committed to party politics.

Show an awareness of recent developments.

That the government recognises voter apathy as a problem can be seen from measures they have taken to re-engage the public with politics, such as various attempts at making voting easier. They have also put citizenship on the national curriculum.

A number of sociological explanations have been put forward to explain this apparent apathy, including class dealignment and the rise of alternative methods of political participation at the expense of the more traditional methods of 'old politics'.

Try to use the correct terminology.

Class dealignment has been studied by Sarlvick and Crewe (1983). This refers to the tendency for voting behaviour to be less obviously based on traditional class positions — the working class identifying with and voting for Labour and the middle class identifying with and voting for Conservative. This breakdown of class alignment can be seen as having also weakened the bonds between people and the political parties as a whole.

Explain why your evidence is relevant.

Similarly the ideological convergence of the main political parties may have led people to feel there isn't enough difference between them to bother voting, or getting involved.

An alternative view is that the rise of New Social Movements and participation in direct action and protest by young people through NSMs suggests that they may not be politically apathetic at all.

Discuss contrasting viewpoints.

Mention relevant studies.

Postmodernists, such as Lyotard (1984), suggest that people's political engagement has become more local and issue-based, and has moved away from the sweeping, party-based ideological politics of the past. This would imply that falling turnout suggests a change in people's political participation rather than a widespread apathy.

While the postmodernist position may well be an exaggeration, there would appear to be substance in the idea that low electoral turnout may well have less to do with political apathy amongst groups within the electorate and more to do with the changing nature of political participation in a globalised world.

Examine the view that it's time to get your revision on...

Oh exams are wonderful things. You spend ages and ages studying a whole array of topics from across the sociological spectrum and then you're expected to get that all down in just a couple of hours. But what that does mean is you need to get used to writing under exam-type conditions — make sure you practise answering questions under timed conditions as part of your revision.

Do Well in Your AQA Exam

04 Assess the view that religion is in decline in the UK.   (33 marks)

Mention relevant studies.

Bryan Wilson (1966) describes a process of secularisation. This is a decline in the significance of religious belief, religious institutions and religious practice in society. Evidence about the influence of religion in society is often open to different interpretations; it is difficult to prove definitively that religion is in decline.

Define the key term or idea that the question asks you about.

Evaluate how reliable data is — don't just take it at face value.

In the 2001 census, 72% of the people in the UK identified themselves as Christian. However, these 72% who identify themselves as Christian do not necessarily hold strong religious beliefs. Some may have been brought up nominally Christian, but have minimal belief in God or the teachings of Christianity.

Church attendance figures are often used to support the view that religion is in decline — the percentage of adults who go to church has fallen from 10% to 7% over the last 20 years. This is a questionable method of judging the extent of secularisation though, as it only deals with religious practice, not religious belief. It's possible to attend church without having faith, just for the social networking aspects, as Herberg suggested. On the other hand, it is possible to believe strongly in God, but never go to church. Davie (1994) claimed that belonging to a church and believing in religion are getting more and more separated.

Have separate paragraphs about different aspects of a topic.

Some argue that religious institutions have lost influence in wider society. Bruce (1995) said that the Church became less important to people as its functions were taken over by other, secular institutions. For example, the Church used to have a strong role in education and welfare — roles which are now primarily filled by secular, state organisations. On the other hand, Parsons claims that even though the Church no longer has all the functions it had back in the Middle Ages, religion can still have an influence on people's everyday lives.

Discuss contrasting viewpoints.

There has been a trend towards religious pluralism (a greater variety of religions practised in British society). This is partly because of the immigration of ethnic minorities, and partly because of new religious movements (NRMs).

Immigrant groups often have a higher level of religiosity than the settled population. Religion contributes to a sense of community and ethnic identity. Davie claimed that identification with a religion was important to South Asian immigrants because it gave a strong sense of cultural identity. Bruce refers to cultural transition — when South Asian immigrants came to the UK, they quickly set up religious institutions to act as a support structure for the immigrant community.

Bring in relevant examples.

Religious pluralism has also resulted from the growth of new religious movements (NRMs) since the 1960s. A large variety of groups and beliefs have been labelled NRMs, from the Moonies to reiki healers. Many sociologists use the growth of NRMs as evidence to argue against secularisation. Sociologists have claimed that the conditions of modernity and postmodernity create insecurity and alienation, and that the growth of NRMs is a response to this. However, it is not easy to use the rise in NRMs as evidence against secularisation. Some NRMs are very vague in their beliefs, and may not count as religions at all.

Explain your opinion on the topic, based on the evidence in the essay.

In conclusion, it is difficult to accurately measure whether religion is declining. Personal belief is a complex topic; for example, even if a person says they are Christian, they may not attend church or believe strongly in God. The rise of NRMs since the 1960s suggests that many people do want some element of spirituality in their lives, but it is arguable whether this is the equivalent of a traditional religion.

Imagine you're doing a covert participant observation study of exam candidates...

The more stuff you learn, the more you'll have to write about. But you have to try to keep it all relevant. It's all too easy to start off answering the question, but end up waffling on about something else entirely. One of the best ways to avoid this is to plan out your answers before you write them. Go through each point you want to make and include supporting evidence.

162

Do Well in Your OCR Exam

*These two pages are all about how to do well in **OCR** exams. So don't bother reading them if you're not doing **OCR**.*

These pages show how the OCR exam papers are likely to be formatted — though there may be a few changes. So it's important that when you take the exams, you **read the instructions and questions really carefully**. Don't assume they'll always follow the same pattern.

You'll have a *1½ Hour Exam* on the *'Power and Control'* unit

This is a **synoptic paper**, which means you'll need to show understanding and awareness of the topics from the whole course — including the topics you studied at AS-Level. The exam is **one and a half hours** long. There are a total of **100 marks** available for this paper.

1) There are four topics included in this paper: **Crime and Deviance**, **Education**, **Mass Media**, and **Power and Politics**.

2) There are usually **12 essay questions** — three on each topic. You have to answer **two questions**. You can choose **any two questions** from the topics you have studied — you can pick them from the **same** or from **different topics**.

3) The questions tend to follow the **same pattern**. They usually start with the words **'Outline and assess...'** followed by a **sociological idea** (a view, explanation or theory). For example: *'Outline and assess functionalist explanations of crime and deviance.'*

4) Each essay is worth up to 50 marks — including marks for **knowledge and understanding** (up to **23 marks**), **interpretation and application** (up to **10 marks**), and **evaluation and analysis** (up to **17 marks**). Make sure your essays include all these skills.

Albert certainly had power — no doubt about that — but just lately he had started to worry that he was all out of control.

There's more about the Assessment Objectives on p.163.

You'll also have an exam on *'Exploring Social Inequality and Difference'*

Again, this is a **synoptic paper**, which means you need to use your knowledge from the **whole course, including your AS work**. The exam is **two hours** long and includes one piece of **research (source material)** on social inequality and difference which the exam questions will use as a starting point. There are **two parts** to the paper:

The difference is, monsieur, that I have someone who sits my exams for me.

- The **first part** is compulsory, and will probably comprise of two questions focused on the key issue of exploring **sociological research** as related to **social inequality and difference**.
- The **second part** is focused on the key issue of **social inequality and difference** related to **social class, gender, ethnicity** and **age**. You will have a choice of questions for this.
- There are a total of **100 marks** available for this paper.

A total of 3½ hours — that's not even enough time to exploit the proletariat...

Although this page doesn't have anything on it about new theoretical approaches or disagreements between rival schools of interpretivist post-Marxism, it's still really important. The more you have an idea of what to expect in the exam the better you'll do in the exam. Get to know the exams and they'll be your friends. You'll still need to learn the sociology stuff though, darn it.

Do Well in Your Exam

Do Well in Your OCR Exam

You Get Marks For...

> AO just means 'Assessment Objective'

You Get Marks for:
AO1 — Showing Knowledge and Understanding, and Communicating Clearly
AO2 — Interpretation and Application, Evaluation and Analysis

1) In the A2 exam, more of the marks are for AO2 skills than they were at AS-Level. However much knowledge you display, if you don't **analyse and evaluate** it you'll miss out on most of the marks.

2) Remember — the A2 is not just studying new and different topics from AS but studying topics in more **depth**. Examiners want to see:

- More evidence of **critical evaluation** and **interpretation**.
- More reflective, **critical understanding** of sociological **theory** and **method**.

You should be well capable of writing your own top/full/easy Marx-based pun by now.

Oh... and don't forget **the basics**.

- Write as **neatly** as you can.
- Use good **grammar** and **punctuation**.
- Check your **spelling** — especially of words to do with sociology.
- Make sure you **answer the question**.

Here's an example of *Source Material* for *Social Inequality and Difference*

The source material for the 'Exploring Social Inequality and Difference' paper **isn't pre-released**, so the first time you see it will be in the **exam** — make sure you read it **carefully**. Here's an example of the kind of thing you might get:

> Women today are increasingly returning to work when their children start school. This can mean they end up combining paid work with childcare. This research explores the experiences of women who have returned to work in the last five years after their child/children had started school.
>
> The methodology focused on the experiences and views of the women themselves and is located within interpretivism. The women in the study were from a variety of ethnic backgrounds. All were married to a husband who was in full-time employment, and all had at least one dependent child in education. The total number of participants was 12 and all participants lived in the Southampton area and worked at least 16 hours per week. The method consisted of two focus groups, each with six participants, and was conducted in a local community hall.   5 ... 10
>
> The research was carried out in May 2008 and the women were encouraged to talk about their experiences of combining caring for a child/children and paid work.
>
> The research found that the women were the main carers in most of the families, and that family life required a great deal of planning: such as making sure children were fed before being taken to out-of-school clubs. Many of the women found that because they worked part-time the main burden of childcare fell to them and that caring for children during school holidays often required reciprocal arrangements with other working mothers. As one participant put it, "Sometimes I feel there is no time for me and that my needs come last to all the other things that have to be done." However, all women expressed the positive aspect of working as a means of building self-esteem and economic independence. "Having gone back to work earning my own money, I wouldn't want to go back to asking for every penny from my husband." It was also found that the women from Asian backgrounds had greater support from wider extended family that lived close by.   15 ... 20
>
> From the findings it was concluded that women want to return to work but that there is a need for greater support to help them with this.   25

> Turn the page for some sample questions and answers based on this source.

Do Well in Your OCR Exam

*These are examples of **OCR**-style exam questions and answers. They're based on the material given on the previous page. They should give you some idea of the kind of answers you'll be expected to write in the exam.*

Here are some sample questions for 'Exploring Social Inequality and Difference'

1 Using the item and your own knowledge, outline and explain the benefits of using focus groups in sociological studies. **(15 marks)**

A focus group consists of a small number of people, six in the case of the mentioned research, and gives the researcher the opportunity of hearing a focused, dynamic discussion between different people on particular issues. Using interpretivist methodology, it allows the researcher to understand why people hold certain views and allows the participants to develop, extend or even modify their views.

The group environment can encourage all the respondents to be involved in the discussion, as generally they have a common interest. This interaction produces rich in-depth information, which can result in points emerging that the researcher had not thought of. The information is valid as it gives a truthful insight into people's views.

In the case of the source material the focus group allowed for the research to focus "on the experiences and views of the women themselves", which makes the findings valid.

A range of benefits of using focus groups are explained — directly answering the question.

You don't need an introduction or a conclusion for short answers.

Use the source material to illustrate your points.

---

3 (a) Outline the evidence that women are disadvantaged in employment. **(20 marks)**

There are many areas of employment in which women appear to be disadvantaged compared to men. Women can be said to face both vertical and horizontal segregation.

Vertical segregation is where women tend to reach a glass ceiling in their careers — they are less likely to be promoted to the most senior and high paying jobs. For example, despite the increase in the numbers of women brought about by the 1997 election, only 18% of MPs returned were women.

Horizontal segregation is where some occupations tend to be carried out by women, and others by men. "Women's jobs", such as primary school teaching, clerical work and catering, are often lower paid than "men's jobs" in professions like construction.

Girls are more likely to pass their A-levels and go to university than boys. Sue Sharpe (1994) found that girls wanted qualifications and careers. The feminist movement in the 1960s and 1970s highlighted gender inequality in the workplace, changing many women's expectations and putting pressure on the government to change the law.

Legislation was put in place to combat gender inequality, such as the 1970 Equal Pay Act and the 1975 Sex Discrimination Act, which show that governments have recognised that women are disadvantaged. However, recent statistics show that the gap between men's and women's earnings for full-time work is starting to widen again after over 30 years of narrowing. This shows that the disadvantages faced by women in society are not just a problem of the past.

Indicate right at the start the focus of your discussion.

The statistics provide evidence to back up the answer.

Explain the meaning of sociological terms.

Shows up-to-date knowledge of the issue.

No, the disadvantaged in society are not just the ones doing exams...

You may not know the exact questions that will come up in your exam, but there's only so much they can ask about. If you learn the different theoretical approaches and the topics you've covered back to front then there shouldn't be too many surprises. The more sociologists and studies you can fire off accurately the better, but just remember to keep it all relevant.

Do Well in Your OCR Exam

Here's an example 'Power and Control' Question and Sample Answer

1   Outline and assess sociological approaches to the solution of crime.   **(50 marks)**

When looking at solutions for crime two modern sociological approaches are particularly important. These are the right and left realist approaches, which focus on the solution to crime rather than the causes of crime.

Always have an introduction to long answers like this to show the examiner you understand the question.

According to right realists Wilson and Kelling (1982) crime is a serious problem which requires practical solutions. They argued that if minor crime (broken windows, litter) goes unchallenged, then more serious crime begins to increase, as it is unchecked.

Refer to specific studies.

Right realists argue that crime results from the decline in respect for authority linked to fatherless families and the negative effects of reduced socialisation.

For right realists the solutions to crime are to be tough on crime with such policies as zero tolerance policing, where the police do not tolerate even the small crimes such as graffiti. This goes hand in hand with more police on the streets and more surveillance, as people are less likely to offend if they are watched.

Refer to other studies that lend support to your comments.

Wilson (1975) argued that people commit crime when the possible gains outweigh the risks. He believed the way to address this was to make punishments for even minor crimes a lot harsher. He argued that punishments should be a deterrent, making the risk of crime seem less attractive.

These ideas were influential on social policy during the 1980s when the focus was on working class male crime. However, that focus resulted in other crimes being ignored. Right realism has been criticised by Matthews (1992) who found no evidence that there is a link between broken windows and crime. Others have pointed out that right-realist-inspired 'zero tolerance' policies have led to a massive increase in the US prison population.

Evaluate the theories as you go.

A very different approach to solutions to crime comes from left realists, such as Kinsey, Lea and Young (1986) who argue that people turn to crime when they suffer relative deprivation, i.e. when they feel less affluent than other people in similar social groups. They believe that a fairer and more just society would lead to a reduction in crime. Kinsey, Lea and Young also argue that improvements are needed in policing, and that these could only come with a stronger role for local communities, who are vital to most successful investigations.

These ideas were influential on Labour policy from 1997 onwards, with the development of a variety of policies that were aimed at tackling the causes of poverty. The left realist approach to crime has been criticised by Hughes (1991), who pointed out that many people who suffer from relative deprivation don't go on to commit crime, and so it can't be the main or only cause.

Use other theories to evaluate.

Marxists have extensively discussed a factor that both left and right realists have tended to ignore, and that is white-collar or corporate crime. They claim the focus on working class crime masks the level of inequality in society and that many crimes committed by the powerful go unchallenged. Although not strictly looking at the solution to crime, they would argue that if inequality was reduced, then crime would go down.

A further criticism of realism comes from feminists who comment that in a patriarchal society, little is done to combat crimes against women and women's fear of crime. The solution for them would be to rid society of male domination.

In conclusion, while realism does provide some ideas about solving crime, a major problem with all theories is that the complexities of crime means that one theory could not be used to adequately explain or solve all crime.

Always finish with a conclusion.

So long sociology — we'll miss you...

So, just two more sociology exams to do and then that's it. Well, sociology is going to miss you too. It hopes you've learnt something and that maybe it's helped you to see things in a slightly different way. Sociology wishes you all the best for your exams, and hopes you are seriously considering going on to study sociology further. But it'll understand if you don't.

Glossary

agenda-setting A practice in journalism where an editor or journalist selects what to include in the news and chooses a particular angle to take when reporting it, so affecting how the story is perceived by their audience.

Althusser Neo-Marxist sociologist who saw education as part of the "ideological state apparatus". He argued that education is designed to produce a docile and obedient workforce.

anomie Durkheim's term for a state of moral confusion in society, resulting from an absence of the common shared norms and values that bind a society together. He argued that this was bad for both individuals (who are uncertain of how to behave in particular situations) and for society as a whole. Anomie (or "normlessness") is a state that is typical of societies undergoing sudden change.

Bandura, Ross and Ross (1963) Conducted psychological experiments that demonstrated how boys imitated aggression in films they had watched. Their research has been used to support the hypodermic syringe theory of the media.

Bourdieu French Marxist who argued that the upper class maintains its position at the top of society by upper class parents passing on cultural capital to their children. He said that the middle class try to develop cultural capital in their children, putting them at an advantage in education, but that working class children don't develop it.

bourgeoisie Marxist term for the capitalist ruling class. They own the means of production (e.g. factories, equipment, raw materials).

Bowles and Gintis (1976) Marxist sociologists who argued that there was a close connection between relations in the workplace and in education — a "correspondence principle". They said that the workplace requires a hard-working, passive and obedient workforce and the education system helps to produce this type of workforce via the hidden curriculum.

British Attitudes Survey (1991) A large-scale study of 1000 married couples which found that, although there was more sharing of child-rearing tasks than in the past, household tasks were still not shared out equally. The survey concluded that there was some movement towards a more equal division of labour but that this was a slow process.

capitalism An economic system based on private ownership of the means of production, distribution and exchange of commodities. In the capitalist system labour itself becomes a commodity which employers buy for wages. Capitalism is associated with free trade and individual enterprise. It started in Europe and the US and has spread to become the dominant economic philosophy in most countries.

catharsis theory This theory suggests that seeing violence on TV helps viewers release tension and violent thoughts, making them less likely to commit violent acts themselves.

censorship The control of the media (TV, newspapers, film etc.) through banning certain works, scenes, images or language from being broadcast or published.

census A government survey of all people within a defined geographical area. The British census is an obligatory survey of the entire population every 10 years. It's an important source of secondary data on the changing characteristics (housing, education, work patterns etc.) of the British population.

civil disobedience Protest action that breaks laws.

class A way of stratifying society, on the basis of people's social and economic status. Class is hierarchical — some classes are more privileged than others. The "class system" is criticised by Marxists.

classical liberalism The view that the market should be free, with minimum state intervention, and that individuals should take responsibility for themselves.

coding Numbered codes for each answer of a question on a multiple choice questionnaire. Coding makes it easy to turn the results into graphs and analyse them.

communism A system of government which is theoretically based on a classless society and where private ownership has been abolished. It is influenced by the ideas of Marx and Engels. During the Cold War, there was conflict between capitalist Western countries and communist countries like the USSR and China. With the end of the Cold War and the break-up of the USSR, many formerly communist countries have moved towards adopting capitalism. To some extent, their reasons for doing this have discredited communism as a viable political philosophy.

conformity Adherence to the norms and values of society. The opposite of deviance.

consensus Fundamental agreement within a society, especially about that society's basic values. Functionalist theory suggests that, as a result of socialisation, the people in a society all share the same norms and values and this contributes to consensus.

correlation The association between two variables where changes in one variable are associated with changes in the other variable, but do not necessarily cause them.

cult A religious group without a fixed set of beliefs. Cults tend to focus on the inner power of the individual and mysticism. They're often short-lived and don't usually have a hierarchy.

cultural capital The cultural skills and knowledge which children learn from their parents. Bourdieu claimed that upper and middle class children are more likely to have cultural capital than working class children and that this puts them at an advantage educationally.

cultural deprivation theory This theory claims that educational achievement and health vary according to social class because some classes lack the cultural values and knowledge which promote a healthy lifestyle and educational achievement.

Glossary

culture The "way of life" of a society or group. Culture is made up of things such as language, customs, knowledge, norms and values. It is passed on by socialisation.

Davis and Moore (1945) Functionalists who believed that modern society rewards ability, effort and intelligence. They claimed that there has to be a system of unequal rewards to motivate people to train for demanding and difficult jobs. The function of the education system is therefore to allocate people to appropriate occupations.

dependency theory A development theory which blames underdevelopment on colonialism.

desacrilisation Religious and spiritual beliefs ceasing to have a place in society.

deviance Something that goes against society's norms and values. Deviant behaviour is behaviour that society doesn't approve of.

Douglas (1964) Studied the link between class and educational achievement. Douglas suggested that both cultural and material deprivation play a part in underachievement at school by working class children. He identified a link between poor living conditions and underachievement, but also claimed that working class parents seemed less interested in the education of their children than middle class parents did.

Durkheim The founder of functionalism. He was one of the three most influential figures in shaping the modern discipline of Sociology, together with Weber and Marx. Durkheim introduced many important sociological concepts, including the "collective consciousness of society" (the shared norms and values that bind a society together) and "anomie" (a state of being without these norms). Durkheim also wrote extensively on the subject of suicide and on the sociology of religion.

Engels A sociologist, philosopher and co-founder of Marxism, Engels was a fierce critic of capitalism. He said women were subordinated through the institutions of private property and monogamy. Engels argued that the family had the economic function of keeping wealth within the bourgeoisie because parents pass it on to the next generation as inheritance.

ethnocentric Centred around the values and interests of one particular ethnic group.

ethnography Research which studies the culture and way of life of a community. It is usually done by observation, and may also use interviews and case studies. Ethnography looks at social relationships, organisations, customs and practices. It is an interpretivist approach to sociological study and so produces qualitative data.

false consciousness Marxism says that workers are in a state of false consciousness about their place in society. They have learnt values and beliefs that support the interests of the ruling class (through their education, the media and religion), and this prevents them from realising how unfair capitalist society is.

false needs Things people think they need but which don't really satisfy them. Marxists say these false needs have been created by a capitalist culture which encourages consumerism.

falsification Proving a hypothesis wrong.

feminism A broad movement which believes that social organisations and culture have been dominated by men to the exclusion of women. Feminists claim that this has devalued and disadvantaged women into a marginalised status. There are many varieties of feminism, e.g. liberal feminism, Marxist feminism, radical feminism and black feminism.

free market An economic system that lets supply and demand control prices, wages etc., rather than the government.

Functionalism An important sociological perspective about how society works, founded by Durkheim. Functionalists believe that society is made up of a number of institutions, each of which has a useful function and helps society to run smoothly, e.g. the family, the education system, religion. These institutions work in harmony because of agreed norms and values, and this is essential for society to survive. Functionalists say that individuals internalise these norms and values (socialisation). Another term for functionalism is "consensus structuralism". So now you know.

gender Sociologists say that gender (femininity and masculinity) is a social construction. Being male or female is the biological sex you're born with, while masculinity and femininity are identities you're socialised into.

Glasgow University Media Group (1976) (1980) (1982) Studied bias in the media. They found that TV coverage of workplace strikes in the 1970s was biased in favour of management and against the strikers in terms of the perspective, the language and what was covered.

globalisation The breaking down of traditional national boundaries as globally people become more interconnected. This happens due to factors such as the growth of multinational companies, improvements in communications and technology, increased migration of people between societies, and the global marketing of cultural products.

Hawthorne effect When participants are aware they are taking part in an experiment, it often affects their behaviour. This is known as the Hawthorne effect.

hegemony The domination of one group of people over others, or of one set of ideas and values over others. Law, religion, media, art, science and literature may all be used to make the dominant group or values legitimate and to discredit the alternatives.

hidden curriculum The social norms and values that are taught at school, but not as part of the regular curriculum, e.g. conformity and respect for authority.

168

Glossary

hierarchy A system which ranks people according to status. Any system where you have a boss in charge of people is a hierarchy.

hypodermic syringe model The idea that the media injects its message directly into the minds of the audience. It claims that all people in the audience are affected in the same way, and that they're powerless to resist or reject the message.

identity An individual's sense of self. This can be influenced by social factors such as class, gender, religion and ethnicity.

ideological state apparatus Institutions like the media, schools, Church and family which can spread the ideology of the state.

ideology A set of ideas and beliefs about the way things should be — often politically motivated.

infrastructure In Marxist theory, the infrastructure is the economic base of society (e.g. labour and manufacturing).

institutional racism When the policies, attitudes and actions of an institution discriminate against ethnic minorities — sometimes unintentionally.

institutions of society Things like the family, the Church, the education system, the health care system.

interpretivism A sociological approach which focuses on the actions and thoughts of individuals. Society is viewed as the product of interaction between individuals. "Interpretivism", "interactionism" and "social action theory" are pretty much the same thing — so don't get confused if you see these other terms being used.

labelling theory This theory says that the labels given to someone affect their behaviour, e.g. someone who is labelled a criminal is more likely to commit criminal acts. Labels also affect how other people treat someone, e.g. teachers might treat a child labelled a "troublemaker" more strictly.

LEDC Less Economically Developed Country.

Left Realism Sociological viewpoint which developed from Marxism. The approach focuses on working within the capitalist framework and aims to direct social policy to help the poor.

Mac an Ghaill (1994) Used overt observation and interviews to study masculinity. He found that many boys formed deviant subcultures because of failure at school and a desire to be "macho" and masculine. He introduced the idea of a "crisis of masculinity" as a cause of the underachievement of boys at school.

Marcuse (1964) Neo-Marxist who wrote about leisure, its consumption by workers and the way it is presented by the mass media. He claimed that the mass media promotes consumerism and gives people false needs (things they think they want but which won't really satisfy them). He said that leisure is based around these false needs, creating "happy robots" who work hard because they're under the false impression that leisure makes them happy.

Marxism A theory and political ideology based on the views of Karl Marx (1818-1883). Marxists are opposed to capitalism, which they believe is based on the exploitation of the working class (proletariat) by the ruling class (bourgeoisie). Original Marxist ideas have been developed and adapted by **neo-Marxists**. Some states have been run politically along Marxist lines, e.g. Cuba under Castro.

mass media Ways of communicating with large numbers of people, e.g. newspapers, TV, magazines, radio, internet.

master status A quality in an individual that comes to dominate the way that they are treated or viewed, to the extent that all their other qualities are disregarded. This quality then takes on the status of a label. E.g. if someone with mental health problems is given the often negative label "mentally ill", and then finds that all their other qualities are ignored, the label "mentally ill" has master status.

MEDC More Economically Developed Country.

media text Any piece of media — e.g. a book, a TV programme, an advert.

meritocracy A system where the best (most talented and hard-working) people rise to the top.

metanarrative An overarching, all-encompassing story which gives meaning to history and events.

moral panic A fear of a moral crisis in society. The mass media have a big role in starting moral panics in modern society.

neo-Marxism In the 20th century, some of Marx's followers revised and adapted his ideas to make them more relevant to modern society. Neo-Marxists often stress the importance of culture in sustaining capitalism, e.g. through the hegemony of capitalist ideas. Neo-Marxists include Gramsci, Althusser and Stuart Hall.

New Right Movement developed in the 1980s. New Right theory believes in the "moral superiority" of the traditional nuclear family, and tends towards the view that sexual tolerance and single mothers are bad for society. Problems like poverty and unemployment are seen to be caused by an over-generous welfare state. New Right sociologists have also claimed that there's been a moral decline in society due to secularisation.

norm A social rule about what is correct and appropriate behaviour within a particular culture, e.g. queuing in a shop.

operationalisation Defining a concept and deciding how to measure it.

patriarchy A society where men are dominant. Feminists often describe male-dominated societies and institutions as "patriarchal".

peer groups People of the same or similar social status and age, e.g. a group of teenagers.

Physical Quality of Life Index (PQLI) A development index that measures infant mortality, literacy and life expectancy.

Glossary

pluralism The belief that society is diverse and reflects the needs and views of everyone via democracy and the free market.

positivism A theoretical point of view which concentrates on social facts, scientific method and quantitative data (facts and figures). The positivist view is that human behaviour is determined by external social factors, and so is outside the control of the individuals in society.

postmodernism Theory which says there is no one objective truth or reality that everyone experiences. Postmodernism rejects the ideas of modernism, such as positivism and metanarratives.

postmodernity The world after the modern age — with flexible working, individual responsibility and people constructing their own identity.

qualitative methods of research Methods like unstructured interviews and participant observation that give results which tell a story about individuals' lives.

quantitative methods of research Methods like surveys and structured interviews that give results you can easily put into a graph or table.

reflexive sociology Research that accepts that the researcher's opinions have an effect on results, and takes this into account.

reliability Data is reliable if other sociologists using the same methods on the same group collect the same data. Quantitative data is usually the most reliable.

representative democracy Rule by the people, via voting in elections for representatives (e.g. MPs).

sanctions Rewards and punishments that reinforce social norms.

secularisation When religion loses its influence in society.

semiotic analysis Looking for hidden meanings in the structure of a text, image or object.

social construct An idea or belief that's created in society, and doesn't come from a scientific fact.

social democrats People who think the state should redistribute wealth, and that there should be a strong welfare state paid for out of taxes. Social democrats believe in social equality.

social policy Government decisions which affect society, e.g. raising taxes, changing the benefits system, privatisation.

socialisation Passing on cultural values and norms from one generation to the next, so that they become internalised, i.e. part of everyone's way of thinking.

stereotype A generalisation about a social group — often inaccurate and insulting.

stratification The way society is divided up into layers or classes.

stratified sample A sample with the same proportions of gender, class, age etc. as the population you're studying.

subculture A group who share values and norms which are different from the mainstream culture. A culture within a culture.

superstructure In Marxist theory, the superstructure is the institutions in a society which aren't economic (such as legal, political, cultural and religious institutions) and the beliefs and values which these institutions propagate. It has a role in maintaining and sustaining the economic infrastructure.

third-way politics A political viewpoint that combines elements of right wing self-sufficiency and left wing social democracy.

triangulation Combining different research methods and data to get the best results.

underclass A social group at the bottom of the social hierarchy. New Right sociologists think they're lazy and dependent on welfare. Left wing sociologists think they're disadvantaged by the welfare system.

validity Data is valid if it gives an accurate picture of what's being measured.

value-free research Research that isn't biased, and isn't influenced by the researcher's beliefs.

values General beliefs in a society about what is important or what is right and wrong, e.g. freedom of speech is a value of Western society.

victim survey Survey asking if respondents have been victims of crime.

vocational education Education that provides the skills needed for a particular job.

Weber (1864-1920) Influential, early sociologist. Weber argued that the better a person's market situation, the better their life chances, wealth and status would be. He also suggested that, as societies developed, secularisation would follow as people came to believe more in science. Weberians are followers of Weber's work and ideas.

Welfare State The British Welfare State was set up in the 1940s with the aim of wiping out the social problems of society (poor health, housing and education, poverty and unemployment). The Welfare State was designed to be free at the point where people actually needed it (e.g. a visit to hospital) and was paid for by people in work contributing to a national insurance scheme.

world systems theory Development theory which looks at the world as a single economic system where some countries have a lot of power and others don't have power.

Index

Symbols

11+ exam 108, 118
1988 Education Reform Act 117, 120
19th century liberalism 93

A

Abbott and Payne 91
Abbott and Wallace 82
aboriginal society 6
Abraham 113
absolute truth 122
Acheson Report 92
activism 24
Adamson 29
advertising 34, 40, 51, 78
age 12, 102
agenda-setting 38
Akers, Ronald 75
Al Qaeda 69
alien 47
Althusser 3, 54, 107, 125
Americanisation 51
amplification of deviance 87
Annan, Kofi 86
anomie 10, 72
anthropology 140
Arber, Dale and Gilbert 95
ascetic ideal 7
Atkinson 89
authoritarianism 68
authority 52

B

Bagdikian 35
Bagehot 58
Bagguley 60
Ball 109, 110
Bandura, Ross and Ross 41, 46, 151
Baptists 9
Barker, Eileen 143, 145
Barker, Martin 41, 46
Baudrillard 37, 49
Bauman 14, 130
BBC 40
Beauvoir, Simone de 7, 12
Becker 74, 109, 110, 139, 146
Beckett 121
being naked 70
Bellah 6
Benyon 62, 97
Berlusconi, Silvio 35
Bernstein 111

Beyer, Peter 14
Biggs 45
bilateral aid 21
binary opposition 42, 51
black feminism 99
black power 64
Black Report 92
Blair, Tony 55, 56, 59, 78
blog 50
Blumler and Katz 48
Bobo doll experiment 151
Bonger 73
Bordua 73
Boserup 29
Bourdieu 107, 111, 143
bourgeoisie 52, 54, 68, 90, 94, 99
Bowlby 71
Bowles and Gintis 107, 116
Bowman and Willis 50
Box 81
Branch Davidians 8
Braverman 96, 116
British Board of Film Classification (BBFC) 41
British Crime Survey (BCS) 80, 141, 146, 148, 149
British National Party (BNP) 63
British Social Attitudes Survey 152
broadcast media 40
Broadcasting Standards Commission 44
broken windows thesis 75
Bronson, Charles 151
Brown 120
Bruce, Steve 8, 9, 11-13, 15, 132
Buckingham 41
Butler and Rose 58
Butler and Stokes 58

C

Callaghan, James 119
Callinicos, Alex 69
Calvinism 7, 8
Cameron, David 56
Campbell 82
Cantril 47
capitalism 6, 16, 36, 52, 54, 55, 61, 69, 73, 76, 77, 94, 99, 101, 102, 125
Carnell 29
Castles and Kosack 101
catharsis theory 41
censorship 34, 40, 41

census data 152
Chambliss 76
charity 22
Charlesworth 157
charts 144
child abuse 70
Chomsky, Noam 69
Christian fundamentalism 9
Chubb and Moe 108, 120
Cicourel 143
citizen journalism 50
City Academies 117, 121
City Technology Colleges 117, 121
civil disobedience 61, 62, 63
civil liberties 87
civil religion 6
civil rights 63, 64, 65
civil service 54
class 43, 58, 59, 61, 63, 65, 73, 76, 81, 82, 83, 90, 91, 92, 94-97, 99, 101-102, 104, 107-108, 110-111, 113, 115-116, 119, 125, 152, 154-155, 157
class dealignment 58
classical liberalism 57, 68
climate change 26
closed systems 129
Cloward and Ohlin 72
Coard 114
coding 139, 144
Cohen, Albert 72
Cohen, Phil 119
Cohen, Stan 41, 45, 87
Cold War 21, 68
collaborative journalism 50
colonialism 20, 24, 31, 33
communism 94
competitive meritocracy 95
comprehensive schools 118
Comte 14, 122, 124
Confederation of British Industry (CBI) 54
confidentiality 136, 137, 149
conflict structuralism 125, 146, 147, 152
conformity 7, 70-72, 116
Connell 152
Connor and Dewson 155
consensus 70, 72, 85, 124
consensus policing 78
consensus structuralism 124, 146, 152
consent 136
conservatism 68

Conservative Party 55-60, 85, 108, 117, 119, 120, 121, 130
consumerism 36
consumerist identity 37
content analysis 34
contradictory class locations 94
Contreras 23
control theory 75
convergence 50
copy cat violence 41
correlation 144
Cottle 44
Crewe 97
Cricher 45
crime 70-89
Crook, Pakulski and Waters 61
Croteau and Hoynes 43
Crown Prosecution Service 85
cults 9, 12
cultural capital 107, 111, 157
cultural deprivation 110, 118
cultural effects theory 47
cultural globalisation 66
cultural hegemony 35
cultural homogenisation 51
cultural imperialism 18
cultural issues 142
cultural reproduction 106
Cumberbatch 43
Cumberbatch and Negrine 44
curriculum 114
cyber crime 86

D

Dahl 52, 54
Dahrendorf 97, 125
Dalmiya and Schultink 23
Darwin, Charles 5
Davie 13-14
Davis and Moore 92, 106, 116
Dawkins, Richard 4
deductive approach 5
demography 28, 29
Denver 58
dependency culture 62
dependency theory 17, 20, 21, 24, 29, 30, 31
deregulation 22
desacrilisation 15
designing research 134
Destutt de Tracy, Antoine 2
determinism 34, 125

Index

development
16, 17, 20, 21, 24, 28, 29, 30, 31, 32, 33
Devereux 51
deviance 70-89, 146
devolution 19
differential educational achievement
112, 113, 114, 115
differentiation 15, 152
direct action 62, 63
disability 44, 63, 103
Disability Discrimination Act 103
disengagement 15
Dobash and Dobash 150
Douglas 89, 110
Downes and Rook 70
Driver and Ballard 115
dual economy theory 24
dumbing down 51
Durkheim
4, 6, 16, 29, 72, 88, 106, 124
Dutton 38

E

economic liberalisation 87
Edgell 94
education 30, 31, 106-121
Educational Action Zones 121
Ehrlich 28, 29
Eisenstadt 7
electoral function 56
elite theorists 53
embourgeoisement 58, 96
empire 17
Employment Equality Regulations 102
Employment Research Institute 117
Engels, Friedrich 2, 6, 54, 68
English Longitudinal Study of Ageing (ELSA) 154, 155
environmental groups 60
environmentalism 65
Equal Opportunities Commission Survey 113
Equal Pay Act 98, 112, 128
equality of opportunity 117, 118
Essex study 104, 105
ethics 136, 137, 149, 150
ethnicity
44, 58, 63, 64, 82, 83, 90, 95, 99-102, 113-115, 152, 154, 157

ethnocentric
16, 17, 18, 24, 111
ethnography 140
Etzioni 75
European Union (EU)
18, 19, 55, 66
evolution 5
experiments 34, 140
Export Orientated Industrialisation (EOI) 25
Export Processing Zones (EPZ) 33
Eysenck 71, 110

F

fair trade 20
false consciousness 6, 125
false needs 36, 52, 59
falsification 5, 122
Featherstone and Hepworth 45
feminism
2, 7, 12, 32, 62, 64, 65, 69, 73, 84, 98, 99, 105, 117, 128, 129, 131, 134, 139, 147, 153
feminist methodology 139
Ferguson, Christopher 41
Ferguson, Marjorie 43
Feshbach and Singer 41
Feyerabend 122, 145
field experiments 140
Field, Frank 130
Fielding 137
Finn 119
Firestone 99, 131
first past the post electoral system 57
Fiske 48
Fletcher and Allen 81
focus groups 140
Foucault 53, 70, 75, 141
Frank 17
Fraser 61, 65
free market
21, 22, 27, 68, 93
free press 40
free trade 17, 21, 33
Friedan 64, 128
Friedman 17
Fröbel 18, 33
Fuller 114
functionalism
3, 6, 31, 53, 72, 76, 85, 92, 93, 95, 101, 102, 106, 116, 117, 124, 127, 134, 143, 147, 153

fundamentalism 6, 9
Furedi, Frank 51

G

G8 23, 67
Gandhi, Indira 69
Gans 38
Garner and Kelly 56
gate-keeping 38
Gauntlett 43
gay pride 64
gender
32, 42, 43, 63, 82, 84, 90, 92, 95, 98, 99, 102, 105, 112, 113, 117, 128, 129, 131, 152-154
Gender Empowerment Measure (GEM) 32
Gender-related Development Index (GDI) 32
General National Vocational Qualifications (GNVQs) 119
generation gap 41
geocentric 18
Gibbs and Martin 88
Giddens
18, 55, 61, 96, 97, 101, 104, 126, 127, 130
Gifford Report 100
Gilroy 83
Glasgow University Media Group (GUMG)
39, 43, 59, 141
Glass 104
Glennon and Butsch 43
global village 51
globalisation
14, 17-19, 64-67, 96, 97, 127
Glock and Stark 12
Goffman 74, 140
going native 142, 150, 151
Goldthorpe 95, 96, 104
Goldthorpe and Payne 92, 105
Gomm, Roger 5
Gordon 76
Gouldner 75
governing function 56
Graef 85
grammar schools 118
Gramsci
3, 52, 54, 59, 76, 125
grand narratives 127
Grant and Marsh 54

green crimes 86
Gross National Product (GNP) 16
Grossberg 38
Gruwell, Erin 151

H

Halbwachs 88
Hall 19, 43, 65, 77, 83, 87
Hallsworth 60
Halsey 110, 111, 118
Halsey, Floud and Anderson 108
Halsey, Heath and Ridge 117
Hargreaves 106, 109, 110
Harrison 28, 29
Hartmann and Husband 44
Harvey and Macdonald 145
Hawthorne Effect 142
Hayek 55
Hayter 20, 21
health education 31
Heath 105
Heelas 11
hegemony
3, 36, 52, 54, 76, 107
Heidensohn 73, 82, 84
Held 67
Herberg 15
Hermes 43
Hewitt 54
Heywood 69
hidden curriculum 107, 116
Hirschi 75
Hirst and Thompson 66
HIV/AIDS 31, 45, 66
Holm, Jean 12
homophobia 116
Hong 23
hooks, bell 64, 99
Hope-Goldthorpe Scale 154
Hoselitz 24
Hughes 79
Human Development Index (HDI) 16
Human Poverty Index (HPI) 16
human trafficking 86
Humphreys 136
hybridity 18
Hyman 111
hypodermic syringe model 46
hypotheses 133

Index

I

identity politics 64, 65
ideological hegemony 59
Ideological State Apparatus (ISA) 3, 54, 125
ideology 2, 3, 54, 59, 68-69
illegitimate opportunity structure 72
Import Substituting Industrialisation (ISI) 25
income 90
individualism 24
inductive approach 4
industrial revolution 24
industrialisation 24-26
infrastructure 125
insider groups 60
international division of labour 26, 97
International Monetary Fund (IMF) 20-22
interpretivism 74, 75, 89, 109, 115, 123, 141, 143, 146, 149, 150, 152, 156
interventionism 25, 84, 85, 103
interviewer effects 139, 142
Islamic fundamentalism 6, 9

J

Jacques, Martin 57
Johal 13
Jones, Nick 37
Joseph Rowntree Foundation 110

K

Karofi and Mwanza 86
Katz and Lazarsfeld 37, 46
Keddie 109, 110
Kellner and Wilby 104
Kelly 113
Kennedy, Charles 59
Kerr 16
King, Martin Luther 6, 63
Kingsbury 26
Kinnock, Neil 59
Kinsey, Lea and Young 78
Klein, Naomi 67
Kuhn 5, 122
Kundnani 63
Kyoto Protocol 19

L

lab experiments 140
labelling 114, 126, 146
Labour Party 56-58, 60, 78, 85, 117, 119, 130
Labov 111, 142, 157
language difference 111, 115
left realism 78-79, 84
left realist square of crime 78
legitimate opportunity structure 72
Lemert 74
Less Economically Developed Countries (LEDCs) 16, 17, 20-27, 30-33
Levi-Strauss 42
Liberal Conservatism 68
Liberal Democrat Party 57, 59
liberal feminism 128, 131
liberalism 2, 98, 118
life histories 141, 152
Lincoln, Abraham 106
linguistic deprivation 157
logical positivists 122
Lombroso, Cesare 71
longitudinal studies 155
longitudinal surveys 139
Lukes, Stephen 52, 53
Lull 48
Lupton and Wilson 53
Lynch, Michael 4
Lyotard 14, 37, 53, 61, 65, 130

M

Mac an Ghaill 113-115, 145
Macintyre 150
Mack and Lansley 130
Macpherson Report 83, 85, 100
macro-theory 124
Maduro, Otto 6
Maguire 81
male underachievement 112
Malinowski 6
Malthus 28
Mannheim, Karl 3
Marcuse 36, 59, 61
marginalisation 14
market principle 108
marketisation 120
Marmot 155
Marsh 82
Marsh and Locksley 54
Marshall and Swift 93
Marx, Karl 2, 6, 16, 52, 54, 68, 90, 94, 95, 97
Marxism 2, 3, 7, 17, 29, 35, 36, 52-54, 59, 60, 68, 73, 76, 77, 83-85, 94-97, 99, 101-102, 107, 111, 116, 119, 125, 127, 134, 147, 153
mass media 3, 22, 34-51, 141
master status 74
Matthews 79
Mayo 142
McBride 51
McDonaldisation 18
McKenzie and Silver 58
McLibel case 67
McLuhan, Marshall 34, 47, 51
McQuail 48
Medhurst 43
media imperialism 51
media texts 48
medical sociology 132
Melton 10
Melucci 61
meritocracy 24, 92, 93, 107, 116, 124
Merton, Robert 72, 82
message trajectory 42
metanarratives 14, 37, 61, 65, 127, 130
method 134
Methodism 8, 9, 13
methodological pluralism 145
Metropolitan Police Authority 85
micro-theory 124
Mies 32
Milgram 136
Miliband 36, 52, 59
Mill, JS 98
Millenarian movements 11
Miller 73, 82
Millett 128
Mirza 113, 114
Mitsos and Browne 112
Mitter, Swasti 32
mixed methods 145
modernisation theory 21
modernity 127
Modood 13, 100
Mods and Rockers 45, 87
Moir and Jessel 71
money laundering 86
Moonies 143, 145
moral panics 41, 45, 46, 87
More Economically Developed Countries (MEDCs) 16, 18, 21, 25, 27, 30, 31
Morley 48
Morris, David 31
Morrison 41
mortality and morbidity 155
Mosca, Gaetano 53
multi-stage sampling 135
multiculturalism 44
multivariate analysis 4
Murdoch, Rupert 35, 59
Murray 62, 73, 79, 97, 101

N

National Front (NF) 63
national identity 66
National Statistics Socio-Economic Classification 91
National Vocational Qualifications (NVQs) 119
nationalisation 57
natural selection 5
Navarro 31
Negrine 50
neo-functionalism 93
neo-liberal 17, 21, 22, 26, 27, 55
neo-Marxism 94, 125
neo-Weberian theory 95
neo-conservatism 68
new age movement 11, 12, 14
new deal 119
New International Division of Labour 18
New Labour Party 55-59, 85, 121
new media 34, 39, 50, 51
new religious movements (NRMs) 10-12
new right 21, 62, 68, 73, 83, 93, 95, 96, 108, 117, 118, 120, 121, 130
new social movements (NSMs) 57, 60, 65, 69
new vocationalism 119
Newly Industrialised Countries (NICs) 17
news 38, 39, 50, 51
Non-Governmental Organisations (NGOs) 18, 22

Index

Norris 58
North Atlantic Treaty Organisation (NATO) 66

O

Oakley 129, 139, 142
objectivity 91, 126, 141, 142, 148, 149, 150, 154
observation 140
Ofcom 40
Office for National Statistics 154
Office for Standards in Education (OFSTED) 120
Ohmae 66
old boys' network 105
old social movements (OSMs) 60
One Nation Conservatism 68
one-tier system 118
open systems 129
operationalisation 133
opinion leader 46
Orbach, Susan 43
organic analogy 124
Ortner 99
outsider groups 60
Oxford Mobility Study 104

P

Pakulski and Waters 95-96
Pantazis and Gordon 81
paradigms 122
parentocracy 120
Pareto, Vilfredo 53
Parsons 6, 92, 102, 106, 124
participant observation 150, 151, 156
participation function 56
particularism 14
partisan alignment 58
patriarchy 7, 77, 99, 128
Patterson 101
Pearce 76
Penn 97
People's Temple 8
philosophies of science 122
Physical Quality of Life Index (PQLI) 16, 31
Pilkington 100, 115
pilot study 135
Plummer 64, 70
pluralism 35-37, 51, 53, 54, 60
Polanyi 4, 5

police 94
police authorities 78
policy function 56
polycentric 18
Popper 5, 122
population 135
population growth 28, 29
positivism 4, 88, 123, 141, 146-148, 151-154
positivist methods 146-148
postmodernism 37, 39, 49, 53, 61, 65, 75, 95, 96, 123, 130
postmodernity 127
Poulantzas 54
Poverty Reduction Strategy Paper (PRSP) 22
power elite 53
predestination 7
Press Complaints Commission (PCC) 40
pressure groups 60, 63
primary data 140
primary deviance 74
primary research 134
privatisation 22, 55, 96
probability sampling 135
process of individualism 75
progressive education 118
progressive liberalism 57
proletariat 52, 59, 68, 90, 94, 96, 153
Protestant Reformation 7
psephology 58
purposive sampling 135

Q

qualitative data, methods and analysis 123, 129, 134, 138-141, 144-147, 150, 152-153, 155-157
quantitative data, methods and analysis 123, 129-130, 134, 138-141, 144-148, 152-155
questionnaires 128, 138, 155
quota sampling 135

R

race 100
racism 64, 83, 101, 116
radical criminology 77
radical feminism 128, 131
random selection 135
rationalisation 18

Reagan, Ronald 79
realism 129
reality TV 49
Reay 157
Redclift 26
redistribution of wealth 57
reflexive research 143
reflexivity 143
Registrar General's Scale (RG Scale) 90, 154, 155
Reiter 57
relative deprivation 78
reliability 134, 148, 154
religion 4, 6-15, 90
religiosity 8, 12-15
religious fundamentalism 68, 69
religious pluralism 8, 14
representative democracy 56
representative function 56
representativeness 154
research design 134-135
research process 132, 133
research questions 133
researcher imposition 142
Resler 96
respondant validation 143
reviewing the field 132
Rex 101
right realism 84
Rist 109
Ritzer 18
Robbins 22
Roberts 96
Rostow 16, 31
ruling class ideology 76
Runciman 97

S

Saeed 13
Saggar and Heath 58
Said, Edward 42
sampling 135
sanctions 70
Sarlvick and Crewe 58
SATs 120
Saunders 93, 96, 101, 105, 110
Savage 152
Savage and Egerton 105
Sayer 129
Scarman Report 100
Schumpeter, Joseph 56
scientific law 122
Scott 96
secondary data 141

secondary deviance 74
secondary documents 151
secondary modern schools 118
secondary research 134
secularisation 14, 15
select committees 60
selective filter model 48
semiotics 34
Seven Up 139
Sex Discrimination Act 98, 112
sex-role theory 73
sexism 7, 82, 98, 116
sexuality 45, 64
Sharpe 112
Signorelli 45
simulacrum 49
Sklair 19, 55
Skocpol 55
Smart, Carol 73
Smith, Dan 27
Snider, Laureen 76
snowball sampling 135
social action theorists 126, 134, 143, 146, 147
social constructs 39, 102, 103
social control 70, 76, 147
social democrats 108, 117, 118, 130
social facts 88
social laws 4
social mobility 104, 105
social networking sites 50
social order 70
social policy 130, 131
social surveys 138
socialisation 106, 124
socialism 32, 55, 56, 68, 69
society in miniature 106
sovereignty 19, 66
spin doctors 59
spiritual shoppers 11
Sreberny-Mohammadi 51
Stanko 84
Stanworth 91
state 54-55, 86
state crimes 86
stereotypes 42-45, 47, 82, 98, 103, 105, 117
Stewart, Frances 27
stratification 90-105, 135, 152-157
stratified random sampling 135
streaming 109
strikes 63
Structural Adjustment Programmes (SAP) 21-23

Index

structuralism
26, 84, 85, 126, 127,
134, 146
structuration 126
structured interpretation model
48
structured interviews 138
subcultures 113, 114, 116
subjectivity
91, 123, 126, 141
subsistence 24
Sugarman 111
suicide 88, 98
superstructure 125
surveys 141, 155
sustainable development 26
Swann Report 114, 115
systematic sampling 135

T

Taylor, Harriet 98
Taylor, Ian 87
Taylor, Laurie 142
Taylor, Steve 89
Taylor, Walton and Young
72, 77
teachers' unions 108
technical schools 118
Thatcher, Margaret 55, 56, 60
theories of science 4, 5
third way politics
55, 56, 121, 130
tiger economies 17, 25
Townsend 130
trade tariff 25
trade unions 33, 60, 63
transnational capitalism 19
Transnational Corporations
(TNCs) 18-21, 23,
30-33, 55, 66-67
Transnational Institute 86
trends 144
triangulation 145
trickle down effect 21
tripartite system 118
triple-systems theory 99
Troeltsch, Ernst 8
Tuchman 43
Tumin 93
Turkle 50
two-party system 57, 58

U

underclass 90, 97, 101, 130
unemployment 27, 83

Unification Church 10
United Nations (UN)
18, 19, 21, 23, 66,
67, 84, 86
universalism 14
unstructured interviews 139,
146, 150, 152, 157
urbanisation 24, 25
uses and gratifications theory
48
USSR 94

V

validity 134, 142, 143
value consensus 70, 106, 124
value free research 123
Van Dijk 44
variable sum model 53
Venkatesh 141, 150
verification 122
verstehen 123
victim surveys 80
victimology 84
Victorian capitalism 5
Viewing the World Report 44
vocational education 119
voter apathy 58
voting behaviour 58

W

Walby 99
Wallerstein 17
Wallis, Roy 10
war 27
Weber 7, 14-16, 52, 94,
95, 101-102, 123,
125, 130, 141
Webster 25
welfare state 55, 56, 130
Welles, Orson 46
Westergaard 96
Westminster model 57
Westwood 73
Whittle, Stephen 64
Whitty 121
Whyte 140
Willis 107, 113, 116, 141,
150, 156
Wilson 14
Wilson and Herrstein 79
Wilson and Kelling 75, 79
Winlow and Hall 150, 157
Wolf, Naomi 43
women's suffrage 65
Woods 110
World Bank 20-22

World Health Organisation
(WHO) 23
world sociology 132
world systems theory 17
World Trade Organisation
(WTO) 67
world wide web 86
Wright 114
Wright, Erik Olin 94
Wright Mills 53

Y

Young 74, 80
Youth Opportunities
Programme (YOP) 119
Youth Training Schemes (YTS)
119

Z

zero sum model 52
zero tolerance 79, 84